DALIT MOVEMENT IN INDIA AND ITS LEADERS

(1857 – 1956)

(SECOND EDITION)

DALIT MOVEMENT IN INDIA AND ITS LEADERS (1857 – 1956)

(SECOND EDITION)

DR R.K. KSHIRSAGAR

PRINTS PUBLICATIONS PVT. LTD.
NEW DELHI

Published by :

Prints Publications Pvt. Ltd.
Prints House, 11, Darya Ganj
New Delhi - 110002
Phone: +91-11-45355555
E-mail : contact@printspublications.com
Website: www.printspublications.com

First Edition : 1994
Second Edition : 2017

ISBN 978-81-927694-0-0

Price : ₹ 995/-

Published and Printed by Mr. Pranav Gupta on behalf of Prints Publications Pvt Ltd at Mohit Enterprises, Delhi.

Contents

Preface to the Second Edition

I am extremely happy to see that the second edition of my book, "Dalit Movement in India and its Leaders" (1857-1956) is being published today.

I am proud to say that the said book of this magnitude was firstly published in 1994 and it has proved to be pioneering one in this field. It has certainly evoked positive and encouraging response from numerous readers.

I, however came to know that the copies of the first edition were already exhausted longback. In view of this, I was inclined to bringout its second edition. Its publisher also evinced interest in this venture. Therefore I was actively involved in the process of reviewing and revising it. Eventually, I had added nineteen more profiles to the previous one hundred fifty five profiles of the leaders.

This book has undoubtedly proved that the Dalit movement was nation-wide, stretching different parts of the country and it was launched by the leaders belonging to various castes and sub-castes among the so called untouchables all over the country.

Even, it has been amply proved in my other book, "Rise of Self-Consciousness among the untouchables in ancient and medieval India," (Kaushalya Publication Hudco, Aurangabad 2008) that the movement was in existence virtually since the very beginning of 'untouchability'. Thus the caste-struggle which had started in the long past came to its logical conclusion under the Constitution of India.

This movement was obviously for nation-building in its true sense, and not merely caste emancipation movement. It was a movement for upliftment of the so called untouchables who were discredited as lower, and join them to the main stream of the society.

On this occasion I must pay my homage to Professor Eleanor Zelliot, Minnesota, U.S.A. (1926-1916) who surprisingly came to my residence to meet me personally in her sojourn on 9th November 1999 for appreciating my work and presenting her book to me with her kind remarks in recognition of my efforts.

I am grateful to Dr. S.N. Busi, IRS (Hyderabad) my teacher and a renowned author for his appreciation of my work.

I am thankful to Advocate Santok Lal Virdhi (Fagwada, Punjab), Dr. S.S. Narwade (Mumbai), Dr. Pradeep Aglave (Nagpur), Dr. S.S. Bansode, Prof. Sushila Mool Jadhav, Prof. B.G. Pawar (Aurangabad) and Mr.Varun (Samantara Publication, Hyderabad) for their co-operation and encouragement in this venture.

I must express my thanks to the Director and Manager of Prints Publications Pvt. Ltd., "Prints House', Daryaganj, New Delhi for having published the second edition of this book in short duration.

Dr. R.K. KSHIRSAGAR

Preface to the First Edition

It was a strenuous task to complete such a comprehensive major research project on *Dalit Movement in India and Its leaders.* It kept me busy virtually for seven years. I, however, do not claim it to be exhaustive. I sincerely feel that it would be helpful in undertaking further in-depth study in this subject.

For completion of this project, I had to depend on the assistance and cooperation of some institutions and individuals. At the outset, I must express my sincere thanks to the authorities of the University Grants Commission, New Delhi for having sanctioned an amount of ₹ 16,000 for completion of this project. Though it was a meagre amount, it would have been very difficult to undertake extensive tours and fieldwork without this help. I am thankful to the Director, Indian Institute of Advanced Study, Shimla, for granting Associateship at the Institute, where I could interact with the eminent social scientists and consult the excellent library of the Institute.

I am thankful to the librarians of Dr Babasaheb Ambedkar College of Arts and Commerce, Aurangabad, and Dr Babasaheb Ambedkar Marathwada University Library, Aurangabad for their excellent co-operation.

I am grateful to several Dalit activists, litterateurs and intellectuals. It is difficult to state the names of all those persons. However, I must express specifically my thanks to Advocate Bhagwan Das, N.G. Uke, Nathilal Shastri (Delhi), Bhante Pradnyanand, Dr Angne Lal, Rajavaidya Mataprasad (Lucknow), Prof R.N. Choudhari (Gorakhpur), Bhante Gyan Prabhakar, Dr Narayan Singh, Prem Pradeep Shilankar (Agra), Umedrao Jatav (Farukhabad), Jatin Bacgchi, S.C. Halder, Mrs Surindar Kaur, (Calcutta), Shri K. P. Waghmare (Balasore), U.N. Sinha (Patna), Rameshchandra Parmar (Ahmedabad), Dr D.R. Jatav (Jaipur),

Rahul Suman Chhawara (Ajmer), Prof P.B. Shegaonkar, Dr Anil Gajbhiye (Indore), M.U. Ramteke (Rajanandgaon), S. Rastrapal, P.R. Venkataswamy (Secunderabad), Prof Sayaji Mahale, Prof B. Parameshwar Rao (Hyderabad), Prof K. Rajalah (Karimnagar), P. Prasad Rao (East Godavari), Dr A. Seppan, S. Babu (Madras), S. Vishwanath (Dharmapuri), Prof Miss Mariamma Joseph, T.H.P. Chantharassery (Trivandrum), K.K.S. Das (Ponkunnam), Prof B.M. Baeen (Gulbarga), I. Loganathan (Mari-Kuppam), M.C. Narayana 'Murthy (Mysore), L. Shivalingiah, A.M. Abraham Ayrookuzhiel (Bangalore), Lekhram, Ishwar Das (Shimla), K.K. Srangal (Jammu), Radheylal Mahul (Chandigarh), L.R. Bailey (Jullundhar), R.D. Gaikwad, Vasant Moon, J.D. Wadekar (Bombay), Prof B.C. Somvanshi (Sangli), H.L. Kosare, P.P. Mool (Nagpur), Gorakh Bhalerao (Pune), Deenbandhu Shegaonkar, Dr Manakikar (Akola), Sanjay Gaikwad (Nasik), Jalindar Jamadar, M.I. Kurane (Kolhapur), Shri Bhimrao Salve (Buldhana), G.K. Veer (Nanded), Dr Gangadhar Pantawane, Prof M.R. Garud and Vithalrao Jondhale (Aurangabad) for their valuable help in my study and field work. I am thankful to Dr S.P. Gaikwad, the honourable chairman of the People's Education Society, Bombay for having encouraged me to complete this project.

My thanks are also due to all those interpreters who came to my help and explained the relevant writings and responses during the interviews expressed in different languages and dialects with which I was not conversant. I am really benefited by the literature published so far pertaining to the subject under study.

I must express my thanks to my wife Mrs Godavari Kshirsagar, daughters Mangala, Sujata, Vasudha and son, Deepak as they had maintained an atmosphere in the family conducive to my study.

I am thankful to Shri Muraleedharan who had typed the manuscript.

1994 **Dr. R.K. KSHIRSAGAR**

Inscribed
to the memory
of all those Dalit leaders
who endeavoured selflessly
for the liberation
of their brethren
from untouchability

—Author

1

Introduction

It is a fact that the evil practice of 'untouchability' has amply proved to be the most injurious to the so-called untouchables in particular and the Hindus in general. Therefore, the struggle for the emancipation of the Depressed Classes from the thraldom of untouchability and casteism has been in continuation for a pretty long time. It is but natural that no community would be willing to remain under cruel subjugation forever, and no society would sustain the shock of inequality and disunity. Several saints, social reformers and political leaders from both the Dalits and non-Dalits had tried their best for the eradication of untouchability from the social fabric. However, the Dalit liberation movement got an impetus during the British period. With the dawn of democratic institutions in India, the Dalit liberation movement steadily became more vocal, assertive and effective. After Independence, untouchability had been legally abolished under Article 17 of the Constitution of India, which states: "Untouchability is abolished and its practice in any form is forbidden. The enforcement of any disability arising out of untouchability shall be an offence punishable in accordance with law." In consonance with this provision the Parliament, empowered under Article 35 of the Constitution, passed "the Protection of Civil Rights Act, 1955" and it has been in implementation since then. Besides, the Constitution has provided certain educational facilities under Articles 15 (4) and 46, reservations in the employment under Articles 16 (4) and 335, and reservations in the central and state legislatures under

Articles 330(1) and 332 (1) for the amelioration of the socio-economic condition of the Dalits.

In the modern period, the liberation movement seems to have started when an untouchable Khalasi expressed his resentment against the denial of *lota* for drinking-water on the ground of untouchability by a Brahmin sepoy in Calcutta in the year 1857. Moreover, he disclosed the fact that the most polluting fat was being used in the cartridges which the sepoys had to remove by their mouth. This incident had, obviously triggered off the Mutiny of 1857. Since then several leaders came forward to contribute to the liberation of the so-called untouchables. However, the struggle for the emancipation of the untouchables was successfully led by Dr Babasaheb Ambedkar during 1919 to 1956. Thus, from 1857 to 1956 the movement was led by several leaders throughout India.

The objective of the Dalit movement was, obviously to liberate the historically known untouchable classes from the most oppressive practice of untouchability observed unscrupulously by the caste Hindus, and to bring the former on a par with socio-cultural level of the privileged classes, so that they could be brought to the national mainstream. Thus, the basic idea involved in this process was of reconstruction of the society on the basis of new values. It is, therefore, necessary to inquire: Who were those leaders, what were their ideologies and approaches to social reconstruction, what was their mode of operation, how could they mobilize the ignorant masses along with them; how they could politicize them, what strategy or tactics they had adopted to raise the involvement of the Dalits in their liberation and in getting the things done at government level; which path or process of social change they had adopted, either sanskritization or desanskritization, westernization or modernization, dialective or the cognitive-historical process; and lastly, how far they became successful in their mission? For this purpose, it is necessary to identify the leaders to take into account their cognitive background, their individual and collective contribution to the movement and their achievements.

Dalit liberation movement is, of course an inseparable part of the politico-cultural history of India, it is true that the Indian

National Movement was determined to liberate the country from the yoke of foreign imperialism, but this process was not going to be complete and final unless all the sections of the society, including the so called untouchables were to be free from the stigma of untouchability. This uphill task of liberation of the Dalits was fulfilled by the Dalit leaders. They were the real precursors of liberty, equality and social justice in India – they commanded attention of the national politicians by their vociferousness and influenced and shaped the national politics in a befitting manner. Their role in setting up the universal human values, narrowing the social distance between the touchables and untouchables and in setting up a democratic polity cannot be easily ignored or underestimated. However, the pity is that the history of Dalit liberation movement has not been properly interpreted and duly recorded in a consolidated and comprehensive manner as such.

The present work is but a humble attempt to give a brief account of the Dalit movement in India and portray with due respect the socio-political profiles of all those leaders who had worked for the emancipation of their brethren from the thraldom of untouchability and caste system, especially during 1857 to 1956.

Untouchability is an ugly canker of Indian society. How did such an institution come into being? It was felt that the causes of its origin definitely merited a study.

Dalit liberation movement had continued simultaneously with the practice of untouchability. However, its existence was felt only in the modern period. How could a community which had lost its very persona till then rise up in protest against the traditional unjust social order is a question. It is very much relevant to go deep into the causes of the origin of the movement.

The history of any society needs to be reviewed and reassessed in its real perspective. The shining deeds of the actors in the history would serve as a beacon to their brethren. If the role played by such actors is ignored, their dedication to the cause would go into oblivion and the society would lose its guiding spirits in finding the future path. Hence, it is proposed to know the history of Dalit liberation, with special emphasis on the role played by the leaders individually and collectively for the liberation of their own brethren and the achievements they had made in their mission.

SCOPE AND LIMITATIONS

Although the history of the struggle for the abolition of untouchability is as old as the custom of untouchability. the present study is, however, limited to the modern period which spreads roughly from the latter half of the 19th century to the first half of 20th century (that is 1857 to 1956).

While taking into account the contribution of the Dalit leaders to the cause of Dalits, one cannot ignore the contributions of non-Dalit leaders. However, the present study is obviously confined to the Dalit leaders who contributed to the movement.

It is, however, not restricted to any particular area or region. It is a macro-level study of the Dalit movement covering the country as a whole.

It covers all the shades or aspects of Dalit movement, and socio-political profiles of all those Dalit leaders and the organizations they established for the purpose of liberation of their brethren. The selection of Dalit leaders for the study is not made on the basis of sample or census, but on the basis of available information of such leaders who could fulfil certain criteria of Dalit leadership. Thus, the study covers almost all the prominent Dalit leaders and their organizations aimed at Dalit uplift. In order to make it more representative, care has been taken to include the contributions made by leaders of various castes or sub-castes from among the exuntouchables including that of women leaders, all over the country.

KEY TERMS

Dalits: For the purpose of the present study Dalit means all those people of different castes and sub-castes among the Depressed Classes who were traditionally subjected to invidious discriminations on grounds of untouchability, and categorized as the untouchables, downtrodden, exterior classes, Depressed Classes or the Scheduled Castes. It is, however, immaterial as to which faith or religion they belonged for the purpose of the study.

Dalit movement: The organizational or institutional efforts made by Dalit leaders for the liberation of the downtrodden masses could be termed as Dalit movement. It is a movement of protest against untouchability, casteism and superstitions. It aims at the uplift of the Dalits to the level of non-Dalits.

Negatively speaking, it stands for the rejection of the old traditional Hindu social order based on untouchability, socio-economic inequality, casteism, unscientific and irrational religious beliefs and customary servitude. Positively speaking, it stands for the acceptance of a new social order based on equality, liberty, social justice, scientific and rational religious or moral principles; and social, economic, cultural and political development of the Dalits.

It is, obviously, the movement to regain self-respect and equal human status in the society. The means by which it could operate were bringing awareness among the Dalit masses about their own 'identity' as human beings equal to other human beings, inculcating in them the attitude of protest against all sorts of injustice and oppressions and raising organizational strength and pressure against all the forces of inequality in a peaceful manner.

Leaders: Unless the context otherwise requires, leaders are those persons, belonging to the Dalit communities, who endeavoured to liberate the Dalits from untouchability, customary servitude and superstitions; and tried to uplift them in social, economic, educational and political spheres to the level of the caste Hindus. The term includes those persons who by their exceptional abilities, position and efforts had raised the pride and status of the community and boosted up the morale of their brethren. They are considered so, irrespective of their ideological and political affiliations and approaches, irrespective of their sphere of activities, irrespective of national level, state or local level activities and popularity, and irrespective of their success or failure in their mission. They should have worked at any length of time during the period under the study.

Dalit consciousness: It is the consciousness of Dalits of their own identity as human beings, equally equipped with physical and mental capacities as other human beings, and equally entitled to enjoy all the human rights without any infringement, abridgement or limitations. It is a staunch feeling of protest against the imposed lower caste status and evil of untouchability. It is a sense of self-respect and selfpride and longing for a new social order based on the sublime values of liberty, equality, justice and fraternity. It is this new awareness, which has been referred to as Dalit consciousness.

RESEARCH AIDS

The present study is, however, based on the available literature on the socio-religious reforms movements in general and the Dalit movement in particular. Especially the biographical literature on the Dalit leaders, though scanty in number and described in different languages, proved to be of great benefit.

The study is, obviously based on personal interviews with Dalit leaders who were alive, and the interviews with the next of kin of such leaders who were not alive.

It was, however, not an easy task. After consulting relevant literature and prominent persons in this field, the leaders were identified. Thus, after having collected the preliminary information about such leaders, efforts were made to contact their relatives and some prominent persons in public life, for collecting their exact addresses. The addresses were collected in a proforma for establishing rapport with them. This process, however, continued intermittently throughout the study period.

Thereafter, the letters were circulated informing all the concerned persons that they would be approached in due course of time for personal interview in this respect. A very few of them responded and appreciated the efforts.

In order to take personal interviews of the respondents, an exhaustive questionnaire was prepared and they were interviewed on that basis. Almost all the respondents were pleased to reveal the required information in this respect, except for one or two persons. It is, however, true that most of the leaders, who were alive, being old and infirm, could not recollect almost all the facts. Many of them had no systematic record or written documents with them. In case of the leaders who were not alive, it was, of course very difficult to collect relevant information about them. The next of kin of such leaders were not fully able to reveal the facts regarding the life and mission of such leaders. However, certain facts collected during the interviews were duly confirmed by consulting other relevant sources.

Apart from that, interviews or discussions with the eminent academicians and activists also proved to be useful in collecting relevant information.

Thereafter, every such leader's role was viewed in the set tests in this respect. The short socio-political profiles of such leaders had been prepared taking into account their contribution to the movement, without prejudice to their caste, region, sex or ideological affiliation, the organizations which they formed to accelerate the movement; and their achievements also got due place in the study. The state-wise profile of the Dalit movement also has been given in the study.

SIGNIFICANCE OF THE STUDY

The Dalits are still subjected to invidious discriminations based on the ground of untouchability. They are the worst sufferers of abject poverty, acute illiteracy, customary servitude, heinous superstitions and intolerable humiliations; and other vices that are incidental to or connected with untouchability.

This study would enable them to analyse, interpret and appreciate the true leadership. It would be useful in developing a sense of brotherhood amongst themselves. They may be able to struggle for their rightful place in history.

Therefore, the history of struggle for the emancipation of Dalits, a sizeable minority, from the age-old ugly and oppressive custom of untouchability cannot be ignored, nor could it be underestimated. Even, the struggle for the liberation of Dalits ought to be treated as equal to the struggle for the Indian independence. Therefore, it is necessary to record it with due respect and with the same sense of gratitude to those leaders and their struggle for the liberation of Dalits, as that of the struggle for national independence.

There are, no doubt, certain books on Dalit movement and its leaders, but they are scanty and scattered. As most of them are written in the regional languages, they are not easily accessible to others. Hence, such leaders and their mission remained unknown to other regions. Most of the books lack critical appreciation. The history of Dalit movement is not found in consolidated form. The present study, however, gives stress upon the role of the individuals, organizations as well as the circumstances in setting the historical events.

It would, of course, be useful as a ready reference to the scholars interested in undertaking intensive research on individual leaders, their thoughts and movement, regional movements and the specific movements. It would be beneficial to those activists who prefer to take lessons from their past. It would be efficacious to the framers of the policy as they would come to know the currents and cross-currents of various thoughts and their linkages in the present. Therefore, it is of great value.

2

Untouchability : A Process of Dehumanization

It is a self-evident fact that untouchability, a most venomous evil of Hindu society, has dehumanized a sizeable section of humanity, called untouchables. The victims of untouchability suffered a lot due to the stigma of untouchability including oppressive servitude, acute illiteracy, grinding poverty, degraded status and sinister contempt. It even marred the progress of the nation to a great extent. Therefore, it had been vehemently opposed by many socially conscious persons including saints, social reformers and political leaders in the past. Eventually, it was abolished under the Constitution of India, which came into implementation on 26 January 1950.

It is, therefore, necessary to know the meaning, nature and origin of that havoc-making infamous evil of untouchability in its real perspective.

MEANING OF UNTOUCHABILITY

Maharshi V.R. Shinde:

"A nation-wide institution indicating three features of often observing pollution, asking to live outside of village and not giving equal legal protection of law"[1] (1933).

---

1. V.R. Shinde, *Bharatiya Asprushyanha Prashna* (Marathi), p. 3 (1976 Edition).

Mahatma M.K. Gandhi:

"Untouchability means pollution by the touch of certain persons by reason of their birth in a particular state of family"[2] (1933).

Dr Babasaheb B.R. Ambedkar:

"Untouchability is the notion of defilement, pollution, contamination and the ways and means of getting rid of that defilement. It is a case of permanent hereditary stain which nothing can cleanse"[3] (1948).

Mr Justice N. Sreenivas Rao:

"The use of the word 'untouchability' refers to the meaning of the term in the context of the historical development of the practice and does not connote its literal meaning.

"A literal construction of the term would include persons who are treated as untouchables either temporarily or otherwise for various reasons, such as their suffering from an epidemic or contagious disease or on account of social observance such as are associated with birth or death or due to social boycott resulting from caste or other disputes. 'Untouchability' in such circumstances has no relation to the causes which relegated certain classes of people beyond the pale of the caste system."[4] (1958).

Prof Marc Galanter:

"In its broadest sense 'untouchability' might include all instances in which one person treated another as ritually unclean and a source of pollution.

"A second somewhat narrower sense of the term would include all instances in which a person was stigmatized as unclean or polluting or inferior because of his origin or membership in a particular group *i.e.* where he is subjected to invidious treatment because of difference in religion and membership in a lower or different caste.

---

2. A.T. Hingorani, (ed.) *My philosophy of life* by Mahatma Gandhi, p. 146.

3. B.R. Ambedkar. *The untouchables.* p. l. 26.

4. AIR 1958. Mysore 84 (Devarajiah V. Padmanna).

"Thus, we arrive at a third and still narrower sense of the term, 'untouchability' as referring only to those practices concerned with the relegation of certain groups 'beyond the pale of the caste system', that is confining it to those disabilities imposed on groups commonly regarded as 'untouchables'.

'Untouchability' then as used in Article 17, is confined to invidious discrimination against certain not readily definable classes of persons"[5] (1969).

The Committee on untouchability etc (Govt of India, Deptt. of Social Welfare, 1969) headed by L. Elayaperumal: "Untouchability is a basic and unique feature of the Hindu social system and order. It is generally held these days that it is an economic backwardness of the people concerned. But the simple fact is forgotten that while economic issues are present in all other countries untouchability is a unique problem confronted in this country only. It does not require much research to realise that the phenomenon of untouchability in this country is fundamentally of religious and political origin. Untouchability is not a separate institution by itself, it is a corollary of the institutions of the Caste system of Hindu society. It is an attitude on the part of a whole group of people. It is spirit of social aggression that underlies this attitude" (1969).

CHARACTERISTICS OF UNTOUCHABILITY

The above said definitions given by various authorities reveal the features of untouchability.

Caste and Untouchability

It is generally observed that untouchability is not an independent institution in itself but is a corollary of the caste system. According to Dr Babasaheb Ambedkar, the "idea of pollution"is by no means a peculiarity of caste as such. It usually originates in priestly ceremonialism and is a particular case of the general belief in purity. Consequently, its necessary

---

5. Prof Marc Galanter. "The abolition of Disabilities-untouchability and the law" In Mahar Michael (ed.) *The untouchables in contemporary India.*

connection with caste may be completely denied without damaging the working of caste. [6]

Caste system is based on Veda, Manusmriti and other religious scriptures, whereas untouchability is based on traditional contempt of Buddhism, and continuation of beef-eating by the so-called untouchables (infra). Caste system prescribes certain rules of "internal behaviour as a distinct unit as such for other castes, whereas untouchability is a rule of "external" behaviour with the so-called lower castes. Caste system divides Hindu society, originally in four Varnas, and later on into thousands of castes and sub-castes; whereas "untouchability" divides the Hindu society into 'Touchables' and 'Untouchables'. Caste system is comparatively more ancient than the institution of Untouchability.

However, caste system has consolidated the institution of untouchability by enforcement of several disabilities and restrictions under the fictitious belief in "purity" of the so- called high caste and "impurity" of the so-called lower castes. As such caste and untouchability are so intertwined with each other that one cannot easily bifurcate them. However, the minute observation reveals that both are separate institutions, at least, at their inception. [7]

UNIQUE ASPECT OF HINDUISM

It is generally observed that untouchability is a unique feature of Hinduism. The Karma theory, expounded in the *Gita*, states that man attains salvation by worshipping God through performance of one's own duties as decided by the religious scriptures. Consequently all the Hindus, including touchables and untouchables, strongly believed that there was no salvation except by complying with the rules of caste system as expounded and interpreted by the Brahmins who had the right to that effect. Almost all the religious gurus and pujaris believed in the

---

6. B.R. Ambedkar, *Castes in India: their mechanism, genesis and development*, p. 7, 1979.

7. Dr R.K. Kshirsagar, *Untouchability In India, law and abolition*, p. 23-26, 1986.

sanctity of untouchability and they had practised and enforced several disabilities based on untouchability. Even as recently as 1969, Shri Shankaracharya of Jagannathpuri is said to have justified the practice of untouchability as a matter of religion in the Vishwa Hindu Dharma Sammelan held at Kashi, Banaras[8]. Therefore, it is necessary to inquire into the fact whether or not untouchability is a part of the principles of Hinduism. Here the important question is, what is Hinduism? What are its main features?

According to a famous Indologist, Sir Monier Williams, the word "Hindu" has a territorial, rather than religious significance. "That part of the great Aryan race" says Monier Williams, "which immigrated from Central Asia, through the mountain passes into India, settled first in the districts near the river Sindhu (now called the Indus)." The Persians pronounced this word 'Hindu' and named their Aryan brethren 'Hindus'. The Greeks who probably gained their first idea of India from the Persians dropped the hard aspirate and called the Hindus 'Indoi'. Further, he observes that although there developed several sects and sub-sects, thoughts and isms, it is "all-tolerant, all-compliant, all-comprehensive, all absorbing."[9]

According to B.G. Tilak, "Acceptance of the Vedas with reverence, recognition of the fact that the means or ways to salvation are diverse, and realization of the truth that the number of Gods to be worshipped is large, that indeed is the distinguishing feature of Hindu religion."[10] Thus, almost all the thinkers including Swami Vivekanand, Mahatma Gandhi, V.D. Savarkar, Dr S. Radhakrishnan and Golwalkar Guruji while defining Hinduism did not stress on untouchability as a distinguishing feature of Hinduism.[11]

---

8. V.S. Nargolkar, Removal of untouchability, goals and attainments. *Indian Journal of Social Work,* Vol. XXX, No. 3, Oct. 1969.

9. Sir Monier William, *Hinduism.* pp. 1-12 (society for promoting Christian knowledge, London, 1894).

10. Samagra Tilak, Vol. 6. p. 791 (Marathi) Kasari Mudranalaya, Pune 1976).

11. Dr R.K. Kshirsagar, *"Untouchability in India, law and abolition"* p. 24-29.

It has been rightly observed by honourable Shri C.J. Gajendragadkar in "Shastri Yagnapurushdasji V. Muldas" (1966) that "unlike other religions in the world, the Hindu religion does not claim any one prophet, it does not worship any one God, it does not subscribe to any one dogma, it does not believe in any one philosophic concept, it does not follow any one set of religious rites or performances; in fact it does not appear to satisfy the narrow traditional features of any religion or creed. It may badly be described as a way of life and nothing more." It is all assimilating and comprehensive of all creeds and untouchability is founded on "superstition, ignorance and complete misunderstanding of the true teachings of Hindu religion."[12] In this respect the Committee on untouchability headed by L. Elayaperumal observes that untouchability "has nothing to do with the Hindu religion in the sense of spiritual principles. Unfortunately however, the basic principles of Hindu religion do not form the governing part of our life in society. It is really the law or codes of rules and regulations that has been mistaken as religion." [13]

Although there is no one founder, one sacred book or a way of worship of Hinduism, Hindus by and large are an identifiable group of people. They observe certain principles and practices distinguishable from other religions. In this sense Hinduism is a religion.

Untouchability, which originated initially in the contempt and hatred of Buddhism by the Brahmanic forces became an integral and essential part of Hindu social habit observed by the caste Hindus all over the country. It has, no doubt intruded into other religions, but by imitation of Hinduism, it cannot be called as an integral and essential part of their religious practices. In this sense untouchability is a unique feature of Hinduism.

Permanent stain: Untouchability was treated as a permanent stain acquired by reason of birth in an untouchable community, and it could not be obliterated by any way. The notion of untouchability was so deeply rooted in the minds of the caste

---

12. AIR 1966, S.C. 1119, "Shastri Yagnapurushadasji V. Muldas Bhunder Das Vaishya".

13. Report of the committee on untouchability, etc. p. 1 Oct. 1969.

Hindus that they thought it was but a religious act. It is their misconceived belief in the pollution or defilement by the touch of untouchables that does not permit them to discard the "custom" of untouchability. In other words, it is their misconceived belief that the so-called untouchables are *ab initio* untouchables, as such there is not a single rite or act which may purify them.

IMPURITY AND UNTOUCHABILITY

Untouchability coincides with the notion of defilement, pollution or impurity. *Manusmriti,* the basic law of the Hindu society refers to a number of instances or events and persons as the sources of impurity. Buhler in his book *The Laws of Manu* enumerates them as follows:

Impurity based on birth: Manu treats birth as a source of impurity. This type of impurity falls on the parents alone. However, the impurity of mother will last for ten days after the birth of a child, and the father shall become pure by bathing. In case of miscarriage a woman was treated as impure for as many days as the months which elapsed after conception.

Impurity based on death: The impurity based on death was very extensive in its range. All the members of the family of the deceased person were treated as impure for ten days or until the bones were collected or for three days or one day only.

Impurity based on Menstruation: Manu treats the period of menstruation as an event of defilement. Menstruating woman becomes pure only by bathing after the menstrual secretion has ceased to flow.

Impurity based on territory: Manu believes in territorial impurity. He states that the country of the *Mlechhas* or Barbarians was impure for the performance of the sacrifices.

The lands or territories fit for the performance of sacrifices *yajnas* were: (a) Brahma Varta, the land lying between Saraswati and Drishadvati rivers; (b) The land of Brahmarishis, the land of Kurus, Matsyas, Panchalas and Sursenakas; (c) Madhya Desa, the territory lying between the Himavat and the Vindhyas; and (d) Arya Varta, the territory between the Himavat and the Vindhyas, which extends as far as the eastern and the western oceans.

The country other than Brahma Varta, Brahmarshis, Madhya Desa and Arya Varta was the Mlechha land which was impure and unfit for sacrifices.

Impurity based on occupation: Manu treats certain occupations as of low status, such as the occupations of actor, singer, physician, seller of meat, oilman, maker of weapons, gambler, shepherd, etc. Persons engaged in lower occupations were treated as impure at the *Shraddha* or sacrifices, and their food was forbidden.

Impurity based on character: According to Manu adultery, prostitution, homicide, mixed marriages, etc, were immoral and punishable acts.

Impurity based on sex: According to Manu, women were the source of impurity. Hence they were not allowed to recite the Vedas. Their presence at the sacrifices would defile it. The eunuchs were also not allowed at sacrifices and their food was forbidden as impure.

Impurity based on physical unsoundness: Persons who were physically sound were eligible to perform religious rites. The mad, dumb, deaf, deformed and blind persons were the sources of impurity or defilement at the time of *Shraddha.*

Impurity based on mixed marriages: Manu in conformity with the Vedas states that there were only four varnas. Each varna was an endogamous group, as such marriages outside one's own varna were not allowed. The progeny of mixed marriages or varna *sankara,* were treated as outside the *Chaturvarna,* and impure.[13(a)]

Impurity based on conversion: This type of impurity was a later development. Those who converted to Islam or Christianity from

---

[13(a)] The impure castes were near about 53. They were Ayogava, Avrita, Avantya, Antyavsin, Abhira, Ahindika, Akarya, Ambastha, Andhra, Apapatra, Asura, Chandala, Dasa, Dasya, Digvana, Dravida, Ghalla, Kaivarta, Kamboga, Karana, Karuara, Karusha, Khasa, Kirata, Kukkutaka, Kina, Koda, Kukku, Madgu, Magadha, Maitreyaka, Malla, Margava, Milecha, Nata, Nishad, Pohlava, Pandusopaka, Panchala, Parad, Parasva, Paundraka, Pushpada, Sopaka, Suta, Svapacha, Saikha, Saka, Ugra, Vaideha, Vena, Viganman and Vratya.

amongst the Hindus were treated as impure and as outcastes on the ground of conversion.

However, "untouchability" and "impurity" described in Manusmriti were different from each other. The points of distinction can be stated as under:

1. Untouchability was a permanent stain. It was observed for all times and for all the occasions, whereas impurity based on birth, death, menstruation, etc, was occasional and temporary. Impurity was also observed at the time of *Shraddha* or sacrifices, and in respect of acceptance of food and in case of recitation of Vedas.
2. Untouchability was observed in respect of a whole class or caste: whereas impurity was observed with regard to the concerned individual.
3. Untouchability was observed with respect to the so-called lower castes, whereas rules of impurity were observed in respect of certain individuals by others irrespective of their caste.
4. Untouchability was not based on any reasonable ground, whereas impurity, with certain exceptions, was based on some reasonable grounds.
5. Untouchability, being a permanent stain, could not be removed, but impurity could be obliterated by performing the purificatory rites, or it might come to an end after the lapse of some time or with the death of the victim.
6. As far as penance was concerned, the untouchable offenders were subjected to harsher penalties than the touchables.
7. The practice of untouchability is not so ancient as compared to the practice of impurity. In the words of Babasaheb Ambedkar, "while the impure as a class came into existence at the time of Dharma Sutras, the untouchables came into being much later than 400 A.D."

Slavery and Untouchability

The slave is "a creature without any rights or any status whatsoever; who is or may become the property of another as a mere chattel, the owner having absolute power of disposal by sale, gift, or otherwise, and even of life or death, over the slave, without being responsible to any legal authority." [14]

According to Manu, the following seven categories of persons were slaves; [15]

1. Persons who were made captive in the war.
2. Persons working for their daily bread.
3. Those who were born in the house as *Dasi pu tra.*
4. Those who were bought.
5. Those who were presented by others.
6. Persons who were inherited from ancestors.
7. Those who were enslaved by way of punishment.

Manu states that slaves were not eligible to hold property. They were allowed to be witnesses only when the other witnesses failed to perform their duties. The Brahmins were allowed to eat the food offered by the slaves. Manu, however, restricts the intercourse with the female slaves. However, afterwards, they were supposed to be impure, and they were not allowed to remain within a distance of 72 paces from a Brahmin and a Nair. In Travancore some of the untouchable castes were literally slaves or serfs and were given away, bought, sold and mortgaged like other property till 1885.[16] However, the differences between untouchability and slavery are discernible.

Untouchability, according to Dr Babasaheb Ambedkar arose out of the contempt for Buddhism and continued habit of beef eating by the Broken Men; whereas slavery had its origin in the capture of defeated men, sale or transfer and born of a dasi. Slavery is quite ancient whereas untouchability came into existence later on. Slavery was more or less universal, but untouchability was a special feature of Indian (Hindu) society only. Untouchables were also unapproachable, and not even fit

---

14. ILR 1980, p. 723 (726), *Empress of India* V. Ramkaur.

15. G. Buhler, *The laws of Manu,* ch. VIII, 415.

16. L.S.S. O'Malley, *Indian Caste Custom,* p. 148 ? (Vikas Publishing House, Delhi, Edition 1974).

to be seen whereas the slaves were allowed to perform domestic services in the houses of their masters, in addition to other menial work. Slaves were the property of their particular master or owner only, whereas the untouchables were the servants of all the high caste Hindus, controlled and dominated by all the villagers.

Untouchability was a permanent stain, but slavery was not so. Untouchability was hereditary, whereas slavery was not so, except in some cases. The slaves were eligible to be free provided they fulfilled certain conditions, for example, the war captives were allowed freedom if they substituted other persons, the debtors were freed if the payment of debt was made. They were manumitted if they saved the life of their master. However, in all these cases of liberation, the tacit consent of the master was necessary.[17]

In 1792, the East India Company issued a proclamation against dealing in slaves in British India.[18] It has been abolished by the Slavery Abolition Act of 1843. Indian Penal Code *inter alia* provides severe punishment for any one dealing in slaves, under sections 370-371.[18(a)] On the other hand the history of legal eradication of untouchability starts from 1938 with the enactment of the Madras Temple Entry Act. The Constitution of India abolished untouchability under Article 17 and declared it as an offence punishable by law.[18(b)]

CERTAIN FORMS OF BEHAVIOUR AND PRACTICES UNDER UNTOUCHABILITY

Following categories or sets of certain forms of behaviour, attitude and practices manifest untouchability:

---

17. Encyclopedia Britannica, Vol. 16. p. 857.

18. L.A. Krishna Iyer. *The Travancore Tribes and Castes,* Vol. II. P. 123 (Govt. Press, Trivandrum, 1939).

18 (a) Dealing with slave is punishable with imprisonment of either description for a term which may extend to seven years, and also a fine.

18 (b) In pursuance of this provision the Parliament has passed the Protection of Civil Rights Act in 1955, which provides imprisonment of minimum one month to maximum six months and also with fine which shall be not less than one hundred rupees and not more than five hundred rupees.

Physical and Notional

Physical and notional untouchability is, obviously, based on religious misbelief, superstitions and contempt for the untouchables. The forms of physical untouchability are avoidance of even the slightest physical contact, unapproachability, keeping them out of sight and asking them to live outside the village. Forms of notional untouchability include a sense of superiority attitude of apathy, hatred and indifference towards the untouchables. It includes the belief in superstitions, thinking of untouchables as a matter of disgrace, a bad omen and a source of some calamity or danger to men and animals.

Overt and Covert

Overt and covert forms of this practice are mainly based on caste purity, hatred, contempt, prejudice and jealousy. Overt forms include not allowing the untouchables to draw water from a common well, not allowing entry in temples and hotels, not admitting in schools, not allowing to wear footwears or ornaments, not allowing to sell goods, not allowing to use common burial grounds, common roads, etc. Covert forms include discriminatory treatment in the schools, or at the public places, preaching or vindicating untouchability on religious, philosophical or historical grounds, calling names by filthy manner, etc.

Exploitative and Oppressive

Exploitative and oppressive forms and practices of untouchability are mainly based on fraudulent and criminal intentions. Exploitative forms of untouchability may include snatching the sources of income, paying less wages, charging more rate of interests, and extracting labour, including menial jobs. Oppressive forms include beating, killing, obstructing processions and other terrorizing activities.

The above description of the forms and practices of untouchability is not sufficient to show the nature of this evil. Untouchability, however, is a comprehensive term which includes each and every practice which aims at suppressing or oppressing the so-called untouchables for no reason. In the words of Mahatma Gandhi, "untouchability is a snake with a thousand mouths through each of which it shows its poisonous fangs. It defies definition."[19]

Untouchability is observed, not only against an individual or a few individuals, but against a group of individuals classed as untouchables. A group of so-called high caste people observes untouchability against all the supposed low caste people. Hence, it has been rightly observed by the Elayaperumal Committee that, "untouchability is an attitude on the part of a whole group of people. It is a spirit of social aggression that underlies this attitude."[20] According to Bhagwan Das, "Untouchability is not merely touch-me-notism, it is much more. It is a prejudice much stronger than the racial prejudice and more dangerous because it is invisible." [21]

ORIGIN OF UNTOUCHABILITY

It is but necessary to inquire into the causes of the origin of untouchability. There are altogether four theories advanced for the explanation of the origin of untouchability. They are discussed hereunder in brief.

The Theory of Taboo

Every caste Hindu, believing in Vedas, believes in varnashram, caste system and caste purity or taboo. It is stated in the *Purushsookta* part of the Rig-Veda, that Brahmin, Kshatriya, Vaishya and Sudra were created by God respectively from the mouth, arms, thighs and feet. The untouchables, however, were not *savarnas*. They were known as *avarnas*. Hence in the hierarchy of the caste system they were more degraded and treated as outcastes, untouchables, whose touch was considered to be profane.

The *Bhagavad Gita* while narrating the duties of each and every Varna states categorically that "by worshipping in through

---

19. A.T. Hingorani, *My philosophy of Life* by Mahatma Gandhi, p. 161, 1961.

20. Report of the Committee (1969), p. 1

21. Bhagwan Das, *"Untouchables and Buddhism"* Thought on Dr. Ambedkar.

the performance of his own duty (Dharma) man attains perfection." Performing one's own duties or Dharma was, thus, made essential for salvation.[22] Therefore, none could afford to challenge the Dharma revealed in the religious books. Ultimately, the habit of untouchability formed *Achar* Dharma of all the caste Hindus.

Thus, Hindus have no explanation as to the origin of untouchability, at the most they try to explain it in terms of fictitious belief in caste purity, taboo and inequality of castes. Therefore, the theory of taboo fails to explain the origin of untouchability.

Race and Occupation Theory

Stainly Rice propounded the theory of race and occupation for explaining the origin of untouchability.[23] According to him the untouchables were non-Aryan and non-Dravidian aboriginals. They were conquered and subjugated by the Dravidians first and thereafter by the Aryans. Accordingly, there were two invasions of India, first by the Dravidians and second by the Aryans. The Aryans vanquished the non-Aryans, reduced them to mere 'serfs' and assigned to them only menial or filthy occupations.

According to Babasaheb Ambedkar, this theory presupposes the homogeneous nature of Aryans, whereas they were divided into Rig-Vedic Aryans and Atharva-Vedic Aryans. The Dravidians were not racially different from the aboriginals. There is no record that the vanquished became untouchables. According to anthropometry test the untouchables resemble the high caste people, most of the names of *Kul* and *Gotra* also are identical to those of untouchables. The filthy and unclean occupations which the untouchables performed were common to all human societies but this practice could not come into existence elsewhere.[24]

---

22. The Bhagavad Gita. Ch. IV.

23. Stainly Rice *Hindu Customs and their Origin* p. B-15 (George Allen Unwin, London, 1937)

24. Dr. B.R. Ambedkar. *The Untouchables*, p. 58.

Multi-causal Theory

According to V.R. Shinde there were five different causes of the origin of untouchability.[25] They were:

1. Those who were living by performing filthy or unclean occupations were treated as untouchables.
2. Those who were independent entities, but later on were vanquished in the wars and became untouchables.
3. Those who were Buddhists and non-believers in God, superstitions and Vedas and did not accept the supremacy of Brahmanism were made untouchables.
4. The tribals not living like civilians also came under this category.
5. The marriage of a high caste female with a low caste male was called *Pratiloma* marriage and it was prohibited. Those who performed *Pratiloma* marriage in contravention of the Dharma Shastras were boycotted and discarded as untouchables.

The Broken Men Theory

According to Dr Babasaheb Ambedkar the untouchables were the Broken Men.[26] The primitive society was mainly tribal. At a later stage they became settled as soon as they switched to agriculture as a means of their livelihood. However, all the tribes did not settle simultaneously. Some tribes were still nomadic when others settled down.

There were intra-tribal wars as well as wars between settled and nomadic tribes. The causes for the intra-tribal warfare were (i) stealing cattle, (ii) stealing women, and (iii) stealthily grazing of cattle in the pastures belonging to others. On the other hand, the causes for the war between settled people and nomadic tribes were: (a) the nomads found it more advantageous to fight against the settlers and steal their wealth, and (b) the settlers were unable to defend themselves from the nomads who were naturally more militant and aggressive.

---

25. V.R. Shinde, *Bharatiya Asprushncha Prashna* (Marathi) p. 78-79, 1976.

26. Dr. B.R. Ambedkar. *The Untouchables,* p. 31-44.

Intra-tribal wars gave rise to divisions among tribes. The defeated tribes were broken into groups. Hence there always existed in primitive times a floating population constituting groups of Broken Tribesmen. On the other hand, the settled versus nomadic war caused loss of property and lives among the former. They were facing acute problem of defence from certain aggressive tribes. Thus the Broken Men were in need of shelter and food whereas the settled were in need of protection of the property and persons. Consequently, they had to come to certain settlement and form an agreement for protecting each other's interests. "Although we have", he states, "no written text of a contract coming down to us from antiquity we can say that the two struck a bargain whereby the Broken Men agreed to do the work of watch and ward for the settled tribes and the settled tribes agreed to give them food and shelter. Indeed it would have been unnatural if such an agreement had not been made between the two especially when the interests of the one required the cooperation of the other."

The primitive settlers, however, were not so liberal as to admit the aliens into their area, hence they allotted the land outside the village to the nomadic tribes. From the protection or strategic point of view, their settlement outside the village was necessary so as to face the prospective dangers. Obviously, because of their living outside the village they were called *Antyaja* or *Antyavasin.*

The second reason for the origin of untouchability according to Dr Babasaheb Ambedkar was the contempt for Buddhism, the religion professed by the Broken Men. The Broken Men who were segregated from the village people must have inclined to embrace Buddhism which was based on liberty, equality and fraternity. The village people who remained in the Hindu fold accepted the supremacy of the Brahmins; whereas the Broken Men discarded the supremacy of the latter and continued to profess Buddhism. This caused strife between the two communities which ended in suppression of the Broken Men and downfall of Buddhism in the later period.

According to Dr Babasaheb Ambedkar the third reason for the origin of untouchability was the habit of beef eating by the Broken Men. The untouchables became habituated to eating flesh of cows, whereas the touchables gave up the same. Even at the later stage the Brahmins not only gave up this diet, but became purely vegetarian so as to outsmart the Buddhists professing the principle of non-violence and compassion to all men and animals. "Unfortunately, beef eating instead of being treated as a purely secular matter, was made a matter of religion. This happened because the Brahmins made the cow a sacred animal. This made beef eating sacrilege. The Broken Men being guilty of sacrilege necessarily became beyond the pale of society."

Thus according to Babasaheb Ambedkar the 'stain' of untouchability was imposed on these people who were Broken Men, Buddhists and beef eaters.

However, there may be three important questions in this respect which need discussion. They are Why did the caste Hindus, especially Brahmins hate only Buddhists? What made the Broken Men who were Buddhists, continue beef eating? Why did they accept filthy occupations in return for the protection of caste Hindus?

1. Buddhism stands for an egalitarian model of society as opposed to Varna model. Buddhist Shramanas were not hereditary. This was in contrast with the theory of Hereditary superiority of Brahmins. The Buddhists opposed the supremacy of Brahmins. Buddhism propounded liberty, equality and fraternity.

   In ancient period there were feuds between Brahmins and Kshatriyas, as both wanted to maintain their own supremacy. Gautam Buddha did not belong to Brahmins. He was the son of a Kshatriya king.

   During his reign there arose a dispute over the use of the waters of Rohini between Sakya and Koliya. Gautam Buddha, then known as Siddhartha, did not accept the advice of the *Sangha* of Brahmins to wage war against the Koliyas. Hence the *Sangha* condemned Siddhartha, and he left the throne and after an intensive search of knowledge he founded Buddhism.

   In the later period Buddhism could appeal to and attract the foreign invaders like Milind and Kanisha, who became Buddhists and propagated this religion.

Naturally there might have developed hatred towards the religion adopted by the enemies of caste Hindu kings.

Although there were several Brahmin *Bhikshus* in Buddha's *Sangha,* they left the *Sangha* when Buddhist, lost royal patronage and when they came to know that they were unable to impose supremacy by Buddhist way.

2. The Broken Men were habituated to eating beef. They could not leave it even after accepting Buddhism. They were allowed to eat the flesh of cows which had died natural death. On the other hand, the Brahmins, in order to establish their supremacy used to practice non-violence and vegetarianism.
3. The Broken Men had lost their importance as far as protection of the village is concerned owing to the fact that the states or kings started to assume the responsibility of the protection of the villages.

This must have caused a loss of profession on the part of the Broken Men, resulting in the loss of source of livelihood. Therefore, the Broken Men had to resort to filthy occupations and beef eating.

Thus, untouchability arose out of contempt and hatred towards the Broken Men who were Buddhists. It was, however, imposed on them by all cunning and coercion. They became gradually victims of caste prejudice, state apathy, acute poverty and inherent ignorance.

PERIOD OF ITS ORIGIN AND GROWTH

Social institutions, however, develop gradually and not all of a sudden. Untouchability is also not an exception to this rule. As it originated in the contempt for Buddhism, it must have grown with the decline of Buddhism in India.

It was, at first recorded by Fa Hien, a Chinese Traveller in India (399-414 AD) that "throughout the whole country the people do not kill any living creature, nor drink intoxicating liquor, nor eat onions or garlic. The only exception is that of Chandala. That is the name for those who are (held to be) wicked men, and live apart from others. When they enter the gate of a city or a market place, they strike a piece of wood to make themselves known so that men know and avoid them and do not come into contact with them."[27] Thus in the beginning of fifth century the custom of untouchability was just emerging. It was observed only in respect of Chandalas, and it might not be known throughout the country.

The next Chinese traveller. Yuan Chung, came to India in 629 AD. He records, "Butchers, fishermen, public performers, executioners and scavengers have their habitations marked by a distinguishing sign. They are forced to live outside the city and they sneak along on the left when going about in the hamlets."[28] Thus in addition to Chandalas some other castes were recorded as untouchables.

Obviously, the decline of Buddhism starts from the period of Pushyamitra Sung and becomes virtually complete in the period when Shankaracharya lived, during AD 788 to 820. Shankaracharya in his final bid to exterminate Buddhism and establish the supremacy of Brahmanism strongly opposed the Buddhists and their religion; absorbed certain principles of Buddhism in Hinduism and moved Brahmanic forces against the Buddhists. He founded four centres of Brahmanism at Shri Badrikedar, Dwarka, Jagannathpuri and Shringeri for the propagation of Hinduism. He could successfully regain the confidence and reverence of the people for Vedas and Varnashram system.

Further he relieved the Sudras from their degraded position and interpreted religious texts in such a way which would give them the right to acquire the knowledge of Itihasa and Puranas, with the exception of the Vedas.[29] During this period probably the so-called Broken Men who were not willing to leave Buddhism and accept the supremacy of Brahmins were

---

27. Legge James *The travels of Fa Hien*. p. 43 (Oriental Publication).

28. Walters, Youn Chwang, Vol. I. p. 147. Quoted by Dr. B.R. Ambedkar in *The Untouchables*. p. 198.

29. Thibant George, *The Vedant Sutras*, Part I. p. 229 (Motilal Banarasidas Delhi. 1962.

gradually brought in place of Sudras and subjected to all the restrictions, prohibitions and disabilities stated in *Manusmriti* in respect of Sudras.[30] Here, it should be borne in mind that *Manusmriti* was written in the long past, presumably after the year 185 BC, when Pushyamitra Sung revolted against Brihdrat of Maurya dynasty. In the words of Dr Babasaheb Ambedkar, "There was no untouchability in the time of Manu. There was only impurity. Even the Chandala for whom manu has nothing but contempt is only an impure person."[31] Manusmriti, of course, states severe restrictions against the Sudras only, which were subsequently imposed on the Broken Men. Therefore, Buddhism, which was passing through a critical position due to the loss of royal patronage and incapable *Bhikshus,* could not sustain this attack as such and it started declining fast thereafter.

However, the decline of Buddhism did not take place throughout the country at once. Buddhism was in existence in western India until the aggression of Mohammad Kasim of Dahir on Sindh in AD 711; in Bengal it was there until 700 to 800 AD, when the Pala dynasty came to an end; in southern India it was in existence till the emergence of Shankaracharya. AD 788 to 820; in Gujarat it was there till 770 AD and in Thaneshwar till the end of kingdom of Harshavardhan, AD 647. Thus, untouchability came into existence as and when Buddhism was declining in different parts of India in different periods.

The next important factor connected with untouchability is the continuation of beef eating by the Broken Men and acceptance of vegetarianism by the Brahmins. The Broken Men, who were Buddhists, did not give up beef eating due to their 'habit' and 'poverty'; they were not allowed to kill the animals for meat by religion but as such they might have continued to eat the flesh of cows which died natural death, whereas the Brahmins switched towards vegetarianism to gain status and importance in an agrarian society. Now, the question is, when did the Brahmins and others accept vegetarianism? In this respect it is necessary to refer to the Chinese traveller Fa Hien.

---

30. C.B. Khairmode. *Dr. B.R. Ambedkar : Biography (Marathi)* Vol. I, ed. 3rd. P. 136, Pratap Prakashan, Girgaon, Bombay.1978.

31. Dr. B.R. Ambedkar. *The Untouchables,* p.186.

He states, "In that country they do not keep pigs and fouls. There are no butchers shop and no dealers in intoxicating drink. Only the Chandalas are fisherman and hunters and sell flesh meat." [32] Thus the Brahmins might have adopted vegetarianism only in the beginning of the fifth century.

Thus, it can be said that untouchability might have originated in the sixth century and spread throughout the country during the sixth to eighth centuries. It even was growing with the new and aggravated forms till recently. Due to ignorance, illiteracy, poverty and helplessness they had to submit to the oppressive will of the majority caste Hindus. Though occasionally they tried to get rid of it, they were again subjected to this evil with new forms and forces.

VICTIMS OF UNTOUCHABILITY

An attempt to enumerate the population of these so-called untouchables was made firstly in the year 1901 by the census authorities. It had divided the Hindu population into three categories, namely (i) Hindus, (ii) Animists, and (iii) Tribals, and the Depressed Classes or untouchables. However, it could not fix the exact number of the untouchables as no criteria of identifying the untouchables were fixed at that time.

The census authorities, however, fixed ten tests for identifying the untouchables in the Census held in 1911. They consisted of those who "(1) denied the supremacy of the Brahmins, (2) did not receive the Mantra from Brahmins or other recognized Hindu guru; (3) denied the authority of the Vedas; (4) did not worship the great Hindu Gods; (5) were not served by good Brahmins; (6) had no Brahmin priests at all; (7) had no access to the interior of the ordinary Hindu temple: (8) caused pollution; (9) buried their dead; and (10) ate beef and did not reverence the cow."

The same criteria were applied in the census which followed thereafter. Thus, the population of the untouchables in the total population and their proportion to the total population in India from the censuses of 1881 to 1961 could be given as under:

---

[32] Legge James. *The travels of Fa Hien*, p. 43.

Table 2.1 : Population Figures: (1881-1961)

SI. No	Census Year	Total Population	Population of the Untouchables	Percentage
1.	1881	248,583,616	43,092,200	17.33
2	1891	277,704,641		
3.	1901	280,875,176	53,196,632	18.93
4.	1911	298,299,527	51,738,673	17.34
5.	1921	301,772,466		
6.	1931	332,507,743	50,250,347	15.11
7.	1941	314,766,865	43,843,000	13.92
8.	1951	356,691,760	51,786,688	14.51
9.	1961	439,235,082	64,511,313	14.68

- Population figures from 1881 to 1931 are exclusive of population of Baluchistan, Burma, NWFP, Baluchistan States, NWFP and Sikkim.
- Compiled on the basis of census figures at various censuses.
- Population figures of 1941 are also exclusive of the population of the region which was partitioned as Pakistan.
- Population figures of 1941 and 1951 are as given in the Report of the Commissioner for SC and ST, 1953 (p. 246).

Altogether 429 untouchable castes were specified in the list of the Scheduled Castes under the Act of 1935. However, the number of such castes in the Schedule under the SC order 1950 became almost double.[33]

CONCLUSION

Untouchability is a notion of defilement, contempt and hatred towards a section of people called untouchables. It was, however, imposed on them by all cunning and coercion. It survived because it formed part of practices of Hinduism.

---

33. For details, see "The Constitution (SC) order 1950".

As a mental attitude it was manifested through several acts which include (i) prevention from entering any place of public worship; (ii) enforcement of disability with regard to access to watering place, public charitable institutions, public conveyance and such other places; (iii) restriction to use of jewellery and finery; (iv) refusal to admit to hospitals, educational institutions and public employment; (v) discriminations to the prejudice of untouchables at public and private places and institutions; (vi) compulsion to perform menial and low status services such as scavenging, etc; and (vii) boycott or perpetration of atrocities on the untouchables as a reprisal or revenge for having attempted to exercise their legitimate rights.

3

Factors Responsible for the Rise of Dalit Movement

The most injurious institution of untouchability, however, came into existence in the remote past, but spread with all its subsequently evolved and aggravated forms almost throughout the country in the recent past. Untouchability, being against the very interests of the so-called untouchables was not acceptable to them. The caste Hindus could successfully exploit the ignorance and helplessness of the untouchables to such an extent that they were made to believe that it was most religious and divinely instituted, and resistance to it would bring divine wrath. Thus their voice could not be audible, rather it was squarely suppressed until recently.

A PEEP INTO THE PAST

Since time immemorial the Hindu society is based on four varnas namely Brahmin, Kshatriya, Vaishya and Sudra. Subsequently, innumerable castes and sub-castes came into existence, obviously due to violation of caste rules and many other reasons. The so-called untouchables who were originally outside the caste system came to be known as 'out-caste' and formed the lowest caste, whose touch, even sight was treated as despicable to the caste Hindus. They were the most exploited and oppressed people in India. Surprisingly enough this non-egalitarian social structure had religious sanction.

However, the Broken Men who were deliberately degraded as untouchables by the Brahmanic forces had never accepted their position. They had started protesting against it from the beginning itself.

At the first, their response to untouchability came to the fore in the form of the 'Bhakti' cult. The Bhakti cult which originated in the 12th century was an antithesis of the Vedantic philosophy propounded by Shankaracharya, who believed in *dnyan* and karma as the only two ways to achieve salvation. The high castes, especially the Brahmins had the monopoly over both the ways of salvation. The saints belonging to the Bhakti cult rose against the Vedantic philosophy; they believed in spiritual equality and Bhakti or devotion to God as one of the means to achieve salvation. They substituted songs, music, dancing and waving of lights for Vedic mantras.[1] They preferred vernacular languages for prayers in place of Sanskrit. Of all the saints of Bhakti cult Shri Ramanujacharya, Madhavacharya, Ramanand, Vallabacharya, Kabir, Tukaram, Meerabai and Chaitanya were prominent. The untouchable saints like Ravidas, Chokhamela, Kanaka, Nandnara and many others were attracted towards the Bhakti cult. It is said that Shri Ramanujacharya opened the Narayana temple in Yadavgiri for the untouchables.[2] The temple of Jagannath at Puri was also opened for the untouchables at the instance of Chaitanya.[3] However, Chokhamela and Kanaka, the untouchable saints were not allowed to enter the temple of Vithal at Pandharpur and the temple of Krishna at Udipi respectively.[4] Thus, they had tried to assert their right of spiritual equality, but in vain.

The untouchables had no right to join martial services. However, during the Muslim rule they were recruited in the military. Some of the valiant and ambitious persons converted to Islam in order to get good positions in the service so as to

---

1. Sir Monier William, *Hinduism,* p. 135-250, 1894.

2. Ganvir Ratnakar (ed.) *Bahiskrit Bharatatil Agralekh,* p. 97 (Ratnanitra Prakashan, Bhusaval, 1976).

3. *Ibid.*, p. 98.

4. K.S. Karant, *four great Saints of India and spiritual equality,* Vol. XXXX. No. 29, 1980.

exploit it for taking revenge on the caste Hindus and rescue the untouchables from the caste tyranny. Some of them rose to be rulers. Kala Pahad, a Bengali untouchable ruler, became a terror for the Hindus in those days.[5] Malik Kafoor who served under Allauddin and trounced the Yadava kingdom at Devagiri in 1307 was a slave brought from Gujarat. Khushru Khan, an untouchable convert became the ruler of the country in 1390. They were mainly instrumental in spreading the Muslim rule throughout the length and breadth of India in those days. Amritnak was a brave warrior and a faithful servant of the Muslim king of Bedar, at whose instance the king recognized the "Charter of 52 Rights" in the year 1129 for Mahars, an untouchable caste.[6] Therefore they got the right to collect their *baluta* or meagre reward for the services they were to render to the caste Hindus as a Mahar or village servant. Though it was a small achievement in a given situation, it proved fatal and ruinous to the untouchables. They got some petty rights, but were expected to do many hazardous and filthy duties as village servants. However, when the untouchables were disappointed due to the indifferent attitude of the Muslims towards their problems they joined the Maratha king Shivaji and fought heroically for the establishment of his kingdom. They continued to be recruited in the Maratha's army subsequently. Nagnak Mahar became prominent in the reign of Rajaram.[7] Shidnak saved the life of Parashrambhau Patwardhan when the latter was in danger in the battle of Kharda.[8] Rainak Mahar fought at the fort of Raigad heroically till the last drop of his blood.[9] When the Brahmins became Peshwas and real rulers of the Maratha kingdom, they stopped recruiting the Mahars in the military, especially in the later period.

When the Peshwa's reign proved to be most harmful to them, they had to go to the East India Company for military

---

5. C.B. Khairmode, *Dr. Bhimrao Ramji Ambedkar: Biography,* Vol. p. 146, 1978.

6. C.B. Khairmode, *Dr. Bhimrao Ramji Ambedkar: Biography,* Vol. I. p. 150.

7. Ibid. p. 150.

8. Ibid. p. 150.

9. Ibid. p. 150.

recruitment. The Company was also in acute need of the martial services of the native people, especially the brave untouchables, hence it enrolled them in its military. The untouchable Pariahs who joined the British troops, fought at the fort of Arcot heroically and won the victory for the Company in 1751. The untouchable Mahars fought against the orthodox and oppressive rule of Peshwas in 1818 at Koregaon and won the victory for the British East India Company.

The untouchables who were getting disgusted due to their all-sided oppression in Hinduism naturally must have inclined to shun it and embrace Islam, which was philosophically more fascinating due to its monotheism and egalitarianism, in addition to being a religion of the ruling community. The rise of Sufism and preaching and propagation of Islamic principles by the Sufi saints in a virtually indigenous and attractive way also must have attracted the untouchables towards Islam.[9(a)] Ramdas, a Maharashtrian saint-poet states categorically in his *Dasbodh* about the situation in medieval India, that "many adore Dawalmalik, many worship Peer, many convert to Islam by their own will." This historical record bears witness to the fact that mass conversions to Islam were held in those days.

European Christian missionaries also attracted the untouchables by their principles of monotheism, egalitarianism and liberalism. Saint Xavier[9(b)] and Father Stephens[9(c)] came to India in the 16th century and started spreading Christianity. The untouchables who were subjected to the aggravated forms of untouchability, especially in South India became Christians in majority and uplifted themselves with the help of missionaries.

The Churha untouchables from Punjab were attracted towards the Sikh religion in the 17th century. They were later on

---

9(*a*) Of all the Sufi saints Khwaja Moinuddin Chisti (1142-1236), Bahauddin Zakaria (D. 1267), Muhammed Gous (D. 1517), Muhamad Farooqui (1563), Sheikh Abdulla Shatari (D.1606), Shah Madar Bodiuddin (D.1542), etc., were prominent. For details see: ***Encyclopaedia of Religion and Ethics.***

9(*b*) St. Xavier was a Portuguese missionary. He came to Goa in 1542.

9(*c*) Father Stephens was from England. He came to India in 1579. He wrote ***Khristpuran*** in Konkani language but in Roman script.

called 'Mazhabis'. The Chamars also followed them. They were called 'Ramdasias'. However, these converts were not treated on equal terms with the high caste converts.

Thus, the untouchables in order to get rid of untouchability and caste tyranny tried to resort to the Bhakti cult, sporadic upsurges and conversions, but in vain. They had of course no right to acquire property, hold weapons, seek knowledge and share political power.[9(d)] Thus, they were most helpless. They, however, tried to denounce, protest against and resist untouchability in their limited capacities and in a given situation, but could not get success to a great extent.

What is the achievement of the Dalit Movement which existed before pre-rebellion period is a pertinent question. It is a fact that the Bhakti cult could create a philosophical base for social equality. However, they could not bring about any substantial change in the existing social structure. Even the right of the untouchables to spiritual equality could not go beyond the singing of Bhakti songs.

The sporadic armed upsurges also proved to be of no use. The untouchable warriors could bring about change in the authority, but not in the social values and social structure. The authorities very cleverly exploited their valour, but as soon as they came to power at any moment of history, they deliberately discarded them. Neither the Muslims nor the British gave them any share in power. They could at the most change the master, but not their own future.

Conversion to Islam and Christianity proved to be good, but only in a limited sense. Muslim community included two classes, namely, Ashraf and Ajlaf meaning high class Muslims and low class Muslims respectively. Even therein existed one more class in the Hindi speaking regions namely Arzal which included persons "engaged in filthy occupations like sweepers, scavengers, such as Sheikhs, Halalkhors, Lalbegis, Abdals, Bediys, Mehtars, Mahars, Mussalis etc"[10] and they were

---

9(d) These restrictions were based on the Code of Manu which were originally meant for the Sudras. They were made applicable to the untouchables at the initiative of Shankaracharya.

10. Bhagwan Das. *Thus Spoke Ambedkar.* Vol. IV. p. 143.

subjected to untouchability. Even among Indian Christians there existed two classes, one converted from higher castes and other from lower castes. It was but a fact that the high caste converts could only derive more and more benefits from the missionaries rather than lower caste converts.

The Bhakti cult, however, created a philosophical base for social equality and set in motion a new trend towards social and spiritual equality. The sporadic armed upsurges and conversions to Islam and Christianity had upset the socio-political balance in the country. It was a sort of protest- blow to Orthodox Hinduism, which caused necessary apprehension in the minds of caste Hindus and compelled them to rethink over the religious orthodoxy.

These movements could provide the probable means and ways of protesting against Hinduism for future generation of Dalits. The same currents of thought of Bhakti, armed upsurges and conversions were rejuvenated in the form of new waves respectively of sanskritization, political aspirations and conversions in future.

It can be stated that the pre-rebellion Dalit movement could not be virtually successful only because it had a premature birth but it generated a new hope that there could be conception in future provided some precautions were taken. Thus the Dalit movement was inherent in the origin and growth of untouchability itself.

Now, the question is what could be the criteria of successful course of Dalit movement, or how the Dalit awakening which existed in post-rebellion era was qualitatively different from that of pre-rebellion era. In this respect following three tests should be applied, namely:

1. Whether the protest was against the social system as a whole.
2. Whether the response of Dalits was ubiquitous in the country.
3. Whether the Hindu society and the existing authorities could take sufficient cognizance of it.

It seems that only the post-rebellion period fulfils these tests of the successful course of the Dalit movement. In other words the Dalit liberation movement could attain momentum after the Mutiny of 1857.

THEORIES OF SOCIAL CHANGE

Dalit movement, obviously contemplates change in the social structure and change in social values of the Indian society. It aims to reform the society on the sublime principles of liberty, equality, justice and brotherhood.

What factors are responsible for bringing about social change? Does social change occur, independent of leadership? Or is it an outcome of leadership? There is a controversy among the social scientists regarding the causation of social change.

There are five major schools of thinkers who had interpreted the causes of social change. According to St. Augustine (354-430 AD) history is only 'an unfolding of a divine plan'. According to August Comte (1798-1857), L.T. Hobhouse (1864-1929), Max Weber (1864-1920)[11] and Emile Durkheim (1858-1917) the religion or culture is important in shaping social structure. Herbert Spencer (1820-1903) believed that an evolution in the society is bound to take place in the course of time. According to H.T. Buckle (1821 -1862),[12] a change may take place in the society because of geographical factors including climate, food, soil and other aspects. According to Karl Marx (1818-1883),[13] the mode of production determines the social structure. He thought that the social structure is but the by-product of the economic structure. It is not the 'intellect' or 'idea', but the pattern of economic production and distribution which shape the structure of a given society.

Thus, it seems that there are two extreme views in this respect, one giving importance to personal factors like reason, morality, ability and one's notion of right or wrong; and other giving importance to impersonal factors like divinity, environment and economic condition.

---

11. Dronberger. *The Political Thought of Max Webber,* p. 278-283, 1971.
12. E.S. Bogardus. *The Development of Social Thought,* p. 278-283, 1964.
13. G.H. Sabine. *History of Political Theory* (p. 766-711), 1961.

In the view of Dr Babasaheb Ambedkar both the personal as well as impersonal factors are important in bringing about social change. However, he thought that the' personal factors are more instrumental than the impersonal factors in this respect. He said very categorically that, it is, "quite wrong in holding that impersonal forces are everything and that man is no factor in the making of history. That impersonal forces are a determining factor cannot be denied. But that the effect of impersonal forces depends on man, must also be admitted. Flint may not exist everywhere. But where it does exist, it needs man to strike Flint against Flint to make fire.. Man therefore, is a factor in the making of history and that environmental forces whether impersonal or social, if they are the first, are not the last things."[14]

In this backdrop of approaches to social change, it is worthwhile to enquire as to which forces were responsible in respect of abolition of untouchability and uplift of the so-called untouchables to the level of other communities. In this respect there were two types of causes or factors: one, the proximate, or endogenous or direct causes and other, the remote or exogenous or indirect causes.

Following were the proximate or endogenous causes for the rise of Dalit movement during the post-rebellion period.

Martial Services

The untouchables including Mahars had a bright history of martial services under the Muslim and Maratha kings. However, their military career came to prominence under the British rule. The East India Company raised two battalions, mainly consisting of Mahara on 4 August 1768.[15] The marine battalion of the Bombay Army was also raised in 1777, in which the Mahars formed a large part. The Company had a special inclination for Mahar soldiers because they knew that the Mahars had a bright military background, they were faithful, reliable, sturdy, vigorous and brave. Moreover, they were quite familiar with the Indian situation including forts, forests and strategic points.

---

14. B.R. Ambedkar, *Ranade, Gandhi and Jinnah,* p. 14.

15. V. Longer, *ForeFront for Ever,* p. 10. 1981.

They were recruited in the Marine Battalion as they had "no inhibitions in serving on the sea or crossing the waves to get to foreign lands." They were expected to be more revengeful against the native rulers as they were deliberately neglected by them. Their assumption and expectation came to be true. The Mahars gave a decisive fight to the Peshwa on the parched battlefield of Koregaon in 1818 and won the victory. They achieved success in Kathiawar in 1826, took part in the first and second Afghan wars, won Gujarat in 1849, fought in the great Mutiny in 1857 and secured victory for the British. They participated in a number of naval conflicts with the pirates off the Indian coast and in the Persian Gulf.

Ini 1852 the total strength of the Indian component of the Bombay Army was 25,938 men; of these 8,789 were from the Mahar community.[16] It was estimated that in 1856 the Mahars comprised one-third of the Bombay Army.

"Bengal army led by Clive in the battle of Plassey consisted mainly of the low caste people like the Dusadh, Dhusla, Doms, Dhanuks etc." "Madras army consisted of low caste Hindus and untouchables."[17]

The Churha untouchables of Punjab who were engaged in sweeping and cleaning were converted to Sikhism. Those converts are called Mazhabis. Ranjit Singh (1780-1839) started recruiting Mazhabis into the Khalsa Army, but due to objections from the high caste Sikhs they were formed into separate companies. After the defeat of the Khalsa in the second Anglo-Sikh war of 1849, many Mazhabis turned to dacoity; as such they were known as criminal class for some time. After 1851 the Dogra Maharaja of Kashmir, Gulab Singh recruited Mazhabis as pioneer troops for his army. They were at first enlisted in the British Indian Army during the Mutiny of 1857.

For a long time, Bengal Army continued to enlist 'low caste' people. It was only after the Mutiny of 1857 that the recruitment of these low caste men was discontinued due to the fear that the

---

16. *Ibid.* p. 16.

17. Bashyam Ardhthe, *Untouchable Soldiers,* p. 3 Ambedker Menorial Society. Bangalore, 1980.

caste Hindu soldiers would not tolerate the untouchable's resurgence in the military.

Martial services, obviously, proved to be a boon to the untouchables in those days when they were deliberately debarred from all walks of life by the Indian society especially the caste Hindus. They could improve their economic condition to a great extent. They could get acquainted with the manners, values and discipline of the British military personnel. The East India Company provided compulsory education for its Indian soldiers and their dependents. When they brought home the victory by exemplifying their bravery in various expeditions, their confidence was raised. They came to know the outside world whenever they happened to go on foreign expeditions. They could get an opportunity to come in contact with each other, share their thoughts, joys and sorrows with their co-brothers. After retirement from military service they could disseminate the new idea of discipline amongst their brethren.

Dalit Reform Movements

A new awareness seems to have been spreading among the Dalits since the latter half of the 18th century. Prominent amongst those who could bring a new awareness to the Dalits through their institutionalized movements included:

Ramdeo Panth: Ramdeo Panth[18] (a sect) was founded by Shri Guru Ramdas who was a resident of village Sithal near Bikaner in Rajasthan. He belonged to an untouchable Dhed community. One Shri Ramdas, Dhed by caste, previously a Kundapanthi (Kundapanthi is a person who eats in an earthen pot or *kunda)* came to Sithal and met Shri Guru Ramdas. Guru Ramdas convinced Ramdas to accept Ramdeo Panth. After becoming a Ramdeo Panthi, Ramdas (1726- 1798) extensively travelled throughout Rajasthan for the propagation of the philosophy of his sect to the masses, especially amongst the untouchables. The tenets of his sect were:

1. Not to have faith in 'Varnashram'.
2. No faith in the incarnation of God.

---

[18] Swami Dayanand, *Satyartha Prakash*, ch. XI. p. 257, Vaidic Sahitya Sadan, Delhi.

3. No salvation without concentrating on *Ram nam*.
4. The Guru was greater than God.
5. The books written by Guru Ramdas were believed to be more valuable than the Vedas.
6. 'Ram' was the 'Sukhsam' Veda.

He established the headquarters of the Panth at Khedapa in Marwad region of Rajasthan. This sect reflects the acute protest against the orthodox Hinduism. It became popular amongst the untouchables in Rajasthan.

Satnami Panth: Satnami movement [19] was founded by Guru Ghasidas. He was born on 18 December 1756 at village Giraud in Bilaspur district of Chattisgarh region in Madhya Pradesh. His father was Mahangu Das and mother was Amrautin. They were religious-minded and agriculturist by profession. Guru Ghasidas married Sofooribai at an early age.

The principles of Satnami movement were:

1. Belief in truth.
2. Prohibition of idol worship.
3. Belief in casteless society.
4. Prohibition of taking meat.
5. Treating wives of others as mother.
6. Prohibition of taking liquor.
7. Love for men and animals.

He believed that "God was one and formless" The only way to realize God, according to Guru Ghasidas, was "to imbibe the spirit of Satnam, the truth". He apparently laid more emphasis on the strong organization of the downtrodden people. However, the reactionaries could not tolerate his radical thoughts, and ultimately murdered him in 1850. His new faith became popular amongst the untouchables living in Chattisgarh region of Madhya Pradesh. His sons and successors also propagated Satnami sect and tried to bring an awareness of the separate identity of the so-called untouchables.

---

[19]. Michael Mahar (ed.). *Untouchables in Contemporary India.*

Naval Dharma: Naval Sahib was born in 1783 at village Harsalla in Nagaur district of Rajasthan. His father Kusal and mother Singari were illiterate and led a simple life.

He came into contact with Karta Ram Maharaj, a religious Guru of Meghwals, a native of the village. The Guru taught Naval the tenets of Nirgun Bhakti preached by Kabir.

Naval Ram began his religious activities among the Bhangis. The orthodox villagers could not tolerate his teachings and began harassing him. Hence he left the village and came to Jodhpur, where he founded his own sect. He set up the headquarters of his sect at Bai-ji-ka-talao and served the community for near about hundred years. He died in Vikram era 1965 at the age of 120. He was cremated in a Bhangi bustee in Jodhpur, which is now known as "Naval Bustee".

The tenets of his new faith were: [20]

1. To forbid idol worship.
2. To worship the creator, Brahma who is 'Nirankar' (without shape).
3. To forbid evil habits, such as drinking, eating beef and traditional customs such as *Mrityu Bhoj*.
4. To believe in equality of human beings.
5. To restrain temptation and anger.
6. To help the poor.

He appointed nine persons, in addition to his son Daya Ram Maharaj to propagate the new faith. They propagated the Naval faith amongst the Bhangis in Rajasthan, Delhi, Maharashtra, Hyderabad, Karachi and Assam.

Warkari Panth: Warkari Panth is a prominent Hindu religious movement in Maharashtra. The saint poet Shri Dnyaneshwar is supposed to be its first propounder. Chokhamela was a Warkari saint poet from the untouchable Mahar community. He lived in Mangalveda near Pandharpur. He was a follower of Namdeva and worshipped Vithal of Pandharpur. He died in 1338 AD. The

20. Shyamlal, *The Bhangis in Transition* (p. 54-65), 1984.

Warkari Panth had been in existence since then even among the untouchables. There were so many saints or gurus among the untouchables throughout Maharashtra. They continued the tradition of Warkari Panth till recently. However, there is no trace of any prominent saint among them during the period under study. The Warkari Panth stressed on purity of heart, cleanliness of body, worship of Vithal of Pandharpur and spiritual equality.

Kabir Panth: Kabir Panth is a prominent religious reform movement which spread in most of the northern part of the country. It was founded by saint poet Kabir (1398-1494) who lived in Kashi. He is said to have belonged to a lower caste known as Julaha. He preached spiritual as well as social equality. Therefore, Kabir Panth became popular among the untouchables. There were several *Maths or* centres and preachers of the Panth. However, prominent among them is not known.

Nasraiah Sect: This sect was founded by Shri Nasraiah, and as such it was named as Nasraiah sect.[21] He was from Andhra region. The main principles of this sect were:

1. To maintain good moral conduct.
2. To worship only one God and not to worship idols.
3. To maintain unity among the untouchables.

He had faith in Islam. He therefore tried to emulate the model of Islam in his sect. His sect became popular among the Nadiga untouchable community living in Vinukonda and Narasoraopet in the present Guntur district of Andhra Pradesh. He died in 1825.

Matua Sect: This sect[22] was founded by Shri Harichand Thakur who was born in 1811 in the Namsudra untouchable community in Bengal. The principles of this sect were:

1. No need to enter the temples of the higher castes for the purpose of worship.

---

21. V. Ramakrishnan, *Social Reform in Andhra,* p. 47, 1983.

22. Dr. Sudhir Kumar Bagchi, Article in *The oppressed Indian*, p. 67, Vol. IV, 1982.

2. Discarding Brahmin priest for any ceremony.
3. To worship only Shri Hari.
4. Not to worship idols and not to visit pilgrimage centres of Hindus.
5. To maintain good moral conduct and lead an ideal family life.

Shri Harichand Thakur's sect became popular in East Bengal, now a part of Bangladesh.

After his death in 1879 his son Shri Guruchand Thakur ably continued the Namsudra movement in Bengal.

These sects were apparently the natural reactions to the orthodox Hinduism. The founders and propagators of the various sects have played a great role in bringing about a new awareness, separate identity, self pride and self confidence amongst the Dalit masses. They had tried to introduce radical changes in the Hindu social system and became successful to a great extent.

Their real evaluation would be possible only when the period in which they had to work is taken into account. The situation for social change was adverse and they had to face many odds. The founders of these sects, being untouchables, could attract more of their untouchable brothers.

Dalit Education

Dalits were deprived of education; as such they had lost everything. Therefore, in right earnest they started to spread education amongst themselves. In this respect the contributions made by the following persons and institutions are creditable.

Mahatma Jyotirao Phule (1827 to 1890) was from the backward Mali caste and once became a victim of relative untouchability imposed by the Brahmins in Pune. Only he could properly realize the importance of education in improving the lot of the untouchables and backward castes. He stated very categorically that, "For want of education intellect deteriorated. For want of intellect morality decayed. For want of morality progress stopped. For want of progress wealth vanished. For want of wealth the Shudras perished. All these sorrows sprang from illiteracy." [23] Thus inspired with the objective of uplift of the untouchables he started one school exclusively for girls in 1848 in Pune, as well as another for the untouchables on 15 May 1848 in their locality itself in Pune. He continued his ceaseless efforts with all missionary zeal for the educational development of the poor masses. Thus, from 1848-1852, he could establish altogether 18 schools in the vicinity of Pune.

His wife Savitribai Phule (1831-1897)[24] worked as an equal partner in his mission of uplifting the poor and oppressed people. Though previously illiterate, she was inspired by Mahatma Phule, her husband and joined school only to teach in the institutions founded by Mahatma Phule as no lady teachers were available in those days to teach girl students. Later, they could procure help from a Muslim lady and some other high caste men for teaching in their schools.

In their missionary zeal and transcending love for untouchables, one Lahujibuwa, a Mang, and Ranoji, a Mahar, came to their help in bringing the students from the untouchable communities to the schools run by Mahatma Phule. Mahatma Phule and Savitribai Phule wrote many thought provoking and inspiring books, poems, etc. Both of them were great educationists of those days, who could come out to criticize the prevailing theory of class education, but in vain. Therefore, they took initiative in starting education for the masses including the untouchables. They had rightly thought that education was an effective instrument of social change and restoration of cultural values.

Mahatma Phule later on established Satya Shodhak Samaj on 24 September 1873 at Pune for the social and religious uplift of the untouchables and other backward communities. He worked throughout his life for the cause of the oppressed people. Hence, he may rightly be called as the father of modern oppressed India. His philosophy of social reformation, eradication of untouchability and restoration of the rule of toilers had a far reaching

---

23. Mahatma Phule, *Samagra Vigmaya*, p. 189, Maharashtra Rajya Sahitya and Sanskriti Mandal, Bombay, 1980.

24. Savitribai Phule, *Samagra Vangmaya* Dr. M.G. Mali (ed), Maharashtra Sahitya and Sanskriti Mandal, Bombay, 1988

influence on the social and political life of Maharashtra and ultimately on India.

The Christian missionaries were also engaged in educating the Indian society, including the untouchables. One cannot ignore their contribution to the spread of education and the progress of knowledge in India.

PROCESS OF CONVERSIONS

The untouchables resorted to conversions as a means to getting rid of Hinduism, which brought all miseries to them. Moreover, they expected to get a new social status which was an obvious motivational force for conversion to Islam, Christianity or Sikh religion, in addition to certain material benefits.

In order to get rid of untouchability and caste system, some of the untouchables, especially the sweepers and Bhangis belonging to Lalbegi and Malkana castes got converted to Islam. Probably, they might have thought or were made to think that they would get the treatment of equality in Islam. However, they were disappointed in this regard. Even the converted untouchables could not discard the age-old Hindu impact on their mind. They adopted Islamic names and rituals, but at the same time retained their old Hindu rituals and ceremonies. The Muslims were reluctant to have blood relationship with them.[25]

Some of the untouchables especially the Churhas in Punjab had converted to Sikhism. It is said the Churhas rescued the body of Guru Tegh Bahadur, the ninth Guru, who was executed by Aurangzeb in 1675. They carried the corpse of the Guru to Amritsar. Thus, after having observed the courage of the Churha sepoys in carrying the corpse of the Guru, the tenth Sikh Guru, Guru Govind Singh, allowed them into the faith; as such they were called Mazhabi or 'faithf ıl'. Most of the Churhas followed the first converts.[26]

The Portuguese missionary, "St. Francis Xavier attempted a large scale conversion of lower classes on the coastal areas of

---

25. T.N. Atre, *Gawa-Gada* Narak Safaichi Gost, p. 25.
26. Bhagwan Das (ed). *Untouchable Soldiers*, p. 44. 1980.

Western India."[27] Later on the Church of England got engaged very actively in proselytization among the lower classes.

The untouchables who were victims of aggravated forms of untouchability especially in Travancore, became Christians in majority. According to 1891 Census there were a total of 2,284,172 Christian converts in India; out of them 1,491,458 were in British Provinces and 792,714 were in Native States.[27(a)] It could presumably be said that the process of conversion to Christianity must have started before the pre-rebellion period.

However, caste status was retained even in the new faith because of caste consciousness especially by the high caste converts. Therefore, the Bishop of Calcutta, Danial Wilson issued a circular in 1823 to all the Anglican missionaries in India, saying that "the distinction of castes must be abandoned, decidedly, immediately, finally." [28]

In 1848 Bishop of Madras namely Bishop Spencer and 84 missionaries resolved to abandon caste as it was opposed to Christianity. Further, the Madras Missionary Conference held in 1850 resolved to abandon caste system in Christianity.

This shows that on the one hand the caste status was being retained by the caste Hindu converts and on the other the genuine efforts of the missionaries to abandon the same were going on. It could presumably be said that the missionaries must have been more successful. Their efforts must have had an educative value which could bring an awakening in the Indian society in general, and among the Christians and lower classes in particular. The process of proselytization could increasingly exert threatening pressure on the high caste Hindus to accommodate certain new values and to get adjusted to the new challenging situation.

Other factors responsible for the rise of Dalit movement could be categorized as exogenous or remote factors. These factors are discussed under two heads: animate and inanimate factors with regard to their nature.

---

27. K.M. Pannikar, *The Foundation of New India*, p. 36.

27(a). George Smith, *The Conversion of India*, p. 201, 1893.

28. G.A. Oddie, *Social Protest in India*, p. 46.

ANIMATE CAUSES OF THE RISE OF DALIT MOVEMENT

Christian Missionaries

Contribution of Christian missionaries to the rise of modern India is of great significance. The first missionary was St.Francis Xavier from Portugal who reached Goa in 1542. Since then the Christian missionaries began to come to India to propagate Christianity.

In 1705, Danish Lutheran missionaries of Protestant Mission named Bartholomew Zieganblag and Henry Plutschau founded the mission in the kingdom of Thanjavur. Zieganblag translated the Bible into Tamil.

In 1792, William Carey of England founded the Baptist mission in Serampur in Bengal. He translated the Bible into Bengali, Sanskrit, Hindi and Marathi. He started the first Bengali newspaper, *Samachar Darpan* in 1818. Claudin Buchanen and Thomas C. Thomson followed him.

In 1813, the East India Company agreed to allow missionaries to work in India. Since then several missionaries came to India and started their missionary activities. Protestant mission was established at Ranchi in 1845; American missionaries formed their centres at Madras and Madurai in 1833, and at Ahmadnagar in 1831. American Presbyterians started their mission at Ludhiana in 1834, Allahabad in 1836, Jullundur in 1846, Ambala in 1848, Lahore in 1849, Sialkot in 1855. They started their activities in Andhra region in 1840 and in Assam in 1841.

The Lutheran Mission started its activities at Mangalore in 1838 and later on at Hubli and Dharwad.[29]

Thus the Christian missionaries started their activities in almost all the parts of India till 1857. They could spend money, time and talent for the propagation of and proselytization to Christianity in India. It was but natural for the oppressed lower castes or untouchables to get attracted to Christianity. Even the missionaries from Bengal in their conference held in 1855 at

---

29. Gazetteer of India, Vol. 1,

Calcutta appealed "to the various missionary societies in Europe and America for more help and cooperation with them and money for pursuing missionary activities more vigorously."[30]

In 1851, there were 339 foreign ordained and 21 native ordained missionaries and 493 native laymen engaged in religious preaching in India. In 1861, there were 479 foreign ordained and 97 native ordained missionaries and 1,266 native laymen engaged in religious preaching.[30(a)]

Further, the process of proselytization was accelerated when the law was passed in 1856 removing disabilities arising out of conversion to Christianity specially in respect of inheritance of property. In most of the schools run by Christian missionaries as well as in those run by the Government, the study of the Bible was introduced.

They subjected Hinduism and its superstition to scathing criticism, thereby lowering the morale of the Hindus. This resulted in acceleration of the proselytization process. Even some of the Muslims were attracted towards Christianity due to certain incentives. Consequently, the "proselytizing activities created a sense of alarm among both the Hindus and Muslims who were specially sensitive in religious matters."[31] It was because of fear of heavy Loss to their religion that they started to think about revival of their respective religions.

Islamic Revivalists

The most affected people due to the arrival of the English were the Muslims, because they had to lose their hegemony over India. Their grievances regarding British resurgence resulted in the formation of a number of organizations.

The first and foremost reaction to British rule came from the Wahabi movement. The Wahabi movement was a protoype of its counterpart founded in Arabia by Muhammad bin Abdul Wahab

---

30. Joshi (ed.), *Rebellion,* 1857, p. 110.

30(a) George Smith. *The Conversion of India,* p. 206.

31. R.C. Majumdar, *British Paramountcy and Indian Renaissance* Part-I. p. 418.

(1703-1792). It was founded in India by Shah Waliullah (died in 1762).

The principles of thc Wahabi movement were:

1. To strictly follow the commands of God.
2. Not to believe, unlike Sufism, in the communion with the God.
3. To pray to God without intermediaries.
4. Disbelief in any innovation like tomb worship, veneration of *pirs,* ascetism, etc.
5. To observe five essential principles: prayer, fast, Hadj, *Zakat* and *Jihad.*[32]

The Wahabi movement was vigorously led by Sir Sayyad Ahmad Barelvi as the Imam and commander of military campaigns. He declared *Jihad* against the Sikhs in 1826.

The British encouraged the Wahabis in their fight against the Sikhs to reap the fruits of war between Sikhs and Muslims. The Wahabis formed their government at Peshawar and then at Sittana. Sayyad Ahmad Barelvi was killed in a battle by the Sikhs in 1831. Thereafter, Wilayat Ali (born in 1790) and Enayat Ali (born in 1794) of the Sidiqipur family of Patna became the leaders of the movement.

When the British spread their hegemony over almost the entire territory from Calcutta to Delhi, the Wahabis declared *Jihad* against them. Consequently the British also revised their policy in respect of the Wahabi movement.

The Wahabis shifted the central headquarters from Sittana to Patna, formed a committee of advisers and appointed itinerant propagators in most of northern India. They maintained contacts with the brother of Nizam of Hyderabad, Nawab of Kurnool, Raja of Satara, Jodhpur and the Nawab of Bhopal for getting cooperation from them in the *Jihad* against the British rule. Ultimately, the Wahabis took a very active part in the rebellion of 1857, but in vain. The British Government successfully suppressed the Wahabi movement by 1871.

---

32. Ahmad Qeyamuddin, *The Wahabi Movement in India,* p. 63, 1966.

The Faraidi movement was founded by Haji Shariatullah of village Bahadurpur in Faridpur district in Bengal in about 1804. It had denounced, like the Wahabi movement, "un-Islamic innovation and customs and declared Bengal which was under the rule of the British, to be a Dar-ul-harb or land of enemy." The Faraidis openly preached the expropriation of the property of landlords without compensation.[33] Most of them were drawn from the "lower classes" and they were demanding social and economic equality. The movement was led by Muhammad Mushin, popularly known as Dudhu Mian (1819-1860). He divided East Bengal into circles called *Halquas* over which a Deputy or *Khalifa* was appointed, whose "duty was to keep the sect together, make proselytes and collect contributions" for furthering the objectives of the sect, "Erazis".[34] Dudhu Mian championed the cause of the labourers engaged in Indigo plantation. He offered protection to the peasants against the levy of unjust cesses.

The movement was active in Bengal from 1830 to 1860, and later it merged with Wahabi movement.

The Aligarh movement was a counter-force to the Wahabi movement. The leaders of this movement were Sir Sayyad Ahmad Khan and Nawab Abdul Latif. They were loyal to the British regime.

Sir Sayyad Ahmad Khan (1820-1898) was a supporter of the Wahabi movement till 1846, but later he turned to be loyalist. He wrote a book *Asar-us-Sandeed.* He supported the British during the rebellion in 1857.

Nawab Abdul Latif (1828) was a pro-British Muslim leader. He was appointed Anglo-Arabic Professor in the Calcutta Madrassa. He gave up teaching in 1849 for a judicial appointment. In 1862 he was nominated to the Bengal Legislative Council.[35]

The Anjuman-i-Islami (Mahomedan Association) was founded on 6 May 1855 at Calcutta. Its leaders were Abdul Bari,

---

33. Joshi (ed). *Rebellion,* p. 75.

34. R.C. Mujumdar, *British Paramountcy and Indian Renaissance.*

35. Mohd. Yusuff Abbasi, *The Genesis of Muslim Fundamentalism.*

the *Qazi, of* Calcutta and Muhammad Abdur Rauf, the editor of *Doorbeen*. It was formed for the purpose of promoting the 'general welfare' of the Muslim community in India. The Association took the side of British in the rebellion of 1857.

Mirza Asadullah Khan Ghalib (1797-1869) was a poet and philosopher. He symbolizes spiritual equality of all. He said categorically "Every son of Adam, be he Muslim, Hindu or Christian, I hold dear and regard as my brother. I do not care if others believe in this or not."[36] He was of the opinion that "God is one, that is our faith. All rituals we abjure. It is only when religions vanish, that belief is pure."[37] He did not involve himself in the rebellion of 1857.

Hindu reformers

Frightened by the horrors of superstitions, graded inequality, abject poverty and political subjugation of the oppressed classes, the thinkers from Hindus came out to criticize the ill-structured Hindu society and tried to reform it to a great extent.

Prominent among them was Raja Ram Mohan Roy (1772 - 1833) who founded the Brahmo Samaj on 20 August 1828 in Calcutta. The principles of Brahmo Samaj were as under:

1. To believe in monotheism.
2. To organize congregational worship of one Brahmo.
3. To remove social evils such as suttee and female child sacrifice, casteism, etc.
4. To discard idol worship.

Even before the foundation of the Brahmo Samaj, he founded Atmiya Sabha in 1816 for the propagation of the above said principles. Atmiya Sabha virtually became defunct in 1823; as such he revived its activities in the name of Brahmo Samaj. He tried to give scriptural evidence in support of the eradication of evil practices prevailing in those days. He wrote many books on Vedant and Upanishad and evils of Hindu society.

---

36. M. Mujeeb, *Mirza Ghalib*, p. 25.
37. *Ibid*. 46.

He began his crusade for the abolition of suttee and in 1829 he became successful in it. Lord William Bentinck, the then British Governor General of India, rendered suttee illegal by the Regulation XVII of 1829.

He firmly advocated English education for the Indians, judicial reforms and freedom of press. It is because of his thoughts and deeds that a new dawn of reasoning arose in India. Hence he is called the father of modern India.

Various other organizations, also aimed at reform, were formed during this period.

The Tattvabodhini Sabha was founded by Devendranath Thakur (1817-1905) in 1838. The principles of Tattvabodhini Sabha were just like those of Brahmo Samaj. This society continued for 20 years, and was united with the Brahmo Samaj in 1859.

Hindu Literary Society was founded in 1830s in Madras by Enugula Veeraswamiah (1780-1836) with the help of P. Srinivas Pillai and others. Its aims were the spread of English education, encouraging widow remarriage, female education and the uplift of the Depressed Classes, and to generate political consciousness among the common masses. The society worked till 1846.

Manav Dharma Sabha was founded by Dadoba Pandurang with the cooperation of Durgaram Manchharam in the year 1844 at Surat. The founders of the Sabha aimed at the abolition of the caste system and idol worship. When Dadoba Pandurang was transferred to Bombay, he shifted the headquarters of the Manav Dharma Sabha to Bombay in 1846 and renamed the Sabha as Paramhansa Sabha. The Sabha continued till 1860.

The British India Association came into existence in 1851 at Calcutta. Its first President was Raja Radhakant Deb. It appealed for inclusion of Indians in the Legislative Council. It demanded equality for all classes and holding civil service examinations in India. Its leaders were Perry Chandra Mitra, Ram Gopal Ghose, Dwarkanath Tagore and many others.

The Society for the Deliverance of Hindu Apostates was formed in 1852 at Calcutta for the purpose of reconverting Hindu converts to Christianity, back to Hinduism[38]

The Bombay Association was founded in 1852 by Jagannath Shankar Shet along with Dadabhai Naoroji, Bhau Daji, Jamshetji Jejeebhoy and others. Jagannath Shankar Shet was its President. The purpose of this organization was to bring political consciousness among the masses and demand political rights. It was an important political organization till the formation of Indian National Congress.

Apart from the institutional contribution, the contributions made by some important individuals to the cause of social awakening should also be taken into account.

Balshastry Jabhekar (1812-1846) was appointed as Assistant Professor in Elphinston College in the year 1834. He started the first Marathi journal *Digdarshan* in 1840. He encouraged widow remarriage, female education and *Shuddhi* or reconversion to Hindu religion.

Iswar Chandra Vidyasagar (1820-1891) was a Sanskrit professor, prolific writer and educationist. He established a school in his native place, Bir Singha in 1853 and up to 1856 he started 20 schools in the four districts of Bengal. He was against child marriage, polygamy and forced widowhood. He was against "the habit of parrot like and dogmatic repetition of old shastras."[39] He was the advocate of modern scientific knowledge.

Gopal Hari Deshmukh, Lok Hit Wadi (1823-1892) wrote many thought-provoking articles in *Prabhakar,* a Marathi weekly journal, from 1848 to 1850 and tried to bring about social awareness among the people.

Samieni Muthoonarasimmah Naido (d. 1856) was district Munsiff in old Madras State. In 1850, he wrote *Hitasoochanee* through which he tried to propagate against social inequalities. He was against worshipping village deities, wasteful expenditure in the marriages and child marriages.

---

38. G.A. Oddie, *Social Protests in India,* p. 72. 1979.

39. Shyamal Chakrabarthy, *Iswar Chandra Vidyasagar,* p. 39, 1971.

The Kuka Movement

The Kuka movement was founded by Bhagat Jawar Mal, generally known as Sian Sahib in the 1840s. Its headquarters were at Hazro in the then Punjab, now in Pakistan. They, while chanting hymns, emit cries (*Kooks*), hence they were called Kukas. the tenets of Kuka movement were:

1. To have faith in Guru Govind Singh as the only true Guru.
2. To remove caste distinctions in Sikhism.
3. To oppose the worship of idols, tombs and ascetics.
4. To abstain from meat, liquors and drugs.[40]

Thus, the main purpose of this movement was to purify Sikhism by removing certain abuses and superstitions that crept into it from Hinduism. The movement became popular among the Namdhari Sikhs. Later on the Kukas went against the British rule. This movement was in existence till 1885.

Parsi Revival

The Rahnumai Mazdayasnan Sabha (the religious reform association) was founded by the young educated Parsis in Bombay in the year 1851. Its aim was to purify and regenerate Zoroastrian religion and introduce certain social reforms like abolition of Purdah system. It encouraged female education. It was led by Dadabhoy Naoroji. The Association published a journal called *Rast Goftar* (truth-teller).

Sir Jamsetji Jijibhoy (1785-1859) was a big and generous businessman in Bombay. He built schools, hospitals and dug wells at his own expenses and used to support the poor and needy not only of the Parsi community but of all the communities.

Rebellious Uprisings

Discontent was growing among the people due to several reasons including poverty, policy of annexation of states and

---

[40]. R.C. Mujumdar, "The Kuka Revolt in the Punjab", In *British Paramountcy and Indian Renaissance*. Part-I, p. 901-904, 1970.

demilitarization of certain castes or tribes. The discontent of the people gave rise to military uprisings.

The significant among them were the uprisings of Bhills in Bombay in 1817, 1825, 1831 and 1846; Kolis in Gujarat in 1825, 1839 and 1844; Ramosis in Bombay in 1826 and Pagal Panthi in Bengal in 1825, 1827 and 1833. Mobilization of forces against the British rule and the feudal lords must have been possible only when some awakening was brought in the minds of the people.

Temperance Movements

In order to restrict the evil habit of taking liquors and to save the people from the menace of drugs, the Christian missionaries belonging to the Bombay missionary union passed a resolution in 1832 to promote temperance. Subsequently several organizations came forward to promote and encourage temperance. The important among them were:

1. The Bombay Temperance Union formed by Hume in 1834-35. It was the first of its kind and an influential one.
2. The Madras Temperance Society founded in 1836.
3. The South Indian Temperance Union established in 1838.
4. The Calcutta Temperance Society founded by Dr Duff in 1841.
5. The Poona Association for the promotion of Temperance, founded by Rev. James Mitchell in 1847.

INANIMATE CAUSES OF THE RISE OF DALIT MOVEMENT

Inanimate causes of the rise of Dalit movement were as follows:

Land Settlement

Before the advent of the British in India, there was no individual peasant proprietorship over the agricultural land. The land belonged to the higher caste owners who were either absentee or non-cultivating owners. At the middle the intermediary class of cultivators existed, and at the bottom the landless labourers were there to actually cultivate the land for their masters. The landless labourers, to a great extent, belonged to the untouchable castes. Thus, there was a relationship between caste hierarchy and differential rights in land.[41] The untouchable castes were landless labourers or serfs or slaves subject to hire or sale or transfer varying from place to place. The feudal lords were to collect the land tax from the village heads for the king on commission basis.

Lord Cornwallis, the then Governor-General of Bengal, introduced the famous Permanent Land Settlement in the year 1793 for Bengal, Bihar and Orissa and later extended it to north Madras. Accordingly, landlords were appointed to collect land revenue under the Permanent Settlement. The tax was calculated to be ten-eleventh of the existing total payments of the cultivators and remaining one-eleventh was left to the landlord as his share.[42] "The purpose of the permanent Zamindari settlement was" in the opinion of R. Palme Dutt, "to create a new class of landlords after the English model as the social buttress of English rule. It was recognized that, with the small number of English holding down a vast population, it was absolutely necessary to establish social basis for their power through the creation of a new class whose interests, through receiving a subsidiary share in the spoils (one-eleventh in the original intention) would be bound up with the maintenance of English rule."[43]

Sir Thomas Munro introduced Ryotwari system (individual peasant proprietorship) in 1820 when he was the Governor of Madras. Ryotwari system was made applicable, apart from Madras, to Bombay, Sind, Berar and Assam. It was a direct settlement with the cultivators.

Thus, permanent zamindari settlement was prevalent in Bengal, Bihar and Orissa and northern part of Madras forming 19 per cent of the total area of British India. Temporary zamindari

---

41. *Gazetteer of India,* Vol. I.
42. R. Palma Dutt, *India Today,* p. 190, 1947.
43. *Ibid* p. 192.

settlement was prevalent in the United Provinces, the Central Provinces (CP) part of Bengal and Bombay, and the Punjab forming 30 per cent of the total area of British India. Ryotwari system was in vogue in Bombay, Madras, Berar, Sind and Assam covering 51 per cent of the total British India.

The new land system, however, had far reaching effects on the socio-economic condition of India. Those effects can be epitomized here as:

1. The new land system marked a departure from the traditional village autarchy.
2. Revenue was settled on the holding of land and not on the produce. Hence it became compulsory to pay the revenue irrespective of good or bad harvest.
3. When the agriculturists were unable to pay the revenue due to famine or otherwise, they were compelled to borrow loan from the moneylender at an exorbitant rate of interests and pay the revenue.
4. Land being recognized as private property, it became a commodity subject to mortgage, lease, sale or purchase.
5. This system gave rise to absentee landlordism. The lesee or sub-lesee or tenants were to cultivate the land.
6. Due to the law of succession by primogeniture, land was subjected to fragmentation.
7. The new land system gave rise to moneylending and thereby to exploitation.
8. Landholders inclined towards commercialization of land got market facilities also.
9. The new land system gave rise to new judicial system in place of old village judicial system.
10. Land became the subject matter of state activity. Protection of land and defence of village were taken over by the State.
11. Due to loss of village autarchy and State intervention in the land system, the villages lost their age-long isolation. They were linked with the State through administrative machinery and means of communication.

New Industries

Industry is one of the agents of social change. There was steady growth in the export of raw cotton. In 1813 it was 9 million pounds, in 1833 it rose up to 32 million pounds and in 1844 it went up to 88 million pounds.

Sheeps' wool export in 1833 was 3.7 thousand pounds, whereas in 1844 it rose to 2.7 million pounds.

Indigo Industry came into prominence under the British. Jute industry also continued to prosper from 1833 to 1850. The Assam Tea Company started its work from 1845. Steel, coal and leather industries also flourished.

The first spinning and weaving mill in India was established by Covasjee Banerji in 1845. Dwarkanath Tagore purchased an English colliery in 1836. The Broach spinning and weaving mill was started in 1855. By 1861 the number of such mills which were in actual operation at Bombay and Ahmedabad rose to seven.

This was the beginning of a new Industrial India. Even this progress in industries must have also contributed to the social change as people of different, castes and communities were employed in the respective Individual establishments.

Means of Communication

Communication has a greater role to play in the process of social change. Railway is a major means of communications. During the Governor Generalship of Lord Dalhousie (1848-56) the Railways made a dent in India. In 1855 the East Indian Railway Company completed 21 miles railway line from Calcutta to Ranigunge and the Great Indian Peninsular Railway Company comprising 37 miles railway line from Bombay to Kalyan. In 1856 the Madras Railways completed 65 miles railway line from Madras to Arcot. Other means of communications were also being developed simultaneously.

New Education

The advent of new education in India in the first half of the 19th century had definitely marked the beginning of the new age in India.

The main features of the new education are summarily stated as under:

1. The State had directly assumed the responsibility of spreading education among the people. Henceforth, several centres of learning were established at the initiative of the State.
2. The new education was imparted through the educational institutions specially manned by well-educated and trained teachers.
3. It was more or less uniform throughout British India.
4. The objective of new education was to educate Indian people in the new knowledge and new values, so that they could be fit, not only to serve the administration, but to serve the nation in bringing about a new awakening among the people.
5. The new education was imparted through the English medium. Therefore, the educated Indians could get access to a wider universe and knowledge.
6. Indians could learn modern science and technology which gave them a new vision and enabled them to imbibe the spirit of criticism.
7. The Indians, through English education, could get acquainted with the Western social, political and economic philosophy, especially the philosophy of liberty, equality and fraternity.
8. The new education was deliberately made available to all the people irrespective of their caste, sex or religion. It marked the abolition of monopoly of a few privileged castes in the field of education.
9. The new education was based on secularism. It was not meant for spiritual salvation, but for mundane living.
10. The new education was more systematic, deliberate and well planned.

While tracing out the history of education in British India, it is necessary to take into account certain landmarks in the educational development. The Calcutta Madarassa was established by Warren Hastings in the year 1781 for the study of

Persian and Arabic along with Muslim theology and law. The next important institution was Sanskrit College at Benaras established in the year 1792 by Jonathan Duncan during the rule of Lord Cornwallis.

It was Sir Charles Grant (1764-1823) who at first in 1797 advocated the introduction of English education among the Indians. The Charter Act of 1813 directed the British Government to provide annually a sum of not less than one lakh rupees for the promotion of knowledge among the inhabitants of British India.

The Hindu College was started at Calcutta in 1817, the Chairman of which was Sir Edward Hyde East. Raja Ram Mohan Roy started Anglo-Hindu School at Calcutta in 1816 and a Vedant College in 1826.

The Bombay Education Society founded by Archdeacon Barnes started six schools – four in Bombay city, one in Surat and one in Broach in 1820. Lord Elphinston founded the Bombay Native Education Society in 1822 with the cooperation of eminent Indian leaders like Jagannath Shankar Shet Murkute, and others.

A Board of Public Instruction was established at Madras in 1826 through which one school at every district and at some Talukas were started in the Madras Presidency. One central school was started at Madras.

During this period a controversy was in vogue on the issue of medium of instruction in the schools. There were two schools, one was of Anglicists and other of Orientalists. The former was protagonist of English medium whereas the latter was of Sanskrit and Arabic languages. Ultimately, the problem was settled in favour of English during the period of Lord Bentinck in 1835 as per the minute submitted by Thomas Babingtom Mecaulay, the then President of Board of Education.

After 1835, education started slowly spreading among the people. However, a few of them were taking benefit of modern education. The educationists were of the opinion that benefits of education would be available to the common masses according to the 'Theory of Downward Filteration'. Most of the girls and the children of the so-called untouchables could not reap the educational benefits. It was Mahatma Phule who could start schools for girls and untouchables. In Bengal, John Drinkwater Bethune and Iswar Chandra Vidyasagar took active interest in spreading education among the girls. In December 1850 the Hindu Balika Vidyalaya was started at Calcutta. Iswar Chandra Vidyasagar established a free school in Birsingha, his native place in 1853. The strength of schools founded by him rose up to 20 till 1856.

During the period of Lord Dalhousie, Sir Charles Wood, the then President of the Board of Control, presented his Educational Despatch, dated 19 July 1854, which is supposed to be the Magna Carta of education in India.[44] The object of Wood's Despatch, however, was to spread western culture in India. According to Wood's Despatch, English was exclusively accepted as medium of Instruction at the higher or collegiate level; however, at the primary and secondary levels both English and vernacular languages were allowed as medium of instruction as per the option of the students. Accordingly, the theory of Downward Filteration was discarded and mass education policy was adopted.

In order to manage the affairs of the college education three universities were founded in the near 1857; the University of Calcutta on 24 January 1857, the University of Bombay on 18 July 1857 and the University of Madras on 5 September 1857. This naturally gave a momentum to education in India.

Press and Publications

In 1799 Lord Wellesley appointed a censor and framed the rules to punish those who infringed the rules. Lord Hastings, however, abolished the press censorship in 1818. Again certain restrictions were imposed on the Press in 1823 by the Governor General Adam. Subsequently Lord Metcalfe made the law in 1835 giving freedom to the Press.

The history of the Press in India starts from the publication of *The Bengal Gazette* in 1780. Some of the important newspapers

---

44. R.C. Mujumdar (ed.), *History and Culture of Indian People,* Vol. X, Part II.

and journals which existed during the first half of 19th century were:

1. *Samachar Darpan* was started by Baptist mission at Serampur in 1818. Its editor was S.C. Marshman.
2. *Sambad Kaumodin* was started in 1821 by Raja Ram Mohan Roy. It was in Persian.
3. *Bombay Samachar* was published in 1822 in Gujarati by Fardoomji Murzban from Bombay.
4. *Enquirer* was started by Krishna Mohan Banerji in English in the year 1840.
5. *Digdarshan* was started by Balshastry Jambhekar in Marathi in the year 1840.
6. *Dnyanodaya* was started in 1842 at Ahmadnagar. Its editor was Henri Balantine.
7. *Prabhakar* was started by Bhau Mahajan in the year 1841.
8. *Dnyan Patrika* was started from Poona in the year 1849.
9. *Tattvabodhini Patrika* was published by Akshaya Kumar Dutt in 1844.
10. *Rast Gojtar* in Gujarati was started in 1851 by Dadabhai Naoroji.

During the pre-Mutiny period a good amount of literature came out in several vernacular languages in addition to English. In 1801 William Carey wrote *Grammar of Bengali* and in 1815 he wrote *Bengali-English Dictionary.* Raja Ram Mohan Roy wrote *Toohphat-at-Muhouddin* in 1803, *Vedant Sootra* in 1815, *Hindu Nari ke Adhikaron ka Hanan* in 1823, *Vajrasoochi* in 1827, etc. Elphinston founded, "the native school book and school society" in 1820 to publish the textbooks. In 1831 Molesworth wrote *Marathi-English dictionary.* At this juncture Winslow wrote *Tamil dictionary.* Iswar Chandra Vidyasagar wrote *Banglar Itihas* In 1848, *Bodhadaya* in 1851 in Bengali, Samineni Muthoonarasimah Naidu wrote *Hita soochanee* in 1850 in Telugu; Lokhit Wadi wrote his *Shatpatre* in Marathi during 1848-50, Ramnarayan Tarkaratna wrote *Kulin-Kula Sarvasva* – a Hindi play in 1854 and there were many other writers who wrote several books which had contributed to the new awakening.

It is difficult to gauge as to how far the Press and publication in India contributed to social change in those days when most of the people were illiterate. However, it could be said that their existence might have not gone without having any bearing on social change. At least some educated people must have been influenced by the existing literature.

New Legal System

Previously, there prevailed canonical law in India. In the civil matter the Hindus were governed by the Code of Manu and usages and the Muslims were governed by the Quran and usages. In the criminal matter both the communities were governed by the Muslim law. Both the communities held that the law of their respective communities was revealed by God himself; and it was perfect and final. The Hindu law was administered by the caste Panchayat or village Panchayat and the learned Brahmins and the Muslim law was administered by the *Qazis*. The criminal law for both the communities was administered by the *Qazis*. In the administration of justice, there was no equality before law nor was there equal protection of law. The higher castes enjoyed more privileges and the lower castes were underprivileged. The laws, especially the Hindu laws were more discriminatory and unjust. Punishment was very severe and harsh. Thus the previous legal system was not in conformity with the ethical standards or those of justice.

With the advent of the British in India, the new era of legal system came into existence slowly but steadily. Previously the law was revealed by the religious text, but later on it was passed by the legislative council. Previously it was administered by the hereditary pandits or *Qazis*, as the case may be. Later on it was administered by the learned and trained judges.

The Governor-General-in-Council was empowered to make the laws for British India. Under the Regulating Act 1773, the Council consisted of four members, but its strength was raised to 12 under the Act of 1853.

Till 1823 three Supreme Courts were established, one each at Calcutta, Bombay and Madras. Their jurisdiction was limited to the respective town and the British subjects in India. The common law which prevailed in England was in operation with certain exceptions and modifications. Outside the three presidency towns of Calcutta, Bombay and Madras the Mofussil courts were established. The courts were bifurcated into two - civil courts and criminal courts. At the time of the Mutiny the highest court of appeal was the Privy Council in England in the civil as well as criminal case. In the civil matter the lowest court was Court of Munsif and the highest court at the provincial level was Sadar Diwani Adalat. So far as criminal matter was concerned Court of District Munsif or Assistant Sessions Judge was the lowest court and Sadar Nizamat Adalat or Sadar Fouzdari Adalat was the highest court in each province.

Under the Indian High Courts Act, 1861, the High Courts of Judicature were established one each at Calcutta, Bombay and Madras and the Supreme Courts and the Sadar Courts were abolished.

During the pre-Mutiny period, the Hindu law and usages were applied in civil matters in which Hindus were involved. The Muhammadan law and usages were applied in civil matters in which Muslims were involved. However, for both, Hindus and Muslims in the criminal matter, the Muhammadan law with certain modifications, was in operation. In cases where no specific law or rule was in existence, the Judges were to act according to justice, equity and good conscience.

After the Mutiny came to an end the Indian Penal Code 1860, the Code of Criminal Procedure 1861 and the Civil Procedure Code 1859 came into universal application.

Those who qualified as barrister were to appear in the Supreme Courts and those who obtained the *sanad* were to appear in the other courts as pleaders.

The laws made before the Mutiny and which were important from the social change point of view are:

1. The Regulation XVII passed on 4 December 1829 declared suttee system to be illegal in the Bengal Presidency. Similar regulation was passed in Madras on 2 February 1830 and in Bombay.
2. The Bengal Regulation XXI of 1775 and Regulation III of 1804 declared infanticide to be murder and punishable as such.

3. The Act V 1843 made slavery illegal in India.
4. The Caste Disabilities Removal Act was passed in 1850 according to which the renunciation of the Hindu or Islam religion was not to entail loss of property on the part of the converts to Christianity.
5. The Hindu Widow-Remarriage Act (Act XV of 1856) was passed on 26 July 1856. It legalized the marriage of widows notwithstanding any custom or rule of Hindu law.

Democratic Process

Till the outbreak of the Mutiny in 1857 there was no development of democratic process in India. However, certain principles which were introduced in the administration had definitely paved the way for democratic process.

During this period the theory of separation of power came into implementation though in a limited sense. The executive branch was headed by the Governor-General in Council in the Centre and Governors in the provinces. Under the Act of 1833 the Governor-General's council consisting of four members was to act as a legislative body. It was expanded in 1853 which included 12 members. The Governor-General in Council was empowered to make laws for the territory under the East India Company. Judiciary was recognized as a separate branch of the Government.

Though the British Government was not fully representative, it was responsive. It slowly and steadily responded to the rising aspirations and expectations of the people in general.

The state is generally said to be the catalyst of any change. It is obviously true in India. It provided a suitable situation for the rise of 'Dalit consciousness'.

Anatomy of Change

Change may take place when any form or structure or value loses its utility or when its absurdity comes to the knowledge of the people. Change, however, cannot be temporary, spatial or isolated. Change gives rise to chains of changes. It is a continuous process. It cannot be limited to a particular space or region or locality. It may spread throughout the nation or even throughout the world. Change cannot remain confined to any particular field like social or economic. It may spread to all the fields of life.

Change is generally vertical and horizontal. It may occur in the higher class and come down to the lower class. It is horizontal in the sense that it may conform to all the classes or groups or associations simultaneously.

However, changes are conveyed from one class or field to another through the mechanism of mutual interaction, imitation of one by another, percolation or filteration from one to another and through direct contact. In a country like India, where 'castes' are closed, how could there be interaction? How the changes which were occurring in the higher castes might have percolated down to the lower castes, is a question. In a closed society also changes can be transmitted according to the above said process; but its process is always slow though steady. The material conditions may be useful in accelerating the process of change. During the pre-Mutiny period, because of the material conditions changes could take place in almost all the fields of social life. The process of social change continued in operation in future. This caused a necessary environment for the changes in the structural and cultural values of the so-called untouchables. The consciousness amongst the Dalits had ignited the gun powder in 1857; as such the explosion took place in the form of rebellion. However, the Mutiny was successfully suppressed by the British forces.

Subsequently, the British Government took over the charge of Indian administration from the British East India Company, by an Act for the better government of India, passed on 2 August 1858. The Queen's proclamation to that effect was formally issued on 1 November 1858 by Viscount Canning, the first Viceroy of India at a special Darbar at Allahabad.

The Queen's proclamation states, "we desire it to be our royal will and pleasure that none be in any way favoured, none molested or disqualified by reason of their religious faith or observance, but that all shall alike enjoy the equal and impartial protection of the law, and we do strictly charge and enjoin in all those who may be in authority under us that they abstain from all interference with the religious belief or worship of any of our subjects on pain of our highest displeasure.

"And it is our future will that, so far as may be, our subjects, of whatever race or creed, be freely and impartially admitted to office in our service, the duties of which they may be qualified by their education, ability and integrity duly to discharge... it is our earnest desire to stimulate the peaceful industry of India, to promote works of public utility and improvement, and to administer the government for the benefit of all our subjects resident therein. In their prosperity will be our strength, in their contentment our security, and in their gratitude our best reward."[45] With this proclamation there commenced the dawn of a new age in traditional India. A new socio-political atmosphere came into existence, which was conducive to free thinking. Later on the Indian people started independence movement from 1885 under the banner of Indian National Congress and eventually they became successful in achieving independence on 15 August 1947.

It is during the post-Mutiny period, the Dalit protest could be developed as a systematic movement for the liberation of Dalits. The movement was, however, led by the able Dalit leadership and supported by the suitable socio-political circumstances.

At the later stage Dr Babasaheb Ambedkar launched a strong, nationwide and relentless struggle for the liberation of Dalits from the bondage of untouchability. He said very emphatically that, "Annihilation of untouchability is my birth right", and believed that, "Lost rights are never regained by begging, and by appeals to the conscience of usurpers, but by relentless struggle."[46] Thus, he prepared his brethren for the struggle and infused a new vigour in the movement so as to enable it to give a decisive fight against the orthodox forces. Ultimately, the movement became successful under his able leadership. It implies that the able and objective oriented leadership based on mass support and relentless struggle will certainly bring about desired social change in a given situation.

---

45. M.V. Pylee, *Constitutional History of India,* p. 27, 1972

46. Keer Dhananjay, *Dr. Ambedkar-Life and Mission* pp. 81, 82, 1971.

CONCLUSION

Although Dalit protest was inherent in the origin of untouchability itself, it became a systematic movement during the post-Mutiny period. It is during this period the movement became more organized, vocal and vigorous. It was, however, based on the strong foundation composed of several social, economic, political and religious factors existing in the pre-Mutiny period. Further, it was well-nourished in the post-Mutiny period by several factors. Obviously, under the able Dalit leadership of Dr Babasaheb Ambedkar the movement became successful in constitutionally securing abolition of untouchability and ushering in a new era of justice, liberty, equality and fraternity.

4

Dalit Organizations

The Dalit consciousness that had been brought about by various factors existing in the pre-Mutiny period could get a momentum in the post-Mutiny period. It was properly institutionalized and formed into a mass-based movement which could be reckoned with as a force.

It was, however, necessary to form organizations to raise the upward mobility of the group as a whole. In the caste-based society individual qualifications and achievements have no significance as such. Hence, the Dalits had to survive to elevate their collective status by forming organizations and raising the moral and material status of their brethren.

This was necessary in order to bring about some structural and cultural changes even among the Dalit masses. It was essential to narrow down the social distance between the castes among the Dalits by coming together and living an associational life. This required communication of new thoughts and values to the masses. This process of socialization was obviously possible through organizations.

The Dalits who were determined to regain their human personality and human rights had to ceaselessly struggle against the traditional social order and the unsympathetic attitude of the government. They had to go through the process of dialecticism. Thus, they felt the necessity of organizing mass satyagraha for temple entry, access to watering places and roads, educational institutions to spread education among themselves, and the conferences to press their demands for employment in civil and military services, certain concessions and statutory safeguards.

In view of growing democratization especially during the later part of the British period, the Dalits were naturally inclined to build up organizational strength for achieving political power for their progress. As a result they attempted to start organizations to put forth their political demands.

In the words of Satish Kumar Sharma, "a social movement emerges out of the historical process of interaction of various socio-structural conditions prevailing in the society. It involves a number of participants who are socially conscious of the existing conditions and wish to transform these conditions either totally or partially. The level of social or collective consciousness is evaluated in terms of its appropriateness for the ends in view. Besides, a certain number of partisans, a social movement is further characterized by an ideology, leadership, certain specified goals, strategies and tactics to achieve the goals and an organizational structure. The relevance of organization in a social movement is vital in view of its function such as mobilization of masses, ordination of the activities, etc."

Thus, during 1857 to 1956, in this decisive phase of Dalit liberation movement, several organizations came into existence to strike squarely at the decaying institution of untouchability and liberate their brethren. It is in the fitness of things to know as to which were those organizations, what were their general and special purposes and how far they became successful in their objective. Therefore, it is proposed to project with available material the socio-political profiles of those organizations. They are namely:

AD DHARM MANDAL[1]

The organization named Ad Dharm Mandal was founded by Shri Mango Ram in November 1926. Its first convention was held at Mugowal in Punjab. Its head office was situated at Jullunder city in Punjab.

---

[1] Juergensmeyer : 1988 : 45-56.

The Mandal was based on a firm philosophic foundation. It is believed that all the so-called untouchables including obviously, the Chamars, Churhas, Sainsis, Bhangres, Bhils, etc, were the original inhabitants of India. Their religion was Ad Dharm. They had a rich culture and civilization. However, the Hindu *qaum* came from outside and enslaved the original people, who were approximately 70,000,000. The Hindus destroyed the original *qaum,* destroyed their history and culture. Therefore, the organization called upon all the untouchables to unite to regain their communal pride *(qaumiat*) and their religion (*mazhab*).

The principles of the Ad Dharm Mandal were:

1. In the beginning when Nature created human beings, there was no discrimination.
2. They adopted non-theistic notion of divinity. Nature has created human beings from the original source, *Adi.*
3. The philosophy of Ravidas ought to be respectfully followed.
4. To follow the Granth or Shastras is a sin.
5. They should engage in *Satsang* (worship services) on the pattern of the Sikhs.
6. They adopted greeting *Jai GuruDev* (Victory to the Divine Guru) to which the response was *Dhan Guru Dev* (blessed be the Divine Guru).

The Ad Dharm Mandal started *Adi Danka* (Drum of Adi people), a journal in Urdu. There were some *Pracharakas* or preachers of the Mandal who travelled in Punjab to preach the philosophy of the Ad Dharm Mandal.

The Mandal had opened its branches at Ferozepur, Chumba, Jullunder, Kangra, Lyallapur, Banaras and Calcutta.

It was because of the efforts of the Mandal and its leader Mango Ram that some of the untouchables were listed as Adi Dharmis and not as Hindus, in the 1931 Census. Their strength was 4,18,789. The Ad Dharm Mandal was active from 1926 to 1946 in some parts of our country. It tried to bring about a new awareness among the people of the Depressed Classes.

ADI-ANDHRA MAHAJAN SABHA[2]

The Adi-Andhra Mahajan Sabha came into existence in November 1917 at Vijayawada in a conference of the Depressed Classes people held under the presidentship of Shri Bhagya Reddy Varma (Hyderabad). It was convened by Shri Guduru Ramchandra Rao.

The conference resolved to call the untouchables as 'Adi-Andhra' in the Andhra region. Several other resolutions were passed in the conference requesting the government to nominate Adi-Andhras to the statutory bodies, right from the Legislative Council down to the Panchayat Boards; to admit their children into common schools and to dig separate wells to provide drinking-water for the Depressed Classes.

Adi-Andhra Mahajan Sabha was very active in Andhra region. It met in several conferences organized at several places. The government accepted the nomenclature of 'Adi-Andhra' vide order No.817 of 25.3.1922. The government nominated N. Devendrudu, S. Venkayya and Gangadhar Sarma, the Adi-Andhra leaders to the then Madras Legislative Council. The Sabha was active till 1940.

ADI-DRAVIDA MAHAJAN SABHA[3]

The Adi-Dravida Mahajan Sabha came into existence in 1890. It was then named as Pariah Mahajan Sabha. The sabha sent a petition to the then Madras Government in 1890 requesting some agrarian concessions to the Pariahs. In 1898 the sabha requested the government to lower the standard of the qualifying test prescribed for admission to subordinate medical services. The government, however, conceded their demand in 1899.

In 1918, the sabha appealed to the government to abandon their disgraceful name 'Pariah' and to give them the highly

---

2. APSH Souvenir : 1976 : 67-71

3. Saraswathl : 1974: 14. 74. 146, 172

respectable name 'Adi-Dravida', denoting the original inhabitants of Dravida land. In 1922, the Provincial Legislative Council passed a resolution recommending that the name Adi-Dravida should be given to the Pariahs. (G.O. 817, Law (Gen.) 25 March, 1922). The Adi-Dravida Mahajan Sabha submitted a memorandum to the Indian Statutory Commission headed by Sir John Simon in 1927 requesting the constitution of separate electorate for the Depressed Classes. Its chief spokesman was Shri M.C. Rajah.

ADI-HINDU MAHASABHA[4]

The Adi-Hindu Mahasabha, which at its inception was known as the Adi-Hindu Jatiyonnati Sabha, came into existence in 1922. It was founded by Shri Arigay Ramaswamy for the purpose of undertaking activities of uplifting the Dalits. Its weekly meetings were conducted regularly at the residence of Konday Venkataswamy, at Kumarguda, Hyderabad. Shri Arigay Ramaswamy, Bhagya Reddy Varma and B.S. Venkatrao used to attend and address the meetings. Shri Konday Venkataswamy was its President and Shri Arigay Ramaswamy was its Secretary.

In the general body meeting held in 1927 in the premises of Chennakeshavaswamy temple, the name 'Jatiyonnati' was replaced by 'Mahasabha'.

The Adi-Hindu Mahasabha arranged Bhajan Mandalis at several places. It organized Panchayats to settle internal disputes, and it formed a batch of 75 persons as volunteer corps under the captainship of P.R. Venkataswamy. He started one gymnasium in the Chennakeshavaswamy temple. The organization played a very important role in the moral and cultural development of the untouchables. It could institutionalize the uplift movement in its early phase at Hyderabad.

---

4. P.R. Venkatswamy : 1955: 18, 21

ADI-KERALOTHARANA SANGHAM (AKS)[5]

The Adi-Keralotharana Sangham was formed in 1927 in a conference of the Depressed Classes people at Calicut. Firstly it was known as Kerala Antyajodharana Sangam (KAS). Later on it was named as Adi-Keralotharana Sangham. It was led by K. Kelappan and C. Krishnan.

The activities of the Sangham were mainly concerned with the education of the Dalits, freedom for them to walk along public roads, and starting hostels for the Dalit students.

ADI-HINDU SOCIAL SERVICE LEAGUE[6]

The Adi-Hindu Social Service League was founded by Shri Bhagya Reddy Varma in 1911 at Hyderabad. However, till 1921 it was known as Manya Sangham. The objectives of this organization were:

1. To eradicate social evil of intemperance.
2. To eradicate the system of animal sacrifice.
3. To eradicate the custom of dedicating girls to deities.
4. To prevent child marriages; and
5. To create friendly relations between all the untouchable castes and the people of the high castes.

For the propagation of these objectives, the organization started an English monthly known as *The Panchama.* It was edited by Shri J.S. Muttiah.

A meeting of the Adi Hindu Social Service league was convened at Adi Hindu Bhawan, Hyderabad on 19 December, 1937. It was presided over by B.S. Venkatarao. The league considered the political demands of the Adi Hindus and decided to submit a memorandum to that effect. Accordingly they submitted a memorandum for reservation of seats in legislature in proportion to their population.

---

5. Joseph Mathew : 1986 : 110
6. P.R. Venkataswamy : 1955 : 39

ADI-KARNATAKA SANGH

The Adi-Karnataka Sangh was formed in Mysore State in 1930. It was working on the lines met by Adi-Dravida Mahajan Sabha in Madras. Shri K. Madiah was its Secretary.

AKHIL BHARAT VARSHIYE NISHAD SABHA

It was founded by Shri Rai Saheb Babu Ramcharanji in 1920 at Lucknow. He was General Secretary of the sabha. The main objective of the sabha was to organize the Mallah untouchable community. He started *Nishad Samachar,* a journal, to bring a new consciousness among the Depressed Classes in the erstwhile United Province.

ALL BENGAL NAMASUDRA ASSOCIATION

It was founded by Jananayak Shri Mukunda Behari Mullick in the year 1912 at Calcutta. As President of the organization, he submitted a memorandum to the Indian Statutory Commission in 1929. He stated that "franchise should be enlarged and all the Depressed classes people paying choukidari tax of ₹ 2/- or payment of a cess of ₹ 1/- or Municipal tax of ₹ l/- should be eligible for election" He advocated that the reservation for the Depressed Classes should be 17 per cent of the total seats of the Legislature. He denounced Rajah-Moonje Pact and supported Dr Babasaheb Ambedkar. The Namasudra Association was mainly instrumental in bringing awareness among the untouchables in Bengal.

ALL INDIA DEPRESSED CLASSES LEAGUE

In the year 1928 Babu Jagjivan Ram formed Ravidas Maha Sabha at Calcutta with a view to uniting the Dalits under one banner and introducing social reforms among them. Later, he joined the Congress. In 1934 in the annual conference of the Ravidas Maha Sabha held at Calcutta, it was decided to establish the Depressed Classes League. Accordingly a conference of the Dalits was organized at Kanpur in 1935, in which it was declared that the said organization had been formed with Rasiklal Biswas as its President and Babu Jagjivan Ram and P.N. Rajbhoj as its

Secretaries. This organization was pro-Congress and spread in almost all the States. It is still in existence.

ALL INDIA RAMNAMI MAHA SABHA[7]

In 1901 Shri Parshu Ram Bhardwaj organized a 'Bhajan Ramnami Mela' for the first time at village Jogideepa near Charpara in Bilaspur district in Madhya Pradesh. The Ramnami Mela is organized every year in Bilaspur and Raipur districts. Shri Parshu Ram Bhardwaj tried to organize all the Ramnami people of the Depressed Classes in the Chattisgarh region of Madhya Pradesh.

The caste Hindus, with a view to opposing the organization of the untouchables, objected to their using the name of Lord Ram. However, Shri Bhardwaj declared that their 'Ram' was not the hero of Ramayana, but the outcome of natural combination of fire, sun and moon.

The principles of Ramnami Maha Sabha were:

1. Not to believe in idol worship.
2. Not to believe in any magic and not to believe in the holiness of Ganga-water for purification of the sins, if any.
3. Not to go to Hindu temples for worshipping their gods.
4. Not to accept Brahmin supremacy and their holy books including *Manusmriti* and *Ram Charit Manas.*
5. To believe in equality and human brotherhood.

The main stress of the Ramnamis has been on improving the moral and materialistic condition of the Dalits. They stress on reducing the marriage expenditure. The parents of both the bride and the bridegroom come to the *mela* spot and perform the marriage under the auspices of the Ramnami Maha Sabha without spending a huge amount.

The Ramnami Mahasabha could successfully organize the untouchables believing in 'Ramnam'. They developed a sort of

---

7. (Awadh Ram Bhardwaj, Gen. Secretary, All India Ramnami Mahasabha)

new theology, thereby arresting the spread of Christianity among the untouchables. It favoured certain social reforms among the community.

ALL INDIA SCHEDULED CASTES FEDERATION

It was the first all India political party which comprised exclusively the Scheduled Castes. It was founded by Dr Babasaheb Ambedkar in a national convention of the Scheduled Castes held at Nagpur during 17-20 July 1942. It was presided over by Rao Bahadur N. Shivaraj, a renowned Dalit leader from Madras.

At the initiative of Dr Babasaheb Ambedkar the All India Scheduled Castes Federation (SCF) was unanimously formed. An executive body of the All India SCF was elected in the convention. Rao Bahadur N. Shivaraj from Madras was elected as President and P.N. Rajbhoj (Bombay) was elected as General Secretary.

Further, the convention passed the following resolutions:

1. Cripps proposals were condemned as they failed to consider the interests of the Dalits.
2. The separate identity of the Dalits be recognized.
3. Special provision should be made in the budgets of respective provinces for the higher education of the untouchables.
4. The untouchables should get adequate representation in the Central and Provincial ministries.
5. Certain seats should be reserved in the government services.
6. The untouchables should get representation in the legislatures and local self-governments in proportion to their population.
7. Their representatives should be elected by separate electorate.
8. There should be provision in the Constitution for the separate settlements of the Scheduled Castes.

9. They should be given arable uncultivated land for their livelihood.

During 1942-46 Dr Babasaheb Ambedkar was Labour Member in the Viceroy's Executive Council and Shri N. Shivaraj and Pyarelal Kuril Talib were nominated members of the Central Assembly.

In March 1946, general elections were held for the provincial assemblies. The SCF, as other political parties, actively participated in the elections. It contested altogether for 51 seats (Madras - 24, Bombay - 5, Bengal - 6, UP - 5, CP and Berar- 11). Of all the contestants one from Bengal (Shri S.N. Mandal) and other from the CP and Berar (Shri R.P. Jadhav) were elected to the respective assemblies.

In order to find a solution to the Indian problem, the Cabinet Mission came to India on 24 March 1946. The representatives of various political organizations, including Dr Babasaheb Ambedkar on behalf of SCF met the Cabinet Mission. The Cabinet Mission declared its plan on 16 May 1946, which contained no reference to the demands of the Scheduled Castes. It was proposed that a Constituent Assembly consisting of 210 members elected by the general electorate, 78 by the Muslim electorate and 4 by the Sikh electorate would be formed to frame the new constitution. It was proposed that there would be an interim government composed of the Congress and the Muslim League. Both the major parties, however, accepted the Cabinet Mission plan.

In view of the apathetic attitude of the Cabinet Mission, the SCF started satyagraha on 15 July 1946 at Poona under the leadership of P.N. Rajbhoj. The satyagrahas were launched at other places as well like Bombay, Nagpur, Kanpur, Lucknow, etc.

Shri J.N. Mandal (Bengal SCF chief) was included in the Interim Ministry under the leadership of Pandit Nehru. In 1946, Dr Babasaheb Ambedkar was elected to the Constituent Assembly, firstly from Bengal and after partition from Bombay Legislative Assembly. He became Chairman of the Drafting Committee of the Constituent Assembly and Law Minister of India. The Constitution drafted by Dr Babasaheb Ambedkar and passed by the Constituent Assembly came into implementation on 26 January 1950.

In the first general elections held in 1952 the SCF contested for 34 Lok Sabha seats (four from Bombay, three from CP and Berar, nine from Madras, two from Punjab, eight from UP, four from Hyderabad, one from Rajasthan, one from Delhi, one from Himachal Pradesh and one from Vindhya Pradesh). Out of them only two candidates were elected. They were Shri P.N. Rajbhoj from Solapur (Maharashtra) and other was Shri M.R. Krishna from Karimnagar (Telangana). However, Dr Babasaheb Ambedkar, who contested from Bombay (north) could not get elected. Again he contested from Bhandara Lok Sabha by-election in 1954, but in vain.

The SCF contested for 215 seats in the legislative assemblies of various States. Of all the 215 seats, the party won 12 seats, five from Hyderabad, two from Madras, one from Bombay, two from Mysore, one from Pepsu and one from Himachal Pradesh.

Dr Babasaheb Ambedkar got elected from Bombay Legislative Assembly to the Rajya Sabha and Shri J.H. Subbiah, the SCF leader from Hyderabad got elected to the Rajya Sabha in 1952.

The Scheduled Castes Federation had witnessed a crucial period in the history of modern India, from 1942 to 1956. The role played by the party during this period could be briefly stated as follows:

The role played by SCF in politico-legal activities is of great importance. It could enlist the participation of the Scheduled Castes (SC) in politics. Its branches were spread in almost all the parts of the country. It tried to aggregate the interests of the SCs and to protect them.

After having assumed the charge of the Labour Department, Babasaheb Ambedkar evolved a new approach called the Tripartite approach that is joint consultation with the representatives of the government, the labour and the management for solving the problems of common interests.

He appointed a Chief Labour Commissioner along with necessary field staff in 1945. A Bill regarding the scheme of insurance was passed in 1948. He introduced suitable amendments to the Workman's Compensation Act, the Indian Mines Act, the Factories Act, etc. He introduced the Minimum Wages Bill in the Parliament on 11 April 1946 which was passed on 9 February 1948.

His services to the nation as Chairman of the Drafting Committee of the Constitution are of great importance. The members of the Committee were: N. Madhav Rao, Sayed M. Sadulla, Sir Alladi Krishnaswamy Ayyer, N. Gopalaswamy Ayyangar, K.M. Munshi and D.P. Khaitan.

As a Law Minister, he introduced several reforms in the Hindu family law called the Hindu Code Bill, on 5 February 1951. However, when he saw the Bill was not being passed with all its provisions, he resigned his portfolio.

As a member of Rajya Sabha he participated in the debates on many Bills. His speeches on the Untouchability (offences) Bill and the Report of the Commissioner for Scheduled Castes and Scheduled Tribes were of specific importance.

In the socio-economic field his services cannot be ignored. He could secure $8^{1/3}$ per cent reservation in appointments in August 1943 for the Scheduled Castes. It was due to his efforts that a special provision was made for the first time in the central budget in 1944 for the grant of scholarship for the Scheduled Castes. This facility was extended to the Scheduled Tribes in 1948.

In October 1943, the Central Assembly passed a resolution moved by Pyarelal Kureel Talib, SCF member for the removal of restrictions on the untouchables in the military forces against holding post of officers.

The satyagraha for uncultivated land by the landless labourers, especially the Scheduled Castes, was launched in the Marathwada region of the then Hyderabad State in 1953 under the leadership of Dadasaheb B.K. Gaikwad and B.S. More.

However, Dr Babasaheb Ambedkar himself desired to wind up the SCF and establish a new party, the Republican Party of India (RPI) which could be able to associate the non- Scheduled Castes along with the Scheduled Castes, work as a strong opposition party to the ruling Congress and strive for the success of democracy. He could not do so due to his sad demise. After his death, his followers, however, established RPI in a special convention held at Nagpur on 3 October 1957. Once again they unanimously elected Shri N. Shivaraj as its President, Babu Haridas Awale as Vice-President and Barrister Rajabhau Khobragade as its General Secretary. However, the party could not remain united after 1959. Presently, it is divided into several factions.

ALL INDIA SHUDRA MAHASABHA

It was founded by Shri Bansilal Ramteke at Rajnandgaon in Madhya Pradesh (in Chhattisgarh region), along with others. The objective of the Mahasabha was to make efforts to bring a new social awareness among the Scheduled Castes in Madhya Pradesh.

ALL TRAVANCORE PULAYA MAHASABHA[8]

It was founded in 1938 at Trivandrum. Its President was T.T. Kesavan Sastry and Secretary was Ayyan Kali. It came into existence to work for the economic and political upliftment of the Pulayas in Travancore. The Mahasabha contributed to a great extent for the liberation of the untouchables in Travancore.

ANARYA DOSH PARIHAR MANDALI

Shri Gopalbaba Walangkar founded Anarya Dosh Parihar Mandali at Dapoli, Ratnagiri district in Maharashtra in the year 1886. The main objective of this organization was to bring about social awakening among the Dalits and unite them to struggle for their human rights. He used to exhort the people to maintain moral and material standards. He used to preach that they should not drink and eat beef. He was of the view that the Aryans purposely imposed several restrictions on the untouchables and reduced them to mere chattel. He gave a call to his brethren to unite and rise against all oppression. He toured throughout Maharashtra and through *Bhajans* or *klrtans* he taught his brethren to unite.

---

8. Joseph Mathew : 1986 : III

ANTYAJ SAMAJ COMMITTEE[9]

The Antyaj Samaj Committee was formed at Ramtek near Nagpur on the occasion of Ramnavami festival in 1906. It was a registered organization, founded and headed by Vithobaji Moon Pande, a saint and social reformer from Nagpur.

The Committee members used to urge the people to raise their moral and material standard. They used to preach that the untouchables should not eat beef and should not drink spurious drinks.

ARUNDATIYA MAHASABHA[10]

In order to organize the Arundatiya or Madigas in the Nizam State, Shri Arigay Ramaswamy founded Arundatiya Mahasabha. Shri Girkala Mallesh Rao and Shri B.S. Venkatrao helped him in the formation of the Mahasabha. It was founded in a specially called for meeting of the Arundatiyas at the Reddy Hostel, Hyderabad on 1 June 1931. This organization proved to be useful in organizing the Arundatiyas in Telangana region of the Nizam state.

ATMA BODHODAYA SANGHAM

The Atma Bodhodaya Sangham was founded by Shri Subhaanand Gurudevan (1882-1950) of Venpala, Chenganoor Taluka, Allapuzha district in Kerala. It was a purely spiritual or religious organization. The Sangham tried to raise the moral and cultural standard of the untouchables in Central Kerala.

AUDIAH MEMORIAL HIGH SCHOOL COMMITTEE

This school was previously named after Sir William Barton, the then President of Hyderabad who donated the land to the

---

9. Kosare 1984 : 23.

10. P.R. Venkataswamy (1) : 1955 : 61

school in Secunderabad. The school was founded by Shri M.L. Audiah, the renowned Dalit leader (1866-1938) in the year 1906. He was President of the School Management Committee and Shri C.V. Padmarao Mudaliar, a sympathizer of Dalits became its Secretary. It was run under the auspices of "The League to Help the Helpless"

Later the Scheduled Castes Trust Fund Bar Board took over the charge of the management, with J.H. Subbiah as its Chairman.

In the year 1961 when K.R. Veeraswamy was appointed as Honorary Secretary of this institution, the name of the school was changed after its founder Shri M.L. Audiah. It was taken over by the Education Department of the Government of Andhra Pradesh.

BAHISHKRIT HITKARINI SABHA[11]

In order to bring about a new socio-political awareness among the so-called untouchables. Dr Babasaheb Ambedkar established 'Bahishkrit Hitkarini Sabha' on 20 July 1924 at Bombay. The aims and objectives of the sabha were as under:

1. To promote the spread of education among the Depressed Classes by opening hostels or employing such other means as may seem necessary or desirable.
2. To promote the spread of culture among the Depressed Classes by opening libraries, social centres and classes or study circles.
3. To advance and improve the economic condition of the Depressed Classes by starting industrial and agricultural schools.
4. To represent the grievances of the Depressed Classes. The founding principles of the sabha were, "Educate, Agitate and Organize".

---

11. Kharat : 1990 : 6-14.

The sabha started one hostel at Solapur for high school students belonging to the Depressed Classes on 4 January 1925. The management of the hostel was entrusted to Shri Jivappa Suba Aydale, a social worker from Solapur.

Dr Babasaheb Ambedkar was nominated to the Bombay Legislative Council with effect from 18 February 1927 for a period of five years. Again he was nominated in 1932 for a period of five years.

He launched the famous satyagraha at Chowdar Tank at Mahad on 20 March 1927. *Manusmriti* was burnt on 25 December 1927. He introduced a Biil to amend the Mahar Vatan in the Bombay Legislative Council on 19 March 1928.

When the Indian Statutory Commission under Sir John Simon came to India, he submitted his statement on 29 May 1928 and gave evidence on 23 October 1928. He demanded adult franchise, joint electorate and reserved seats for the Depressed Classes. However, the Commission did not take due cognizance of those demands. He launched the famous temple satyagraha at Kalaram temple, Nasik on 2 March 1930. He represented the case of Dalits in the Round Table Conference during 1930-32. He emphatically declared on 13 October 1935 that he would not die as a Hindu.

It worked very effectively in bringing about social awareness among the Dalit masses. It was on its foundation that the Independent Labour Party came into existence.

BAHUJAN SHIKSHAN SANGH[12]

The Bahujan Shikshan Sangh was formed in 1928 at Ahmednagar in Maharashtra. The main objective of the Sangh was to spread education amongst the Depressed Classes. Initially the Sangh was named as Ahmednagar Jillha Bahishkrit Samaj Seva Sangh.

Though it was established in 1928, it became practically active in 1948 when Shri D.T. Rupvate took charge of it as its President and Shri R.K. Gaikwad as its Secretary.

---

12. Silver Jubilee Souvenir: 1974.

The Sangh opened its first hostel for the Depressed Classes students in June 1948 at Sangamner in District Nagar. It was named as 'Siddharth Boarding'. Presently the Bahujan Shikshan Sangh runs Janata High School, Pune (1967), Siddharth Vidyalaya, Sangamner (1965), Sambodhi Vidyalaya, Nagar (1962), Siddharth High School, Sangamner (1970), Mahatma Phule Vidyalaya, Ghulewadi (1970) and 23 hostels at various places in Nagar, Pune, Aurangabad and Thane districts in Maharashtra. The Sangh has been doing commendable work for the girls' education also. It has celebrated its Silver Jubilee in 1974. The contribution made by the Sangh to the uplift of the Dalits cannot be ignored.

BHARAT SANT SAMAJ

The Bharat Sant Samaj (the Saints' organization) was founded in a meeting specially called for by Shri Patit Pawan Das at Shri Kshetra Ramtek on 10 April 1927. The saints from among the untouchables were present at the meeting. They had decided to build a *dharmashala* for the comfortable stay of the saints and pilgrims at Ramtek.

The next such meeting was held at Akola on 18 February 1934 under the presidentship of Mahant Mangal Tulsiram Gajbhiye. It was attended by several saints and social reformers. They decided to support Babasaheb Ambedkar and to propagate his thoughts among the untouchables, to preach against superstitious habits and tradition and to stress the importance of education.

The next meeting of the saints was held at Indora, Nagpur on 8 November 1936. It was presided over by Shri Dasrath Gajbhiye, a Kabir Panthi saint. The saints assembled there unanimously resolved to support the conversion move of Dr Babasaheb Ambedkar. Thus, the Sant Samaj tried to educate their traditional followers in the new ideology.

BHARATIYA DUSADH MAHASABHA[13]

It was founded by Shri Hari Govindji Bhagat of Bihar in the year 1914. The objective of the Mahasabha was to organize the

---

13. Sachchidananda : 1977 : 154

Dusadh community and reform it. The Dusadh Mahasabha propagated against the payment of dowry, eating non-vegetarian food and drinking wine. It stood for discouraging divorce and encouraging adoption of sacred thread and spread of education. The Dusadh Mahasabha stated that the Dusadhas were a branch of Rajputs or Kshatriyas.

BIHAR RAJAK SANGH

The Bihar Rajak Sangh was founded in early 1940's. Shri Nayantara Das was the General Secretary of this organization from 1947 to 1951. The main objectives of this organization were as under:

1. To educate the children.
2. Not to take liquor at least on ceremonial occasions.
3. Not to send young girls to collect the clothes from the customers' houses.
4. Not to give or accept dowry.
5. To maintain cleanliness in the locality.

BOMBAY STATE INFERIOR VILLAGE SERVANTS ASSOCIATION[14]

The Bombay State Inferior Village Servants Association was established by Dr Babasaheb Ambedkar on 31 August 1955. Its office was at Gokuldas Pasta Road, Dadar, Bombay. The main objectives of the Association were as follows:

1. The Vatan land should be given to the inferior village servants.
2. The inferior village servants should be treated as government servants for the purpose of salary and other benefits.
3. The duty time and particulars of their work should be decided.

It was obviously meant for hereditary village servants such as Mahar, Mang, Ramoshi, Jugale, Bhill, and Koli. Its membership fee was ₹ 10 for all the servants of the village. The

---

14. Kharat : 1990 : 335-338.

Maharki and other hereditary jobs were very much exploitative and oppressive for the so-called untouchables in Maharashtra. Hence Dr Babasaheb Ambedkar was bent upon to abolish the same. He, however, introduced a Bill to amend the Bombay Hereditary Offices Act of 1874 on 19 March 1926 and again on 17 September 1937 in the then Bombay Legislature, but in vain. Ultimately, the Mahar Vatan was abolished under the Bombay Inferior Village Vatans Abolition Act 1 of 1959 under the provision of Article 23 of the Constitution.

BUDDHIST SOCIETY OF INDIA

The Buddhist Society of India was founded in 1955 by Dr Babasaheb Ambedkar. It was under the auspices of this society that he was initiated into Buddhism at Nagpur on 14 October 1956 along with his five lakh brethren.

The objectives of the society were:

1. To spread the knowledge of Buddhism in India.
2. To build viharas at as many places as possible in order to strengthen the faith of the new converts.
3. To establish schools and colleges where education will be provided in Buddhist literature and philosophy.
4. To establish orphanages and hospitals and undertake other social work.
5. To train workers to carry the message of Buddhism to all parts of India and to establish study circles for the purpose.
6. To encourage the comparative study of religions in order to foster the study of Buddhism in right perspective.
7. To publish popular literature in Buddhism including pamphlets, brochures, etc.
8. To form a new monk order in India.
9. To hold conferences of Buddhists in India to bring about uniformity in religious practices, rites and ceremonies.

After the death of Babasaheb Ambedkar, the first conference of the Buddhist Society of India was held at Nagpur on 3 October

1957 under the presidentship of Shri Yashwantrao Ambedkar. Presently, Smt Meeratai Y. Ambedkar is the President of the Society.

The movement of conversion of the Scheduled Castes to Buddhism was made active under the auspices of the Society.

Charamar Daiva Sabha (Church of God of Charamars — Pulayas)[15]

It was founded by a Pulaya Christian named Solomon Markose. He observed that the treatment which the Syrian Christians gave to the untouchable Christians was discriminatory and unchristian. Therefore, Shri Markose founded his new faith called Charamar Daiva Sabha. The Sabha was active during 1950's and got enough followers.

CHERAMAR MAHA JAN SABHA

The Cheramar Maha Jan Sabha was founded in Kerala by Pampady John Joseph on 14 January 1921. He was of the view that the caste name 'Pulaya' was disgraceful as it denoted pollution, therefore, he named it *Cheramar* which means 'son of the soil' of Kerala.

The Cheramar Maha Jan Sabha attracted the converts and non-converts towards it. It gave a new awakening to the untouchables in Kerala.

DALIT HARIJAN SAMAJ

It was formed by Muldas Vaishya in 1948 at Ahmedabad. Its objectives were:

1. To organize Dalit communities in Gujarat.
2. To revive traditional occupations like tanning and weaving to improve their economic conditions.
3. To remove untouchability within Dalits and abolish social customs which degenerated them.
4. To take steps to obtain political rights.

---

15. Michael Mahar : 1969 : 157.

5. To start indigenous games for physical development of the Dalits.
6. To give ethical education.
7. To organize cooperative societies and to get loans to develop business.

DALIT SEVA ASHRAM

The Dalit Seva Ashram was established by Shri N.R. Shende in 1943 at Bhandara. He opened 27 centres of mass education in Bhandara district in Maharashtra on behalf of the Ashram and tried to educate the people belonging to Depressed Classes.

DEPRESSED CLASSES ASSOCIATION

The Depressed Classes Association was founded in 1928. Rao Bahadur M.C. Rajah (Madras) was its President and Ganesh Akhaji Gawai and G.M. Thaware (Vidarbha region) were its Secretary and Joint Secretary respectively. The Association was active in Vidarbha region and some other parts of the country. It was, however, not popular due to its opposition to the Ambedkarite movement. It, however, continued till 1942. In that year Shri M.C. Rajah joined the SCF at Nagpur.

DEPRESSED INDIA ASSOCIATION[16]

It was founded by Ganesh Akkaji Gawai in 1917 at Pune. However, it came into existence in Vidarbha region of Central Provinces and Berar in 1922.

The main objectives of the Association were:

1. To spread education among the Depressed Classes.
2. To develop their moral and material condition.
3. To introduce social reforms.
4. To protect the interests of the industrial and agricultural labourers.
5. To safeguard the political interests of the Depressed Classes.

---

16. Kosare : 1984 : 115. 122.

In order to achieve those objectives it decided to convene meetings and conferences, open hostels and schools for girls and boys and run a newspaper to vent the grievances of the Depressed Classes both in India and outside.

DRAVID KAZHAGHAM

The Dravid Kazhagham (Association) was formed by John Rathnam at Madras in the year 1892. The main objective of this Association was to unite the Depressed Classes in Madras and to act as a pressure group to get the demands of the untouchables fulfilled.

It was, however, in 1944 that the South Indian Liberal Federation at Salem under the leadership of E.V. Ramaswamy Naicker, adopted the name 'Dravida Kazhagham' in place of South Indian Liberal Federation. It was a leading non- Brahmin movement in Madras State.

However, the real pioneer of the non-Brahmin organization was Shri John Rathnam, an untouchable leader. Later on, the Depressed Classes people adopted the name of their community as 'Adi-Dravidian', which was accepted by the government in 1922.

HIMALAYA SCHEDULED CASTES ASSOCIATION

It was founded by Shri Anokhi Ram Betab (1922) at Shimla in the year 1945. This organization tried to bring a new awareness among the Scheduled Castes in Himachal Pradesh. Later on, it was renamed as Himachal Scheduled Castes Federation in 1948. Its President was Shri Bhagat Ram and Secretary was Anokhi Ram Betab. Later on, it was merged into Republican Party of India. Shri Anokhi Ram, Teluram Baidwan and Bhagat Ram were its leaders.

HYDERABAD STATE DEPRESSED CLASSES ASSOCIATION

The Youth League of Ambedkarites was formed by P.R. Venkataswamy and B.S. Venkatarao at Hyderabad on 17 May 1936. Shri B.S. Venkat Rao was its President and Shri P.R. Venkataswamy was its Secretary, with its office in Hyderabad.

The aims and objectives of the League were:

1. To organize the youth of the Depressed Classes under one banner.
2. To support Babasaheb Ambedkar in his mission to lead the community out of Hinduism.
3. To enlighten the community on the evils of Hinduism.
4. To obliterate existing caste differences among them.
5. To start a vigorous campaign to ameliorate their social and economic disabilities.

However, it was decided on 29 May 1938 to rename the League as Hyderabad State Depressed Classes Association. The objectives of the Association were just like those of the League. It was done so because they wanted to expand its activities in view of the proposed reforms in the Hyderabad State. Shri B.S. Venkat Rao was elected President of the renamed organization.

The Association submitted a memorandum on 7 May 1939 to Sir Akbar Hydari, President of the Nizam's Executive Council. They demanded, among others, separate electorate and educational facilities for the Depressed Classes.

However, after the merger of Hyderabad with India in 1948, the Depressed Classes Association was merged with the Scheduled Castes Federation. Further, it joined with the All India Depressed Classes League affiliated to the Congress.

HYDERABAD STATE SCHEDULED CASTES FEDERATION

At first, the Hyderabad State Adi-Hindu Mahasabha came into existence on 1 June 1941 in a meeting of the Adi- Hindus at Jamsed Hall, Hyderabad. It was presided over by B.G. Madre.

The aims and objectives of the Mahasabha were:

1. To revive and develop the ancient culture of the Adi-Hindus and foster the spirit of brotherhood among them and to organize them into one united body.
2. To remove their social disabilities, to strive for their economic betterment and their educational advancement.

3. To achieve their legitimate political rights by peaceful and constitutional means.

Later on, it came to be known as Hyderabad State Scheduled Castes Federation, and affiliated to the All India Scheduled Castes Federation which was founded by Dr Babasaheb Ambedkar at Nagpur in 1942.

INDEPENDENT LABOUR PARTY (ILP)

It was founded by Dr Babasaheb Ambedkar on 15 August 1936 at Bombay. He himself was its President and Treasurer, Shri M B. Samarth was its Secretary, and Shri K.V. Chitre and S.A. Upashyam were its Joint Secretaries. It was the first political party of the Dalits and exploited people in India.

The ILP declared its manifesto before the general elections to be held in 1937. Accordingly, the party stood for a representative and responsible government in India. It was to develop agriculture, credit system through banks, industries, technical education and even state management of industries. It promised to undertake suitable social reforms and abolish compulsory labour.

The ILP participated in the provincial elections held on 17 February 1937. In the Bombay Presidency, the ILP could win 14 seats (11 reserved and three general seats). Dr Babasaheb Ambedkar was among the successful candidates. He was elected from Bombay city (north).

In the Central Province and Berar seven candidates were elected on reserved seats and none on general seats.

Apart from this, two members were nominated by the Governor to the Bombay Legislative Council.

The role played by ILP in the politics of Bombay, CP and Berar, and in the national politics is of great importance. However, the party had a very short life. The British Government declared India's participation in World War II without consulting Indians. Therefore, the Congress declared its non-cooperation to the Government. During the war the whole political situation in India came to a standstill.

The ILP was not treated by the majority of non-Dalit workers as their own party. In this situation, Dr Babasaheb Ambedkar decided to freeze the activities of the party and started a new party. Thereafter, he founded All India Scheduled Castes Federation in 1942.

INDEPENDENT SCHEDULED CASTES FEDERATION

This organization came into existence at Hyderabad on 23 June 1945. Its aim was to strive for the unity of the Depressed Classes organizations.

A memorandum of demands was submitted by its leaders to Sir Mirza Ismail, President of the Executive Committee of the Nizam's Government in October 1945.

JAGAN MITRA MANDAL

It was founded in 1906 by Shri M.V. Bhagya Reddy Varma at Hyderabad. The organization, used to arrange *Harikatha* programmes and afterwards, Shri Bhagya Reddy Varma would explain to the untouchables that "they were the real and original inhabitants of India and that the others have migrated from Central Asia for their livelihood and that the main cause of their backwardness was their ignorance and illiteracy." It was the pioneering organization of the Depressed Classes in Hyderabad State. It inspired a new awakening among the people.

JAMMU-KASHMIR HARIJAN MANDAL

The Jammu and Kashmir Harijan Mandal was organized on the pattern of All India Scheduled Castes Federation founded by Dr Babasaheb Ambedkar. Babu Milkhi Ram was its leader. Babu Milkhi Ram (1926–1989) contested on behalf of the Mandal in 1952 for the Legislative Assembly of Jammu and Kashmir but in vain. Again he contested on the ticket of the Mandal in 1957 Assembly Election and got elected. Later, he joined the Republican Party of India and worked throughout his life for the mission of Babasaheb Ambedkar. It was because of Ambedkarite mission under Babu Milkhi Ram's leadership that the Scheduled Castes were treated as eligible to all the safeguards under the Constitution of India.

JATAV VEER MAHASABHA

This party was founded in 1917 at Agra by Prabhutanand Vyas and Pandit Sundarlal Sagar. Its objectives were, "to motivate the Jatavs toward education, sanskritization of their way of life and change of their identity." It demanded representation for the Jatavs in the Legislature. Thus, in 1920, Shri Khemchand Bohare was nominated a member of the UP Legislative Council. It was a great achievement for the Mahasabha. Though it spread throughout Agra district and the neighbouring districts, it came to an end in 1928 due to internal dissensions. However, a new organization called Jatav Youth League came into existence in 1930, which worked for the same aims and objectives, which the Jatav Veer Mahasabha endeavoured for in the past.

JAT-PAT TODAK MANDAL[17]

Jat-pat Todak Mandal (organization to break caste) was founded by Shri Sant Ram B.A. (1887-1988) in 1922. The main objective of the organization was to break caste system by arranging and promoting inter-caste marriages.

Previously, the Mandal was under the influence of Arya Samaj. However, it came out of it later on. The Jat-pat Todak Mandal was very popular in Punjab. Once its leader Shri Sant Ram invited Dr Babasaheb Ambedkar in 1936 to deliver his presidential address in the annual meeting of the Mandal. However, he did not go to deliver his address as it was not acceptable to some of the members of the Mandal.

KARNATAK BAHISHKRIT SANGH

It was founded by Swami Deorai Ramji Ingle, School Board Member, Belgaon, in 1922. He used to propagate among the Depressed Classes people, especially those living in the villages that they should struggle for their human rights. He used to propagate among all the untouchables including Mahar, Mang, Chambhar and Dhor, and tried to unite them for all social activities. The Sangh was active till 1930.

---

17. Juergensmeyer : 1988 : 39.

KHET MAZDOOR SABHA[18]

The Khet Mazdoor Sabha (Agricultural labourer organization) was founded by Shri Jagjivan Ram in the State of Bihar in 1930s. It was one of the first agricultural labour organizations in the country. Its main base was among the agricultural labourers belonging to Dalits in Bihar. The Khet Mazdoor Sabha aimed to protect the interests of the agricultural labourers. It, however, turned against the All India Kisan Sabha which was working under the left leadership and posing a great challenge to the Congress.

LOK SEVA NATYE MANDAL

Shri Deenbandhu Shegaonkar (1926) founded Lok Seva Natye Mandal in 1942 at Akola in Maharashtra. It was an association to undertake cultural activities like staging dramas, organizing Bhajan parties and bringing a new awakening among the Dalit masses. The Mandal was active till 1953. Thereafter, it was named as Deenbandhu Kala Pathak. The Kala Pathak tried to spread the message of Dr Babasaheb Ambedkar through cultural programmes. The Kala Pathak was very much popular in Akola and the neighbouring districts.

MADHYA PRANT VARHAD BIDI MAJOOR SANGH

It was founded in a conference of the *bidi* labourers at Kamathi, near Nagpur in the year 1925. Its main objective was to strive for the welfare of the *bidi* labourers in the erstwhile Berar region of Maharashtra.

MAHABODHI ASHOK MISSION

The Mahabodhi Ashok Mission was founded by Mrs Quin Moi Rahul and Rahul Suman Chhawara at Ajmer in the year 1955. They had built a big Mahabodhi Ashok Vihara at Ajmer. The Mission runs a school in the Vihara and a monthly *Right View* from Ajmer. The Mission is spreading Buddhism among all the Depressed Classes, especially the Koris or Kolis in Rajasthan.

---

18. Gail Omvedt: 1982 : 23, 106.

MAHANUBHAV PANTHIYA ASPRUSHYA SAMAJ

It was established in the month of January 1935. Its President was Raosaheb Thaware. The main objective of the Samaj was to organize the untouchables converted to Mahanubhav Sect.

MAHAR DNYATI PANCHAYAT SAMITI

It was founded by Sambhaji Tukaram Gaikwad in the year 1942 in Bombay. It has been renamed as Boudh Jan Panchayat Samiti. It is still in existence. The Mahar Dnyati Panchayat Samiti strove to propagate the thoughts of Babasaheb Ambedkar in the society.

MAHAR TARUN MANDAL

The Mahar Tarun Mandal (Mahar Youth League) was founded by Shri Fathuji Bapuji Shende (1880-1922) at Nagpur in the year 1904. On behalf of the Mandal, he opened a school for boys and another for girls. The Mandal strove to root out the old bad customs and habits of the Depressed Classes.

MARWAR MEHTAR SUDHAR SABHA

This organization came into existence in 1945. Shri Prabhu Das Gharu was its President. Bhagwan Das Gund was its Vice-President and Shri Ram Sarvate was its Secretary.

The said Sabha prepared a chapter of demands in 1946. Accordingly, its objectives were confined to the Mehtar Community of the Marwar region of Rajasthan.

The main demands of the organization among others, were as follows:

1. They wanted to be treated as permanent servants.
2. They wanted to get brooms for sweeping.
3. They demanded one month's leave in a year with full salary.
4. They wanted to have *pucca* houses and separate wells to be dug for them.

The demands of the Sabha were very genuine, but due to the apathetic attitude of the government, they had to go on strike for six days to press for their demands.

MEGHWAL SUDHAR SABHA

Meghwal Sudhar Sabha was founded to reform Meghwal community in Rajasthan. Shri Barupal Pannalal was President of the Sabha.

MEHTAR KAMGAR UNION

It was established by Shri Chouthmal at Nagpur in 1944. The main purpose of this union was to solve the basic problems of the Mehtar community and inspire them to take up education. He led a strike of thousands of people to press for the demands of the Union.

MUNICIPAL KAMGAR SANGH

It was founded by Dr Babasaheb Ambedkar at Bombay. He himself was the President of the organization, and Shri Ganpatbuwa alias Madakebuwa was its working President. Its head office was situated at Nana building, Parel, Bombay.

Shri Madakebuwa organized all the class IV employees of the Bombay Corporation under one banner. The organization could successfully fight for the welfare of the employees.

MUSHAR SEVAK SANGH[19]

The organization was formed by Shri Somar Ram in 1953 with its headquarters at Ranchi in Bihar. He was the President for seven years. The objective of the organization was to awaken Mushar community in Bihar.

NAMASUDRA WELFARE ASSOCIATION[20]

Guruchand Thakur, son of Harichand Thakur started Namasudra Welfare Association. He called an All Bengal Namasudra Conference at Duttadanga in the district of Khulna (at present in Bangladesh) in the year 1881.

---

19. Sachchidananda : 1977 : 156.

20. ***The Oppressed Indian,*** July 1982, Vol IV. pp. 6-7.

Guruchand Thakur was the President of the conference. Guruchand Thakur advised his people to start schools in the areas densely populated by them. His next movement was to remove the disgraceful term "Chandal" (which was then attributed to Namasudra by the higher caste Hindus) from the census report. He was successful in the same. The term "Chandal" was removed from census report of 1911. In 1907 he appealed to the then Governor of Bengal and Assam for employment of the Namasudras in government services.

NAV YUVAK KALA MANDAL

It was started by Shri Jawahar Lal Gund at Udaimandir Bustee in the year 1950. Its main purpose was to reform the Bhangi community in Rajasthan by undertaking artistic performances at various places.

PANCHAMA KALVI ABHIVARTHI – ABHIMANA SANGH[21]

This was an organization of the untouchables in Madras Presidency. The organization appealed to Montague, the then Secretary of India when he visited India in 1917, that the untouchables should be saved from "the yoke of Brahmins"

PASCHIM KHANDESH DALIT SHIKSHAN PRASARAK MANDAL, DHULE

The institution came into existence with the inspiration of Dr Babasaheb Ambedkar in the year 1939 at Dhulia in Maharashtra. Its founder was Shri P.L. Lalingkar. The main purpose of the institution was to spread education among the Dalits in the region. The institution had started its first hostel in the year 1939-40 at Nandurbar (Dhulia) with 10-12 students. The institution could construct four rooms of its own for the hostel. Since 1960 Shri Raosaheb Niley (1924- 1986) took over the charge of the institution. Presently, the said Mandal runs four high schools, two hostels and a law college.

---

21. Keer : 1971 : 33.

PEOPLE'S EDUCATION SOCIETY, BOMBAY[22]

Education is the *sine qua non* of the liberation of any community and especially of the Dalits. Considering the importance of education in the liberation of Dalits, Dr Babasaheb Ambedkar founded the People's Education Society at Bombay on 8 July 1945. The aims and objectives of the society are as stated below:

1. To provide facilities for education—secondary, collegiate, technical, physical and the like.
2. To start, establish, conduct educational institutions such as schools, colleges, hostels, libraries, playgrounds, etc, at suitable places in the State of Bombay as well as in any other part of India, or give aid to such institutions.
3. To provide facilities for the education of the poor.
4. To create and foster a general interest in education amongst the Scheduled Castes and in particular to give them special facilities, and scholarships for higher education in India and abroad.
5. To promote science, literature and fine arts and to impart useful knowledge.
6. To cooperate, amalgamate or affiliate the society or any institution or institutions run by or belonging to the society, to any other institution or society with a view to securing further advancement of the aims and objects of the society.

The society was registered under the Society's Registration Act XXI of 1860, No. 1375 of 1945-46 dated 9 July 1945 and the Bombay Public Trust Act 1950 (Bom XXIX of 1950) Registration No. F. 303, dated 2 June 1953.

At present the Governing Body of the Society consists of the following members:

1. Dr S.P. Gaikwad, G.C.A.M. – Chairman
2. Shri S. S. Rege, B.A., Dip. Lib. Sc. – Dy.Chairman

---

22. PES Reports.

3. Shri K.B. Talwatkar, M.A.LL.M. – Member
4. Dr J.V. Deshpande, M.Sc., Ph.D. – Member
5. Shri M.V. Rao, B.A., LL.B. – Member
6. Dr P.T. Borale, B.A., LL.B. – Member
7. Shri M.B. Tambe – Member
8. Shri M.S. Moray – Member
9. Prof S.K. Mohgaonkar – Member
10. Hon'ble Shri K.H. Rangnath – Member
11. Dr M.L.Shahare, M.SC., Ph.D. – Member

The office of the society is located at Anand Bhawan, Dr. Dadabhai Naoroji Road, Fort, Bombay.

It is running the following institutions:

Colleges

1. Siddarth College of Arts, Science and Commerce, Bombay (1946).
2. Siddharth College of Commerce and Economics, Bombay (1953).
3. Siddharth College of Law, Bombay (1956).
4. Dr Ambedkar College of Commerce and Economics, Wadala, Bombay (1971).
5. Dr Ambedkar College of Law, Wadala, Bombay (1978).
6. Milind College of Arts, Aurangabad (1950).
7. Milind College of Science, Aurangabad (1950).
8. Dr Babasaheb Ambedkar College of Arts and Commerce, Aurangabad (1960).
9. Dr Ambedkar College of Law, Aurangabad (1968).
10. Physical Education College, Aurangabad (1984).
11. Dr Babasaheb Ambedkar College of Arts and Commerce, Mahad, Dist. Raigad (1961).
12. Dr Ambedkar College of Arts and Commerce, Yerwada, Pune (1985).

Diploma Institutes

13. Siddharth College of Mass Communication, Bombay (1965)
14. Siddharth College of Industry and Administration, Bombay (1967)

Schools

15. Siddharth Night School, Bombay (1947)
16. Milind High School, Aurangabad (1955)
17. Milind Primary School, Aurangabad (1975)
18. Matoshri Ramabai Ambedkar High School, Aurangabad (1965)
19. Goutam Vidyalaya, Pandharpur (1974)
20. PES Vidyalaya, New Bombay (1978)
21. Nagsen Vidyalaya, Nanded (1981)
22. PES High School, Bombay (1983)
23. Nagsen Vidyalaya, Bangalore (1984)

Hostels

24. Sant Gadge Maharaj Chokhamela Hostel, Pandharpur (1949)
25. Matoshri Ramabai Ambedkar Students' Hostel, Dapoli (1962)
26. Subhedar Sawadkar Vidyarthi Ashram. Mahad (1978)
27. Siddharth Vihar Hostel, Wadala, Bombay (1964)

The People's Education Society has done yeoman's service to the cause of Dalit uplift through education.

PRATYAKSHA RAKSHA DEIVA SABHA

The Pratyaksha Raksha Deiva Sabha (PRDS) was founded by Poykayil Yohannan (Poykayil Sree Kumar Devan) in 1908. He saw that the untouchable converts were not treated equally with the other Christians. Hence he came to the conclusion that "the Bible is not meant for this generation and it shall not provide any solution for the problems of Depressed classes." Ultimately, he himself founded a new faith called PRDS.

The principles of the PRDS were:

1. To reject Christianity and Hinduism.
2. To believe that God will incarnate to liberate the untouchables.
3. To believe in liberty, equality and fraternity.
4. To pray in the name of the Creator, but not to offer sacrifice.
5. To pray in separate temples.

The PRDS is still working for the moral and spiritual development of the downtrodden communities in Kerala. Its head office is situated at Tiruvalla in Pattanamtitta district in Kerala.

RAJPUTANA MEHTAR SUDHAR SABHA

The Rajputana Mehtar Sudhar Sabha was founded by Shri Gopalanand Maharaj in 1948 in the conference held at Udaimandir Bhangi Bustee, where the representatives of the Bhangi community from various places in Rajasthan were present. Shri Nagarmal from Churu and Ghasi Ram were elected President and Secretary respectively.

The objectives of the Sabha were:

1. To promote the spirit of unity among the community members.
2. To promote social and material welfare of the members of the Bhangi community.
3. To preach importance of education.

They aimed to promote social change by way of sanskritization.

ROHIDAS DNYANODAYA SAMAJ

It was founded by Shri R.B. Chandorkar in 1923. It was renamed as Rohidas Sudharak Mandal in 1933. Its headquarters were in Bombay.

SADHUJAN PARIPALAN YOGAM

The Sadhujan Paripalan Yogam (the organization to protect the poor people) was formed by Shri Ayyan Kali (Kerala) in the year 1905. He tried to organize the untouchables in Kerala under the banner of this organization. The members of the organization were to assemble on every Sunday in open space where they prayed to God, but not to the idols. Ayyan Kali used to preach to them at such congregations to maintain cleanliness and maintain high moral standard. It was to act as a court to punish those who violated the rules and teachings of the Yogam. Shri Keshwan and Kunjan Krishnan were to assist him. The Sadhujan Paripalan Yogam was a comprehensive organization which tried to unite almost all the untouchable castes or sub-castes in Kerala. It gave a new awakening to the untouchables. It tried to regain all the civil rights which the untouchables were not allowed to enjoy.

SAFAI MAZDOOR SANGH

It was founded in 1937 in Punjab. Its founders were Chunilal Thapar, Bal Mukund, Mohtan Singh and Sant Ram. They staged at first a strike in 1938 which was led by Sant Ram. The agitation spread to many cities of Punjab. It was for improving the service conditions of the sweepers.

SAHITYA CHARCHA MANDAL, NAGPUR[23]

The Sahitya Charcha Mandal or Literary Study Circle was founded at Nagpur on 9 November 1941. The objectives of this organization were to encourage writings and to undertake several literary activities.

SAHODARAN SANGHAM

The Sahodaran Sangham (Association of Brotherhood) was founded by Ayyappan. He preached equality among all castes among the untouchables. He wanted all the untouchables to mix together, move forward together, interdine and even intermarry. It was popular in Kerala.

---

23. Kosare : 1984 : 391.

SAMASTHA COCHIN PULAYA MAHASABHA[24]

The Samastha Cochin Pulaya Mahasabha came into existence in 1913. Shri Krishnadiyasan was its President and Pandit K.P. Karuppan and P.C. Chanchan were its Secretaries. Its office was at Ernakulam.

The Mahasabha engaged in liberating the Pulayas in Cochin region of Kerala. The organization revolted against the tradition of denying entry to the untouchables in the city of Ernakulam. It started some schools and night schools for the untouchable students. It tried to bring a new awakening among the untouchables in Cochin.

SAMATA SAINIK DAL

The Samata Sainik Dal was founded by Dr Babasaheb Ambedkar in March 1927. It was to enlist support for the Mahad satyagraha and maintain discipline in the satyagraha and in the society. Previously it was known as Swayam Sevak Dal and it was not a centralized organization. It was led by Sitaram Gangaram Gangurle in Nasik, Shri Sasalekar in Bombay, Shri Lalingkar in Khandesh and R.R. Patil in Nagpur.

It was, however, formally organized at a national level on 20 July 1942 at Nagpur. The convenor of the first organization was Shri H.L. Kosare. Its first conference was held under the presidentship of Sardar Gopal Singh of Punjab. Dr Babasaheb Ambedkar addressed the conference.

The activities of the SSD were revived in 1957. The SSD was a very strong and well-disciplined organization, which gave a new vigour to the Dalit liberation movement. It is again being revived by leaders such as Bhagwan Das and L.R. Bali.

SANMARG BODHAK NIRASHRIT SAMAJ

The Sanmarg Bodhak Nirashrit Samaj was founded by Shri Kisan Fagu Bansod in 1903 at Nagpur. The objectives of the Samaj were as under:

---

24. Joseph Mathew : 1986 : 110.

1. To spread education among all the Depressed Classes.
2. To preach against drinking spurious liquor and against beef eating.
3. To oppose conversion to other religions.
4. To organize all the Dalits under one banner.
5. To propagate moral and religious principles.
6. To reform the untouchable society.
7. To struggle for human rights.

This organization was popular among the untouchables throughout the Vidarbha region of the present Maharashtra.

SANSKRITI CHAKRA

In 1949, Shri Jyotin Bagchi founded at Calcutta a cultural organization, called "Sanskriti Chakra" to awaken the cultural consciousness among the backward classes. From the very inception, he discharged the responsibility as the General Secretary for seven years. Besides, dancing and singing activities, practice of recitation, practice to oratorial skills were also included in the programme of this organization.

He published a monthly magazine *Patheya Patrika* with a view to encouraging young and promising writers especially from the downtrodden people.

SARVAJANIK VYAYAMSHALA

The Sarvajanik Vyayamshala was established by Shri Vasant Lal Chouhan at Hirpur, Ahmedabad in the year 1940. The main objective of the *vyayamshala* (gymnasium) was to develop physical strength of the Scheduled Castes and organize them so that they may be able to face the attacks of the caste Hindus.

He established *vyayamshalas* at various places in Ahmedabad. He used to give physical training and discourses for bringing awareness among the Scheduled Castes at such places.

SATNAMI MOVEMENT

This organization was founded by Shri Ghasi Das in Chattisgarh region in 1830's. According to its teaching all men are equal irrespective of caste. He believed in one Creator or *Satnam.* He had no faith in Hindu deities. He preached against consuming liquor and tobacco. He preached vegetarianism, and asked his people to maintain high moral and cultural standard.

After the death of Ghasi Das in 1850 his successors, Agar Das and thereafter Agam Das and Muktawan Das continued the movement.

The head of the Satnami movement is known as 'Guru'; at the intermediate level there are *Mahants* and at the bottom of the organization there are *Bhandaris* (after Bhandar, a village which became the seat of the Satnami cult).

The Satnami movement became very much popular in the Chattisgarh region of Madhya Pradesh. The movement tried to bring about a new awakening among the ignorant masses of the region. It could raise the self-pride of the untouchables. The movement is still in existence. However, it could not spread to other parts of the country. It also suffered from internal dissensions. However, its contribution to the Dalit uplift movement cannot be ignored.

SCHEDULED CASTES STUDENTS UNION, HYDERABAD[25]

A Scheduled Castes Students' Convention was called on 11 August 1950 at Nallagunta Temperance centre. In the conference an organization named "Scheduled Castes Students Union" was formed with K. Narayan Rao as President. The Union was meant to solve the problems of Scheduled Caste students.

SHRI CHOKHAMELA SAMAJ[26]

Shri Chokhamela Samaj came into existence on 5 September 1920. Its first meeting was held at the residence of Shri Vithoba

---

25. P.R. Venkataswamy : 1955 : II. 651-653.
26. Kosare : 1984 : 111-113.

Mistri at Nagpur. The persons present at the meeting were Kisan Fagu Bansode, Umaji Master, Bodi Buwa, Raghunath Shambharkar and others. The main purpose of the Samaj was to develop the untouchables socially, politically, culturally and educationally.

The next meeting of the Samaj was held under the presidentship of Shri Dashrath Laxman Patil. It was attended among others, by Vishramji Sawaitul, Hemchandra Khandekar, V.D. Makesar, U.G. Khandekar, Sambhaji Godghate, Hariprasad Buwa. In the meeting they passed certain resolutions regarding compulsory education and representation of the Dalits in the legislature. They thought that the increasing cooperative movement would be harmful to the Depressed Classes.

The Samaj established Chokhamela Boarding for the Scheduled Caste students at Navivasti, Nagpur in about 1920.

SHRI CHOKHAMELA SAMAJ GIRLS EDUCATION SOCIETY, NAGPUR[27]

Shri Chokhamela Samaj Girls Education Society was formed in 1922 at Pach Pawali, Nagpur, by the Dalit leaders named Shri Tukaram Borkar, Shri Vithobaji Pantawane, Shri Ramaji Dongre and Vithalrao Sawaitul. The main objective of the Society was to spread education amongst the girls belonging to the Depressed Classes. The Society established at first a girls night school in 1922. Later on in 1960 it started a high school and then a junior college for the girl students. Presently near about 3,000 girl students are taking education in the Society's institutions at Nagpur.

Presently its President is Advocate Sukhdeve, Vice Presidents are S.R. Dongre and Nagorao Pantawane, Secretary is Shri B.P. Shende and Dr Gangadhar Pantawane, Dr Bhau Lokhande, Haribhau Choure, A.B. Dev are its executive body members and its Treasurer is Shri Shyam Kamble. The SCs Girls School is known as a pioneering institution in the matter of spreading of education among the Dalits.

---

27. Gangadhar Pantawane, Aurangabad, interviewed on 21.11. 1992.

SHRI SHANKAR PRASADIK SOMAVANSHIYA HITCHINTAK MITRA SAMAJ

It was founded by Shivaram Janaba Kamble in 1904 at Poona. The main purpose of this organization was to unite and organize the Depressed Classes and to inspire them to try their best to improve their social status.

Shivaram J. Kamble proposed to establish a school and one library for the Depressed Classes. He believed that only education could bring some solace to the untouchables.

The Samaj tried to bring about social reforms among the untouchables. It gave stress on maintaining cleanliness and high moral standard. It was against Devadasi system. Kamble appealed to the government to start recruiting the untouchables in government services including police and military services.

SOUTH INDIA BUDDHIST ASSOCIATION

It was founded by an untouchable leader, Pandit Iyodhi Dass in the 1890s. It was primarily concerned with the betterment of its untouchable members.

On 21 November 1920, P. Lakshmi Narasu presided over a conference held at Mayo Hall, Bangalore. The conference requested the Government of India to initiate for the Depressed Classes, political reforms and free compulsory education, and facilities for higher education.

In a booklet published in 1954, the South India Buddhist Association claimed nine branches in Madras State, namely, Pudapet and Royapettah in Madras city; Vannivadu, Valathore, Gudiyatham. Thirupathore and Palikondai in North Arcot district; and Angambakam and Enathore in Chinglepet district. The three branches in Mysore State were located at Champion Reef and Marikuppam in the Kolar Gold Fields, Bangalore city and Hubli. It could reach even outside India to Indonesia and Africa. Natal, Durban and Zululand were the African areas where Tamil speaking labour had migrated.

The South India Buddhist organization tried to revive Buddhism in South India because of which a good many untouchables were attracted towards this religion.

THAKAR BAPPA ASHRAM, NIMAKHANDI

The Thakar Bappa Ashram was founded at Nimakhandi on 11 November 1952 by Shri Mohan Nayak (1921-1983). Shri Nayak was a great liberator of the untouchables in Orissa. He participated in Indian independence movement. The Thakar Bappa Ashram was founded to undertake such schemes which would have relevance to the socio-economic development of the Scheduled Castes.

THE CENTRAL PROVINCES AND BERAR DEPRESSED CLASSES EDUCATION SOCIETY

This Society was established by Shri G.M. Thaware at Nagpur in 1922 with the objective of spreading education among the Depressed Classes. The Society runs a number of schools in Nagpur and Bhandara districts. It was renamed as 'Yugantar Education Society' on 12 March 1960 at the instance of Shri Nasikrao Tirpude, the then and present President of the Society. The Society's office and its educational institutions are situated at Tiger-Gap Ground Civil Lines, Nagpur.

VALMIKI SABHA

It was founded at Jullunder in Punjab as early as 1910. Mahatma Fakir Chand and Shri Gendu Ram were its founders. They tried to organize the sweepers (Churhas) under the banner of this organization. It became active after 1932 as most of the sweepers left the Ad-Dharm movement and joined the Vaimiki Sabha. It was formed to achieve 'cultural' and 'social' organization of the Churhas. Later on, it was led by Shri Sant Ram, Chunnilal, Balmukund, Mohtan Singh and many others.

VIDARBHA ASPRUSHYA SAMAJ SUDHARAK SEVA MANDAL

This organization was founded by Shri Sambhuji Ansuji Khandare at Akola on 1 December 1926.

The main objectives of the Mandal were as follows:

1. To struggle for religious equality, and to reconvert those who had converted to Islam or Christianity.

2. To propagate against sub-casteism among the untouchables to encourage inter sub-caste marriages; to propagate against drinking and beef eating.
3. To spread education amongst the untouchables by opening schools, hostels, and to spread technical education.
4. To work for getting due representation on the District Boards and legislature.

The Mandal proved to be very useful in uniting all the Depressed Classes in Vidarbha region of Maharashtra. It started several schools in the remote villages and appointed 17 teachers in the schools. It tried to reform the Depressed Classes. It tried to propagate for high moral, material and cultural standard among the Depressed Classes.

Table 4.1 : State-Wise and Period-Wise Number of Dalit Organizations

SI. No.		I 1857-1890	II 1891-1918	III 1919-1956	Total
1.	Andhra Pradesh	–	4	6	10
2.	Assam	–	–	–	–
3.	Bihar	–	1	4 (2)	5
4.	Jammu & Kashmir	–	–	1	1
5.	Karnataka	–	–	2	2
6.	Kerala	–	3	6 (3)	9
7.	Madhya Pradesh	1	1	1 (1)	3
8.	Maharashtra	1	5	23 (1)	29
	Gujarat	–	–	2	2
9.	Orissa	–	–	1	1
10.	Punjab	–	1	3	4
	Haryana	–	–	–	–
	Himachal Pradesh	–	–	1	1
11.	Rajasthan	–	–	5 (1)	5
12.	Tamil Nadu	2	1	2 (1)	5
13.	Uttar Pradesh	–	1	1	2
14.	West Bengal	1	1	2	4
		5	18	60 (9)	83

(Note: No period is known of the foundation of those organizations whose number is given in brackets in column No.5, but they are inclusive of the total).

Table 4.2 : State-Wise Number of Organizations Working in Different Fields

SI. No.	States	Social	Political	Religious	Cultural	Educational	Economic	Total
1.	Andhra Pradesh	7	2	–	–	1	–	10
2.	Assam	–	–	–	–	–	–	–
3.	Bihar	4	–	–	–	–	1	5
4.	Jammu & Kashmir	–	1	–	–	–	–	1
5.	Karnataka	2	–	–	–	–	–	2
6.	Kerala	6	–	3	–	–	–	9
7.	Madhya Pradesh	1	–	2	–	–	–	3
8.	Maharashtra	16	2	1	2	5	3	29
	Gujarat	1	–	–	1	–	–	2
9.	Orissa	1	–	–	–	–	–	1
10.	Punjab	2	–	1	–	–	1	4
	Haryana	–	–	–	–	–	–	–
	Himachal Pradesh	–	1	–	–	–	–	1
11.	Rajasthan	3	–	1	1	–	–	5
12.	Tamil Nadu	4	–	1	–	–	–	5
13.	Uttar Pradesh	2	–	–	–	–	–	2
14.	West Bengal	3	–	–	1	–	–	4
		52	6	9	5	6	5	83

Note: There was only one All India level political party namely the All India Scheduled Castes Federation. Others were its branches. There were state level branches of the SCF in almost all the states.

WEST BENGAL HARI JATI KALYAN SAMITI[28]

This organization came into existence in 1948. Its office is in Calcutta. The objective of this organization is to strive for the educational and social uplift of the Dalits.

CONCLUSION

There were several organizations which aimed at liberating the so-called untouchables. However, it is difficult to give their profiles in detail, due to want of sufficient information about their nature, working and achievements. With the exception of a few, those organizations were confined to the uplift of their respective castes. Many of them were local level organizations. A great majority of them were not registered. It is not known as to how long they continued to work.

For the convenience of study of the Dalit movement during 1857 to 1956, it could be divided into three phases. The first phase starts from 1857 and ends in 1890, second from 1891 to 1918 and the third and final phase starts from 1919 and ends in 1956. Table 4.1 gives the state-wise and period-wise number of Dalit organizations included in the study. Table 4.2 shows the statewise number of organizations working in different fields.

---

28. Dalit Vikas Samiti : 1990 : 68.

5

Chronology of Events and Achievements

Dalit consciousness that originated, among others, from the acute discontent of the Dalits with their wretchedness, could not remain dormant. This widespread feeling was manifested through several organizations and struggles for the emancipation of Dalits. With the passage of time it became increasingly vocal, vigorous and effective. It started with Khalasi's demand for a *lota* for drinking water and the following Mutiny in 1857; and culminated in the commencement of the Constitution of India in 1950 and conversion to Buddhism in 1956 of Dr B.R. Ambedkar and his followers. This span of hundred years was full of struggles and achievements of the Dalit movement.

The study of the Dalit movement would not be complete unless the chronology of events and achievements of the same are not duly recorded. Therefore, it is proposed to enumerate in brief certain important events and achievements of the Dalit movement. Of course, untouchability being a multi-faceted phenomenon, including within its scope social discrimination, religious restrictions, educational deprivation, economic exploitation and political persecution, it is proposed to state the events and achievements respectively pertaining to those forms of untouchability.

CIVIL RIGHTS

Since long the Dalits were forbidden almost all the civil rights. They were denied access to the locality of the *savarnas*, the roads or footpaths in the *savarna* locality and in the vicinity of the temples, public and private wells, bathing ghats, burial grounds, etc. They were not even allowed to wear fine clothes, footwears, grow upward moustaches, use ghee in the feasts, give honorific names to their children and to speak good language. In some parts of the country they were not allowed to walk along the streets in the day time on the pretext that their very sight or shadow would pollute the *savarnas*. Thus, the so-called untouchables were treated as the most despicable and contemptible people by the caste Hindus.

The Dalits had to wage a war against this social tyranny. The chronology of events of the said struggle and the milestones of their achievements could be traced as under:

1. Dalit consciousness which was, however, growing slowly in the first half of the 19th century, could not remain dormant. Its outbreak, though not entirely deliberate, originated in the episode when a low caste untouchable Khalasi, asked a Brahmin sepoy to let him drink from his *lota*. The Brahmin sepoy refused to give the *lota* thinking that the Khalasi's touch would defile it. Then the untouchable Khalasi said, "You think much of your caste, but wait a little, the Sahib *log* (Englishmen) will make you bite cartridges dipped in cow and pork fat, and then where will your caste be?" Thus, the Brahmin sepoy incidentally came to know as to how they were being polluted by the British who made them open the cartridges covered with fat. That Brahmin sepoy named Mangal Pande ran through the barracks and instigated the soldiers to rise in rebellion against the British as they were said to have been secretly defiling the Hindus as well as the Muslims. The soldiers followed him in the name of religion. The rebellion spread throughout northern India like a volcano within a short time. The princes and nawabs thought to exploit the situation to regain their respective kingdoms taken over by the British Government. However, the rebellion could not succeed

against the mighty British power. But, the British Parliament taking into account the inability of the East India Company to rule over the vast British Indian territory took over the administration of British India. This was followed by Queen Victoria's Proclamation promising a beneficent rule for all the people.

2. In 1868, Mahatma Jyotirao Phule allowed the untouchables to fetch water from the water tank in the premises of his house.
3. In 1870, Shri Kokkonda Venkata Ratnam Panthulu founded the Hindu Sreyobhi Vardhini Sabha at Madras. He used to arrange lectures for bringing awareness amongst the untouchables.
4. In the same year Shri Shashipad Bandopadhyaya, a Brahmo social reformer in Bengal formed a club of the Chandal untouchable labourers near Calcutta. According to Mangudhar he tried to teach good moral habits to the untouchables. He inspired them to sing devotional songs, educate their children and not to drink.
5. In 1872, a meeting of the Namasudra heads of villages was held in Bengal, in which they made the following decisions:
   (i) Not to send women to bazaars,
   (ii) Not to serve higher castes, and
   (iii) Not to accept the food prepared by the higher castes except that of Brahmins.
6. The special Marriage Act was passed in 1872 which made it possible for an Indian of any caste or creed to enter into a valid marriage with a person belonging to any caste or creed.
7. Mahatma Phule had established Satyashodhak Samaj at Pune on 24 September 1873 to emancipate the Sudras and untouchables from casteism and superstitions. At the same time 300 people decided to be members of the said organization.
8. In 1890 Gopal Baba Walangkar established Anarya Dosh Parihar Mandali, an organization to improve the lot of Dalits.

9. In 1891 Shri R. Srinivasan founded Adi Dravida Mahajan Sabha at Madras to organize the members of the Depressed Classes.

10. In 1892 John Rathinam, an untouchable convert in Tamil Nadu started an Association of Dravidians, Dravida Kazhagham in Madras.

11. In 1893, R. Srinivasan convened a conference of the untouchables in Wesley School, Royapetta, Madras.

    This was the first conference of this sort convened in the whole of India.

12. Pandit Iyodhi Dass (Madras) had founded the Paraiyan Mahajan Sabha in 1895 in order to organize the Paraiyan untouchables in the then Madras State.

13. The Maharaja of Mysore issued an order in 1899, stating that the dancing girls of Srikanteswaraswamy temple at Nanjangud be stopped from dancing.

14. According to Khairmode in 1902 Shri Govind Mukunda Mahar, an untouchable fetched water from a common well for drinking water at Ahmadnagar. Therefore, the orthodox caste Hindus filed a case against him in the Court under Section 277 of IPC. Eventually, the Judicial Magistrate second class convicted him of the charge and awarded two weeks simple imprisonment and fine of ₹ 8. However, at the initiative of the District Collector, an appeal was made to High Court of Bombay which acquitted him. Many Mahars supported the accused in his trial.

15. At the initiative of Maharshi Vithal Ramji Shinde an organization named The Depressed Classes Mission Society was established under the Presidentship of Shri Chandavarkar on 18 October 1906. Margudkar states that the main objectives of this organization were to eradicate untouchability and to propagate education among the untouchables.

16. A conference of the Namasudras took place in the sub-divisional town of Narail, Jessore in 1908. It stressed the need for education and social reform within the community so as to raise the social status of the caste.

17. An anti-untouchability conference was held at Ferguson College, Pune, in October 1912 under the presidentship of Dr Ramkrishna G. Bhandarkar. As described by Khairmode it was attended by 350 untouchables and 50 caste Hindus. The prominent leaders who attended it were Dr Kurtkoti and the Maharaja of Ichalkaranji. All the leaders who attended the conference dined together. It was the first occasion when untouchables and caste Hindus dined together as a first step to eradicate untouchability.

18. Shri M.B. Dadabhoy moved a resolution in the Imperial Legislative Council on 16 March 1916 for the uplift of the untouchables to the level of general masses. However, the said resolution was withdrawn on the positive assurance of the Congress.

19. A meeting of Pulaya castemen and women was held at Quilon in 1916. It was presided over by Changanasserry Parameswaran Pillai, a Nair social reformer. According to Mathew in that meeting Aiyyan Kali, the leader of the Pulaya untouchable community asked his castewomen to throw away the bead necklaces, a custom which was of "primitive nature". Hundreds of women publicly threw away their bead necklaces in protest against the attitude of the caste Hindus in Kerala.

20. In 1917 Swami Sahajanandan from Madras organized the untouchables and claimed the right of access to the water of a tank at Omekalam.

21. The Congress at its annual session held at Calcutta on 26 December 1917, passed a resolution against the ugly age-old practice of untouchability. It was presided over by Mrs Annie Besant. The resolution was moved by G.A. Natesan of Madras, and it was supported by Bhulabhai Desai, Ranga Iyer and Asaf Ali. The resolution was as follows:

    "This Congress urges upon the people of India the necessity, justice and righteousness of removing all disabilities imposed by custom upon the Depressed classes, the disabilities being of a most vexatious and oppressive character, subjecting those classes to considerable hardship and inconvenience."

22. All India Depressed Classes Conference was held on 23 and 24 March 1918 in Bombay. It was convened by Karmaveer V.R. Shinde on behalf of the Depressed Classes Mission Society of India. Maharaja Sayajirao Gaekwad of Baroda presided over the conference. It was attended by prominent leaders like M.R. Jaikar, Vithalbhai Patel, Bepin Chandra Pal, B.G. Tilak and others. The Chairman of the Reception Committee was Sir Narayan Ganesh Chandavarkar. At the conclusion of the Conference an All India Anti-Untouchability Manifesto was signed by all the prominent leaders to the effect that they would not observe untouchability in their everyday affairs. B.G. Tilak, however, did not sign it, allegedly on the ground of pressure from his followers.

23. The next conference was held at Bijapur under the presidentship of B.M. Kamat on 6 May 1918. Khairmode states that it was also attended by many prominent leaders. It passed a resolution to eradicate untouchability at the public places like schools, hospitals, watering places and in the temples.

24. Chhatrapati Shahu Maharaj of Kolhapur declared on 27 July 1918 that the untouchables in his State would be able to enjoy all the civil rights without any hindrance on the ground of untouchability.

25. On 21 March 1920, a conference of the untouchables in princely state of Kolhapur was held at Mangaon under the presidentship of Dr Babasaheb Ambedkar. Chhatrapati Shahu Maharaj of Kolhapur was the chief guest of the occasion. It was organized by Shri Appasaheb Dadgonda Patil, a Jain head of the village, with the cooperation of the untouchable leaders like Dattoba Powar, Tukaram Ganeshyacharya, Gangaram Kamble, Shri Abaji Gawali and others in Kolhapur State. It was followed by common dinner. However, the caste Hindus of that village boycotted Shri Appasaheb Dadgonda Patil and the untouchables of that village. They were, however, taken

back when Chhatrapati Shahu Maharaj threatened to arrest them if they continued with this attitude.

26. A conference of the representatives of the untouchables was held at Nagpur on 30-31 May and 1 June 1920. It was presided over by Chhatrapati Shahu Maharaj of Molkhapur. Shri Kalicharan Nanda Gawali (Gondia) was the Chairman of the Reception Committee. It was attended by 500 representatives coming from Bombay, Madras, Madhya Pradesh and Bera. Dr Babasaheb Ambedkar, S.N. Shivatarkar, S.J. Kamble, Kisan Fagu Bansod and others addressed the Conference.

27. The Government of Madras had formed a labour Advisory Board in the year 1920. One European Gilbert Starter, one Brahmin K. Ramanujachariar and one Adi-Dravida M.C. Rajah were its members.

28. On 24 October 1920, a dinner was arranged at Mangalore where about 150 people of all castes including the Pariahs, Mohammadans and Christians were present.

29. In 1922 the Madras Provincial Legislative Council passed a resolution recommending that the name Adi-Dravida should replace Panchama or Pariah. Accordingly, an order was issued on 25 March 1922, directing that the term Adi-Dravida in Tamil districts and Adi-Andhra in Telugu districts should be adopted in official documents in place of the words 'Panchama or Pariah or similar names'. It was, however, a long standing demand of the concerned communities that they should be called by the new name instead of the old disgraceful name given by the caste Hindus.

30. At the initiative of Shri S.K. Bole (Bombay), a famous social reformer, the Bombay Legislative Council on 4 August 1923, adopted the resolution, "the untouchables classes be allowed to use all public watering places, wells and Dharmashaias which are built and maintained out of public funds or administered by bodies appointed by Government or created by Statute, as well as public schools, courts, offices and dispensaries". Accordingly the

Bombay Government issued directives to that effect to all the Departments on 11 September 1923.

31. According to Keer, Dr Babasaheb Ambedkar established Bahishkrit Hitkarini Sabha in a meeting held at Dadar, Bombay, on 20 July 1924. Its President was Sir Chimanlal Satalwad. Its cardinal principal was "educate, agitate and organize".

32. In 1924, the untouchables of Travancore State attempted to assert their right to the use of the roads which skirted the temple at Vaikom. These roads were public roads maintained by the State, but as they were proximate to the temple, the untouchables were not allowed to use them. Ultimately as a result of satyagraha, the temple compound was enlarged, so that even if the untouchables used it, it would not be within the polluting distance of the temple.

33. Keer states that Dr Babasaheb Ambedkar launched a satyagraha for asserting the Civil rights and access to water at Choudar Tank, Mahad (Kolaba) on 20 March 1927 along with many of his brethren.

34. On 4 July 1927 an All India Anti-Untouchability Conference was held at Bangalore under the presidentship of Shet Jamnalal Bajaj.

35. The practice of dedicating girls to temples was made punishable in Mysore under the Hindu Religious and Charitable Endowment Act, 1927.

36. A Committee was constituted by the Bombay Government under the Chairmanship of Starte in 1929 in pursuance of the resolution moved by Dr P.G. Solanki, to inquire into the educational, economic and social conditions of the Depressed Classes and the aboriginals in the Bombay Presidency.

37. Mahatma Gandhi established the All India Anti-Untouchability League on 28 September 1932. It was renamed as Harijan Sevak Sangh in December 1932.

38. On 7 November 1933 Mahatma Gandhi began his countrywide tour to propagate against the evil of untouchability. The tour was started from Wardha and

ended at Varanasi. He toured for nine months covering more than 20,000 kilometres, addressing meetings, collecting funds and making the caste Hindus aware of the adverse effects of untouchability on Hindu society.

39. A bride and bridegroom belonging to the untouchable Dom caste were carried in a palanquin through the inhabited area of a village near Allahabad on 23 December 1933. The caste Hindus thought that it was contrary to the village or caste custom to do so. They filed a case against the concerned under Section 153 of IPC. Eventually, the High Court of Allahabad acquitted the accused in 1936 saying that caste Hindus could not prove that the custom had the force of law.

40. On 13 June 1936, a meeting of the Devadasis and Jogins was called at Damodar Hall, Bombay. It was addressed by Dr Babasaheb Ambedkar. He advised them to abandon their contemptuous way of life and lead an honourable life.

41. On 16 March 1937, the Bombay High Court gave the decision in favour of Dr Babasaheb Ambedkar in a case filed against him on account of his satyagraha at Choudar Tank, Mahad, in 1927.

42. The Arya Marriage Validation Act was passed in 1937 in order to recognize and remove doubts as to the validity of intercaste marriages current among Arya Samajis.

43. Dr Babasaheb Ambedkar introduced a Bill to abolish the Mahar Vatans (servitude based on birth in the untouchable Mahar caste) on 17 September 1937 in the Bombay Legislative Assembly. The same was introduced by Shri S.C. Joshi (ILP) in the Legislative Council. However, it was not passed at that time. It was finally abolished under the Bombay Inferior Village Vatans Abolition Act 1 of 1959.

44. In January 1939, the Harijan Sevak Sangh secured the management of the Criminal Tribes Settlement at Gorakhpur in Uttar Pradesh. The settlement was renamed as Harijan Basti. The Doms who lived there were taught

rules of hygiene, and started spinning for them. They were taught Bhajans and religious principles.

45. The ruler of Dewas Senior, gave instructions to observe Harijan Day on 26 March 1939, and to remove the stigma of untouchability. The Maharaja himself participated in the community dinner on that day.
46. In July 1939, the Maharaja of Dewas Junior granted the *sanad* of a Mankari Assami to a Mahar, presented him with a dress of honour and offered him a seat in the Durbar.
47. In October 1939, a law was passed in Baroda State for removing social disabilities of the Depressed Classes.
48. On 19 March 1940, Dr Babasaheb Ambedkar, alongwith his followers, near about 15,000, celebrated 'Independence Day' of the Depressed Classes at Mahad.
49. In July 1940, the Maharaja of Indore gave a grant of ₹ one lakh from his privy purse for building 91 tenements for the sweepers.
50. Some of the provincial governments and princely states passed the anti-untouchability laws. They were:

    The Central Provinces and Berar Removal of Untouchability Act, 1934.

    The Madras Removal of Social Disabilities Act, 1938 (XIII of 1938).

    Baroda Social Disabilities Removal Act, 1939.

    Mysore Removal of Social Disabilities Act, 1943 (XLII of 1943).

    Orissa Removal of Civil Disabilities Act, 1946 (X of 1946).
    The Bihar Harijan (Removal of Civil Disabilities) Act, 1946.

    The Bombay Harijan (Removal of Social Disabilities) Act 1946 (Bom. 1947).

    The Central Provinces and Berar Scheduled Castes (Removal of Civil Disabilities) Act, 1947.

    The United Provinces Removal of Social Disabilities Act, 1947.

The East Punjab (Removal of Religious and Social Disabilities) Act, 1948.

The West Bengal Hindu Social Disabilities Removal Act, 1948.

The Hyderabad Harijan (Removal of Social Disabilities) Regulation 1358 F.

The Saurashtra Harijan (Removal of Social Disabilities Act) Ordinance Act, 1948.

The Travancore Cochin Removal of Social Disabilities Act, 1125 K.

The Coorg S.C. (Removal of Civil and Social Disabilities) Act 1949.

51. On 29 April 1947, the Minorities and Fundamental Rights Committee of the Constituent Assembly decided that "Untouchability in any form is abolished and the imposition of any disability on that account shall be an offence." The resolution was moved by Sardar Vallabhbhai Patel. Thus the age-long ugly system of untouchability constitutionally came to an end. The Constituent Assembly eventually passed the said provision on 29 November 1948.

    The Constitution of India, which came into implementation on 26 January 1950 provides under Article 17 as given below:

    "Untouchability is abolished and its practice in any form is forbidden. The enforcement of any disability arising out of untouchability shall be an offence punishable in accordance with law."

52. The Parliament of India had passed the protection of Civil Rights Act, 1955 which came into force on 1 June 1955. The said Act provides punishment for the offences committed on account of untouchability.

RELIGIOUS RIGHTS

The untouchables were called Hindus, but they were denied religious equality on a par with the touchables. They were not allowed to enter the temples and worship the deity in the temple.

They were not allowed to read or even listen to Vedas and learn Sanskrit. They were not entitled to take the sacred thread. They had their separate gods and priests. Their religious manners, rituals and ceremonies were more or less different from those of the touchables. Brahmin did not officiate at religious ceremonies at the houses of untouchables. The untouchables had their own priests to perform the worship or rituals. The untouchables had to worship God in the touchables' temple from outside the temple, if at all they wanted to. Dalit movement raised the banner of revolt against religious inequality and restrictions imposed by the Hindu religion.

1. The Castes-Disabilities Removal Act was passed in 1850 which facilitated conversion to another religion without forfeiting the convert's right to inherit the ancestral property.

2. The Churha untouchables of Punjab who were converted to Sikhism were called Mazhabis. However, distinctions were made between them and the descendants of the original converts. According to Bhagwan Das (1980), in 1873, the Singh Sabha was split on the question of admitting the Mazhabis into the Golden Temple, Gurudwara of Amritsar.

3. In 1874, the Shanars (Madras) tried to establish their right to enter the Meenakshi Temple at Madurai, but in vain.

4. Pandit C. Iyodhi Dass, an untouchable social reformer from Madras converted to Buddhism in 1890. He was ordained by Ven. Sumangala Maha Nayak, Principal, Vidyodaya College in Ceylon. He was the first Indian untouchable to convert to Buddhism in Modern India.

   He established The South Indian Buddha Sakkiya Sangh in 1902 in Madras.

5. By 1910, over 36,000 Meghs (untouchables) from the Sialkot area became Arya Samajis.

6. Shri Poykayil Yohannan (Kerala) founded a new faith named Pratyaksha Raksha Deiva Sabha (PRDS) in the year 1910. He tried to convince the Christian and Hindu untouchables to embrace the new faith.

7. In 1917, about 2,000 Pulayas led by Chakola Kurumban forcibly entered Chenganoor Temple.
8. In 1920, the Indian Buddhists of Madras met in a vihara at Perambur, Madras and issued a statement that if the untouchables converted to Buddhism, they would be no more untouchables.
9. On 30 March 1924, the Kerala Congress Committee decided to launch a satyagraha in Vaikom, a village in Travancore, where even the roads to the temple of Lord Shiva were forbidden to the untouchables, leave apart the entry into the temple. The satyagraha movement lasted for a year.
10. In 1924, the All Kerala Buddhists Conference was held in Calicut.
11. In 1926, Shri Babu Mangu Ram (Punjab) founded "Ad-Dharm Mandal" for the uplift of the untouchables. Its head office was at Jullunder in Punjab.
12. Dr Babasaheb Ambedkar publicly burnt *Manusmriti* which initially denied religious rights and privileges to the Sudras and later on to the untouchables, on 25 December 1927 at Mahad in Maharashtra.
13. In August 1927, the satyagraha was launched to enter the temple of Ambadevi at Amravati by Babasaheb Ambedkar, Punjabrao Deshmukh, Nanasaheb Gawai and many others.
14. At the initiative of Dr Babasaheb Ambedkar, the temple entry satyagraha was launched at Parvati temple in Pune, on 13 October 1929. It was led by Shri P.N. Rajbhoj, S.J. Kamble and others.
15. Dr Babasaheb Ambedkar launched temple entry satyagraha at Kalaram temple at Nasik on 2 March 1930, which continued intermittently for five years, but in vain.
16. Shri Kelappan had started a fast on 20 September 1932 in front of the temple of Krishna at Guruvayur to press upon the Zamorin, the Hindu king of Calicut to throw open the temple for the untouchables. However, he discontinued

his fast on its tenth day on the intervention and assurance of Mahatma Gandhi that if the temple was not opened for the untouchables, he could carry on with his hunger strike. Ultimately, on the advice of Mahatma Gandhi, a referendum was taken that he could carry on with his hunger strike in the Ponnani Taluka to decide the issue of temple entry. Majority of the people voted for temple entry to the untouchables. But the king did not accept the verdict of the people.

17. Shri Ranga Iyer introduced the Temple Entry Bill in the Central Legislature on 24 March 1933, but due to the apathetic attitude of Congress and the Government, he had to withdraw the bill.

18. On 4 November 1934, a meeting of Malkana Halalkhor caste was convened at Miraj by Shri Babulal Lad. The caste members decided to adopt certain reforms like remarriage, common religious behaviour and communal unity among the members of the caste.

19. In the year 1934, the Government of Bombay passed Bombay Devadasis Protection Act in order to put an end to the Devadasi system. Any person found guilty of an offence of dedicating or abetting in any move to dedicate any woman as a Devadasi became liable to punishment.

20. Dr Babasaheb Ambedkar lost his hope of getting religious equality; as such he declared that, "I will not die as a Hindu" in a conference of untouchables held at Yeola in Nasik district on 13 October 1935. It was a historic decision which shocked the Hindus and was appreciated by the non-Hindus.

21. On 6 January 1936, a satyagraha was started for entering the temple of Vishveshwar at Varanasi, in UP.

22. On 30-31 May 1936, a conference of the Mahars in Bombay Presidency was called at Dadar, Bombay. Shri Revji Dolas welcomed the delegates and Rao Bahadur B.S. Venkat Rao (Hyderabad) presided over the conference. Dr Babasaheb Ambedkar advised his brethren to discard their Hindu

religion which had inflicted on them innumerable miseries. He emphatically said, "I tell you, religion is for man and not man for religion. If you want to organize, consolidate and be successful in the world, change this religion. The religion that does not recognize you as human beings, or give you water to drink, or allow you to enter the temples is not worthy to be called a religion. The religion that forbids you to receive education and comes in the way of your material advancement is not worthy of the appellation 'religion'. The religion that does not teach its followers to show humanity in dealing with its co-religionists is nothing but a display of force. The religion that asks its adherents to suffer the touch of animals but not the touch of human beings is not religion but a mockery. That religion which precludes some classes from education, forbids them to accumulate wealth and to bear arms, is not religion but a mockery. The religion that compels, the ignorant to be ignorant and the poor to be poor, is not religion but a visitation!"

Finally he advised his brethren to seek refuge in reason. In the words of Lord Buddha he exhorted, "Be thy own light" *(Atta Deep Bhava).*

23. The Maharaja of Travancore Sir Bala Rama Varma declared on 12 November 1936, "Profoundly convinced of the truth and validity of our religion believing that it is based on divine guidance and on an all comprehending toleration, knowing that in its practice it has, throughout the centuries, adapted itself to the needs of changing times, solicitous that none of our Hindu subjects should, by reason of birth or caste or community, be denied the consolation and solace of the Hindu faith, we have decided and hereby declare, ordain and command that, subject to such rules and conditions as may be laid down and imposed by us for preserving their proper atmosphere and maintaining their rituals and observances, there should henceforth be no restriction placed on any Hindu birth or religion on entering or worshipping at the temples controlled by us and our Government."

24. On 24 March 1939, satyagraha for entering the temple of Gopal at Indore in Madhya Pradesh was launched under the leadership of P.N. Rajbhoj.

25. Some of the provincial governments and princely states passed the religious disabilities removal laws in their respective states. They were as under:

    The Temple Entry Proclamation, Nov. 1936 (Travancore-Cochin).

    Bombay Hindu Temple Worship (Removal of Disabilities) Act, 1938 (XI of 1938).

    Madras Temple Entry Authorization and Indemnity Act, 1939 (XXII of 1939).

    Malabar Temple Entry Act (XX of 1938).

    The Bombay Harijan Temple Entry Act, 1947.

    The Madras Temple Entry Authorization Act, 1947.

    The Orissa Temple Entry Authorization Act, 1948.

    The East Punjab (Removal of Religious and Social Disabilities) Act, 1948.

    The Hyderabad Harijan Temple Entry Regulation 1358 F.

    The Mysore Temple Entry Authorization Act, 1948.

    The Coorg Temple Entry Authorization Act, 1949.

    The Travancore Temple Entry (Removal of Disabilities) Act, 1950.

26. The Constitution which came into implementation on 26 January 1950 states under its Article 25 the following:

    "(1) Subject to public order, morality and health and to the other provisions of this part, all persons are equally entitled to freedom of conscience and right freely to profess, practice and propagate religion."

    (2) Nothing in this Article shall affect the operation of any existing Law or prevent the state from making any law.

    (3) Providing for social welfare and reform or the throwing open of Hindu religious institutions of a

public character to all classes and sections of Hindus."

Explanation II. In sub-clause (b) of clause (2) the reference to Hindus shall be construed as including a reference to persons professing the Sikh, Jain or Buddhist religion, and the reference to Hindu religious institutions shall be construed accordingly.

27. On 4 May 1955, Dr Babasaheb Ambedkar founded Bharatiya Boudha Maha Sabha to undertake preaching and propagation of Buddhism.
28. Dr Babasaheb Ambedkar ultimately embraced Buddhism at Nagpur on 14 October 1956 on the occasion of Vijaya Dashami. The monk or Bhikshu Chandramani had officiated at the ceremony. Then Dr Babasaheb Ambedkar gave Buddhism to his brethren comprising approximately five lakhs, at the same place. It was but a unique, unparalleled and unprecedental occasion when five lakh people converted to a new faith at a time in the world history.

EDUCATIONAL RIGHTS

Untouchability was a cunningly created cage for confining the so-called untouchables to their low status. They had no right to admission in the schools, learn Sanskrit and acquire knowledge. Therefore, Dalit movement was primarily directed towards regaining the right to education as a *sine qua non* for their total emancipation.

Following are the important events and achievements of the Dalit movement in this respect.

1. In August 1848 Mahatma Phule, the great social revolutionary opened the first school in Pune for the girl students. He opened the first school for the students of untouchable communities in Pune in the year 1852. In 1856 the number of such schools rose to three and the number of students became 300. Altogether eight teachers were serving in those schools. In 1858, he opened a hostel for the poor untouchable students in Pune wherein 25-30 students were accommodated every year.

2. In June 1856, at Dharwad, in the then Bombay province, a Mahar, untouchable boy was denied admission in the school on the ground of untouchability. Therefore, the Bombay Government had to declare that all the schools receiving government grants should be opened to all the students irrespective of their caste or creed. This was declared in the year 1858.
3. In 1865, Shri Shashipad Bandopadhyaya (Bengal), a staunch Brahmo opened a school for the poor labourers and the untouchables at Baranagar near Calcutta.
4. On 19 October 1882, Mahatma Jyotirao Phule submitted a memorandum to the Education Commission, Bombay headed by Mr Hunter in which he requested the government to make primary education compulsory for the children of the untouchables. Further he advocated separate schools for them as they were not allowed to sit along with the caste Hindus owing to caste prejudices.
5. Since 1883, separate schools were being opened for the students of the untouchables in Baroda State. Mangudkar (1976) state that in 1910 the number of such schools rose to 297, and the number of students studying in these schools rose to 13,703.
6. In 1886, John Rathinam, an untouchable leader, started a Model School in Thousand Lights area of Madras for the untouchable students and in 1899 started one hostel for them.
7. Pandit C. Tyodhi Dass started several schools in Madras city in 1889, with the help of Colonel Olcott, Mary Balbare and Annie Besant.
8. In 1890, separate schools for the Panchamas (Untouchables) were opened in the Mysore princely State at Mysore, Bangalore and Anekal.
9. In 1891, separate primary schools were established for the Pariahs.
10. Colonel Olcott opened his first school for the untouchable students in Madras in 1894; second school in 1898 and

third school in 1899. In 1901, 384 boys and 150 girls were taking education.

11. In 1895, Shri Januji K. Khandare opened a free hostel for the students of the Depressed Classes at Akola in Maharastra. He got the land for the purpose from the government, built the building at his own. It was the first ever hostel in Vidarbh.
12. Mangudkar (1976) states that in 1897, Raosaheb K. Rangarao, the Secretary of Bramho Samaj, Mangalore started his first school for the untouchable students in Mangalore.
13. In 1904, Shri Ayyan Kali started a school at Katakala near Venganoor in Kerala for the students of the untouchables.
14. The Maharaja of Kolhapur promulgated an ordinance on 28 November 1906 to run right schools in Kolhapur for the untouchable students.
15. In 1906, Shri M.L. Audiah started a school at Secunderabad for the students of the Depressed Classes. It was named after Sir William Barton, the then Resident of Hyderabad.
16. Shahu Maharaj of Kolhapur opened a school in Kolhapur for the girls belonging to Chambhar and Dhor untouchables on 4 October 1907.
17. At the instance of Chhatrapati Shahu Maharaj of Kolhapur a school for Mahar students was opened at Udagaon on 1 May 1909.
18. In 1910, Shri Kalicharan Nandagavali built a school building at his own expense at Gondia in Bhandara district (Maharastra) for the girl students of the untouchable community.
19. The Depressed Classes Mission of India founded by Maharshi V.R. Shinde undertook the task of starting schools for the untouchables from the year 1911.
20. Pandit Palaniswami started Dravid School in 1917 in Madras for the untouchable students.

21. Mrs Jaibai Choudhari, a staunch lady social worker at Nagpur, established a school named Chokhamela School, at Nayabasti, Nagpur in 1922. It was to impart education exclusively to girl students belonging to the untouchables.
22. The Arya Samaj opened a school for the benefit of Bhangi children in 1923 in Jodhpur.
23. M.R. Jaikar moved a resolution in the Legislative Assembly on 23 February 1928 recommending to the government "to provide special facilities for the education of the untouchables and other depressed classes and also for opening all public services to them specially the police." The resolution was adopted with minor amendment.
24. On 14 June 1928, Dr Babasaheb Ambedkar started the Depressed Classes Education Society to spread education among the untouchables.
25. Under the Poona Pact, 1932, it was agreed to earmark an adequate sum for providing educational facilities to the members of the Scheduled Castes in every province.
26. The Harijan Sevak Sangh started giving scholarships to the students of the Depressed Classes since 1936-37. It gave scholarships to 94 students in that year.
27. By 1939, there was an institute called The Jatav Men's Educational Institute at Agra, which was running five schools for boys and one for girls in Agra district.
28. In June 1941, the Harijan Sevak Sangh started Harijan Kanya Vidyalaya at Sabarmati.
29. A special provision was made for the first time in the central budget in 1944 for the grant of scholarships for the Scheduled Castes. This facility was extended to the Scheduled Tribes in 1948.
30. Dr Babasaheb Ambedkar founded the People's Education Society (PES) on 8 July 1945 at Bombay. The said Society started its first college named Siddharth College at Bombay on 20 June 1946. It started Milind Maha Vidayalaya at Aurangabad on 19 June 1950.

31. The Constitution which came into implementation on 26 January 1950 states under its Article 29(2) that "No citizen shall be denied admission into any educational institution maintained by the State or receiving aid out of state funds on grounds only of religion, race, caste, language or any of them."

Article 15 (4) states, "Nothing in this article or in clause (2) of article 29 shall prevent the state from making any special provision for the advancement of any socially and educationally backward classes of citizens or for the Scheduled Castes and the Scheduled Tribes."

Article 46 of the Constitution states: "The State shall promote with special care the educational and economic interests of the weaker sections of the society, and in particular of the Scheduled Castes and Scheduled Tribes..."

ECONOMIC RIGHTS

Untouchability includes economic exploitation, oppression and deprivation of economic opportunities. Untouchables had no means of production, nor had they any right to acquire them. Their main professions were servitude or *vethi*, tanning leather and making footwears, drum beating, scavenging, sweeping and agricultural labour. They had no right to change their ancestral profession imposed upon them by the Shastras and the tradition.

1. Slavery was rampant in some parts of the country. It had been abolished by the Slavery Abolition Act of 1843.
2. Indian Penal Code (Act No.45) of 1860 *inter alia* provides severe punishment for any one dealing in slaves, under Sections 360-371. Accordingly, any person dealing in slaves is punishable with imprisonment for a term which may extend to seven years, and also fine.
3. The industrial progress has a good bearing on social change. In this respect it should be noted that the Empress Cotton Mill was started in 1877 at Nagpur, which naturally attracted many poor persons of Scheduled Castes, in search of employment. Many of them took to

cotton trade. This had a good effect on their economic condition.

4. In 1904, Shri Ayyan Kali led the strike of agricultural labourers against the landlords in Kerala. The strike proved to be very successful and effective. The caste Hindus agreed to treat the untouchables as equals.

5. On 15 May 1920, Chhatrapati Shahu Maharaj had declared that *vet begar* (forced labour) would be no more in existence. Mahar *Vatan* was abolished and the *vatan* lands were given to the Mahar on ryotwari basis *(Maharaki* or *veti* was abolished by law in the rest of Maharashtra in 1959).

6. In 1921, Mysore State accepted the recommendations of Sir L.C. Miller (CJ of Mysore) Committee appointed in 1918, regarding appointments of the non-Brahmin castes in the services of the State, and issued orders to provide special concessions to such eligible persons.

7. On 24 January 1922, the exploitative system of *begar* was formally declared to have been abolished in Kumaun region of Uttar Pradesh.

8. In 1927, the Madras Government passed the communal Government Order (GO) according to which certain posts were reserved for the backward communities including the Depressed Classes in the state services.

9. On 19 March 1928, Dr Babasaheb Ambedkar introduced a bill, to amend the Bombay Hereditary Officers Act, 1874; but in vain. The said Bill aimed to abolished *Maharaki* of the Mahars. Again he introduced the Bill to that effect on 17 September 1937 in the Bombay Legislature but failed again.

   Ultimately the Mahart *Vatan* was abolished under the Bombay Inferior Village Vatans Abolition Act 1 of 1959.

10. Under the Poona Pact concluded on 25 September 1932, an assurance was given to secure fair representation of the Depressed Classes in appointments to the public services, subject to such educational qualifications as may be laid down in that respect (Clause 8).

11. In 1943, due to the efforts of Dr Babasaheb Ambedkar, the then Labour Member in the Viceroy's Executive Council, the Scheduled Castes got 8.33 per cent reservations in the government services. In June 1946 the percentage of reserved seats was raised to 12½ per cent corresponding to their percentage in the population (12¾ per cent) in undivided India.

    The percentage was raised to 16⅔ per cent of posts filled on other than open competition in August 1947.

12. The Minimum Wages Bill was introduced in the Central Assembly on 11 April 1946. It was passed on 9 February 1948. The Act provides for fixing and revising, at suitable intervals, the minimum wages for workers in various scheduled industries, including agriculture.

13. The Constitution of India, which came into implementation on 26 January 1950, declares (*Vide* Article 19 [1]) that all the citizens equally have the right to practise any profession or to carry on any occupation, trade or business. This right is a part of fundamental rights and all the citizens are equally entitled to have it. Moreover, it is the duty of the state to secure a social order in which social and economic justice would be possible. The state has to see that "the operation of the economic system does not result in the concentration of wealth and means of production to the common detriment."

14. The so-called untouchables were denied the right to get employment under the government. The present Constitution of India, however, provides equal opportunity to employment to all the people. It even empowers the State to make the provision of reservation in services for the backward classes, under its Article 16 (4).

    Further it states under Article 23(1) that, "Traffic in human beings and begar and other similar forms of forced labour are prohibited and any contravention of this provision shall be an offence punishable in accordance with law."

15. On 18 June 1951, the Constitution (first Amendment) Act was passed by the Parliament. It inserted Ninth Schedule to the Constitution due to which the Bihar Land Reforms Act, 1950, the Bombay Tenancy and Agricultural Lands Act, 1948, the Bombay Talukdari Tenure Abolition Act, 1949, the Bombay Khoti Abolition Act, 1950, the Bombay Paragana and Kulkarni Watan Abolition Act, 1950, the Madhya Pradesh Abolition of Proprietary Rights (Estates, Mahals, Alienated Lands) Act, 1950, the Madras Estates (Abolition and Conversion into Ryotwari) Act, 1948, the Uttar Pradesh Zamindari Abolition and Land Reforms Act, 1950, the Hyderabad (Abolition of Jagirs) Regulation, 1358 F, and the Hyderabad Jagirs (Commutation) Regulation, 1358 F. were exempted from the operation of the Right to Property, Article 31 of the Constitution. Thus, they were declared as valid under the Constitution.
16. On the advice of Dr Babasaheb Ambedkar the SCF Marathwada unit launched satyagraha demanding land for the landless agriculturist, on 16 October 1953. it was led by Shri B.S. More. Thousands of people took part in the satyagraha. Approximately 1,700 people courted arrest.
17. Traffic in women for immoral purposes, was made a punishable offence under the Suppression of Immoral Traffic in Women and Girls Act, 1956.

RIGHT TO FREEDOM OF THOUGHT AND EXPRESSION

The untouchables had no right to think and express their views and grievances. They were forced to believe in the supremacy of the Shastras and superstitions. Due to lack of education, awareness and resources they could not express their feelings and grievances. Therefore, they remained ignorant, unheard and uncared for centuries together. They were, however, made aware of their plight in the following stages.

1 On 1 August 1861 the book in Marathi *Jatibhad Viveksar* written by Tukaram Tatya Padwalkar was published at Pune.

2. In the year 1866 (1788 *Shaka)* one Mahar untouchable saint Balakdas, resident of Padegaon in Pune district wrote a book named *Mhar Mhatmya* in which he had stated that original man of Mahar was Samaji, their God was Shiva, their land was Marwad and saint was Markandeya and the Mahar and Musalmans belong to one Chandravanshi or Somvansh. The manuscript of this book was found in 1907 by V.R. Shinde and it was written in Marathi.

3. In 1885, Mahatma Jyotirao Phule wrote a book *Asprushyanchi Kaiphiat* depicting the wretched socio-economic condition of the Mahars and Mangs, the two important untouchables castes in Maharashtra.

   In 1869, he wrote *Brahmanche Kasab* (Priestcraft Exposed) exposing various tricks of the Brahmins for exploiting the people.

   In 1873, Mahatma Phule wrote *Gulamgiri* (Slavery) in Marathi. The main objective of writing tliis was to attract the attention of the people in general and rulers in particular towards the wretched condition of slavery imposed by the Brahmins in the name of religion over the Sudras and untouchables, and to get redressal through the British Government.

4. In 1885, John Rathinam, an untouchable convert, started a magazine *Dravidan Pandian* (Dravidian King) from Madras.

5. In 1888, Gopal Baba Walangkar had written *Vital Vidhwansan* to bring about social awareness amongst the untouchables.

6. In 1893, Shri R. Srinivasan started one magazine, namely, *Parayan* in order to bring a new awakening among the untouchable masses in Madras.

7. In 1902, Colonel Olcott published his book *Poor Pariah.* In this book he stated that once upon a time the Pariahs were Buddhists.

8. Shri Shivram Janba Kamble (Pune) wrote one *Soochi Patra* in 1903 and distributed its copies to his brethren freely to awaken them.

9. In 1907, Pandit C. Iyodhi Dass started the magazine *Tamizhan.* This had wide circulation in India and also in overseas countries like Sri Lanka, Burma, Singapore and South Africa.

10. Barrister V.D. Savarkar wrote a play in Marathi, named *Ushap* on the social life of an untouchable in the year 1908. He tried to educate Hindus against untouchability so as to arrest conversions to Islam and Christianity and strengthen Hinduism.

11. In the year 1908, Shri Shivaram Janaba Kamble (Pune) started a fortnightly in Marathi named, *Somvanshiya Mitra* from Pune. This journal continued for two years from 1 July 1908 to 1 June 1910. It was being published from Pune.

12. In the year 1909, Shri Rashbehari Roy started *Namsudra Darpan* from Calcutta.

13. In the year 1910, Shri Kisan Fagoji Bansod (Nagpur) started a Marathi weekly named, *Nirashrit Hind Nagrik* from Nagpur.

14. Shri Trimbak Narayan Atre wrote a book *Gawa Gada* in 1915, in which he described the village life especially in Maharashtra, and categorically said that unless the caste system and its offshoot, slavery are abolished, villages would not be developed.

15. Shri Tarak Chandra Sarkar wrote the life history of Guru Harichand, called *Sri Harililamrita,* a book of poems, which was published posthumously in 1916, two years after his death.

16. In 1916, Bharat Chandra Sarkar started *Namsudra Hitaisi* (well-wisher) from Calcutta.

17. In 1917, Mukund Behari Mullick started *Flag* from Calcutta.

18. In 1917, Shri Mangipudi Venkata Sarma of West Godavari District in Andhra Pradesh composed a treatise in poetry *Niruddha Bharatam* wherein the miseries and sufferings of the untouchables were described.

19. On 31 December 1918, an English monthly *The Panchama* was started by Shri J.S. Muthaiah an untouchable member of the Manya Sangham, from Hyderabad.
20. In order to bring about socio-political consciousness amongst the so-called untouchables Dr Babasaheb Ambedkar started a weekly in Marathi, named *Mooknaik* at Bombay on 31 January 1920. Its editor was Shri Pandurang Nandram Bhatkar of Amravati. Chhatrapati Shahu Maharaj of Kolhapur had donated ₹ 2,000 for starting the paper.
21. Shri Nanasaheb Gawai also started a monthly named, *Bahishkrit Bharat* from Amravati in the year 1920 itself.
22. In 1922, Shri Unnava Laxminarayana, a Telugu writer wrote a novel, *Malapalli* on the social life of the untouchables.
23. In 1924, Pandit Sundarlal Sagar (Agra) wrote *Jatav Jeevan* a book on the Jatava untouchables.
24. In the year 1926, Shri D.M. alias Dadasaheb Shirke started *Garud,* a weekly from Kolhapur and continued it for a period of 22 years consistently.
25. On 3 April 1927, Dr Babasaheb Ambedkar started *Bahishkrit Bharat,* a fortnightly in Marathi. It continued for near about three years.
26. Shri P.N. Rajbhoj started *Dalit Bandhu,* a weekly in 1928. It continued for near about 20 years. It was published from Pune.
27. On 24 November 1930, Dr Babasaheb Ambedkar started *Janata,* a weekly which continued for near about 26 years. During this long period Shri Devarao Naik, B.R. Kadrekar, G.N. Sahastrabuddha, B.C. Kamble and Yeshwantrao Ambedkar served as its editors.
28. In 1930, Shri Bhagya Reddy Varma started a Telugu fortnightly *Bhagya Nagara Patrika* devoted to the uplift of the untouchables. The same fortnightly was renamed as *Adi Hindu* in 1937.
29. On 21 November 1932, the famous Hindi writer and editor of *Jagaran,* Shri Premchand wrote in the editorial on the

problem of temple entry for the so-called untouchables. Further, on 26 December 1932 he wrote in the editorial on 'Harijan Day' which was observed in response to the call given by Mahatma Gandhi. He described the Harijan Day as *Pavan Tithi* (holy day) for all the Hindus and expressed deep concern over the problems of the so-called untouchables.

30. In February 1933, Sir George MacMunn wrote a book *The Martial Races of India* in which he stated that the Pariahs were a martial community.
31. Shri Mulk Raj Anand wrote *An Untouchable,* a novel in English on the wretched life of a scavenger in the year 1935.
32. In the year 1936, a famous film producer, Shri V. Shantaram produced "Dharmatma", a Marathi film on the eradication of untouchability.
33. In 1938, Mr Alexander Robertson wrote a book named *Mahar Folk, A Study of Untouchables in Maharashtra* in which he had given an account of social life of the Mahars.
34. In 1940, Ranjit Mone's "Achhut" a Hindi film on the social condition of the untouchables was produced by Chandulal Shaha.
35. In 1942, Shri Ramnarayan Yadvendu (Agra) wrote *Yaduvansh Ka Itihas,* a book of the history of the Jatav untouchables.
36. Dr Babasaheb Ambedkar wrote *What Congress and Gandhi have done to the Untouchables* in 1945.
37. Dr Babasaheb Ambedkar's famous Treatise on *The Untouchables* was published in 1948.
38. The present Constitution of India states very categorically under Article 19 that, "All citizens shall have the right (a) to freedom of speech and expression, (b) to assemble peaceably and without arms, (c) to form associations and unions."

RIGHT TO MARTIAL SERVICES

The untouchables were not allowed to enter the police and military services of the State. Their duty was to serve the State by performing certain menial duties. However, Chhatrapati Shivaji Maharaj could skilfully utilize the martial qualities of the untouchable Mahars. The British East India Company also utilized the fighting qualities of the untouchables, especially those of Mahars and Pariahs. However, after the outbreak of the Mutiny of 1857 they had changed their policy of recruiting the untouchables in the military in the year 1892. The Dalit movement, therefore, was directed to get the injustice remedied in the field of martial services.

1. When the British military attacked Jhansi in the 1857 Mutiny, one heroic lady of the untouchable Kori caste, named Jhalkaribai, fought against the enemy in the guise of Rani Laximibai till her last; due to her sacrifice the true Rani Laxmibai could run away safely along with her adopted son. Had there not been Jhalkaribai, Rani Laxmibai would have been killed by the British.
2. According to Khairmode, Shri Sonnak Tannak, a Mahar sepoy belonging to 19th Bombay Infantry, along with one Major Sydney James Waudby and Elahi Bux died on 16 April 1880 while fighting heroically in defence of the Durbas post in Afghanistan. They fought against 300 soldiers for three hours and killed many soldiers of the enemy in the Indo-Afghan war. In honour of their heroism a tablet had been placed in Fort area, Bombay by the Regiment.
3. In order to alleviate the rising discontent and prejudice among the caste Hindu soldiers against the untouchable soldiers in the post-Mutiny period, the British Government decided on May 1892, to discontinue recruitment of the untouchables in the military.
4. The Mahars resented the Government's decision to prohibit the untouchables entry in the military. The first petition was submitted to the Government on 21 June 1894 by Shri Shivram Govind Waikar Master on behalf of Mahar military personnel of Satara district in Maharashtra and requested that the decision be favourably reconsidered.
5. The next petition was sent to the Government by Shri Gangnak Sanjnak, on behalf of Anarya Dosh Parihar

Mandali, Ratnagiri, an organization founded by Gopal Baba Walangkar, a retired military personnel and a social reformer, urging the Government to allow the entry of the Mahars in the British military, on 11 April 1895.

6. Subedar Major Ramji Maloji Sakpal, the illustrious father of Dr B.R. Ambedkar, had submitted a petition in 1902 to the British Government appealing for the recruitment of Mahars in the British Army. He got the petition nicely drafted by Justice M.G. Ranade, a famous social reformer in those days.
7. Shivaram Janba Kamble, a famous Dalit leader from Pune, submitted an appeal in 1904 to the Governor of Bombay requesting for the recruitment of the Mahars in the British Army.
8. A conference of Mahars was held at Pune in 1910 under the presidentship of Subedar Bahadur Gangaram Krishnaji to request the Government to start recruitment of the Mahars in the army. It was convened by Shivaram Janba Kamble. Almost all the 1,500 Mahars attending the conference unanimously approved the petition addressed to the Secretary of State for India. The petition signed by 1,500 persons was submitted to the said authority, on 14 December 1910.
9. During the First World War, in January 1917 the British Government decided to recruit the Mahars and ordered them to join two Madras Battalions at St.Thomas Mount. In June 1917, a battalion, the 11th Mahar was raised.

   The Mazhabis of Punjab also continued to be recruited, with a 'special effort' made during the First World War to recruit them.
10. After the end of the First World War, the British Government decided to discontinue the recruitment of Mahars in March 1921. A petition was submitted, among others by Shri J. Pappanna of Belgaum to the Governor of Bombay on 24 December 1921 for reviving the policy of disbandment of the Mahars. However, the petition had no effect on the Government. The recruitment of Mazhabis also was discontinued after the First World War on the

grounds of economy. The last Mazhabi unit was disbanded in 1932.

11. When the Second World War was at its height, the Viceroy had set up a Defence Advisory Committee at the end of July 1941. Dr Babasaheb Ambedkar was appointed as a member on the said committee. Making the best use of this opportunity. Dr Ambedkar appealed to the Government to start the recruitment of the untouchables in British military and his demand was conceded favourably. Accordingly, the first Mahar Battalion was raised in September 1941. At the instance of Dr Babasaheb several Mahars joined the British military and served the nation. The Mazhabis and Ramdasis Sikhs also were recruited in the British Army during the Second World War.
12. The UP Government removed the disqualification on the recruitment of Dalits to the Police. Two untouchables were appointed as Deputy Superintendent of Police in 1937-38.
13. The first battalion of the Mahar Regiment was raised at Nanawadi in Belgaum on 1 October 1941. It moved to Kamptee near Nagpur, in February 1942. The second battalion was formed at Belgaum on 1 August 1942, and the third battalion was raised at Nowshera in the then NWFP on 1 November 1943. The Mahar Regiment was renamed as Mahar Machine Gun (MMG) Regiment from 1 October 1946. The Regimental Centre moved from Kamptee to Arangaon near Ahmadnagar on 15 October 1946. The Regimental Centre was shifted from Arangaon to Sangar in Madhya Pradesh on 1 December 1948. Till now it is there.
14. In October 1943, the Central Assembly passed a resolution moved by Pyarelal Kuril Talib (SCF) for the removal of restrictions on the Scheduled Castes in holding posts of Officers in the military forces.
15. Hawaldar Rawoo Kamble of the 1st Battalion, the Mahar Regiment fought heroically in the Jammu and Kashmir operations of 1947-48. He was commanding the MMG sub-section. When the raiders came from the rear and

chopped off his head with a sword; his body fell forward on the gun in front of him and as a result his gun continued to fire on the enemy.

16. No. 718 Naik Krishna Sonawane of the 1st Battalion, the Mahar MG Regiment, had shown his courage, determination, bravery and devotion to duty in the war against Pakistan in 1948 for which he was honoured with Mahavir Chakra. He inflicted 700 casualties on the Pakistan raiders and saved a vital position. He was the first Mahar to have won Mahavir Chakra.

POLITICAL RIGHTS

Untouchability, obviously includes deliberate denial of political rights to the untouchables. It, however, originated out of the suppression of the Broken Men who were Buddhists, and out of the establishment of the supremacy of the Brahmins. They had no access to power and authority. They were never treated as citizens or even as human beings, but as mere untouchables having no rights whatsoever. Therefore, the Dalits gave more stress on securing political power.

The major events and achievements of Dalit movement in this respect are given here;

1. After the successful suppression of the Mutiny, the British Government took over the administration of British India from the East India Company in the year 1858, and proclaimed the aims and objectives of the new government, which included, among others, to provide religious freedom, maintain religious equality and not to interfere in the religious matter of the Hindus or the Muslims, and to administer the government for the benefit of all the Indian subjects.

   This proclamation is a very important document in the history of modern India. It is from this period that India could witness a dawn of modern age and beginning of the responsible government. It has a special bearing upon the socio-political life of the so-called untouchables too.

2. In 1860, Indian Penal Code was passed which treated all persons equally, irrespective of caste or creed.

It, however, obliterated the traditional penal law based on *Manusmriti* which treated human beings unequally. It was the most discriminatory and derogatory writing aimed against the Sudras and the untouchables.

3. In 1861, the Indian Council Act was passed, which laid the foundation of representative and responsible government in India.

   The Governor-General was to be assisted by an Executive Council consisting of seven members including the Governor-General himself. The Act created one Legislative Council consisting of near about 16 members. Though it was not a fully representative body, it laid the foundation stone of parliamentary government in India. The Privy Council (in UK) was the highest Court of Appeal for India and the High Courts were also established in place of Diwani and Foujdari Adalats. Thus a new system of government came into operation in British India.

4. In 1872, Indian Contract Act was passed, which gave right to all the legally competent persons to form contracts with any member of the society in furtherance of their interests at their own free consent.

5. The Government of India Act, 1909 ushered in a new era of representative form of government in India. However, this perturbed the Muslim minority who felt that they would be outvoted by the Hindu majority. Therefore, they insisted in 1909 that the so-called untouchables should not be enumerated as Hindus in the census of 1911. The census authorities also deliberately or otherwise did not mention the untouchables as Hindus, but as "untouchables."

6. The Hindus who were already perturbed because of the conversions of the untouchables got one more "jolt" from the census of 1911. They were afraid of the 'Politics of number' in which they were presumably to lose power. Therefore, they met in a conference held in Haridwar in 1915 under the presidentship of Shri Munindra Chandra Nandi where they formed an organization of the Hindus called Sarvadeshik Sabha, the object of which was, *inter alia,* to eradicate untouchability.

On 20 December 1916, the non-Brahmin movement under the name of South Indian Liberal Federation was formed and a manifesto was issued under the signature of its Secretary, Rao Bahadur Pitty Theogaraja Chettiar, claiming a due share in government appointments and political power.

7. A conference of the Depressed Classes was held at Madanpura in Bombay on 11 November 1917, under the presidentship of Sir Narayan Chandavarkar. The conference by its resolution appealed to government to protect the interests of the untouchables by granting them the right to elect their own representatives to the legislatures in proportion to their population.

   After a week a second meeting took place under the presidentship of Bapuji Namdeo Bagade, a leader of the non-Brahmin party and again stressed upon due representation to the Depressed Classes in the legislatures.

8. The British Government had appointed a committee under Lord Southborough in the year 1919 to suggest suitable reforms in the franchise.

   Dr Babasaheb Ambedkar, among others appeared before the Committee on 27 January 1919 and pleaded for reservation of seats in proportion to the population of the untouchables, with separate electorate. Thus he stated that the untouchables from Bombay Province should elect nine representatives to the provincial legislative council and one representative to the Imperial Legislative Council.

9. According to Government of India Act, 1919, the Depressed Classes got the representation as under:

   In the Central Legislative Assembly there were altogether 103 elected members and 41 nominated members. Out of the 103 elected members, 51 were from general constituencies, 30 from Muslims, 2 from Sikhs, 7 from landlords, 9 from Europeans and 4 from businessmen.

   Out of 41 nominated members, 26 were official members and remaining were nominated members. The Depressed Classes got only one seat in the Central Legislative Assembly.

The number of members in the various provincial Assemblies (Act of 1919) are given in Table 5.1

All the members belonging to the Depressed Classes were to be nominated from among the non-official Depressed Classes people. They were altogether 20.

10. In 1920, Shri Faguwa Rohidas, a cobbler, was elected to the Central Provinces Legislature. He was elected on Congress ticket.
11. Shri M.C. Rajah was elected as an MLA of the Madras Legislature in 1920.
12. Shri M.C. Rajah (Madras) was nominated as a member of the Central Legislative Assembly in 1922. He was the first untouchable to be nominated to the Central Legislative Assembly.

Table 5.1: Number of Members

Sl. No.	Province	Elected representatives	Nominated Rep. non-official	Nominated Depressed Classes	Nominated	Total
1.	Assam	39	7		7	53
2.	Bombay	86	9	(2)	19	114
3.	Bengal	114	16	(1)	10	140
4.	Bihar-Orissa	76	12	(2)	15	103
5.	Central Provinces	55	8	(4)	10	73
6.	Madras	98	11	(10)	23	132
7.	Punjab	71	15	—	8	94
8,	United Provinces	100	6	(1)	17	123

13. R. Srinivasan, an untouchable leader, was elected to the Madras Legislature in 1922.
14. Shri Dhruvanak D.Gholap from Satara (Bombay) was nominated as a member of the Bombay Legislature in 1926. He was the first untouchable to be nominated to the Bombay Legislature.

Dr Babasaheb Ambedkar was nominated as a member of the Bombay Legislative Council, on 18 February 1927.

15. A special convention of the representatives of the Depressed Classes all over India was held in New Delhi on 22-24 December 1927 to discuss the question of reforms and to accord welcome to the Simon Commission. Swami Achhutanand was the Chairman of the reception committee. It was a great success. M.C. Rajah presided over the session. Shri G.A. Gawai (Nagpur), Bhosle (Bombay) and Janaki Das (Delhi) delivered speeches at the session. It resolved, among others, to have separate electorate for the Depressed Classes.
16. The British Government appointed the Indian Statutory Commission under the chairmanship of Sir John Simon to study the Indian constitutional problem. The Commission reached Bombay on 3 February 1928. Due to its non-Indian character, the Congress boycotted it. Altogether 18 Depressed Classes gave evidence before it. About 16 of them pleaded for separate electorates. Dr Babasaheb Ambedkar also submitted a memorandum to the Simon Commission, on behalf of the Bahishkrit Hitkarini Sabha. He demanded joint electorates with reservation of seats for the Depressed Classes. However, the demands put forth by him were rejected by the Simon Commission.
17. A special UP Depressed Classes conference was held on 14-15 April 1928 at Agra. It was convened by Chandradhar Johari, Secretary Achhutodhar Committee and Pandit Shri Krishnadutta Paliwal. The conference passed a resolution condemning the Adi-Hindu movement and supporting the boycott of the Simon Commission.
18. The Executive Committee of the All India Depressed Classes Association met at the Royal Hotel in Simla in July 1930. It was attended by M.C. Rajah (Madras), G.A. Gawai and G.M. Thaware (CP), B.C. Mandal (Bengal), Devi Das Jatav (Delhi), Choudhary Bali Ram (Punjab), Swami Achhutanand and Nanak Chand Dhuria (UP). The committee decided not to accept the proposals of the commission in the absence of separate electorate.

19 In 1930 election Shri Guru Gosain Agamdas and Balaraj Jaiswar were elected to the Central Province's Legislature. Both belonged to the Chamar community. Both were Congressmen. In the same year Shri Bansilal Choudhary, a sweeper, got elected to the Punjab Legislature on the Congress ticket.

20. The first conference of the All India Depressed Classes Congress was held at Nagpur on 8-9 August 1930 under the presidentship of Dr Babasaheb Ambedkar. It was the first representative conference of the Depressed Classes in India. It resolved, *inter alia,* to get adequate representation in the legislature.

21. The second conference of the All India Depressed Classes Congress was held at Kamathi, Nagpur on 7-8 May 1932 under the presidentship of R.B. Muniswamy Pillai (Madras). It was attended, among others, by Dr Babasaheb Ambedkar, R. Srinivasan, N. Shivaraj (Madras), M.B. Mallick, R.L. Biswas (Bengal), Swamy Achhutanand (UP), and Babu Mangu Ram (Punjab). This conference emphatically claimed for "special representation as a matter of natural rights necessary for their protection." At the end the delegates formed The All India Depressed Classes Federation and elected V.I. Muniswamy Pillai (Madras) and Rasik Lai Biswas (Bengal) as President and Secretary of the Federation respectively. Its office was located at Calcutta.

22. In order to discuss and decide the nature of the future Constitution of India, the British Government convened the First Indian Round Table Conference in London from 12 November 1930 to 19 January 1931 in which 89 delegates, including Dr Babasaheb Ambedkar (Bombay) and R.B. Srinivasan (Madras) from among the Scheduled Castes had participated. The Congress, however, boycotted it.

    The second Round Table Conference was convened from 7 September 1931 to 1 December 1931. This time the Congress took part in the conference. The representatives of the Scheduled Castes, Dr Babasaheb Ambedkar and R.B. Srinivasan strongly advocated for separate electorate for the Scheduled Castes. Mahatma Gandhi, however, opposed the demand for separate electorate for the Scheduled Castes.

Eventually, the British Government headed by Mr Ramsay Macdonald announced 'the Communal Award' on 17 August 1932. The award envisaged separate electorate for the Depressed Classes, along with Muslims, Europeans, Sikhs, Indian Christians, Anglo-Indians and even the Marathas. Hence, Mahatma Gandhi went on a historic fast in protest against the Communal Award, especially in respect of the Depressed Classes. Ultimately, Dr Babasaheb Ambedkar had to come to a compromise due to exigency of the situation created by heavy pressures exerted by opposite circles. The issue was settled between the two contending parties at Pune on 24 September 1932. This agreement later became famous as the 'Poona Pact'.

Pandit Madan Mohan Malaviya was the principal signatory on behalf of the caste Hindus, and Dr Babasaheb Ambedkar on behalf of the Depressed Classes. Many other important leaders among both the groups also signed the Poona Pact.

23. Text of the Poona Pact 1932

(1) There shall be seats reserved for the depressed classes out of the general electorates seats in the provincial legislatures as follows:

Madras	30
Bombay with Sind	15
Punjab	8
Bihar and Orissa	18
Central Provinces	20
Assam	7
Bengal	30
United Provinces	20
Total	148

These figures are based on total strength of the Provincial Councils announced in the Prime Minister's decision.

(2) Election to these seats shall be by joint electorates, subject however, to the following procedure:

All the members of the Depressed Classes registered in the general electorate roll in a constituency will form an electoral college, which will elect a panel of four candidates belonging to the depressed classes for each of such reserved seats, by the method of the single vote; the four getting the highest number of votes in such primary election, shall be candidates for election by the general electorate.

(3) Representation of the depressed classes in the central legislature shall likewise be on the principle of joint electorates and reserved seats by the method of primary election in the manner provided for in clause (2) above, for their representatives in the Provincial Legislatures.

(4) In the Central Legislature, eighteen per cent of seats allotted to the general electorate for British India in the said legislature shall be reserved for the depressed classes.

(5) The system of primary election to a panel of candidates for election to the Central and Provincial legislature, as herein before mentioned, shall come to an end after the first ten years, unless terminated sooner by mutual agreement under the provision of clause (6) below.

(6) The system of representation of the depressed classes by reserved seats in the provincial and central legislatures as provided for in clauses (1) and (4) shall continue until determined by mutual agreement between the communities concerned in the settlement.

(7) Franchise for the Central and Provincial Legislatures for the depressed classes shall be as indicated in the Lothian Committee Report.

(8) There shall be no disabilities attaching to anyone on the ground of his being a member of the depressed class in regard to any elections to local bodies or appointment to the public services.

Table 5.2 : Representation of the Scheduled Castes in the Federal Assembly

Provinces	Total Number of Seats	Total for Gen. Seats	General Seats Reserved for SC	Sikh Seats	Muslim Seats	Anglo Indian Seats	European Seats	Indian Christian Seats	Commerce & Industry	Land lords	Seat for Rep. of Labour	Women's Seats
Madras	37	19	4	–	8	1	1	2	2	1	1	2
Bombay	30	13	2	–	6	1	1	1	3	1	2	2
Bengal	37	10	3	–	17	1	1	1	3	1	2	1
United Province	37	19	3	–	12	1	1	1	–	1	1	1
Punjab	30	6	1	6	14	–	1	1	–	1		1
Bihar	30	16	2	–	9	–	1	1	–	1	1	1
Central Provinces	15	9	2	–	3	–	–	–		1	1	1
Assam	10	4	1	–	3	–	1	1	–	–	1	–
Orissa	5	4	1	–	1	–	–	–	–	–	–	–
North-West Frontier Province	5	1	–	–	4	–	–	–	–	–	–	–
Sind	5	1	–	–	3		1	–	–	–	–	–
Baluchistan	1	–	–	–	1	–	–	–	–			
Delhi	2	1	–	–	1	–	–	–	–	–	–	–
Ajmer	1	1	–	–	–	–	–	–	–			
Coorg	1	1	–	–	–	–	–	–	–	–	–	–
Non-provincial seats	4	–		–		–	–	–	3	–	1	–
Total seats	250	105	19	6	82	4	8	8	11	7	10	9

24. The third session of the Indian Round Table Conference was held from 17 November 1932 to 24 December 1932 to confirm and finalize the decisions taken in the previous sessions. This time the Indian National Congress boycotted the conference.

25. According to the Government of India Act, 1935 the Scheduled Castes got the representation in Federal Assembly as well as in the provincial legislative assemblies.

    The representation of the Scheduled Castes in the Federal Assembly under the Act of 1935 is given in Table 5.2.

26. Dr Babasaheb Ambedkar founded the first ever political organization of Dalits named, Independent Labour Party in August 1936. Its head office was at Bombay. It contested 13 reserved seats and 7 general seats for the Bombay Legislative Assembly and 10 reserved seats and 5 general seats for the CP and Berar Legislative Assembly. The elections were held on 17 February 1937. The ILP could win 11 reserved seats and 3 general seats for the Bombay Legislative Assembly and 7 reserved seats for the CP and Berar Legislative Assembly.

27. The elections to the Provincial Assemblies were held in February 1937. The Scheduled Castes representation is given in Table 5.3

28. On 19 March 1939, the Independent Labour Party had observed Independence Day, for on that day in 1927, Dr Babasaheb Ambedkar, while addressing a mammoth gathering of near about 10,000 untouchable men and women at Mahad, had declared that he would launch satyagraha for regaining their civil rights.

29. The Maharaja of Mysore announced constitutional reforms in 1939. Accordingly, the Depressed Classes secured 30 out of the 300 seats in the Assembly and 4 out of 68 in the Council.

30. Dr Babasaheb Ambedkar was included in the Viceroy's Executive Council as a Labour Member on 9 July 1942. He was the first untouchable to get such a coveted post in the

Imperial Executive Council. He held this post till the third week of June 1946.

Table 5.3 : Scheduled Castes Representation

SI. No.	Province	Total No. of Seats in the Lower House for SC	SC Ministers	SC Parliamentary Secretaries
1.	Assam	7	1	–
2.	Bengal	30	2	–
3.	Bihar	15	1	1
4.	Bombay	15	–	–
5.	CP & Berar	20	–	–
6.	Madras	30	1	1
7.	NWFP	–	–	–
8.	Orissa	6	–	–
9.	Punjab	8	–	1
10.	Sind	–	–	0
11.	UP	20	–	2
	Total	151	5	5

31. The third conference of the All India Depressed Classes Congress was held at Nagpur on 18-20 July 1942 under the presidentship of R.B.N. Shivaraj (Madras). Dr Babasaheb Ambedkar addressed the conference. It urged the government to protect the interests of the Scheduled Castes in the future constitution of India.

    At the end, the conference unanimously established "All India Scheduled Castes Federation" under the presidentship of R.B.N. Shivaraj. It was the first national level political party of the Dalits.

32. Dr Babasaheb Ambedkar was invited to the Pacific Relations Conference to be held at Quebec in Canada in December 1942. He wrote a paper for the said conference on the plight of the so-called untouchables. He, however, could not go due to his engagements. He, therefore sent

Shri N. Shivaraj to present the paper on his behalf at the conference. The said paper was later on published under the title *Mr. Gandhi and the Emancipation of the Untouchables.*

33. In the Interim Government of India constituted under the leadership of Pandit Jawaharlal Nehru in August 1946, Shri Jagjivan Ram (Bihar) was included among the Scheduled Castes by the Indian National Congress, as Labour Minister.

    The Muslim League which joined the Interim Government subsequently included Shri Jogendra Nath Mandal (Bengal) among the Scheduled Castes, as Law Minister, on 21 October 1946. Thus, the Scheduled Castes got two seats in the Central Cabinet in the year 1946.

34. Dr Babasaheb Ambedkar was elected as a member of the Constituent Assembly from the Bengal legislature on 19. July 1946. However, he lost his membership due to the partition of India. Therefore, he was re-elected to the Constituent Assembly, from the Bombay legislature on 23 July 1947.

35. Dr Babasaheb Ambedkar was included in the first cabinet of free India as a Law Minister on 15 August 1947.

    On 29 August 1947 he was appointed as the Chairman of the Drafting Committee of the Constituent Assembly. The draft of the constitution became ready by 14 November 1949 and the Constituent Assembly finally approved it on 26 November 1949. It came into implementation on 26 January 1950.

36. The Constitution of India provides under Article 330 and 332, reservation for the Scheduled Castes in proportion to their population, in the House of People and the State Assemblies respectively.

    Table 5.4 shows the number of seats reserved for the Scheduled Castes in the House of People and State Assemblies in the year 1952.

Table 5.4 : Number of Seats Reserved for the Scheduled Castes In 1952

SI. No.	Name of State	House of People				State Assemblies			
		Gen. seats	Seats for SC	Seats for ST	Total	Gen. seats	Seats for SC	Seats for ST	Total
1.	Assam	9	1	2	12	77	5	26	108
2.	Bihar	42	7	6	55	251	44	35	330
3.	Bombay	37	4	4	45	259	27	29	315
4.	Madhya Pradesh	22	4	5	29	173	32	27	232
5.	Madras	62	12	1	75	309	62	4	375
6.	Orissa	13	3	4	20	91	21	28	140
7.	Punjab	15	3	–	18	104	21	–	125
8.	Uttar Pradesh	69	17	–	86	347	83	–	430
9.	West Bengal	26	6	2	34	186	40	12	238
10.	Hyderabad	21	4	-	25	142	31	2	175
11.	Madhya Bharat	8	2	1	11	70	17	12	99
12.	Mysore	9	2	–	11	80	19	–	99
13.	Pepsu	4	1	–	5	50	10	–	60
14.	Rajasthan	17	2	1	20	139	16	5	160
15.	Saurashtra	6	–	–	6	55	4	1	60
16.	Travancore–Cochin	11	1	–	12	97	11	–	108

Table 5.4 : Number of Seats Reserved for the Scheduled Castes In 1952

SI. No.	Name of State	House of People				State Assemblies			
		Gen. seats	Seats for SC	Seats for ST	Total	Gen. seats	Seats for SC	Seats for ST	Total
17.	Ajmer	2	–	–	2	24	6	–	30
18.	Bhopal	2	–	–	2	23	5	2	30
19.	Bilaspur	1	–	–	1	–	–	–	–
20.	Coorg	1	–	–	1	18	3	3	24
21.	Delhi	3	1	–	4	–	–	–	–
22.	Himachal Pradesh	2	1	–	3	28	8	–	36
23.	Kutch	2	–	–	2	–	–	–	–
24.	Manipur	2	–	–	2	–	–	–	–
25.	Tripura	2	–	–	2	–	–	–	–
26.	Vindhya Pradesh	4	1	1	6	48	6	6	60
		392	72	25	489	2571	471	192	3,234
		80.16%	14.72%	5.12%	100%	79.50%	14.56%	5.94%	100%

NOTES

1. The anti-slavery issue caused civil war in USA in the year 1861. President Abraham Lincoln successfully united the USA and signed the Proclamation of Emancipation of the Blacks on 22 September 1862.
2. In 1871, the Government of Japan promulgated the "Emancipation Edict" and declared the discontinuation of the discrimination against the lowest social class – Buraku.
3. In 1859, J.S. Mill wrote on liberty and in 1867, Karl Marx wrote *Das Capital.*
4. The Banaras Hindu University came into existence under Banaras Hindu University Act, 1915 and Aligarh Muslim University came into existence under the Aligarh Muslim University Act, 1920. Both these universities were established for Hindus and Muslims respectively.
5. In 1912, Bulgaria, Greece, Serbia and Montenegro formed themselves into a Balkan League and declared war on Turkish imperialism. In this war Turkey was completely defeated and the Balkan League got freedom.
6. In 1914, the First World War started.
7. On 26 October 1917, Communist Revolution took place in Russia, under the leadership of Lenin, Trotsky and Stalin.
8. In 1923, the Hindus intensified their *Shuddhi* programme.
9. Sir Muhmmed Iqbal in his presidential address at the session of the All India Muslim League held at Allahabad in 1930 declared his 'two nation theory'.
10. The Justice Confederation held at Tiruvarur in August 1940 under the presidentship of E.V. Ramaswami Naicker passed a resolution to have a separate Dravid land for the Dravidians.
11. The Muslim league at its session held in March 1940 at Lahore under the leadership of M.A. Jinnah resolved to have a separate land for the Muslims in India.
12. On 10 December 1948, the United Nations Organization made an historic universal declaration of Human Rights.
13. Jews, the persecuted minorities scattered in various countries got the separate land, Israel in the year 1948.

6

Principal Dalit Leaders

Any social movement is but an organized endeavour to accomplish certain well-defined objectives. It requires a well-dedicated and capable leadership to lead it. The objective of Dalit movement was, obviously, to liberate the Dalits from untouchability and other incidental vices. It was not an easy task. However, the movement could achieve a great success in regaining the civic personality and all the civil rights for the Dalits.

Who were those leaders who worked for their brethren? What was their perception of the oppressive Hindu social system? What ideology had they adopted? How far could they mobilize the ignorant and illiterate masses into a potential power? What role had they played in the movement? How far did they succeed in their mission? In order to know this, it is necessary to consider their socio-political profiles.

The Dalit movement was, undoubtedly, led by several persons belonging to Dalit as well as non-Dalit communities. The present study is, however, confined to the role played by some of the eminent Dalit leaders only who could strive for the substantial part of their life during 1857 to 1956 (born during 1800 to 1920 only). The socio-political profiles of all those leaders, irrespective of their caste, creed, sex, region or ideology are given succinctly as under:

AMBEDKAR, B.R.[1] (1891-1956)

Dr Bhimrao Ramji Ambedkar, popularly known as 'Babasaheb', was born on 14 April 1891 at Mhow in the vicinity of Indore in Madhya Pradesh. His father's name was Ramji and mother's name was Bhimabai. His ancestral village was Ambadave in Mandagad Taluka in the district of Ratnagiri in Maharashtra. He belonged to an untouchable Mahar community. He came of a valiant and cultured family. His father Ramji, and grandfather Maloji were in the British Army. His mother belonged to Murbad village in Thana district in Maharashtra and her family also had the tradition of military service.

At the time of his birth his father Ramji was serving as Headmaster in Military School at Mhow and had attained the rank of Subedar-Major. He retired from service when Bhim was two years old. After retirement his father came to Dapoli in Ratnagiri district in the year 1894. Soon his father was appointed as storekeeper in Ratnagiri and later on transferred to Satara in the year 1896. Later on his family shifted to Bombay in 1904 and lived in a room in Dabak Chawl at Lower Parel, with his two brothers, Balaram and Anandrao, two sisters, Manjula and Tulsa, and his aunt Meerabai.

Ramji was a staunch follower of Kabir Panth. He used to read and recite devotional songs of saint-poet Chokha Maharaj and Tukaram Maharaj. He used to read *Bhagavad Gita, Ramayana* and *Mahabharata*. He was a teetotaller and vegetarian. He was economically poor, but maintained cleanliness, discipline and religious atmosphere in the family.

Bhimrao completed his primary education at Satara in 1904. Then he was admitted to Elphinston High School, Bombay, from where he had completed his matriculation in the year 1907. He passed his B.A. in 1913 from Elphinston College, Bombay. Then with the kind help of Maharaja Sayajirao Gaikwad of Baroda, he went to prosecute his further education in the famous Columbia University, New York in July 1913. He was awarded M.A. in Economics in June 1915 on his thesis, "Ancient Indian

---

1. Source of Information :

Keer Dhananjay. *Dr. B.R. Ambedkar : Life and Mission* (Bombay 1974) and many other sources.

Commerce". Simultaneously, he continued his research leading to Ph.D. He submitted his thesis "National dividend of India - A historic and analytical study" to the Columbia University in June 1916 on which he obtained Ph.D. degree.

His thirst for knowledge was not quenched. He went to London and joined there in London School of Economics and Politics, in October 1916. He was awarded M.Sc. for his thesis, "Provincial Decentralization of Imperial Finance in British India", in June 1921. He was awarded D.Sc. on his thesis, "The Problem of Rupee", in the year 1923. In the meantime he joined Gray's Inn where he became Barrister-at-Law.

He had earlier married Ramabai, daughter of Bhiku Walangkar, resident of Dapoli in Ratnagiri. At the time of marriage Bhim was 14 years old and Ramabai was 9 years old. Her father was a poor labourer belonging to Mahar community. They got a son by name Yeshwant. Ramabai was illiterate. She managed her family with a meagre amount and maintained very healthy atmosphere in the family. She died on 27 May 1935 due to ill health. Later, Babasaheb Ambedkar, on medical grounds, married Dr Sharada Kabir, a Saraswat Brahmin lady doctor, on 15 April 1948 at New Delhi.

At first he joined as a Lieutenant in the Baroda State Forces in 1913. When he came to know that his father was seriously ill he came to Bombay, within a few days of joining the service. However, Ramji breathed his last before his arrival in Bombay. Then he did not return to Baroda to join the service as he was frustrated by acute untouchability threat which he had to face. Again, when he returned to India after completing higher education in USA and UK in July 1917, he joined the Maharaja's service at Baroda as a Military Secretary. It was obligatory for him to serve the Baroda State for a period of ten years as per the bond signed by him as a precondition for obtaining the grant of scholarship for prosecuting higher studies in foreign countries. He was again subjected to discrimination on the grounds of untouchability by the staff in the department. He could not get residential accommodation also. Therefore, he had to leave the service in November 1917. He returned to Bombay.

He was appointed as a Professor of Political Economy in Sydenham College, Bombay on 11 November 1918. He resigned his professorship on 11 March 1920. Again he went to London in September 1920 to complete his studies. He was there till 1923.

After returning from England he started his legal practice at the Bombay High Court in June 1923. From June 1925 to March 1928, he served as a part-time teacher in Mercantile Law in Batliboi's Accountancy Training Institute, Bombay. From June 1928 to March 1929 he served as a Professor of Law in Government Law College, Bombay. He served as Principal of the same college from June 1935 to June 1938. Thereafter, he resumed his full time legal practice and socio-political work till his last.

He started his mission from 1919 onwards. On 27 January 1919, he gave evidence before the Southborough Committee on Franchise and strongly advocated separate electorate with reserved seats in the legislature for the Depressed Classes. In order to bring socio-political awakening to the Depressed Classes he started *Mook Naik* (leader of the Dumb), a fortnightly in Marathi from Bombay on 31 January 1920. It continued till 1923. He presided over a conference held at Mangaon near Kolhapur on 21 March 1920 where the Maharaja of Kolhapur, Shahu Chhatrapati addressed the conference.

The first All India Conference of the Depressed Classes was held at Nagpur on 30-31 May and 1 June 1920. It was presided over by Chhatrapati Shahu Maharaj and Dr Babasaheb Ambedkar, among others, addressed the conference. It was attended by delegates from Bombay, CP and Berar, Madras and Bengal. The conference resolved, among others, to have true representatives of the Depressed Classes in the legislature.

After spending two and half years from September 1920 to February 1923 in England for higher studies he returned to India and resumed his mission. In order to institutionalize the socio-political activities for the emancipation of the Depressed Classes, he formed the Bahishkrit Hitkarini Sabha (Depressed Classes Welfare Organization) on 20 July 1924 at Bombay. Its President was Sir Chimanlal Setalvad, managing committee Chairman was Babasaheb Ambedkar and its Secretary was S.N. Shivtarkar. The Sabha started one hostel at Solapur for high school students belonging to the Depressed Classes, on 4 January 1925. The management of the hostel was entrusted to Shri Jivappa Subha Aydale, a social worker from Solapur.

He was nominated to the Bombay Legislative Council with effect from 18 February 1927 for a period of five years. He was renominated in 1932 for a period of five years.

In order to assert the right to equality, he undertook a unique satyagraha at the Choudar Tank at Mahad, alongwith his followers, on 20 March 1927. They burnt *Manusmriti* at Mahad on 25 December 1927 as a protest against inequality preached by it. During this period he started *Bahishkrit Bharat,* a fortnightly on 3 April 1927. It continued up to 15 November 1929. He formed Samaj Samata Sangh (Social Equality Organization) on 4 September 1927 and Samata Sainik Dal (Equality Volunteer Army) in December 1927 to bring a new vigour and militancy to the march of equality.

He introduced the Bill No. XII of 1928 to amend the Bombay Hereditary Offices Act, 1874, in the Bombay Legislative Council on 19 March 1928. Again, he introduced the Bill to that effect in the Bombay Legislative Assembly (Bill No.XXlII of 1937) on 17 September 1937. The objects of the said Bill were to make the better provisions for the remuneration of the *Vatandars;* to allow commutation of *vatans;* to free the inferior *Vatandars* from the obligation to serve the iyots; and to define the duties of officiating *Vatandar.* Moreover, he introduced the Bill No.XX of 1937 to abolish the *Khoti* system in the Bombay Legislative Assembly, on 17 September 1937. The main objective of this Bill was to abolish the exploitative *Khoti* system prevailing in Konkan area and give the inferior holders the status of occupants. However, these bills were not passed by the Bombay legislature.

When the Indian Statutory Commission under Sir John Simon came to India, he submitted the statement on 29 May 1928 on behalf of the Depressed Classes and gave evidence on 23 October 1928. He demanded adult franchise, joint electorate and reserved seats for the Depressed Classes. However, the commission did not take due cognizance of his demands.

He founded Depressed Classes Education Society at Bombay on 14 June 1928. The Bombay Government accorded sanction to five hostels, established at Panvel, Thane, Nasik, Pune and Dharwad for the special benefit of high school students belonging to the Depressed Classes.

In order to assert the right to religion and religious equality he launched the Temple Entry Satyagraha at Kalaram temple, Nasik on 2 March 1830. The satyagraha was in continuation, of course intermittently, for a period of five years, but in vain. It ultimately culminated in his famous declaration renouncing Hinduism, at Yeola on 13 October 1935.

In the meantime he presided over the All India Depressed Classes Congress held at Nagpur on 8-9 August 1930. The conference reposed its faith in the leadership of Dr Babasaheb Ambedkar. The second All India Depressed Classes Congress was held on 7 and 8 May 1932 at Kamathi, near Nagpur. It was presided over by R.B. Muniswamy Pillai of Madras. Shri L.N. Haridas presented the welcome address. Dr Babasaheb Ambedkar, R.B. Srinivasan, R.L. Biswas, Swami Achhutanand, M.B. Mullick, Hansraj, N.C. Dhusia and many others addressed the conference. The conference accepted the leadership of Dr Babasaheb Ambedkar and reiterated the demands put before the Round Table Conferences, by Babasaheb Ambedkar and R.B. Srinivasan. The conference finally elected one All India Working Committee in which R.B. Muniswamy Pillai was elected as President, R.L. Biswas as General Secretary and T.C. Sakhare and Raisaheb Ram Sahai as its Joint Secretaries.

In order to discuss and decide the nature of future constitution of India, and resolve the communal problem, the British Government convened the Round Table Conferences in London, and invited, among others. Dr Babasaheb Ambedkar and R.B.R. Srinivasan as representatives of the Depressed Classes to the said conferences. This was, of course, the first occasion when the British Government recognized the Depressed Classes as a separate element in Indian politics, which could rightly be attributed to the strenuous efforts of Dr Babasaheb Ambedkar. He, however, participated in the Round Table Conference, the first from 12 November 1930 to 19 January 1931; the second from 7 September 1931 to 1 December 1931 and third from 17 November 1932 to 24 December 1932. The British Government conceded the demand for separate electorate to the Depressed Classes put forth by Babasaheb Ambedkar in the first and second conferences. However, due to Mahatma Gandhi's epic fast against it he had to accept the Poona Pact of 1932 which envisaged joint electorate with reserved seats. During this period he submitted his Note to the Indian Franchise Committee known as Lothian Committee on 1 May 1932.

Once again he started one fortnightly namely *Janata* (The People) on 24 November 1930. It became weekly from 31 October 1931 and it was renamed as *Prabuddha Bharat* from 4 February 1956.

In order to protect the political interests of the Scheduled Castes and other weaker sections, he founded the Independent Labour Party on 15 August 1936. When general elections were declared under the Act of 1935, he fielded his candidates for certain reserved and non-reserved seats in the Bombay Presidency and in CP and Berar. He contested from Bombay (East) reserved constituency. The other contestants to the same seat were Baloo Palvankar (Cong.), P.N. Rajbhoj and Deorukhkar. Dr Babasaheb Ambedkar was declared elected on 17 February 1937. He took very active interest in the proceedings of the Legislative Assembly. However, the Assembly was prorogued in 1939 in the wake of the outbreak of the Second World War.

When the Industrial Trade Dispute Bill virtually banning strikes was introduced in the Bombay Legislature in September 1938, near about 60 labour unions declared a token strike for a day on 7 November 1938 in protest against the said Bill. Dr Babasaheb Ambedkar also actively participated in the strike along with other labour unions.

He founded the first national level political party called All India Scheduled Castes Federation in a special convention held at Nagpur on 18-20 July 1942. R.B.N. Shivaraj (Madras) was elected as its President and P.N. Rajbhoj (Pune) as its General Secretary.

Dr Babasaheb Ambedkar had got the unique opportunity of being appointed as Labour Member in the Viceroy's Executive Council with effect from 27 July 1942. He continued to be Labour Member till July 1946. During these days he rose to the height of popularity and contributed substantially to the uplift of the Scheduled Castes and the labourers. However, the caste Hindus in general went against him. Therefore, no candidate of his SCF could get elected in the general elections held for the provincial assemblies in 1945.

In order to spread higher education among the Scheduled Castes in particular, among others, he founded 'People's Education Society' at Bombay on 8 July 1945. On behalf of the said society he started Siddharth College of Arts and Science (1946), Siddharth Night School (1947), Siddharth College of Commerce and Economics (1953), Siddharth College of Law (1956) – all at Bombay, and Milind Mahavidyalaya (1950) and Milind Multipurpose High School (1955) at Aurangabad.

According to the Cabinet Mission plan the elections to the Constituent Assembly of India were to be held in July 1946. However, Babasaheb Ambedkar had no hope of getting elected from Bombay Legislature. Hence, he got elected to the Constituent Assembly from the Bengal Legislature, on 19 July 1946, with the help of his lieutenant J.N. Mandal and the Muslim League members. However, due to the proposed partition of Bengal in 1947, he lost his membership which he had got with great effort. However, after realizing the intellectual capacity, legal knowledge and staunch nationalism of Dr Babasaheb Ambedkar, the Congress nominated him from the Bombay Legislature and got him elected to the Constituent Assembly, on 23 July 1947.

He got another unique opportunity of being nominated as the first Law Minister of free India in the cabinet of Pandit Jawaharlal Nehru. Further, he was elected as Chairman of the Drafting Committee of the Constituent Assembly, on 29 August 1947. He drafted the constitution and presented it to the Constituent Assembly on 26 November 1949 for its acceptance. The same constitution, after having been accepted with certain modifications by the Constituent Assembly, came into implementation on 26 January 1950.

Due to differences of opinion with Pandit Nehru on certain issues like Hindu Code Bill, foreign policy, etc, he submitted his resignation on 28 September 1951 which came into effect on 6 October 1951.

In the general elections held in January 1952, he contested for Lok Sabha from Bombay (north) parliamentary constituency. Shri N.S. Kajrolkar (Congress), was his opponent. Babasaheb Ambedkar was defeated in the election. Again he contested from Bhandara parliamentary constituency (reserved – double member) in the by-elections held in 1954. This time Nama Arjun Borker (Congress) was his opponent. This time also Babasaheb Ambedkar was defeated and his opponent got elected. In the meantime, he was elected to the Rajya Sabha from the Bombay Legislature in March 1952. He was member of Rajya Sabha till the end of his life.

On 6 June 1952 the Columbia University, New York awarded him LL.D. for being the successful architect of the Constitution of India. The Osmania University of Hyderabad also honoured him with the degree of D. Litt on 12 January 1953.

In 1953 he advised his followers in Marathwada region to launch a massive satyagraha for getting wasteland for agricultural purpose. Therefore, thousands of his followers launched satyagraha in which 1,700 people courted arrest. However, he withdrew the satyagraha in November 1953.

It became clear by the end of April 1950 that he was inclined towards Buddhism. Therefore, he was invited as a delegate to the World Buddhist Conference held at Colombo, Sri Lanka on 25 May 1950. He participated in it. He also participated in the World Buddhist Conference held at Rangoon (Burma) in December 1954. He founded Boudha Maha Sabha in 1955. He almost completed the writing of the *Buddha and his Dhamma* by the end of February 1956.

Ultimately, Babasaheb Ambedkar embraced Buddhism along with his family members on 14 October, 1956 at Nagpur. Rev. Bhikshu Chandramani of Kushinara officiated at the ceremony. Soon after that, Babasaheb Ambedkar, himself converted millions of his followers who came from several parts of the country, to Buddhism. On 16 October 1956, he gave *Deeksha* of Buddhism to his followers at Chandrapur.

He went to Kathmandu (Nepal) to participate in the World Buddhist Conference held on 15 and 16 November 1956 and returned to New Delhi on 30 November 1956.

He breathed his last on 6 December 1956 at his residence at 26 Alipore Road, New Delhi at the age of 65. The next day his body was put on the funeral pyre at Dadar crematorium, Bombay.

His son Yeshwantrao alias Bhaiyasaheb Ambedkar was also a leader of the Scheduled Castes and Buddhists in India. Presently, his son Prakash Y. Ambedkar is leading the movement.

Dr. Babasaheb Ambedkar was a prolific writer. His books are:

Caste in India: Their mechanism, genesis and development (1916).

The Problem of Rupee: Its origin and its solution (1923).

The evolution of provincial finance in British India. A study in the provincial decentralization of imperial finance (1925).

Annihilation of caste (1936).

Federation versus freedom (1939).

Pakistan or the partition of India (1940)

Mr Gandhi and the emancipation of the untouchables (1942).

Ranade, Gandhi and Jinnah (1943).

Communal deadlock and a way to solve it (1945).

What Congress and Gandhi have done to the untouchables (1945).

Who were the Shudras? How they came to be the fourth Varna in the Indo-Aryan society (1946).

States and minorities: What are their rights and how to secure them in the Constitution of free India. (1947).

Maharashtra as a linguistic province (1948).

Thoughts on linguistic States (1955).

The Buddha and His Dhamma (1957) (Posthumous).

Riddles in Hinduism – An exposition to enlighten the masses, (1987) (Posthumous).

The untouchables (1987) (Posthumous).

Philosophy of Hinduism (1987) (Posthumous).

Revolution and counter revolution (1987) (Posthumous).

Buddha or Karl Marx (1987) (Posthumous).

His whole life was a mission aimed at the emancipation of the Depressed Classes from untouchability, casteism, ignorance, irreligion, poverty and exploitation.

His philosophy is so wide and comprehensive that it covers social, economic, political, educational, religious and cultural aspects of human society. His philosophy stands for a new social order based on liberty, equality and fraternity.

It is but a fact that his thoughts and movement had great impact on contemporary Indian society. Though he was misunderstood by some people, he was a true nationalist, humanist and rationalist of his times. He, however, rendered invaluable services to the nation as a whole. Therefore, the Government of India honoured him (posthumously) by awarding the nation's highest civilian award, Bharat Ratna on 14 April 1990, and declared the year 1990-91 being his birth centenary year, as the year of social justice.

Appaduraiyar, G.[2] (1890-1961)

Shri Gabriel Appaduraiyar was born on 15 May 1890 at Salem in Tamil Nadu. His father, Shri Gabriel who belonged to Adi-Dravida caste, was converted to Christianity. Though Appaduraiyar was born as a Christian, he converted to Buddhism in the year 1911. He was a Tamil Pandit. He was serving as a high school teacher in Tamil at Kolar Gold Field (KGF) till his retirement in 1940.

He presided over the first Buddhist Conference held at Madras in 1917. Later, he presided over the fourth Buddhist Conference held at Madras in 1945. He represented the Depressed Classes and the Buddhists in the Congress Committee Convention at Belgam in 1924.

He edited a Tamil weekly *Tamilian* in 1928 for bringing a new awakening to the untouchable masses. It continued till 1932. It is

---

2. Source of Information :
Personal Interview with
Shri I. lognathan
4, Sarojini Compound, Mari Kuppam, KGFon 6.6.1989

said that the writings and speeches of Pandit Appaduraiyar had influenced E.V. Ramaswamy Naicker.

Pandit Appaduraiyar had written a book on Buddhism in Tamil known as *Buddhar Arularam* in the year 1950. He preached and propagated Buddhism among the Scheduled Castes in KGF and nearby areas. He had a daughter named Annapurni who married a Mudaliar member of Self-Respect Movement.

He met Dr Babasaheb Ambedkar when the latter visited KGF in 1944. Dr Babasaheb Ambedkar was pleased to see the religious uplift run by Pandit Appaduraiyar.

Shri Appaduraiyar expired on 21 January 1961 at the age of 71.

Arigay Ramaswamy[3] (1885-1973)

Shri Arigay Ramaswamy was born in 1885 at Ramankole, in Ranga Reddy district. He belonged to Mala Caste. His father Arigay Balayya was a tonga driver in Secunderabad.

Arigay Ramaswamy was sent to Baptist Mission School, Secunderabad, but could not continue his education due to acute poverty. He joined the Nizam's Railway service as office boy. He was for sometime a number taker at Purna. Later on, he was promoted as ticket collector at the Bolaram railway station.

He was addicted to the evil habit of drink in his youth. However, he came under the influence of his Guru Mandippela Hanumantha Rao, an exponent of Achala Bodha' in 1912. Thereafter he left drinking and meat-eating.

He founded Suneethi Bala Samajamu and carried on his social reform activities, especially in Kummarguda, a locality in Secunderabad, where he lived. He exhorted his brethren to abandon spurious drinks and eradicate the Devadasi system from the community. He preached against animal sacrifices and child-marriages.

---

3. Source of Information :
Personal Interview with his son
Arigay Bhaskar Rao
8-2-314, Komuariguda, Secunderabad on 22.11.1988.

He believed in Achal Siddhant and Brahmo Samaj. He firmly believed that the Adi-Hindus were separate from the Hindus. He stood for abolition of sub-castes among the untouchables.

In 1922, he formed, Adi-Hindu Jatiyonnati Sabha. Its President was Konday Venkataswamy, and J. Papiah and Arigay Ramaswamy were its Secretaries. The Jatiyonnati Sabha was named as Adi-Hindu Mahasabha in April 1927. Shri B.S. Venkatarao, Madari Govindraju, C.S. Ethirajan, P.R. Venkataswamy and others were its members. The organization was in existence up to 1930.

He was a member of the Hyderabad Municipal Council from 1933-1940. He was one of the delegates to the All India Depressed Classes Conference held at Nagpur under the presidentship of R.B.N. Shivaraj, on 18-20 July 1942. He was elected President of Independent Scheduled Castes Federation founded by him in 1944. In 1949 he formed Dalit Jatiya Sangh on the advice of Swami Ramanand Tirth, a veteran freedom fighter and a Congress leader.

He was nominated as a member of the Constituent Assembly and then to the Provisional Parliament from 1950-52.

He contested as Congress nominee in the first general election (1952) for Hyderabad Legislative Assembly from Vikarabad (General or G and SC) seat and got elected. He was nominated as Deputy Minister for Agriculture and Civil Supplies, Government of Hyderabad from 1954 to October 1956. He was elected for the Andhra Pradesh (AP) Assembly as Congress candidate in 1957 from Vikarabad Assembly constituency. Again he was elected unopposed from the same constituency in 1962. Again he was elected to the AP Legislative Assembly from the same constituency in 1967. He was Minister for Social Welfare, Government of Andhra Pradesh from April 1967 to July 1969.

He married Rajamma who died in 1921. Then he married Lalitabai in 1929. He had three sons.

He was a good speaker in Telugu. He was a great social reformer, efficient administrator and a great politician. He expired on 26 January 1973 at the age of 88 at Hyderabad.

AUDIAH, M.L.[4] (1866-1938)

Shri Madari Audiah was born in 1866 at Ghasmandi, Secunderabad. His father was Madari Laxmiah. He belonged to Mala caste. After his schooling he joined the Queen's Own Sappers and Miners Engineering School at Secunderabad and got through it with credit.

He began his career as an overseer in PWD in Nizam State and rose to the position of an Assistant Engineer. It was under his supervision that the magnificent buildings like the Hyderabad High Court, Victoria Zanana Hospital, City College and Osmania General Hospital were constructed.

He was a great social reformer among the untouchables. He organized Manya Sangham at Ghasmandi under the leadership of Shri Bhagya Reddy Varma, the pioneering social reformer in the Nizam State. Shri Audiah very sincerely strove to eradicate the age-old customs of drinking and eating meat at social occassions, and in marriage and funeral functions; he achieved success to a great extent.

Later on he formed another organization named, Sangliabhiwrudhi Samajamu. The main purpose of the organization was to conduct regular weekly Bhajans and awaken the people. It proposed unity of all the untouchable castes. It was opposed to the Choudharies who exploited the people. It also opposed alcoholism.

In order to spread education among the untouchables, Shri Audiah started a school in 1906. At the initial stage there were only 15 students and one lady teacher in the school. Later Rao Bahadur C.V. Padma Rao Mudaliar, a well-wisher of the untouchables became its honorary Secretary. The school was named after the then Resident of Hyderabad, Sir William Barton who donated the land to the school.

---

[4] Source of Information :
Personal Interview with his grandson
Shri H.N. Jaigopal
Building No. 14, H.No. 7-3-158/262
Audiah Nagar, Secunderabad on 22.11.1988

He constructed Channa Keshavaswamy temple for the untouchables, where weekly Bhajans were sung. The marriages were to be celebrated in the temple.

He married Kishtamma and had four sons and three daughters.

Shri M. L. Audiah worked for the social and cultural uplift of the untouchables. He devoted his time, energy and money for the uplift of his brethren.

He breathed his last in December 1938, at the age of 72. In recognition of his high contribution to the social cause, the Ghasmandi area where he resided is named as Audiah Nagar and the school he started is renamed as Audiah High School by his admirers and disciples.

Aydale, J.S.[5] (1895-1946)

Shri Jivappa Aydale was born in 1895 at Jat Taluka Sangli district in Maharashtra. His father Shri Sudhana Aydale was head of the Mahar community in erstwhile Jat Sansthan, who was to give justice in the disputes of the community. He had some *Inam* land for his livelihood. Shri Jivappa Aydale was educated up to matric. For some time he was appointed as a teacher in the city municipality of Solapur.

At first Shri Aydale concentrated on reformation of the Dalits. He asked his brethren in Jat Sansthan to abandon beef-eating, carrying dead animals and Devadasi system. He was, however, opposed by his own castemen as well as the caste Hindus. Ultimately, he could successfully convince the Maharaja of Jat to take necessary steps to reform the society.

In order to spread education among the Dalits, he founded Depressed Classes Education Society at Solapur in 1916. He was Secretary of the Society up to 1921. He started three night schools for the adults belonging to Depressed Classes under the auspices of the Society. He also started a school for the children

---

5. Source of Information :
Personal Interview with his grand daughters husband
Shri Bhagwant M. Shingle
195 Forest, New Tiregaon, Sholapur, Maharashtra, on 8.5.1989

of Depressed Classes. However, he handed over the night schools and the primary school to the Municipality, Solapur in 1922.

He was a member of the Solapur Municipality and its school board up to 1928. He started Bahiskrit Anath Vidyarthi Ashram for the Depressed Classes students in 1925 and ran it till 1928. He founded the Satya Prasarak Bhim-sena Mandal, which organized a troop of 380 persons for maintaining discipline in the community.

When Babasaheb Ambedkar started a hostel for the untouchable students at Solapur under the auspices of the Depressed Classes Education Society, Shri J.S. Aydale was appointed as Superintendent of the hostel there. He held this post from 1930 to 1936.

When Babasaheb Ambedkar founded the Independent Labour Party, Shri Aydale joined it. In the elections held in 1937 to the Bombay Legislative Assembly, he contested on ILP ticket from Solapur (North east) (R) constituency and got elected. He took active part in the proceedings of the Assembly.

He believed in Warkari Panth. He used to sing devotional songs and explain them to his brethren.

He married Godabai and had a son and a daughter. His brother Shri Setappa and uncle Lingappa also were active in the movement.

He died in May 1946 at the age of 51.

Ayyan Kali[6] (1863-1941)

Shri Ayyan Kali was born on 28 August 1863, at Venganoor in Neyyattinkara, Trivandrum district in Kerala. He belonged to

---

6. Source of Information :
Personal Interview with his grandson
Shri P. Sasidharan, IPs,
Ashirwad Vrindavan Gardens, Pattom,
Trivandrum (Kerala)
on 21.4.1991

Pulaya caste. His father Shri Ayyan was a poor agricultural labour. Shri Ayyan Kali had not received any formal education. He was physically strong and well versed in martial art.

In those days the position of the so-called untouchables was very poor, pitiable and precarious. Untouchability was observed by the caste Hindus very strictly. They were not allowed to take formal education, and to enter the temples or public places. They were not even allowed to walk along the streets. However, if that was unavoidable they had to make a sound for alerting the high caste people and they had to keep at a pace of about 30 feet from the road, till the high caste man passed ahead. They were not allowed to wear full clothes. Even the women had to be half naked, leaving the upper and the lower parts of the body uncovered. They were not allowed to wear ornaments or new garments. If they had to wear new clothes, they had to sprinkle dirty water over these before wearing them. This adverse situation and his own experiences with the acute and virulent form of untouchability motivated Shri Ayyan Kali to undertake the task, though it was very difficult, to liberate his brethren from untouchability and casteism.

In 1893, Shri Ayyan Kali started his fight against untouchability. At first he sought to regain the right to walk along the streets. He bought one bullock cart, tied bells around the neck of the bullocks for alerting the people on the street and used to travel in that bullock cart, along with his brothers (who were strong enough and well armed, to face the challenge, if any), with a view to securing the right to use the public roads. The caste Hindus did not dare to challenge him. However, there occurred a clash between the untouchables and caste Hindus at Aralum Mood, in which the untouchables defeated the caste Hindus. Thereafter, the caste Hindus did not dare to prevent the untouchables from walking along the public streets in the vicinity of Trivandrum.

In order to bow down the caste Hindus observing untouchability, the untouchable agricultural labourers went on strike in 1904. It was, of course, led by Shri Ayyan Kali. It became very much successful. The caste Hindus had to lose paddy production for that year. Thenceforth, they decided to treat the untouchables as equals.

In 1904, he started a primary school at Katakala near his village. There were only two students in the school at first. Later, the school was set ablaze by the miscreants. He started another school at his own village, Venganoor.

In the year 1905, Shri Ayyan Kali founded Sadhu Jana Paripalana Yogam, an organization of the Dalits. The main principles of this organization were to pray to God, but not to the idol; to worship or pray to God in the open space as the untouchables were not financially well off to construct the temples; not to sacrifice the animals for propitiating God; to educate the children; to practise cleanliness; to take daily bath and use sandal paste on forehead, and to settle the disputes, if any, among themselves without filing complaints with the police or filing suit in the court, which would otherwise cause great loss. Almost all the untouchable people irrespective of their sub-castes became the members of SJPY. They followed their leader Ayyan Kali. They settled the disputes under the auspices of the SJPYs court, presided over by Ayyan Kali. Shri Keshwan acted as writer and Kunjan Krishnan acted as assistant to the President of the court.

The king of Travancore came to know of the activities of Shri Ayyan Kali. Hence the proclamation was issued by the king to allow the untouchable students to enter the schools.

In 1912, the Maharaja nominated him as a member of the Sri Moolam Praja Sabha (the Legislative Assembly). He was consecutively the member of Shri Moolam Praja Sabha from 1912 to 1941, the year of his death. During this period he could secure the right to hold agricultural land. Previously, there was *Adimattom* (slavery); as such the untouchables were not allowed to hold the land. They were slaves subject to sale, lease or mortgage along with the land. The Maharaja granted 1,000 acres of land for its distribution among the untouchables.

Shri Ayyan Kali could secure fee concessions, mid-day meals and other facilities for the students. At the request of Ayyan Kali, the king agreed to appoint the untouchables as peons, watchmen, gardeners, etc.

He asked his brethren to live with self-pride, clothe their bodies fully. He sold his one acre of agricultural land and purchased the *rowkas* (blouses) for the women and distributed them among the women at Perinad. He asked the women to throw their bead necklaces.

He could convince the Maharaja to throw open the temples to the untouchables. Therefore, the Maharaja made the Temple Entry Proclamation on 12 November 1936. Accordingly, the untouchables got the right to enter any Hindu temple in the State of Travancore.

He was, however, against conversion of the untouchables to Christianity. Shri Ayyan Kali could save Hinduism from probable loss of its followers to Christianity.

Once Mahatma Gandhi, while on Kerala tour, came to meet him in January 1937 at Venganoor and asked him as to what he wanted. Shri Ayyan Kali replied that he did not want anything for himself but he wanted to see at least ten graduates from among the untouchables before he breathed his last. This shows his concern for the educational progress of the Scheduled Castes.

He married Chellamma. He had six sons and a daughter. He died on 18 June 1941 at the age of 78 years.

Babu Ramcharanji,[7] (1889-1935)

Rai Saheb Babu Ramcharanji was born in 1889 at Khalashi Lane, Kanpur in Uttar Pradesh. He belonged to Nishad caste. His mother took him to Lucknow at the age of seven and got him admitted in Mission School, Hasanganj, Lucknow in 1895. He passed his B.A. in 1912 and LL.B. in 1914 at Allahabad. He got employment in Railway Department in 1902; and in Audit office in 1908. He had to seek employment at an early age due to

---

7. Source of Information :
Swami Bodhanandji Mahasthveer, Mool Bharat Varshaur Arya, Lucknow, 1930.

poverty. However, he had an indomitable urge for education, and could complete his studies.

He started his legal practice at Lucknow and started taking part in the uplift of the Dalits. He joined Swaraj Party. He contested for the membership of Municipal Council, Lucknow in 1923, but could not get elected. He failed to get elected in 1926 also.

Shri Babu Ramcharanji was very much influenced by Swami Bodhanandji, a renowned Buddhist monk at Lucknow. Shri Babu Ramcharanji had faith in Buddhism.

In 1920, he founded the All India Nishad Maha Sabha and he was elected as its General Secretary. He started a paper *Nishad Samachar* in 1920.

In 1925, he joined the Adi-Hindu movement. He was elected President of Adi-Hindu Sabha in 1927. He believed that the Depressed Classes were the original inhabitants of India. They must be entitled to all the rights in their own Land.

He was nominated as member of Legislative Council of UP on 27 December 1927. He thought that the Depressed Classes should get certain facilities for their educational development. He proposed that at least 50 students at college level should get Rs 20 each every year; at least 300 students at secondary level should get Rs 10 each every year; at least 600 scholarships of RS one each should be instituted at the primary level education; minimum one Deputy Inspector and two supervisors in each district should be appointed to take care of education of the Depressed Classes and education ought to be open and free to all the students.

When the Simon Commission visited India, he gave evidence before the same on behalf of the Depressed Classes, on 6 December 1928.

He married at an early age. After the death of his first wife, he married Shivaratna Devi. He had three sons and two daughters.

He was honoured by the British Government by the title of Rai Saheb in the year 1927.

He died on 15 June 1935 at relatively young age of 46 years.

Baidwan, Teluram[8] (1914-1990)

Shri Teluram Baidwan was born on 14 January 1914, in Shimla, Himachal Pradesh. He belonged to Balmiki community. His parents were Shri Punnu Ram and Smt Pyaridevi. Shri Teluram was not well educated but could read and write English apart from Hindi.

He began his social work from 1930 onwards. He was General Secretary of the Balmiki Nawjawan Achhut Sabha, Shimla which awakened the Balmikis and other Scheduled Castes communities. He was elected General Secretary of the Balmikis Depressed Classes League.

He took part in the sweepers strike at Ludhiana in 1939. Shri Teluram Baidwan had joined the Scheduled Castes Federation in 1942 itself and became the President of District branch of Shimla. When Lord Wavell convened the conference of all the political parties at Shimla in the last week of June 1945, Shri Teluram Baidwan and his coworkers had organized a mammoth gathering of the Scheduled Castes at Shimla which was addressed by R.B.N. Shivaraj and Shri P.N. Rajbhoj, the President and Secretary respectively of the SCF.

In the year 1948 he led the strike of the sweepers in Shimla, which became very successful and effective. He found in Chanan Ram Kalyanpuri a selfless and active companion.

On 14 April 1961 he declared the conversion of Scheduled Castes Federation into Republican Party of India, (RPI) Shimla unit. He served as General Secretary of the Himachal Pradesh unit of the RPI. He followed and tried to spread the philosophy of Babasaheb Ambedkar in Himachal Pradesh.

In 1953, he became a member of Shimla Municipality. Later on, he contested on RPI ticket from Ambala Lok Sabha (R)

---

8. Source of Information :
Personal Interview with his son
Shri Ranbir Sinh Baidwan
at Block No. 5. House No. 8, Bamloe Estate, Shimla on 8.7.1992

constituency in 1957 and 1962, but could not get elected. He became General Secretary of RPI Himachal Pradesh in 1970 and its President in 1977. He continued to be so till his death.

He was a selfless dedicated social worker of the Scheduled Castes in Himachal Pradesh. He tried to spread the sociopolitical and religious philosophy of Dr Babasaheb Ambedkar for whom he had a high regard.

He married Krishna Devi and had two sons and two daughters. He breathed his last on 11 December 1990 at the age of 76. He was honoured posthumously by the Government of Himachal Pradesh on 14 April 1991 for his contribution to the uplift of the Scheduled Castes.

BALKRISHNAN, S.C.

Balkrishnan was born in 1909 at village Ayakudi, Palani taluka, Dist. Madurai in Tamil Nadu in a poor scheduled caste family. His father's name was Saliappuli Chinaa Karuppanam. Mr. Balkrishnan was educated at Municipal High School, Palani.

He joined Indian National Congress and participated in the national freedom movement. He was a member of Legislative Assembly of Madras from 1937 to 1939.

He was President of Madurai Dist. Depressed classes league. He was elected to the Lok Sabha in 1952 on congress ticket. He opened two Hostels for the poor boys and girls belonging to the schedule castes.

He wrote (1) "Harijans in Independent India", in Tamil and (2) "Lotus in Mire" a Tamil Drama.

He married Mariammal and they had two sons.

BALMIKI, KANHAIYALAL

Shri Kanhaiyalal Balmiki was born on 14 March 1919 at village Khanai in Baluchistan, now in Pakistan. He was a Balmiki. His father's name was Shri Chainta Ram. His family came to Bulandshahar in UP and settled there. Shri Kanhaiyalal passed his matriculation from DAV High School, Bulandshahar and Intermediate from Allahabad.

He joined the Congress in 1940. He actively participated in the Quit India Movement of 1942. When the police was in search of him, he went underground from August 1942 to May 1943. However, he was sentenced to imprisonment from 1943 to 1945. He became member of the DCC Bulandshahar in 1950.

He was active in Dalit liberation movement. He organized the sweepers in Bulandshahar. He was elected as President of the All India Mehtar Mazdoor Sangh in 1950. He became President of Delhi Provincial Municipal Workers Sangh in 1951. Later, he became General Secretary of All India Balmiki Maha Sabha. He tried to solve their problems and advised them to educate their children and maintain high moral and cultural standards.

He was very active in election politics also. He was elected member of the Provisional Parliament from 1950-52. In the first general elections held in 1952 he contested on Congress ticket for the Lok Sabha from Bulandshahar (G and SC) constituency and got elected. In 1957 also he got elected from the same Lok Sabha constituency. In 1962, he contested from Khurja (SC) Lok Sabha constituency and got elected. Again he contested in 1968, 1971 and 1980 from the same constituency, but could not get elected.

He married Ramavati Devi in 1941 and had a daughter. He had faith in Arya Samaj and strictly observed all the principles of Arya Samaj.

BANSOD, KISAN FAGUJI[9] (1879-1946)

Shri Kisan Faguji Bansod was born on 18 February 1879 at village Mohapa near Nagpur in Maharashtra. He belonged to Mahar caste. He passed normal school teachers training, but turned to social service.

In order to organize the Dalits and make them conscious of their rights, he founded one Sanmarg Bodhak Asprushya Samaj at Nagpur in 1901. The Samaj became popular throughout the

---

9. Source of Information :
Shyamrao Kisanji Bansaod, 'Pradeep'.
Usha Niwas, Siraspeth, Nagpur.

Vidarbha region. He tried to bring awareness to the people under the banner of this organization.

He wanted to spread education not only among the boys, but among the girls too. Therefore, he established one Chokhamela Girls School, at Pachpawali, Nagpur in the year 1907. He stood for equality, moral conduct and self-dependence. He tried to improve the overall condition of the untouchables.

He was against caste system, superstitions and myths. He was influenced by the philosophy of Brahmo Samaj. Therefore, he embraced Brahmo Samaj on 1 October 1909.

He could properly realize the importance of Press in making the people socially and politically conscious and organizing them under one banner. He started the journal *Nirashrit Hind Nagarik* in 1910; *Vital Vidhvansak* in 1913, *Majur Patrika* in 1918 and *Chokha Mela* during 1931-36. He started one press at Pachpawali, Nagpur in 1910. His wife Mrs Tulsibai Bansod shared the press work and helped him in bringing out the above said journals. He wrote many articles in the papers which were being published in those days in Maharashtra.

He was one of the two secretaries of the reception committee of the first All India Depressed Classes Conference held at Nagpur on 30-31 May and 1 June 1920. In this conference he spoke against the ill-treatment of the Dalits by the caste Hindus. He said very categorically that he was prepared to give his daughter in marriage to a Bhangi, and to accept a Brahmin girl for his son. Thus, he expressed his opinion on social assimilation. However, the caste Hindus became very furious at this statement and burnt his printing press.

He stood for national freedom. When the non-cooperation movement was started at the initiative of Mahatma Gandhi in 1920, he actively participated for its success in the then CP and Berar Province along with other Congress leaders.

He tried to organize the labourers and to express their grievances. In this respect Shri G.A. Gawai and G.M. Thaware came to his assistance.

Though he had good relations with Mahatma Gandhi, he was opposed to the name 'Harijan', given by the latter to the untouchables.

He was a keen student of literature written by the saints and social reformers. He wrote a book in Marathi named, *Shri Sant Chokhamela Charitra* in the year 1942. He wrote two plays, named *Chokhamela* and *Satyashodhak Jalsa.* He composed many poems, which aimed to inspire the Dalits to protest against traditionalism. He said very categorically that, "Mahars would not achieve salvation, unless they struggle" *(Maharashi Anti, Nahi Ladhanyavina Mukti)*.

He had a daughter and four sons. He worked ceaselessly throughout his life for the uplift of his brethren. He died of cancer at the age of 67, on 10 October 1946 at Nagpur.

BARMAN, UPENDRANATH

Shri Upendranath Barman was born on 1 December 1899 at Gopalpur district, Cooch Behar in West Bengal. He was a Rajbanshi. His father's name was Shri Biranarayan Barman. Shri Upendranath Barman passed his B.A. from Victoria College Cooch Behar and LL.B. from University Law College, Calcutta. He started his legal practice at Jalpaiguri.

He joined Indian National Congress and was an elected member of Bengal Legislative Assembly from 1937 to 1945. During this period, he was Minister from 1941-43. He was elected by the Bengal Legislative Assembly as a member of the Constituent Assembly. In the first general elections held in 1952, he contested from North Bengal (G and SC) Lok Sabha constituency and got elected. Again he contested from Cooch Behar (G and SC) Lok Sabha constituency in 1957 and got elected. Again, he contested in 1962 on Congress ticket from Cooch Behar (SC) Lok Sabha constituency, but he was defeated by FBL candidate Shri D.N. Karjee.

He conveyed his message of good wishes to the conference of the All India Depressed Classes held at the initiative of Babasaheb Ambedkar at Nagpur in 1942.

He made it clear in the Constituent Assembly that the Scheduled Castes should put their "legitimate claims before the Government, before the public and also before our august organization. If even after that, our legitimate claims and demands are not conceded, then it would be our duty to stand on our own leg and try our level best to get our just share."

Shri Barman was President of Dhupguri High School and Helapankhuri High School in Jalpaiguri district.

He had the unique honour of being included in the Indian Parliamentary delegation to the Commonwealth Conference held in London in October 1948.

He was a great thinker and writer. *He wrote History of Rajbanshi Community* and *History of Rajbanshi Literature.*

He married Kshirodebala Debi in 1926. He had two sons and four daughters.

BATHULA, SUMITRA DEVI[9(a)] (1918-1980)

Smt. B. Sumitra Devi was born on October 9, 1918 at Hyderabad, Telangana State. She passed matric and started taking part in Depressed Classes upliftment activities.

Smt Sumitra Devi was running a school and a hostel for the untouchable girls at Hyderabad.

Previously she was in the scheduled castes federation. However, she came out of the SCF and joined the Congress. She became secretary of Dalit Jatiya Sangh. She was active in the freedom movement also. She became successful in the election to the Secunderabad Municipality in 1951.

In the first general elections held in 1952. She contested as INC candidate from Huzurnagar (SC) constituency for the Hyderabad Legislative Assembly, but could not get elected.

Again she contested in 1957 on INC from Jubilee Hills (G + SC) Constituency for the Andhra Pradesh Legislative Assembly and got elected.

She got elected in 1962 from Hyderabad East (SC) Assembly Constituency, in 1967 from Medchal (SC) Assembly Constituency, in 1972 from Medchal (SC) Constituency and in 1978 from Ibrahim Pattanam (SC) Assembly Constituency. She was married to Deviprasad.

She died in December 1980 at the age of sixty two.

9(a). Source of Information

Our *struggle for Emancipation* (1955) by P.R. Venkatswamy. (Hyderabad).

BERUPAL, PANNALAL[10]

Shri Pannalal Berupal was born on 6 April 1913 at Ramdeo Pathshala, Bikaner in Rajasthan. He was a Meghwal. His father's name was Shri Modaram Berupal. Shri Pannalal Berupal had no formal education. He was a cultivator and petty businessman.

He was President of Meghwal Sudhar Sabha and Rajasthan Provincial Depressed Classes League. He was a member of Harijan Welfare Board in 1944. He worked for the abolition of *Jagirdari* and *Begar* or bonded labour. He used to compose songs with messages aimed at bringing social awareness among the Scheduled Castes.

He joined the Congress in 1940. He contested in 1952 for the Lok Sabha as the Congress candidate from Ganganagar-Jhunjhunu (G and SC) and got elected. He contested consistently in 1957 (Bikaner), 1962 (Ganganagar), 1967 (Ganganagar) and 1971 (Ganganagar) and got elected. He contested in 1977 from Bayana (SC) and in 1980 from Jalore (SC) for the Lok Sabha as an independent candidate, but could not get elected both the times.

He married Laxmi Devi. He is survived by an adopted son.

He wrote *Hindu Samaj Jin ko Achhoot Manta Hai, Kya Weh Achhoot Hain? Jati Pati aur Varna Vyavasta ka Rahasya; Harijan Pukar; Meghwal (Chamar) Jati ki Utpati aur Rasam Rivaj and Alakhiya Sampradaya.*

BHAGYA REDDY, M.V.[11] (1888 - 1939)

Shri Madari Bhagiah, renamed as Bhagya Reddy was born on 22 May 1888 in Hyderabad. He had not received any formal

---

10. Source of Information :
Who's who in Lok Sabha.

11. Source of Information :
Personal Interview with his son
Shri. M.B. Gautam, ex-MLA
Adi-Hindu Bhavan, Chadarghat Bridge, Hyderabad
on 23.11.1988
and other sources.

education, but he could read and write Telugu. He was a Mala by caste.

At first, he was in the domestic service of a Goanese businessman in Hyderabad. Later, he joined the Electricity Department as a wireman. Later, he was appointed as preacher in the Jeevanraksha Mandali of Lalji Meghji on a monthly salary of Rs 60, with a motor cycle for his conveyance.

After having seen the pitiable condition of his own untouchable brethren, he switched over to their uplift. At first he founded Jagan Mitra Mandali in 1906 to enlighten the illiterate masses through *Harikatha* performances and Bhajans. In the year 1912, he founded Manya Sangham which after a decade was given the name of Adi-Hindu Social Service League. Shri Bhagya Reddy was its President. The main object of the organization was to eradicate the evil habits that had crept into the society, such as drinking, sacrificing the animals, dedicating the girls to the deities, and performing child marriages.

In order to achieve these objectives he organized a band of 35 volunteers, named, Swastik Dal. His volunteer corps worked very hard and thereby earned both name and fame. He took over the Panchayat system of the community and saved them from litigation. He founded an organization called, Adi-Hindu Murali Nivaran Mandali to eradicate prostitution.

The Adi-Hindu Social Service League apart from its social reforms activities, made a commendable contribution to the spread of education among the untouchables. It started about 40 primary schools in Hyderabad for the untouchable students. However, due to paucity of funds those schools were handed over to the government. He constructed a hostel building for the students of the Adi- Hindu community with the generous help of some philanthropists.

Shri Bhagya Reddy was the pioneer of Adi-Hindu movement in Andhra. In 1917 he was invited to preside over the first Andhra-Panchama Conference at Vijayawada. In his presidential address Bhagya Reddy observed that the Depressed Classes were the original inhabitants of India and ought to be called Adi-Hindu instead of Panchama. Consequently, the conference adopted the name of Adi-Andhra Maha Jan Sabha. He was invited to preside over the Adi-Andhra conferences held successively at Masulipatnam in 1919, Eluru in 1925, Anantpur in 1925 and Nagpur in 1933. He participated in Adi-Hindu conferences held at Allahabad and Lucknow also.

He had no faith in Hinduism. He, however, believed in Brahmo Samaj. He was attracted towards the philosophy of Lord Buddha, as he preached liberty, equality and fraternity. He started celebrating Buddha Jayanti on every Vaishakh Poornima, since 1913.

He exhorted that the caste differences even among the Depressed Classes ought to be removed.

He supported Dr. Babasaheb Ambedkar who demanded separate electorate for the Depressed Classes.

He opened a printing press of his own and started a Telugu weekly *Adi-Hindu* in the year 1930.

He married Lakshmi Devi. He had one son, named M.B. Goutam, who is also a great leader of the Scheduled Castes in Andhra.

Shri Bhagya Reddy breathed his last on 18 February 1939 at the age of 51 only.

BHANDARE, R.D.[12] (1916-1988)

Shri Ramachandra Bhandare was born on 11 April 1916 at Vita, Satara district in Maharashtra. He was a Mahar by caste and his father's name was Shri Dhondiba Bhandare. Since his family shifted to Bombay, Shri Ramchandra Bhandare completed his primary education at North Varali Primary School, middle school education at Kolabavadi and high school education at Maharashtra High School, Bombay. He completed his B. A. from Elphinston College and M.A. and LL.B. from Bombay University.

Thereafter, he started his legal practice at Bombay; and simultaneously worked as Professor of Law. He was Secretary of Bombay Municipal Kamgar Sangh from 1942 to 1945, Vice-president of Bombay Textile Workers Union from 1952-1954.

---

12. Source of Information :
Dharma Iyoti, May 1973.

He was President of Nav-Bharat Mazdoor Maha Sabha from 1963-66.

He was President of Inferior Village Servants Union from 1949-1952 under the leadership of Babasaheb Ambedkar.

He joined the Scheduled Castes Federation from its inception itself. He was President of Bombay Pradesh SCF. When Mahatma Gandhi arrived at Bombay to reside at a Mehtar's house at Varali with a view to showing his brotherly attitude towards the untouchables, Shri R.D. Bhandare and his followers showed black flags to Gandhi and resented that 'show' of Mahatma Gandhi. This resulted in a fiery clash between the caste Hindus and the Scheduled Castes. During those riots Shri R.D. Bhandare stood very strongly with the Scheduled Castes. Hence, he became very popular leader of the Scheduled Castes in Bombay.

During 1945 to 1957 he was an elected member of Municipal Corporation, Bombay. He started one library at Varali in 1946, and Talim Sangh in almost all localities of Bombay. He was instrumental in starting Ambedkar birth anniversary celebration on large scale with all gaiety and enthusism. He started one weekly named *Nirdhar* on 14 April 1950. It continued for two years.

In the first general elections held in 1952 he contested on SCF for the Bombay Legislative Assembly from Naigaon-Wadala constituency, but he was defeated by Congress candidate Shri S.N. Shivatarkar, who was previously follower of Babasaheb Ambedkar. He, however, got elected on SCF for the Bombay Legislative Assembly in 1957. From 1960 to 1962 he got an opportunity of acting as leader of the opposition parties on the floor of Bombay Legislative Assembly.

In 1962 he contested on RPI ticket for Lok Sabha from Miraj (G) constituency, but could not get elected. Again, he contested Lok Sabha election in 1967 from Bombay Central (G) constituency as Congress candidate and got elected. In 1971 also he got elected to the Lok Sabha from the same constituency. He could not get elected in the elections held in 1977.

During 1973-1976 he got a unique opportunity of being appointed as Governor of Bihar and during 1976-1978 as Governor of Andhra Pradesh.

He was in the Scheduled Castes Federation from 1942 to 1957. He was one of the founder members of the Republican Party of India. However, due to differences and increasing dissensions in the party, he left RPI and joined Congress on 15 August 1966.

He was a staunch Ambedkarite. He worked under his leadership and earned a name. He converted to Buddhism at the initiative of Dr Babasaheb Ambedkar at Nagpur on 14 October 1956. He remained a staunch Buddhist and worked for the Buddhists. He convened a conference of Buddhists in 1968. He presented memorandum of demands to Prime Minister Indira Gandhi and urged her to treat the Scheduled Castes converted to Buddhism on a par with the Scheduled Castes.

His work on the floor of Bombay Legislature and Lok Sabha as well as his work as Governor and the leader of the Buddhists in India need a special study.

He married Shakuntala, daughter of a military man on 23 April 1939. He had three sons and one daughter.

He expired on 5 September 1988 at the age of 72.

BHATKAR, L.S.[13] (1901-1970)

Shri Laxmanrao Bhatkar was born in 1901 at Thugaon, Amravati district in Maharashtra. His father Shri Shravan Bhatkar was a hereditary village servant Mahar—at Thugaon. Shri Laxmanrao Bhatkar was educated up to the eighth class at the Depressed Classes Mission High School, Bombay, which was run by Maharshi V.R. Shinde.

Shri Laxmanrao Bhatkar started his career as a member of Satyashodhak Samaj under the leadership of Pandharinath Patil and Anand Swami, the leaders of non-Brahmin party, at Buldhana.

---

13. Source of Information :
Personal Interview with his son
Shri Ravindra Laxman Bhatkar
Ambedkar Nagar, Ward N0. 13
Chikhali : Dist. Buldhana (Maharashtra)
on 11.10.1988

He used to propagate the philosophy of non-Brahmin movement in the district of Buldhana through ballads and *jalasa*. He used to compose folk songs and write *Vag* or folk stories and would play them. They proved to be very effective.

He had very rightly thought that unless the untouchables were educated, they would not find salvation. They were, of course, unable to take education due to poverty. Therefore, he started Shri Chokhamela Hostel at Chikhali in the year 1921. At first there were only 15 inmates in the hostel started in a big hut at Chikhali in Buldhana. He used to beg for the inmates in the morning and then feed them. Shri G.A. Gavai and Kalicharan Nandagawali, both members of the CP and Berar Legislative Council had inspired, encouraged and helped him in running the hostel.

Shri Bhatkar was elected as Vice-president of Municipal Council, Chikhali in the year 1933. He contested in 1937 as a candidate of non-Brahmin party from Chikhali constituency and got elected.

Due to the downfall of the non-Brahmin movement from 1938 onwards, he was inclined towards the Congress. He joined the Congress in 1938 and was elected President of the Vidarbha Depressed Classes League in 1959 and continued to be in that post till his end.

In the year 1946, he contested on Congress ticket from Chikhali (R) assembly constituency, but he was defeated by Shri Raibhan Punaji Jadhav of SCF. However, Shri Bhatkar was elected by the Legislature of CP and Berar to the Constituent Assembly in 1946. In the first general elections held in 1952 he contested on Congress ticket from Buldhana - Akola (G and R) Lok Sabha constituency and got elected. Again he got elected from Akola Lok Sabha (R) constituency respectively in 1957 and 1962. Thus, he had the honour of being a member of the Lok Sabha for a period of 21 years. During his membership of Parliament, he participated many times in its discussions and worked on various committees.

He participated in many satyagrahas. He led the satyagraha at Lonar in Buldhana district for taking water at a common watering place. He participated in the Quit India Movement for which he was sentenced to imprisonment for one month.

He believed in Satyashodhak Samaj and Prarthana Samaj. He had no faith in idol worship. He was influenced by the thoughts of a social reformer and saint Shri Gadagebaba, who preached social equality and rationalism. He was against Brahmanism.

At first he believed in the utility of separate electorate for the Scheduled Castes. He was, however, inclined towards Gandhism after the downfall of non-Brahmin movement.

He married Jaibai in 1916. They had five sons and two daughters. He expired on 7 February 1970 at the age of 69 at Chikhali.

BHATKAR, P.N.[14] (1890-1962)

Shri Pandurang Bhatkar was born in 1890 at Keliveli in Akot, Akola district in Maharashtra. He was a Mahar by caste. His father Nandram Bhatkar was an agriculturist. He owned a good house in the village and ten acres of land. One of his brothers was in the military.

Shri Pandurang Bhatkar passed his matriculation from Government High School, Akola and Intermediate from Furguson College, Pune, in the year 1908. He was well conversant with Sanskrit and English apart from Marathi.

During his stay at Pune, he came into contact with Maharshi Vithal Ramji Shinde. When Shri V.R. Shinde started a hostel at Pachpawai, Nagpur, on behalf of the Depressed Classes Mission, for the Dalit students, in the year 1908, Shri P.N. Bhatkar was appointed to manage the affairs of the hostel.

He started Shri Chokhamela Boarding at Nagpur, probably in the year 1917. It was taken over by the Depressed Classes Association founded in 1928. Later on, it was handed over by Shri P.N. Bhatkar to Swastik Sikshan Sanstha, Nagpur on 29 March 1959.

---

14. Source of Information :
Personal Interview with his eldest daughter.
Mrs. Parvatibai Namdeo Ingle
Shyam Nagar, near Maltekdi, Amravati (Maharashtra)
on 19.10.1988

Dr Babasaheb Ambedkar started publishing *Mook Nayak* from 31 January 1920. While leaving for England for higher education on 5 July 1920, he asked P.N. Bhatkar to undertake the responsibility of publishing the *Mook Nayak* in his absence. However, the managing committee of the journal handed over its editorship to Shri D.D. Cholap in 1920 itself.

He was in favour of the separate electorate for the Depressed Classes. He was a staunch follower of Babasaheb Ambedkar. From the very beginning he was in favour of Buddhism. He embraced Buddhism along with his family members at Nagpur on 14 October 1956 itself.

He thought that inter-caste marriages were necessary for the eradication of caste. He advised Devdasis to get married.

He married Ambubai from whom he had one son and two daughters. However, again he married Venutai, a Brahmin widow residing in the Ashram run by V.R.Shinde.

He came to Amravati in 1934 and settled there permanently. He breathed his last on 24 May 1962 at the age of 72.

BHINGARDEVE, L.B.[15] (1908-1986)

Shri Lakshmanrao Bhingardeve was born on 25 January 1908 at Vita in Khanapur, Sangli district in Maharashtra. He belonged to Mang community. His father Shri Babaji Bhingardeve was engaged in sheep rearing. Shri Lakshmanrao Bhingardeve passed his B.A. in 1934 and LL.B. in 1939 from Bombay University. Thereafter, he started his legal practice at Sangli.

Shri L.B. Bhingardeve was very much influenced by Karmaveer Bhaurao Patil. He started his social uplift activities in 1932 at the age of 24. In those days it was necessary on the part of Mang, Ramoshi and some other castes to report every day their

---

15. Source of Information :
Personal Interview with his son
Shri Ravindra Lakshmanrao Bhingardeve
Village Vita, Taluka Khanapur,
Sangli district (Maharashtra)
on 29.7.1989

attendance at the nearest police station as they were suspected to be involved in criminal activities. This practice was unjust and oppressive. Therefore, Shri Bhingardeve raised his voice against it.

He tried to bring about reformation in the society. He asked the *Potraj* to abandon that ugly system. Due to his efforts the barbers started cutting the hair of the untouchables. He started to celebrate festivals such as Krishna Ashtami and Lahuji Vastad Punyatithi. He read Gita and *Dhammapada* with great devotion. He used to celebrate Buddha Jayanti. He advised his brethren to maintain cleanliness and high moral culture in the family. He started several hostels and schools in Sangli district.

He joined the Congress in his youth. He was a follower of Mahatma Gandhi. He supported the scheme of joint electorate with reserved seats for the untouchables. He took part in Quit-India Movement. He contested for the Bombay Legislative Assembly in 1946 as a Congress candidate from Karnala-Barsi (R) constituency and got elected. He contested in the first general elections held in 1952 from Khanapur assembly constituency and won. In the general elections held in 1957 he got elected to the Maharashtra Legislative Assembly. He contested in the general elections held in 1962 on Congress ticket from the Man assembly constituency and got elected.

In the year 1962, he founded one organization, named Bharatiya Dalit Vikas Sangh at Bombay. He was its President, Balasaheb Bharaskar and Dr Devram Kamble were its Vice-presidents and Shri R.B. Sarode was its Secretary. Its activities were spread in many parts of Maharashtra. The said Sangh started hostels at Pune, Udgir, Vita, Solapur and ran some technical institutes.

He founded a political party, named Bharatiya Majdoor Paksh, and submitted a memorandum of demands to the then Home Minister of India, Shri Y.B. Chavan, on 17 August 1968. The memorandum contained several demands for the amelioration of the economic condition of the Dalits for social and political justice and for abolition of forced labour.

He started *Dalit Samachar* from Pune in the year 1965. It was a weekly newspaper.

He devoted his remaining life to running various educational institutions and writing articles on various socio-political subjects in the papers and journals.

He had two sons and three daughters. He expired on 5 August 1986 at the age of 78.

BHOLE, R.R. [16] (1913-1993)

Shri Rajaram Bhole was born on 11 February 1913 at Bolaram near Hyderabad in Andhra Pradesh. He belonged to Mahar caste. His father's name was Shri Ramji Bhole. Shri Rajaram Bhole passed his matriculation from a high school at Secunderabad and B.Sc. from Furguson College, Pune. Later, he passed his LL.B.

Shri Rajaram Bhole happened to meet Babasaheb Ambedkar and to listen to his speech at Solapur. He was very much "overwhelmed" by the "instructions and advice" of Baba Saheb Ambedkar.

It was because of Babasaheb Ambedkar, that Shri Rajaram Bhole could get a scholarship from the Nizam Government to prosecute his engineering education, but owing to his long illness he could not complete it. Shri Rajaram Bhole was well acquainted with Mahatma Gandhi also. He got an opportunity to stay for a year in the Sewagram Ashram at Wardha.

After having seen the abominable condition of the Scheduled Castes in those days, Shri Rajaram Bhole decided to work for them. At first he organized a conference of Dalit youths at Pune in 1935 under the presidentship of Dr Babasaheb Ambedkar.

In the provincial assembly elections held in 1937, he contested for the Bombay Legislative Assembly from Pune (West) as a candidate of Independent Labour Party and got elected. He was a very active member of the Assembly.

---

16. Source of Information :
Personal Interview with Justice R.R. Bhole
411, Shalaka, Maharshi Karve Road, Bombay
on 30.6.1991,

In the first general elections held in 1952, he contested as SCF candidate from Kolhapur-Satara Double Member parliamentary constituency but he could not achieve success in the election.

Later on he joined the judiciary as a District Judge in the year 1955. He was appointed as one man commission by the Government of India in 1962 to report on the firing in Port Blair in Andaman Islands. His report was accepted by the government. He was the first Judge of the High Court of Bombay from among the Scheduled Castes. He retired from his post on 11 February 1975 at the age of 62.

He was appointed as the Chairman of the Commission for the revision of pay scales of the employees of the Maharashtra Goverment. The report of the Commission was accepted by the government.

He was appointed member of the famous Backward Classes Commission constituted under the chairmanship of Shri B.P. Mandal, on 20 December 1978. It submitted its report to the President of India on 31 December 1980.

In the Lok Sabha elections held in 1980 he contested from Bombay on Congress ticket and got elected.

He had rendered a very valuable contribution to the mission of Babasaheb Ambedkar and the educational development of the Dalits as a Member of the Governing Body of the Peoples Education Society, Bombay, founded by Babasaheb Ambedkar from 1945 itself. After the sad demise of Babasaheb Ambedkar, the founder and first Chairman of the People's Education Society, the mantle of chairmanship fell on the shoulders of Shri R.R. Bhole on 14 January 1957. In that crucial period, he gave very able leadership to the People's Education Society. He was elected as its Chairman for the next term in 1959 and that position he graced till 1962. Again he was elected as its Chairman in 1972 for the next term till 1974. Again he graced the same position for three consecutive terms from 1978 to 1985.

Shri Justice R.R. Bhole is survived by a son. Justice Bhole died on 24 August 1993. He has proved his exceptional capabilities as a leader of the Depressed Classes, as a legislator and parliamentarian, as a judge and as an educationist. He tried to accelerate the wheel of Buddhism as Chairman of the Buddhist Council of India.

BOHARE, KHEMCHAND[17] (1875-1960)

Shri Khemchand Bohare was born in 1875 at Namak ki Mandi, Shahganj, Agra in UP. His father's name was Shri Nannu Sinh Bohare. He was a well-to-do and respectable person of Jatav community. Shri Khemchand Bohare completed his education at Saint Jone's College, Agra in 1898. From 1900 to 1901 he worked as contractor in Great Indian Peninsula (GIP) Railway, between Bilaspur to Gondia and Nagpur section.

Shri Khemchand Bohare left his profession and came to Agra in 1910. After having seen the pitiable condition of the untouchables he started working for their uplift. He was one of the founder members of the Jatav Mahasabha which came into existence in 1912 at Agra. Under the said organization, he successfully fought for replacing disgraceful caste name 'Chamar' by 'Jatav'.

He was nominated as a member of the Municipality of Agra in 1918 and continued his membership till 1936. He was appointed to the District Board of Agra from 1922 to 1930. In the year 1922 he was nominated as a member of the Legislative Council (MLC) of UP. He continued as MLC till 1936.

Shri Khemchand Bohare proposed in the Council that one member of his community be appointed to each district Board in UP. The motion was admitted. He further proposed that one member of his community be nominated to every Municipal Board. The motion was passed. He gave testimony before the Simon Commission Electoral Committee in 1928.

He was elected Vice-president of All India Depressed Classes Association founded in 1925 under the presidentship of Shri M.C. Rajah (Madras).

In the provincial assembly elections held in 1937 he contested from Agra district constituency, but he was not elected. Dr Manak Chand Jatav of NAPA, his main rival, got elected in that contest.

---

17. Source of Information :
Sri. P.P. Shilankar
Press Reporter, Agra.

Shri Khemchand Bohare died on 14 January 1960 at the age of 85.

BOJJA APPALA SWAMY[17(a)] (1912-2005)

Bojja Appala Swamy was born on 19, August 1912 at Bojjavaripeta, on the outskirts of Kandikuppa village, Katrenikona Mandal, East Godavari District in Andhra Pradesh. His parents were Bojja Govindu and Venkamma. He belonged to Adi-Dravida, an untouchable community.

He studied at Maharaja's School at Pithapuram. He was influenced by the liberal thoughts and reformative measures adopted by benevolent Maharaja of Pithapuram, speeches of Ragupati Venkataratnam Naidu, Devulpally Krishna Shastri and other eminent social thinkers.

In such a liberal tradition also there prevailed acute untouchability. Even Bojja Appala Swamy also was asked by the caste Hindus to occupy a separate seat in a theatre, but by dint of courage and popular support from his brethren he did not succumb to the casteist threats.

Bojja Appala Swamy was deeply influenced and inspired by the philosophy of Dr.Babasaheb Ambedkar and his liberation movement spreading all over the country. He started forming Adi Andhra Associations and bringing a new awareness among the so called untouchables. He became active in the Ambedkar movement from 1940 onwards.

After the formation All India Scheduled Caste Federation by Dr.Babasaheb Ambedkar at Nagpur in 1942, Bojja Appala Swamy started working under its banner in the Godavari belt of Andhra Pradesh. Although the Brahmo Samaj movement as well as the communist movement were popular in that region, he could not get attracted towards them. He could not allow any other movement other than, Ambedkarite movement in the oppressed communities in that region. It was his real contribution to the Ambedkarite movement.

17(a). Source of Information

Dr. B.Vijaya Bharati, Daughter in Law of the Leader, Flat No. 304, Mehta Towers, Ashok Nagar, Hyderabad.

In the first General Elections held in 1952, he contested for Madras Legislative Assembly from Amalapuram double member constituency, as SCF candidate and got elected. After the formation of separate Andhra State in 1953 he again contested and got elected from Amalapuram (SC) Constituency. Later in 1955 he contested from Allavaram Constituency and got elected.

He organized the movement for land less agriculturists and acquired the uncultivated land for them. Therefore, the men in society and in Government were suspecting of his veracity as an Ambedkarite, but he proved, beyond any doubt, to be an Ambedkarite.

He married Mavulamma and had two sons and a daughter. People called him. Adi Andhra Ratna'with love and veneration.

He breathed his last on 19 August 2005 at the age of 93 years.

BUTTI RAJARAM[18] (1911-1975)

Shri Butti Rajaram was born 2 May 1911 at Karimnagar in Andhra Pradesh. His father's name was Butti Ramayya. Shri Butti Rajaram was illiterate and belonged to Mala Caste. For some time he served in Nizam's constabulary as a sepoy at Karimnagar. He left his job and became a fruit contractor.

He registered his protest against traditional Hinduism by accepting Arya Samaj. Pandit Prem Kumar and his other relatives at Hyderabad, who were Arya Samajis, successfully influenced him to accept Arya Samaj and work for the uplift of the Depressed Classes from the drudgery of untouchability, which was quite severe in the feudal State of Nizam of Hyderabad. Shri B. Rajaram started his social service from 1930

---

18. Source of Information :
Personal Interview with his grandson
Shri B. Vinod Kumar
(Salestax Officer)
5-2-132, Fattepura Colony, Karimnagar, AP
on 20.11.1988.

onwards through Arya Samaj. He started educating the people in vegetarianism, temperance and cleanliness. He purchased some land and donated it to the weaker sections for housing purposes. He came to the help of the people in representing their grievances to the local authorities for their redressal.

He joined the Scheduled Caste Federation. He arranged a public meeting at Karimnagar which was addressed, among others, by J.H. Subbiah in the year 1946. He arranged another public meeting on 18 November 1948 at Karimnagar under the presidentship of Shri K.R. Veeraswamy, the Organizing Secretary of Scheduled Caste Federation. He arranged several meetings in Karimnagar district for awakening the people.

In the first general elections held in 1952, Shri Butti Rajaram contested on SCF ticket for the Hyderabad Legislative Assembly seat from Jagtial (R) constituency and got elected.

In those days the SCF became very weak in Hyderabad. Hence he joined Congress. He contested for the Assembly as a Congress candidate from Sultanabad (R) constituency in 1957 and got elected. Again, he contested in 1962 from Peddapally (R) constituency, and in 1967 from Nusthulapur (R) constituency and got elected. Thus from 1952 to 1972 for a period of 20 years Shri Butti Rajaram represented the community in the Assembly.

He married Lakshmma. He had four sons and four daughters. He died on 11 April 1975 at Karimnagar at the age of 64 years.

CHAKOLA DEIVATHAN[19] (1880-1927)

Shri Chakola Deivathan was born on 26 January 1880 at Aranmula in Pattanamthitta district in Kerala. His father Shri

---

19. Source of Information :
Interview with his nephew
Shri Krishnan (Retd. Teacher)
Vanchiyoor, Trivandrum
on 22.4.1991

Kurumban and mother Smt Adegi were serfs in the service of a landlord. He belonged to the Pulaya caste. Due to untouchability, he was not admitted in any school.

However, an astrologer taught him secretly. His teacher was severely beaten by the caste Hindus for his offence of educating an untouchable.

Shri Chakola Deivathan was greatly influenced by Shri Mulur Padmanabha Panicker, a revolutionary Ezhava poet, and Shri Ayyan Kali, a pioneer of Dalit movement in Kerala. Shri Deivathan became Joint Secretary of Sadhu Jana Paripalan Yogam, founded by Shri Ayyan Kali.

Shri Deivathan was a revolutionary poet. He used to sing his revolutionary songs before the audience and they had a great impact on them. He exhorted his brethren to educate their children and get rid of serfdom of the landlords. He taught them the martial arts and to successfully combat the orthodox caste Hindus whenever they prevented the untouchables from exercising civil rights. He taught them to remain organized.

After having taken into account his active participation in public life and his revolutionary spirit the Maharaja of Travancore nominated him as a member of Sri Mulam Popular Assembly in the year 1917. He was consecutively nominated to the Popular Assembly till 1927. He supported the demands made by Shri Ayyan Kali for the uplift of the Depressed Classes.

Shri Deivathan married Deivatal. He had two daughters and one son.

Shri Chakola Deivathan died on 18 April 1927 at the age of 47.

CHANDORKAR, R.B.[20] (1901-1968)

Shri Ramchandra Chandorkar was born on 3 October 1901 in Pune. His father Shri Baloji Chandorkar belonged to village

---

20. Source of Information :
B.S. Hate, *Jith Pani Petala,*
Bombay, 1977

Chandor, Goregaon in Raigad district of Maharastra. Shri Baloji Chandorkar, a Chambhar by caste, was in 117th Maratha Light Infantry as a Jamadar.

Shri Ramachandra Chandorkar came to Bombay with his mother as his father had expired at Pune. His mother Smt Tulsabai R. Chandorkar got employed as a teacher in the Corporation's School, at Bombay. Shri R.B. Chandorkar completed his education up to matriculation. Thereafter, he devoted himself to the uplift of the Dalits.

He was a staunch follower of Dr Babasaheb Ambedkar. He along with his companions like R.S. Wanmali, Babaji Wanmali, K.G. Shiradkar and Keshav Chandorkar undertook an extensive tour to Pune, Nasik, Thane, Kulaba, Ratnagiri and other places for propagating the philosophy of Dr Babasaheb Ambedkar. It had greatly influenced the masses in deciding their course of action in their social life.

Shri R.B. Chandorkar took an active part in the Choudar Tank satyagraha at Mahad in the year 1927. He offered satyagraha, along with his brethren at the water tank at Goregaon. He took part in the Kalaram Temple Entry Satyagraha at Nasik in the year 1930.

In order to organize his brethren, he founded an organization, named, Rohidas Dnyanodaya Samaj in the year 1923. However, due to differences among its members, it had to be closed. Subsequently, he founded Rohidas Sudharak Mandal in the year 1933. The main objective of these two organizations was to bring about a new sociopolitical awareness among the untouchables and to unite them under one platform.

Shri Chandorkar was a staunch supporter of the demand for separate electorate for the Scheduled Castes made by Dr Babasaheb Ambedkar in the Round Table Conference. During those days he sent a telegram to the Prime Minister at London conveying his support to Dr Babasaheb Ambedkar.

Shri Chandorkar died on 10 September 1968 at the age of 67 after serving the society for a period of 37 years. Due to his dedicated service to the Depressed Classes throughout his life, the Bombay Municipal Corporation renamed a road in Bhaikhala area after him.

CHAVDA, KHEMCHANDBHAI SOMABHAI[21]

Shri Khemchandbhai Chavda was born on 4 October 1919, at Dhinoj in Chanasma, Mehsana district in Gujarat. He passed his B.Sc. from Baroda College, Ahmedabad.

He was the President of Mehsana Prant Hari Harijan Yuvak Mandal from 1947-51. He was Vice-president of Harijan Kalyan Sangh Trust, Ahmedabad since 1964. He was elected to the Bombay Legislative Assembly in the first general elections held in 1952. He was a member of Rajya Sabha from August 1960 to 9 March 1971. In the year 1971 he was elected to the Lok Sabha as a candidate of Congress (O) from Patan (SC) constituency. Again he was elected in 1977 as a candidate of Bharatiya Lok Dal from the same Lok Sabha constituency.

Later, he joined Janata Party and contested from the same Lok Sabha constituency in 1980 and 1984. but could not get elected both the times.

He started a fortnightly named *Tankar* in 1952 and it continued up to 1957. Throughout he had special interest in amelioration of the Scheduled Castes and the weaker sections of the society.

He attended the conference of the World Assembly for Peace held in Helsinki in the year 1955 and travelled in many foreign countries.

He married Smt Hiraben in 1946 and had four sons and three daughters.

CHIKKALINGAIAH, M.[22] (1901-1966)

Shri Malavalli Chikkalingaiah was born in 1901 at Malivalli district, Mandiya in Karnataka State. He was an Adi-Karnataka

---

21. Source of Information :
Lok Sabha
Who;s Who : 1971

22. Source of Information :
Personal Interview with his nephew
Shri M.C. Narasinhmurthy
8/II DFRL Qts. Mysore
on 4.6.1989

by caste. His father Dodda Lingaiah was a small farmer at village Malivalli. His family name was Tippayan Kathe. Shri M. Chikkalingaiah had passed his B.A. from Maharaja's College Mysore in 1930. He, being the first graduate among the Scheduled Castes in erstwhile Mysore State, the Maharaja honoured him.

He was appointed as District Special Officer for the Scheduled Castes by the Maharaja of Mysore in 1932. He resigned his post in 1951. In those days the untouchables of Malavalli were not allowed to fetch drinking-water from the local water tank. Once in 1934, there arose a scuffle between the untouchables and the caste Hindus when the former were not allowed by the latter to take water. Then Shri M. Chikkalingaiah took the issue to the Diwan of Mysore, who asked the IGP, Bangalore to take immediate action against the offenders. Thereupon, the caste Hindu culprits were arrested by the police who remanded them. The drinking-water tank *(Kunneru Katie)* in question was thrown open to all the communities.

He started one hostel for girls and another one for the boys belonging to the untouchable communities at Malavalli. He entered the temple of a goddess in Malavalli along with his followers. The caste Hindus opposed him, but he could enter the temple with the help of the police.

Shri Chikkalingaiah contested in the first general elections held in 1952 as a SCF candidate from Malavalli assembly constituency (R) and got elected. Again, he contested from the same constituency on SCF ticket in the general elections held in 1957, but he was not elected. In 1962, he contested from Kirugavalu (R) assembly constituency on PSP ticket, but could not get elected.

Shri Chikkalingaiah married Chikkamadamma in 1932, but they had no issue. He died in 1966 at the age of 65.

CHOUDHARY, JAGLAL[23] (1895-1975)

Shri Jaglal Choudhary was born in 1895 at village Garkha,

---

23. Source of Information :
S.P. Sen (ed.) Dictionary of National Biography, Vol. I (1972) Institute of Historical Studies, Calcutta.

Saran district in Bihar. He belonged to the Pasi caste. His father Shri Mushan Choudhary was a toddy- seller.

After passing the lower primary examination in 1903, he was admitted to the Chapra Zilla School and passed the matriculation in first division in 1912. He passed his Intermediate (Science) examination in 1914 from Patna College. Thereafter, he was admitted to Medical College, Calcutta. However, he left; his education and joined the Non-cooperation Movement in 1921 at the call of Mahatma Gandhi. Soon, he became a member of the District Congress Committee, Saran. During the Salt Satyagraha he courted arrest. He was equally interested in the movement of Dalit liberation.

In the provincial elections held in 1937 he was elected on Congress ticket to the Bihar Legislative Assembly. Soon he became the Minister for Public Health and Excise. Taking into account the adverse effects of liquor in general and on the Depressed Classes in particular, he introduced prohibition in the districts of Saran, Ranchi, Muzaffurpur, Haribagh and Dhanbad.

In November 1941, he was arrested and sentenced to imprisonment for offering individual satyagraha. During the Quit India Movement 1942, he led a satyagraha and captured the post office and police station at Garkha. He was arrested on 23 August 1942 and sentenced to five years' imprisonment. During this movement one of his sons was shot dead by the British force. On 30 March 1946 he was released from jail.

In the elections held in 1946, he was elected to the Bihar Legislative Assembly. Soon he became Minister for Public Health and Harijan Welfare in the second Congress ministry formed in the Province in 1946.

In the first general elections held in 1952, he got elected to the Bihar Legislative Assembly. He contested with success in 1957, 1962, 1967 and 1969 elections to the Bihar Legislative Assembly (Garkha SC).

In 1953, he wrote a book entitled *A Plan to Reconstruct Bharat.* He stood for equal rights and opportunities for men and women of all classes. He thought that the caste system was "the greatest curse of the Hindu society". He was of the view that each family of five or six members should possess only three acres of land, with no right to sell them. He was a strong protagonist of prohibition and sanitation. He did not believe in the sacred thread.

He married Jageshwari Devi and had three sons and three daughters.

He breathed his last in 1975.

CHOUDHARI, JAIBAI [24] (1892-1964)

Mrs Jaibai Choudhari was a great educationalist and social worker among the Mahars. She was born on 2 May 1892 at Umrer, near Nagpur. Due to the havoc played by the famine of 1896, her parents came to Nagpur in search of labour. There she could complete her primary education. She was married to Bapuji Choudhari of Nagpur in 1901 at a very tender age. Due to acute poverty she had to work as a coolie carrying luggage on her head from Nagpur to Kamptee, a distance of ten miles. She came in contact with Miss Gragory, a Christian missionary, by whose good offices she got teacher's job at Mission School, Timki, Nagpur. She was to get ₹ 4 only per month. However, the caste Hindu students boycotted the school as their parents could not tolerate an untouchable lady teacher teaching their kids. Therefore, she had to leave the service. Consequently, she firmly decided to fight against untouchability and the caste system. She thought that education could be used as a means to achieve that end. She had firmly decided to spread education among the untouchable girls and awaken the women. With this determination she opened a school for the untouchable girls, named Sant Chokhomela Girls School at New Colony (Mangalwari Bazar), Nagpur, in the year 1922. She fully dedicated her time and energy to the development of the school. From 1922-1954 it was a primary school, from 1954 to 1980 it became a secondary school and now it is a full-fledged intermediate college.

---

24. Source of Information :
Personal Interview with her grandson
Shri Sudhakar Shravan Choudhary
(Principal, Jaibai Choudhary JR. College)
Raj Nagar Plot 3, Katol Road, Nagpur
on 22.10.1988

She was devoted to the overall uplift of the untouchables. She was a secretary of the reception committee of the first Dalit women conference held at Nagpur on 8-9 August 1930.

She was moving from place to place for educating the untouchable women and motivating them to adopt new lifestyles, cleanliness and rationalism.

Jaibai Choudhari was a member of the reception committee of the All India Depressed Classes Womens' Conference, held at Nagpur in the year 1942. The conference was addressed, among others, by Dr Babasaheb Ambedkar.

She was a member of the Scheduled Castes Federation. She participated in the satyagraha for political rights in 1946 at Nagpur. She converted to Buddhism in 1956.

She led a happy married life. She had two sons and one daughter. She died on 11 October 1964 at the age of 72.

CHOUDHARY, MULKIRAM[25] (1910–1954)

Shri Mulkiram was born on 11 April 1910 at village Bhatiyana in Hapud, Meerut district in Uttar Pradesh. His father's name was Choudhari Dansahay. Shri Mulkiram completed his primary education at his native place, high school education at Hapud and college education at Meerut. He was appointed as Superintendent in the Department of Rural Development in the year 1936. In 1939, he passed his PSC examination conducted by UP Government and soon on 1 November 1940 he was appointed as Deputy Collector at Hardoi. For some time he served as Director of Social Welfare, Department of the UP Government.

Choudhari Mulkiram got the unique honour of being appointed to a high post, but he was always concerned with the welfare of his brethren. As a protest against orthodox Hinduism, he accepted Arya Samaj and observed almost all the practices of

---

25. Source of Information :
Personal Interview with his son-in-law
Shri R.D. Sonkar, IAS
Chief Administrator, Dr. Bhimarao Raniji, Ambedkar University Project, Lucknow, UP on 12.6.1991

Arya Samaj very strictly. He was a staunch nationalist. He used to show full sympathy to the leaders of national movement whenever they were arrested and presented before him for legal action against them.

He came in contact with Shri Krishna Datt Paliwal, a well-known leader of Agra. Shri Choudhari Mulkiram proved to be a good friend and guide of several educated and uneducated Dalits. He gave encouragement and inspiration to his brethren to shake off their 'untouchable' status and struggle to achieve their moral and material progress.

Shri Mulkiram was a poet and philosopher. He stated very rightly that the Indian society is very much caste-ridden. He thought that they should come out of it. He was of the view that no one ought to tolerate injustice at any cost. He exhorted his brethren to educate their children and revolt against injustice. He wanted to reconstruct human society on the values of liberty, equality and fraternity. His poetry reveals his love for humanity and human values.

He married Smt Nathodevi and had two daughters and one son. He died on 21 August 1954 at the age of 44 only. An anthology of his poems, *Hridayodgar,* has been published posthumously.

CHOUDHARI, NANDLALJI (1862-1941)

Shri Babu Nandlalji Choudhari was born in March 1862 at Allahabad in Uttar Pradesh. He belonged to Jaiswar (Chamar) caste. His father's name was Shri Gopal Lal. He passed his matriculation from Government High School, Allahabad. He was employed in the meteorological observatory.

After having seen the adverse effects of untouchability and casteism on his community, he decided to try to fight against untouchability. He used to advise his brethren to maintain high moral and cultural standards and send their children to schools. He had faith in saints and Sant Ravidas especially was his spiritual preceptor. He used to propagate the tenets of saints whenever he could find time.

Later, he became a staunch propounder of the Adi-Hindu movement. He laid the foundation of Adi-Hindu movement in Allahabad and UP along with Swami Achhutanandji.

He became Choudhari of his community and gave judgement and settled the disputes between the parties of his community. He was very much respected in the society.

He wrote *Panch Bhasha* a book containing decisions of the *Panch* or judges given in a number of disputes. He had fascination for poetry. He himself was a poet. He composed *Radhika Virah Aur Udho-Upadesh* a book containing his poems.

He died on 16 September 1941 at the age of 79.

CHOUDHARY, SADHU RAM[26] (1909–1975)

Shri Sadhu Ram Choudhary was born in January 1909 at village Domeli, Kapurthala district in Punjab. His father's name was Shri Jawahar Mal. Shri Sadhu Ram was educated at Khalsa High School, Domeli in the same district. He belonged to Chamar caste.

He was a businessman, but he took active interest in the uplift of his brethren. He joined Ad Dharm movement founded by Shri Mangoo Ram. However, later on there arose a rift in Ad Dharm movement in 1930. Shri Sadhu Ram led one group and Shri Mangoo Ram led another group. Shri Sadhu Ram formed his faction of Ad Dharm, known as All India Ad Dharm Mandal, with Lyallpur as its headquarters. Shri Vasant Singh was its President and Shri Sadhu Ram was its Secretary. The Sadhu Ram faction, however, survived only for three years. Later Shri Sadhu Ram joined the movement led by Dr Babasaheb Ambedkar. He joined the Scheduled Castes Federation in 1942 itself and became President of its princely state unit of Punjab.

In 1946, he joined the Congress. He joined Depressed Classes League and became its convenor for the PEPSU State in 1954. In the first general elections held in 1952 he contested on behalf of Congress from Phagwara (G and SC) constituency for the PEPSU Legislative Assembly and got elected. He became Deputy

---

26. Source of Information
Who's who In Lok Sabha and other sources

Minister for Home Affairs of the PEPSU. In the second general elections held in 1957 he got elected in Lok Sabha from Jullunder (G and SC) constituency. He got elected in 1962, 1967 and 1971 for the Lok Sabha from Phillaur (R) constituency. He was a member of the Committee on Welfare of the Scheduled Castes and Scheduled Tribes during 1968-70. He was a member of many other committees also.

He married Smt Rao Kaur in 1927 and they had four sons and two daughters. He expired on 1 August 1975 at the age of 66.

CHOUHAN, VASANTLAL[26(a)]

Shri Vasantlal Chouhan was born on October 21, 1921 at village Bhanav, taluka Siddhapur, Dist. : Mehsana in a Rohit Chamar family in Gujarat. His father Shri Tulsibhai Chouhan was a Mill Worker at Siddhapur. Shri Vasantlal Chouhan could complete only primary education.

His economic condition compelled him to work in the mill at Siddhapur at the age of twelve. His family shifted to Ahmedabad in 1935. Though, Ahmedabad was mainly industrialized place, untouchability and casteism was prevailing there to a great extent.

Shri Chouhan concentrated on the physical development of the Dalits. He thought that the Dalits should be physically strong and well organized to face the probable attacks of the high castes. Therefore, he started one Sarvajanik Vyayamshala (Public Gymnasium) at Hirpur, Ahmedabad in the year 1935. He established Vyayamshalas at many places in Ahmedabad, where the Dalits were getting physical training as well as social discourses.

At first he joined the scheduled castes federation, in 1943 under the leadership of V.T.Parmar. He left the SCF in 1948 and joined the S.S.P. under the leadership of Ram Manohar Lohia.

26(a) Source of Information—

Personal Interview with his Son Jayantibhai Vasantlal Chouhan, 235, Govt. Colony, Sukhram Nagar, Gomtipur, Ahmedabad on 6-11-1989.

Further, he joined the Communist Party under the leadership of Indulal Yadnik, in the year 1963.

He participated in the quit India movement in 1942. He used to inspire the youths who were taking physical training in his Vyayamshala, to take part in the quit India movement. Therefore, he was arrested by the Police in the Gomatipur area of Ahmedabad.

He took part in the temple entry Satyagraha at the Swaminarayana Temple, Ahmedabad, on January 14, 1948, under the leadership of Muldas Bhudardas Vaishya.

He participated in the Satyagraha of the landless peasants in 1964, under the leadership of Karsandas Parmar (the R.P.I. Leader in Gujrat) and Indulal Yadnik (the Communist Leader). Therefore, he was arrested on December 29, 1964. He was released from the jail on September 27, 1965.

He wrote three plays : "Doshit Kaun", "Panchayat Koni" and "Sudharonke Kudharo" in Gujarati.

In view of his social work he was honoured with a memento and an amount of Rs.Twenty Five Thousand on October 22, 1989, by the 'Vasantlal Chouhan Sanman Samiti.'

He married Kankuben. They had four sons.

DANI SHANTABAI[27] (1918–2002)

Shrimati Shantabai Dani was born on 1 January, 1918 at Nasik in Maharashtra. Her father Shri Dhanaji Dani of the Mahar caste was a poor milkman and used to sing devotional songs. Smt Shantabai Dani passed her matric from Pune and teachers' training from Nasik.

She was appointed as a teacher at Vinchur in Nasik district, but she left her job for social work. In 1942 she listened to the speech of Babasaheb Ambedkar and met him along with Shri B.K. Gaikwad. She joined the Scheduled Castes Federation in 1942 itself. She was elected as President of SCF Nasik district unit in 1943. She participated in the second conference of SCF at

27. Source of information:

Personal Interview with Smt Shantabai Dani, Purandare Colony, Nasik on 2.5.1989

Kanpur in 1945. She got the unique honour of presiding over the SCF Women's conference at the same time.

In 1946, she contested for Bombay Legislative Assembly from Niphad constituency, but could not get elected. After that, she participated in the satyagraha launched by the SCF, at Pune in 1946. In 1947 she went to Raipur along with Shri P.N. Rajbhoj to bring about new consciousness among the Satnami untouchables. However, they were misunderstood as the agents of Nizam and imprisoned in Jabalpur jail for a period of three weeks.

She contested for Bombay Legislative Assembly on SCF ticket in 1952 from Sinnar-Niphad constituency, but could not get elected. She was defeated by Congress candidate Amritrao Dhondiba Rankhamble, who was previously a lieutenant of Babasaheb Ambedkar.

In 1962, she contested from Malegaon (G) Lok Sabha constituency as RPI candidate, but could not get elected. During 1968-1974 she was a nominated member of Maharashtra Legislative Council. She contested for the Lok Sabha in 1980 from Nasik, but could not get elected.

She was one of the founding members of the RPI at Nagpur. She was working with B.K. alias Dadasaheb Gaikwad till 1971, then she joined Shri R.S. Gawai's faction. She took part in the landless peoples' satyagraha in 1959 and 1964.

She thought that the spread of education was a must for the development of the untouchable society. Therefore, in 1959, she started Takshashila Vidyalaya and Goutam Chhatralaya at Nasik. She started Ramabai Ambedkar Girls School at Nasik in 1965. These educational institutions are being run in good condition.

She remained a spinster and dedicated herself fully to the cause of Dalit liberation movement. She converted to Buddhism in 1956, itself and since then she has been propagating Buddhism in Maharashtra.

She has got utmost cooperation from Miss Londhe, Geetabai B. Gaikwad, Dadasaheb Roham and Shri Lalingkar.

She breathed her last on, 9 August 2002.

DAS. BELI RAM[27(a)] (1908-1969)

Beli Ram Das was born in October 1908 in Barpeta in Assam. He belonged to a poor untouchable community.

Having seen the pitiable social and economic condition of his brethren, he started their liberation movement.

He was elected to The Provincial Assembly of Assam in the year, 1937. After independence, he contested for the Lok Sabha seat from Barpeta unreserved Constituency in the general elections held in 1952 on congress ticket. He contested for the Assam Legislative Assembly in 1966 on Congress ticket from Marigaon S.C. Reserved seat and got elected.

In his student life he received Gandhi Scholarship instituted by Harijan Sevak Sangh.

He was active in social and political life of Assam till his death on 14 January 1969.

DAS, MOHINI MOHAN[28] (1886-1949)

Shri Mohini Mohan Das was born on 14 August 1886 at Chandsi district Barisal (now in Bangladesh). He was a Namashudra. His father Shri Padma Lochan Das was a medical practitioner. Shri Mohini Mohan Das was educated up to matric at Goila School, Barisal.

He started his social activities from 1910. He preached against beef-eating, superstitions, idol worship, child marriage, untouchability and casteism.

[27(a)] Source of Information :
1. History of the Harijan Sevak Sangh, P. 144
Harijan Sevak Sangh, Kings Way Delhi. (1971)
2. RC SC ST 1953 P.107.
Govt. of India, New Delhi .

[28]..Source of Information:
Personal interview with his son
Shri Amiya Bhushan Das 2C Flat Regent
Tower. 121/1 N.S.C. Bose Road Calcutta on 27.10.1988

He led the Temple Entry Satyagraha at Kali temple in Dhaka in the year 1930. He was arrested along with his wife and other colleagues and was later on released.

He was a lover of classical music. In order to develop classical music in the society in general and the Depressed Classes in particular he started one school at Barisal.

He joined the Congress under the leadership of Chittaranjan Das. Later on he joined the Swaraj party founded by Shri Chittaranjan Das in 1923. He was elected member of Bengal Legislative Assembly from 1922 to 1929.

He was a writer. He wrote a book in Bengali, named *Pashan Putra* and a book of poems, named *Pathayar.*

In order to bring a new socio-political awareness among the untouchables, he started a monthly *Sadhak* in 1923. It was in continuation till 1929. He wrote many articles in *Amrit Bazar Patrika* and *Bongwani.*

He thought that a separate electorate system would be beneficial to the untouchables.

He married Sutrishna in 1909 and after her death in 1923 he married Sonomani. He had two sons and two daughters. He died on 27 October 1949 at the age of 63 at Calcutta.

DAS, NAYANTARA

Shri Nayantara Das was born on 1 January 1915 at Purani Gunj, Monghyr in Bihar. His father Shri Sonu Ram was an agricultural labourer. Shri Nayantara Das was educated up to matric at Ripon Collegiate School, Howrah.

Shri Nayantara Das was member of the District Working Committee of the Depressed Classes League, Monghyr from 1939-1951. He became President of Rajak Sangh Monghyr district from 1945-1950. He was elected General Secretary of Bihar Prantiya Rajak Sangh from 1947-51.

He was elected to the Lok Sabha in 1952, 1957 and in 1962 from Monghyr (SC) constituency and in 1967 from Jamui (SC) constituency on the Congress ticket. He, however, could not succeed in the general elections held in 1971 and 1977. He married Sharada Devi in 1940 and they got four sons and three daughters.

DAS, PATITPAWAN[29] (1901-1942)

Shri Patitpawan Das was born in 1901 at Tigaon, Wardha district. His real name was Keshav Narayan Deo. He belonged to the Mahar caste. He was influenced by the philosophy of Satya Shodhak Samaj founded by Mahatma Phule and the Depressed Classes Mission founded by Maharshi Shinde. Initially, he aimed to uplift the Dalits through these organizations. However, he led a saintly life and also tried to bring salvation to the Dalits by spiritualism. He tried to instil awareness among the people through the *Bhajans* and *Kirtans* (devotional songs). He used to compose such songs for awakening his brethren.

When he came to know that Dr Babasaheb Ambedkar planned to insist upon his right to civil equality at Mahad on 20 March 1927, he went there to participate in the satyagraha. He was of the view that Hinduism should adopt certain reformative measures for its survival.

In order to motivate the saints belonging to the untouchables to work for the uplift of their brethren, he convened a meeting of the Dalit Sadhus at Shri Kshetra Ramtek on 10 April 1927. In the meeting one Bharat Sant Samaj was founded.

He participated in the Kalaram Temple Entry Satyagraha at Nasik on 30 March 1930. He was Chairman of the Satyagraha Committee. The said satyagraha was in vogue intermittently for near about five years and ultimately it culminated into the declaration of conversion to another religion by Babasaheb Ambedkar. Shri Patitpawan Das also favoured this idea. He held a number of meetings to support the conversion movement.

He participated in the Depressed Classes conference held under the presidentship of Muniswamy Pillai (Madras) at Nagpur on 7-8 May 1932.

In 1935, he went to Lucknow to preside over the conference of the Dalits. He pointed out various defects in Hinduism in his

---

29. Source of Information: :
H.L. Kosare, *Vidharbhatil Dalit Chalvalicha Itilhas,* Nagpur (1984).

presidential address and appealed to the Dalits to stand by Dr Babasaheb Ambedkar.

On 29 December 1935 he was elected as President of CP and Berar Depressed Classes conference held at Amravati. The conference passed a resolution in support of the conversion proposal.

In the public meeting held at Kamathi near Nagpur under his presidentship, the Hindu scriptures and idols were publicly burnt to express their symbolic protest against Hinduism.

In a meeting at Tiroda (Bhandara district) held on 22 October 1936, under his presidentship a resolution was passed to support the conversion proposal made by Babasaheb Ambedkar.

In order to awaken the Dalit masses, he started a weekly, named *Patit Pawan* on 5 September 1936 from Nagpur. It continued for a period of two years. He was editor of *Patit Pawan* for one year and thereafter Shri K.S. Shambharkar became its editor

In the year 1937, he contested from the CP and Berar Legislative Assembly from Hinganghat (Wardha district) constituency as a nominee of the Independent Labour Party, but he was defeated.

He died in 1942 at the age of 41.

DAS, SANTANU KUMAR[30] (1917–1993)

Shri Santanu Kumar Das was born in September 1917 at Jeypore in Orissa. He was educated at Government High School, Jeypore.

He took up social work for the liberation of the criminal tribes under the guidance of Shri Thakkar Bapa. He worked with him from 1936 to 1938.

He was elected member of Jeypore Municipality in 1938. He took part in the national freedom movement under the banner of

---

30. Source of Information:
India's Who's who-1969 and other sources.

Congress. He participated in the Quit India movement for which he was jailed.

He was the Founder President of the Orissa Depressed Classes League, and the State Scavengers Welfare Committee.

He was elected member of the Orissa Legislative Assembly in 1946. Subsequently, he was elected to the Constituent Assembly. He was member of the Constituent Assembly and the Provisional Parliament from 1946-1952.

In the first general elections held in 1952, he contested on Congress ticket for Orissa Legislative Assembly from Jeypore (SC) constituency and got elected. He became Deputy Minister of Orissa in 1952 for local Self-government, Co-operation and Fisheries.

He got elected from the same constituency in 1957 and in 1962. He was Deputy Minister from 1957 to 1959.

He joined Jan Congress in 1966 and contested as Jan Congress candidate from Jeypore constituency in 1967 and got elected. He was again Minister from 1967 to 1971 for Tribal and Rural Welfare and Excise.

Again he contested in 1971 as Jan Congress candidate and in 1974 as Congress candidate from the Jeypore (East) (SC) constituency but he could not succeed in both the elections.

He got elected in 1977 from Binjharpur (SC) assembly constituency on Janata Party ticket. He contested in 1980 for Lok Sabha from Jeypore (SC) on JNP but could not get elected.

He wrote three books in Oriya. They are *Bhai Bhai, Ashwan* and *Bhitamati.* He expired on 3 Oct. 1993.

DASS, IYODHI[31] (1845-1914)

Shri Iyodhi Dass was born in 1845 at Nilagiri in Tamil Nadu. His father's name was Candasamy. He was an Adi- Dravida.

---

31. Source of Information:
Interview with his grandson B.R. Asokan
1 / A Rajaji Nagar, Coonoor, Nilgiris. Tamil Nadu on 26-8-1991.

Shri Iyodhi Dass was a scholar in Tamil and Pali. He was a reputed native medical doctor. He owned a dispensary named Buddhist Medical Hall, at Royapettah, Madras. He used to give free medical aid to the poor people.

Previously, he was a Vaishnavite. Later, he decided to learn the truth contained in other religions. So, he devoted his time to the study of Christianity, Jainism and Buddhism. He, however intended to leave Hinduism which is based on inequality, unreason and exploitation. He wanted to revive Buddhism, based on liberty, equality and fraternity. In the year 1891, Pandit Iyodhi Dass along with his followers met Colonel H.S. Olcott and requested him to help revive Buddhism in India. Thereupon, Colonel Olcott took Iyodhi Dass to Sri Lanka, where he was ordained by Ven. Sumangala Maha Nayaka, the then Principal of Vidyodaya College, Sri Lanka.

Inspired by Colonel Olcott, Madam Blatvasky and Ven. Angarika Dharmpala, Pandit Iyodhi Dass began his missionary work under the auspices of the South Indian Sakya Buddhist Association established by him in 1900 at Madras. He was instrumental in establishing a branch of the said association at Marikuppam in 1907 and another at Champion Reef Mine, KGF in 1914. He thought that the untouchables were originally Buddhists, and their salvation lay in Buddhism.

He felt that the untouchables must be educated. It was at his instance that four schools were started in Madras for the Depressed Classes children by Colonel H.S. Olcott.

In order to create social awakening, he started a weekly newspaper, *Tamizhan* in 1907. He used to publish important extracts from *London Times,* depicting the incidents of atrocities on the untouchables, the Congress politics, etc. He was editor of the paper till his death.

He was a great thinker and writer, he wrote *Buddhar Adivedam; Tiruvalluvar Aaraichi; Kural Kadavul Vazhthu; Ambikai Amman; Murugakadavul; Harishandran Poigal; Indirar Desa Saritram; Yadhartha Yesha Brahmana Vibaram; Gajamukha Moorthy Unmai; Kabaleeshwar Vibhuthi Aaraichi* and *Trikural.* All these books are in Tamil and they expose the myth of Brahmin superiority, irrational Hindu literature and exploitative caste system.

Later on, Prof. Laxmi Naresh and Advocate Shri Singarvelu came to his help in his social and religious activities. In the year 1910, they had organized the South Indian Buddhist Conference.

He married Dhanalakshmi, the younger sister of Dewan Bahadur R. Srinivasan, who represented the Depressed Classes with Dr Babasaheb Ambedkar at the Round Table Conference.

Pandit C. Iyodhi Dass had four sons and two daughters. One of his sons Shri I. Rajaram went to Natal, South Africa and tried to spread Buddhism there. Later on, Shri A.C.P. Perriaswamier founded the Natal Buddhist Society in the year 1920.

Pandit Iyodhi Dass was the first Buddhist revivalist in India among the untouchables. He breathed his last on 5 May 1914 at the age of 69.

DASS, RAM[31(a)]

Ram Dass was a dedicated social worker. He stood for the upliftment of his brethren from untouchability and servitude. He was from Ramnagar in HP.

He contested from Solon Constituency in Himachal Pradesh for the H.P Assembly as a SCF candidate and he got elected.

He joined R.P.I after its formation. He remained in the Dalit Liberation movement till his last. He died on 15th July 1988 at Rampur (H.P.)

DEORUKHKAR, BALKRISHNA[32] (1884-1947)

Shri Balkrishna Deorukhkar was born on 30 October 1884 at Khadki near Pune. He belonged to Chambhar community. His ancestors were from Ratnagiri in Konkan. His father Shri Janoji Deorukhkar was an officer in the 8th Battalion. Shri Balkrishna

---

31(a). Source of Information :
Subah-i-Jammu
July 16, 1988.

32. Source of Information:
Bhau Lokhande. Dr. Ambedkari Krantiveer. Kalyan, 1983.

Deorukhkar was educated up to sixth (English) standard. He got employment in 158th Battalion as head clerk. Later, he resigned from service after the death of his father and came to Bombay. There he was employed in Railways Head Office. He settled permanently at Parel, Bombay.

He started his socio-political career as a Congressman, but later on he joined Dalit liberation movement under the leadership of Dr Babasaheb Ambedkar. He joined ILP. He was elected member of Bombay Municipal Corporation on ILP for ten years.

He became Vice-president of SCF, Bombay in 1942. He was very much cooperative, eloquent and hard worker. He died in a murderous attack made by some *goondas* in Bombay on 18 January 1947. In his memory, a road in Naigaon, Bombay is named after him.

DESHBHRATAR, ANJANIBAI[32(a)]

Smt. Anjanibai Deshbhratar was born in 1912 in a poor Mahar family at Nagpur. She was married to Krishnarao Deshbhratar. Both of them were interested in spreading education amongst the Dalit girls.

Both of them founded a hostel specifically for the poor Dalit girls who were to come from different places to Nagpur for education in the year 1933. Anjanibai shouldered the responsibility of superintendent of the hostel. Initially there were only three girls in the hostel. They however endeavoured to collect girls students from different places and continued to run the hostel. Previously it was at New Shukrawari area of Nagpur. Later on it was shifted to a selfowned building on a spacious 1.4 acre land at North Ambazari Road, Nagpur.

32(a). Source of information :

1. *Amhihi Itihas Ghadvala* by, Urmila Pawar- Meenakshi Moon, Stri-Vuvach, Mumbai, 1989.

2. *Asmitadarsh'* editor Dr. Gangadhar Pantawane

Aurangabad. *"Dalit Stree"* Special number 1981. Articles by H.L. Kosare and Sugandha Shende.

It is because of their firm determination and strenuous efforts, the strength of the hostellers rose to two hundred. The contribution of this couple in educating the poor scheduled caste girls student is of great value. After her death the hostel was being run by Shri Khemrajji Hirekan; a social worker. It is fully aided by the Government of Maharashtra.

Anjanibai Deshbhratar was serving as a Teacher in Nagpur Municipal Corporation for her livelihood and for the self-less aid to the hostel. She was anyhow managing her family and supporting her ailing husband. Even though she was not getting disappointed.

She was equally interested in social activities. She had organized Central provinces and Berar girls students conference on 24-25 May 1936 at Nagpur Cotton Market. She exhorted them to take education for their development.

She was one of the founders of 'Asprushya Sudharak Lagna Sahayak Mandal' at Nagpur. It was founded in August 1936 for counselling the marriageable girls and boys. It's president was Hariprasad Deorao Manake and Anjanibai Deshbhratar was its Joint-Secretary.

In a meeting presided over by Mrs. Janakibai Phule at Imamwada on 26 April 1937 one "Asprushya Mahila Sudharak Mandal" was formed. Miss Virendrabai Tirthankar was elected as President and Mrs. Anjanibai Deshbhratar became its Vice - President. The meeting was attended by a good number of Dalit Women. Thus, she was active throughout her life in the upliftment of the Dalit Women in the Madhyaprant - Berar region.

DHARAM PRAKASH[33] (1900-1972)

Shri Dharam Prakash was born in November 1900 at

---

33. Source of Information:

Personal Interview with his son. Shri Kishore Bhai, Office Secretary. Bharatiya Depressed Classes League, 12, Dr. Rajendra Prasad Road, New Delhi on 19.3.1990

Mohalla Jatavpura in Bareilly in Uttar Pradesh. His father Shri Mohan Lal was a leather worker and head of the Jatava community at his native place. Shri Dharam Prakash was educated up to matric at Bareilly. He studied Homeopathy and practised the same at Bareilly and Meerut.

He was influenced by Dr Shyam Swarup Satyavrat of Bareilly, who was an Arya Samaji. Dr Dharam Prakash accepted Arya Samaj in 1920 and strictly observed all the principles of Arya Samaj throughout his life. He was strictly vegetarian and teetotaller.

From 1926 to 1927 he was supervisor of schools. He founded Kumar Ashram at Meerut in 1928. He was member of the District Board, Meerut during 1930-32.

In order to organize the Dalits, he founded Bharatiya Depressed Classes League, at Lucknow in 1935. Its first President was R.L. Biswas (Bengal), General Secretary was Jagjivan Ram (Bihar) and Secretary was P.N. Rajbhoj (Maharashtra). Its branches were opened in UP, Delhi, Rajasthan and Hyderabad.

He was against conversion of the untouchables to other religions. He tried to reconvert those untouchables who converted to either Islam or Christianity in the past.

He was active in national freedom movement also. He participated in Quit India Movement in 1942 for which he was imprisoned till 1944.

He was elected to the Constituent Assembly in 1946. He had actively participated in the Constituent Assembly. He was a member of the Provisional Parliament from 1950-52. He was an elected member of Rajya Sabha from 1962-68.

In order to make the Dalits socially and politically conscious, he started a weekly, named *Adhikar* from Bareilly. It was in existence from 1935 to 1940. Later on, he started another paper, named *Manav Kalyan* from Delhi, which was in existence from 1952 to 1962. He married Saraswati Devi. He had a son and a daughter.

He breathed his last in July 1972 at the age of 72.

DHANVE, SOPANRAO[34] (1914–1990)

Shri Sopanrao Dhanve was born in 1914 at Kalsambar in Bhir district. His father's name was Baliram Dhanve. He was a Mahar by caste. Shri Sopanrao Dhanve passed his matriculation in 1933 and entered social service. After having seen the pitiable situation of the Dalits, he decided to struggle against the feudal society.

He tried to improve the condition of the persons engaged in *veth begar,* a system of traditional bonded labour imposed on the Mahars among the untouchables. He tried to increase the *baluta* or wages of the Mahars engaged in *veth begar.* He advised his followers even to take away the field by force, if a landlord did not pay reasonable wages. This had a great effect on the landlords.

There was oppression and exploitation of the untouchables in the Nizam State. The Hindus were exploiting the untouchables, whereas the Muslims were converting them to Islam by applying undue influence. In this respect a delegation of the leaders went to Bombay to meet Dr Babasaheb Ambedkar in the year 1936 under the leadership of Sopanrao Dhanve. After seeking advice and inspiration from him, they returned to Bhir and started to organize the Dalit masses and infused in them a new vigour.

In order to spread education among the Dalits, he opened near about 20 primary schools in Bhir and Osmanabad districts in the year 1936. He demanded that the Dalits ought to be educated in separate schools run by their own teachers.

He was President of the Depressed Classes Association at Bhir. He was against conversion of Dalits to Islam. He feared if he did not favour Nizam the Dalits would either be forcibly converted to Islam or massacred. Therefore, under the leadership

---

34 . Source of Information:

Personal interview with Shri Sopanrao Dhanve, A-120, 10/10 CIDCO, Nanded on 24.10.1989`

of Rao Saheb B.S. Venkatrao and B. Shyamsunder, he favoured the Nizam.

A conference of the Dalits was held at Parbhani on 30-31 May 1942 under the presidentship of B. Shyamsunder. It was addressed by B.S. Venkatrao also. Shri Sopanrao Dhanve was Chairman and Shri Tukaram Gade was Secretary of the reception committee of that conference. Therefore, the next conference was held at Latur in 1943 and it was presided over by Sopanrao Dhanve.

He was nominated to the Hyderabad Legislative Assembly on 17 January 1947. He played an important role along with other Scheduled Caste members in securing the sanction for the Scheduled Caste Trust Fund of Rs one crore.

After the famous police action in Hyderabad in 1948, his activities came to a standstill.

In the year 1962, he started *Zunjar Neta* a journal from Bhir. It was in existence only for two years.

He died in 1990 at the age of 76. He had two sons. He served the people throughout his life.

DHULDHOYE, GANGARAMJI[35] (1888-1973)

Shri Gangaramji Dhuldhoye was born in about 1888 at Mhow, Indore district in Madhya Pradesh. His father Shri Nanaji Dhuldhoye was in the British Army. Shri Gangaramji was educated up to seventh standard. He worked as head fitter in Malwa Cotton Mill, Indore for near about 50 years. Thereafter, he was busy in social work. He belonged to Mochi community.

He started social uplift work from 1942 onwards. He joined the Scheduled Castes Federation in 1942. Later in 1952 he joined the Congress.

---

35. Source of Information:
Personal Interview with his son Shri Bansilal Dhuldhoye
23. Jagjivan Ram Mohalla. Ravipura. Indore. MP on 14.9.1989

He participated in the famous satyagraha for political rights in 1946 and he was imprisoned also. He started a school in Ravipura, Indore for the untouchable students.

He was a good singer. He used to play several musical instruments. He was an artist. His *Noutanki* was very much famous. He used to educate the masses through his *Noutanki.*

He was very liberal in giving charity to the poor and needy brethren. He tried to work along with Shri Shankarrao Mhasde and Sajjansinh Vishnav.

He was active in labour unions. He led Dalit Majdoor Kisan Union, Indore.

He married Moti Devi from whom he had six sons. He died on 17 January 1973 at the age of 85.

DONGRE, SULOCHANABAI[35(a)] (1919-1945)

Sulochanabai Dongre was born at village Nagapur in Yeotmal district in Maharashtra State on 6 November, 1919. She was born in a Mahar, an untouchable caste, but it was a well to do family. She had completed her primary education at Indore at her maternal uncle's place; Shri G.D. Borkar. He was a Brahmo Samajist Member. She was given in marriage to Sadashivrao Dongre. She completed her intermediate education in Moris College, Nagpur. She was appointed as Hostel Superintendent in a Depressed Classes Girls Hostel. She became very popular among the hostellers due to her loving and cooperative nature.

From the early age she was interested in social work alongwith the family responsibility. She was inspired to undertake social work and Dalit upliftment movement by Jaibai Choudhari, a renowned social worker, Nagpur.

On 20-04-1940 a convention of The Umred Taluka S.C. Women's Federation was held under the Presidentship of

---

35(a).. Source of Information :

Urmila Pawar and Meenakshi Moon Amhihi Itihas Ghadvala (1989)
H.L.K. Kosare, Vidarbhatil Dalit Chalwalicha Itihas. (1984)

Sulochanabai Dongre. She exhorted and inspired the Dalit Women to work for Dalit liberation movement prevailing under the able leadership of Dr. Babasaheb Ambedkar. She inspired the women to take part in Samata Sainik Dal and give a moral strength to the women, especially the women living in villages. It was under her presidentship a resolution was passed to provide for reservation for the Dalit women in the Constitution which was soon to come into existence. She urged the government to start hostel for Dalit Girls and to start payment of scholarships to the students.

When the national level convention of the Scheduled Castes was organized to establish scheduled caste federation at Nagpur on 18th to 20th July 1942 under the leadership of Dr. Babasaheb Ambedkar and under the presidentship of Rao Bahadur N. Shivraj, the women's convention was also held on the same occasion on 20th July 1942 under the Presidentship of Sulochanabai Dongre. It was a memorable occasion which was presided over by Sulochanabai Dongre in her early age. She gave a very befitting speech on the dias of the conference on 20th July 1942 in the August presence of Dr.Babasaheb Ambedkar and before the mammoth gathering of thousands of women attending the conference. The conference had passed, certain resolutions including the resolution to provide one month's paid leave, pension and casual leave of twenty one days to all the working women in Bidi factory, Railways and Municipalities on par with other working women in government establishments and public undertakings.

As President of the All India S.C. Women's Federation, she had the privilege of participating in the conference held at Kanpur (UP) in 1944.

She died in 1945 in early age

Her husband Shri Sadashiv Dongre, worked as Army Recruitment Officer during 1956-62. After retirement he served for some time as Rector of the boy's hostel of Milind College of Science at Aurangabad. He died at Aurangabad on 7 April 1987 at the age of 82.

Mr. and Mrs. Dongre had two daughters and a son. They were well placed.

EALY VADAPALLY[36] (1911-1972)

Shri Ealy Vadapally was born on 11 August 1911 at Nandapeta in East Godavari district, Andhra Pradesh. He was an Adi-Andhra. His father Ealy Naganna was a farmer.

Shri Vadapally passed his matriculation in 1928. He chose the field of social work for the uplift of his untouchable brethren. In his youth he believed in teachings of the Brahmo Samaj. However, under the leadership of Dr Babasaheb Ambedkar, he embraced Buddhism.

In order to spread education among the untouchables, he tried to instil in the masses an awareness of the importance of education. In 1940 he started one Ashram or hostel for the students of the community. He begged in order to feed the students. He established Lakshmi Industrial Training School at Ramchandrapuram.

In order to bring political awareness and unity, he organized many meetings and conferences of the Scheduled Castes at various places in East Godavari district. In 1944, he organized a mammoth rally in Ramchandrapuram, (with the cooperation of Nandanara Harishchand, a great Dalit leader) which was addressed by Dr Babasaheb Ambedkar.

Shri Vadapally joined the Scheduled Castes Federation and organized the party at district level with great efforts and zeal. Later on, he joined Republican Party of India.

Shri Vadapally was Councillor of Ramchandrapuram Municipality for near about two decades. He contested as SCF nominee in the first general elections held in 1952 for the erstwhile Madras State Legislative Assembly from Kakinada (G and SC), but could not succeed in the election. He contested for the Lok Sabha seat in 1957 as SCF candidate from Kakinada (G and SC), but in vain. He again contested for the Andhra Pradesh Legislative Assembly seat from Tallarevu (SC) in 1967 as a Congress candidate and became successful in the election.

---

36. Source of Information::

Mrs Jyothi Rao, daughter, and E. Prem Prasad, son of the leader: Ramachandrapuram, 27.2.1989

For some time he published *Jaibheem* from Ramchandrapuram. He wrote *Nimna Jathula Charitra,* the story of Scheduled Castes and Gandhi and untouchability. He composed poems, through which he depicted the social life of the Scheduled Castes.

He married Shankhamma in 1939. He had two sons and five daughters.

Shri Vadapally was honoured by his admirers and followers with the title of *Sevadhurandhar.* He died on 11 November 1972 at the age of 61.

GAIKWAD, B.K.[37] (1902-1971)

Shri Bhaurao Gaikwad was born on 15 October 1902 at village Ambe, Taluka Dindori, Nasik district in Maharashtra. His father Shri Krishnaji Gaikwad was an agriculturist and he was well-to-do. He belonged to the Mahar caste. Shri Bhaurao Gaikwad was educated up to matric at Nasik.

Soon he was appointed as a clerk in the post office at Nasik in 1918. He served the Excise Department from 1919-20. Thereafter, he was appointed as Superintendent of the Shahu Chhatrapati Vidyarthi Ashram at Nasik in 1920 where he worked till 1926. During 1942-46 he served as Welfare Officer, Western Aviation Circle, Bombay. In 1947, he served as Officer on Special Duty for refugees at Jullunder and Kurukshetra. For some time he was honorary supervisor of the institutions run by the People's Education Society, Bombay.

He was a staunch disciple of Dr Babasaheb Ambedkar. He joined the Independent Labour Party. He joined the Scheduled Castes Federation in 1948 and worked as President of its Bombay provincial unit from 1948 to 1956. He was elected as a member of the Presidium formed on 31 December 1956 after the death of Babasaheb Ambedkar. He was one of the founding members of the Republican Party of India which came into existence on 3

---

37. Source of Information:

Mrs Bhavana Bhargava, *Padmashri Dadasaheb Gaikwad,* Nasik, 1968, and Haribhau Pagare, *Dadasaheb Gaikwad: Jeevan Karya,* Nasik, 1987.

November 1957. He was elected as its President in 1964 after the death of Shri N. Shivaraj and continued to be so till the end of his life.

At first he was nominated as a member of the Nasik Municipality in 1926. He was nominated as a member of the District Local Board of Nasik in 1928. In the elections held in 1937, he contested for the Bombay Legislative Assembly as ILP candidate from Nasik (R) constituency and got elected. In the elections held in 1946 for the provincial assemblies, he contested on SCF ticket from Nasik constituency, but he could not get elected. In the general elections held in 1952, he contested for the Bombay Legislative Assembly from Nasik-Igatpuri constituency, but he was not elected. In the elections held in 1957 he contested for the Lok Sabha from Nasik (G) constituency, and got elected. He was defeated in the elections held in 1962 for the Lok Sabha seat. He was, however, elected to Rajya Sabha in 1962 for a period of six years. He was again elected to Rajya Sabha in 1968 for the next term.

He had participated in the Choudar Tank Satyagraha on 20 March 1927 at Mahad under the leadership of Dr Babasaheb Ambedkar. He was Secretary of the Temple Entry Satyagraha Committee, under which banner the satyagraha was offered at Kalaram temple, Nasik on 2 March 1930 and it continued intermittently till 1935. He was arrested in 1932 when satyagraha was at its height. He led the satyagraha for wasteland in Marathwada region in 1953 along with Shri B.S. More and others for which he was arrested and imprisoned for four months at Harsul jail, Aurangabad. He led the satyagraha of landless peasants in Maharashtra in the year 1959. He led a huge rally at Parliament House on 21 October 1964 and submitted a charter of demands to the then Prime Minister Shri Lai Bahadur Shastri. When the demands were not conceded he led the nationwide satyagraha from 6 December 1964. The satyagraha was unique one, in which more than three lakhs of people participated and it continued for two months. The Prime Minister was very much impressed by it and he called the leaders of the satyagraha to meet him. Accordingly, a delegation under the leadership of Bhaurao alias Dadasaheb Gaikwad met the Prime Minister and submitted the charter of ten demands to him. They could be epitomized as under:

1. A portrait of Dr Babasaheb Ambedkar, the architect of the Constitution of India be placed in the Parliament Hall.
2. Land should be given only to the tillers.
3. Waste or uncultivated land should be given to the landless people.
4. The increasing prices should be controlled and essential commodities should be supplied through the public distribution system.
5. The economic condition of the people living in hutments should be improved.
6. The Minimum Wages Act, 1948 should be made applicable to all the industries, establishments and agricultural labourers.
7. All the special facilities provided for the Scheduled Castes should be extended to the converts to Buddhism.
8. Effective measures should be taken to curb atrocities on the Dalits.
9. The Untouchability Offences Act, 1955 should be strictly implemented.
10. The seats reserved for the Scheduled Castes and the Scheduled Tribes should be filled up by the candidates of those communities.

The Prime Minister, however, assured the delegation that he would sympathetically consider these demands.

It is because of those demands that the statue of Babasaheb Ambedkar was installed in front of the Parliament House and the Scheduled Castes converts to Buddhism were treated as eligible for the post-matric scholarships.

It is, however, true that the Republican Party of India was divided twice in his period. It was divided once in 1959 and second time in 1968. He, however, failed to unite the party.

He formed an alliance with the Samyukta Maharashtra Samiti in 1957 and thereafter with the Congress in 1967. Both alliances proved to be fatal to the party as both times the party was divided.

His contribution to the field of education is worth admiration. He was President of Nasik district School Board for the year 1941-42. He founded Ramabai Ambedkar Boarding in 1944 at Nasik. In the year 1957 he founded Takshashila Vidyalaya and Goutam Chhatralaya at Nasik. He founded Dr Ambedkar College at Deekshya Bhoomi, Nagpur.

He was one of the members of the Committee on Untouchability constituted in 1967 under the presidentship of Shri L. Elayaperumal. The Committee submitted its report to the President of India in 1969.

He organized the conference of the untouchables at Yeola in Nasik district on 13 October 1935, where Dr Babasaheb Ambedkar declared his decision to quit Hinduism. He embraced Buddhism at Nagpur on 14 October 1956. Since then he had been dedicated to the spread of Buddhism in India.

He widely toured throughout India for propagating the thoughts and mission of Dr Babasaheb Ambedkar. He brought about rise of new leadership in the party through certain agitations and satyagraha.

He had two wives, namely, Mrs Sitabai Gaikwad and Mrs Geetabai Gaikwad, but had no issue.

Due to his dedicated services to the society at large, he was honoured with Padmashri by the President of India on 16 April 1968.

He died of heart attack on 29 December 1971 at New Delhi at the age of 69.

GAIKWAD, S.T.[38] (1864-1949)

Shri Sambhaji Tukaram Gaikwad was born in 1864 in Mahar community, at Poud, Kolaba district in Maharashtra. Due to utmost poverty he could not get any formal education. He came to Bombay at the age of 20 and learnt motor mechanism. He became an expert motor mechanic. He was working in a motor company in Bombay on the salary of ₹ 350 per month.

---

38. Source of Information:
H.G. Bhau Lokhande, Dr Ambedkari Krantiveer III Kalyan 1983.

Since 1918, he started taking part in the Dalit uplift movement. When Dr Babasaheb Ambedkar started Dalit liberation movement around 1920, Shri Sambhaji Tukaram Gaikwad joined him as a follower and an activist. When Babasaheb Ambedkar founded the Bahishkrit Hitkarini Sabha in 1924, Shri S.T. Gaikwad became its member. He used to organize several meetings of the untouchables in Bombay and tried to awaken them.

When Dr Babasaheb Ambedkar decided to launch satyagraha at Choudar Tank, Mahad, Shri Gaikwad extended his fullest cooperation to him. He moved from place to place in the vicinity of Mahad to propagate the idea of satyagraha and enlisted the cooperation of a good many people. When the first conference of the Depressed Classes was organized at Mahadon 19-20 March 1927 at the initiative of Babasaheb Ambedkar, Shri Sambhaji Tukaram Gaikwad was elected as Chairman of the reception committee of the said conference. It was because of the cooperation of such social workers that the Mahad satyagraha succeeded.

He was instrumental in enlisting the cooperation of the saints belonging to various sects such as Kabir Panth, Ramanand Panth, Nath Panth and Warkari Panth to the cause of Mahad satyagraha. He arranged a conference of all such saints at Bombay and convinced them that they should cooperate with the Dalit liberation movement under the able leadership of Dr Babasaheb Ambedkar.

Shri S.T. Gaikwad founded an organization called, Mahar Samaj Seva Sangh with a view to uniting his brethren under a banner and tried to awaken them.

On 15 November 1929, he gave evidence before the Starte Committee appointed by the Government of Bombay to investigate into the socio-economic condition of the Depressed Classes.

Shri Gaikwad was very much active during the Kalaram Temple Satyagraha, Nasik. When Babasaheb Ambedkar declared at Yeola on 13 October 1935 to convert to another religion, Shri Gaikwad strongly supported him. He was active in arranging the Mahar Parishad at Bombay in 1936.

He started a library for the untouchables in BIT Chawl where he was residing. The library is still in existence.

He founded an organization, named Mahar Dnyati Panchayat Samiti in 1942. It is still in existence under the name of Boudhajana Panchayat Samiti.

He died on 7 March 1949 at the age of 85.

GAWAI, G.A.[39] (1888-1973)

Shri Ganesh Gawai was born on 26 October 1888 at Thugaon in Bhakuli Amravati district in Maharashtra. His father Shri Akkaji Gawai was a hereditary village Mahar servant at Thugaon. Shri Ganesh Gawai was educated at Akola. He, however, did not reach up to matric level. At Akola he resided in Janoji free boarding institute from 1900-1904.

He was influenced by Maharshi V.R. Shinde. In those days, the Christian missionaries especially the Roman Catholic missionaries were very active in converting the Dalits in Amravati district. Shri Ganesh Gawai wanted to arrest the conversion movement. He thought that the untouchables should fight against untouchability and casteism, but should not convert to another religion.

In the year 1909 he became a member of Brahmo Samaj. He had, of course, manifested his resentment against Hindu orthodoxy, but he was against conversion to another religion.

In order to bring about a new awareness to the people, he started a library at his native place. In 1910 he formed Mahar Sudharak Mandal at Amravati to reform and unite the people. He started a fortnightly, named *Bahishkrit Bharat* from Amravati in the year 1914.

Shri Ganesh A. Gawai participated in the Conference of Depressed Classes held in Bombay on 11 November 1917. It was presided over by Sir Narayanrao Chandavarkar. In the said conference it was decided, *inter alia,* to support the Lucknow Pact. However, Shri G.A. Gawai opposed it saying that, if the

---

39. Source of Information:
Personal interview with his son Shri Hemchandra Gawai, Hanuman Mandir Chawl, Fraizerpura, Amravati on 19-10-1988.

Hindus demanded Swaraj, which meant the rule of Hindu bureaucrats, then what was the use of such Swaraj to the Depressed Classes.

In order to unite all the Depressed Classes under one banner, he formed Depressed India Association at Bombay on 12 January 1918. However, it was registered on 10 April 1940.

After having observed the zeal of Gawai in the uplift of the untouchables, the Government nominated him to the CP and Berar Legislative Assembly in 1920. He continued to be its member -till 1945, for a period of 25 years. He moved the Anti-untouchability Bill in the Assembly in 1934 and it was passed.

On the issue of separate electorate for the Depressed Classes, he differed from Dr Babasaheb Ambedkar. Shri Gawai was of the view that the untouchables being dependent on the caste Hindus, could not be separated from them. If they were politically separated from the Hindus, their life would be miserable. He supported Rajah-Moonje Pact which proposed to have joint electorate with reserved seats for the Scheduled Castes. He was, however, one of the signatories of the Poona Pact, 1932.

He was one of the main founders of All India Depressed Classes Association at Nagpur in 1928. Shri M.C. Rajah was elected as its President and Shri G.A. Gawai was elected as its General Secretary. Shri G.A. Gawai was its General Secretary till its dissolution in 1944.

Shri G.A. Gawai did not support the declaration of conversion made by Dr Babasaheb Ambedkar in 1935. Though Babasaheb Ambedkar said explicitly that he was inclined towards Buddhism, Shri Gawai was under the wrong impression and apprehension that the former would convert to a religion other than Buddhism. Subsequently, Shri Gawai, under the influence of Dr Moonje and Barrister Savarkar, joined the Hindu Maha Sabha and continued to be its member till his end.

He married Kesharbai. He had four sons and a daughter. He breathed his last on 27 July 1973 at the age of 85 years.

GEDDALA, BRAHMAIAH[39(a)] (1912-1950)

Shri Geddala Brahmaiah was born in 1912 in a Adi-Andhra untouchable caste in East Godavari District of Andhra Pradesh. He was a social reformer and a devoted leader of the Adi-Andhra movement. He moved from place to place in the district to propagate the importance of the Adi-Andhra movement and to instil in the people the zeal to work for the upliftment of the down trodden people.

He edited 'Adi-Andhra Patrika', and tried to bring about a new consciousness among the downtrodden people. He revived the Adi-Andhra Sangham and strengthened it. Shri Brahmiah was elected its Secretary in 1935. He successfully organized the conferences of the Adi-Andhras in 1938, 1939 and 1940 in the district.

In recognition of his yeoman services, people conferred on him 'Adi-Andhra Ratna' in Ramchandrapuram conference.

He died in 1950.

GILL, MIHAN SINGH[39(b)]

Mihan Singh Gill was a very staunch and devoted leader of the scheduled castes in the erstwhile PEPSU region of Punjab. He joined Scheduled Castes Federation founded by Dr. Babasaheb Ambedkar in 1942 at Nagpur. He became President of the Pepsu Unit of AISCF. He organized a public meeting of the party at Patiala on 29 October 1951. It was addressed by Dr. Babasaheb Ambedkar himself.

Shri Mihan Singh was SCF candidate from Amloh-Payal in Patiala and East Punjab Assembly Constituency in 1952. He was elected in the election for Pepsu Assembly.

39(a). Source of Information :

The Champions of The down Trodden in Andhra Pradesh; an article by V.B. Raju in Andhra Pradesh State Harijan Conference, Souvenir, April 1976, Hyderabad.

39(b) Source of Information :

1. Radhey Lal, Sector 15A Chandigarh Punjab.
2. Adv. Santok Lal Virdhi, Fagwada, Punjab.

Later, in the General Elections held in 1957 he contested from Sirhind (SC) Assembly Constituency on Indian National Congress ticket and got elected to the Punjab Legislative Assembly. Later, he contested from Payal (SC) Constituency in 1962 but could not win. Again he contested from Khanna (SC) Assembly Constituency, but could not win.

Details about him are not known.

GOPINATH MAHARAJ[40] (1881-1951)

Shri Gopinath Maharaj was born in 1881 at Algud, Basavakalyan Taluka, in Bidar district (erstwhile Hyderabad State, now Karnataka). His father's name was Shri Narsingdeo Kamble. He was a Nath Panthi by birth. He received no formal education, but he was conversant with Marathi, Kannada and Sanskrit. He was well versed in Hindu scriptures. He was a Mahar by caste.

At the age of 12 he left his village, but came back after four years. He got married at the age of 16 years to Sitamai, but had no issue. After marriage both of them left their village and came to Mahur in Nanded district. They remained at Shri Kshetra Mahur for about 12 years. There he performed *tapasya* with strict austerity and studied the religious literature. Then, the *Mahant* of the Datta Mandir, Mahur, advised him to serve people and preach spiritualism. Thereupon, Gopinath Maharaj came to Aundha (Nagnath) in Hingoli in Parbhani district(Maharashtra), probably in the year 1924 and settled there. However, he was moving from place to place for preaching spiritualism and bringing a new consciousness to his untouchable brethren.

He constructed a rest house and a well for the use of the Dalit pilgrims at Aundha. A meeting was arranged at Aurangabad on 17 December 1929 in which persons from various places decided to support him in his proposal of raising funds for starting schools, building rest-houses for pilgrims and constructing wells.

---

40 · Source of Information :
Interview with Jaikiran Nakul Kamble (his nephew),
Kholeshwar College, Ambajogal, Bhir, Maharashtra.

Later on, he was attracted towards the movement of Dr Babasaheb Ambedkar. He inspired the saints amongst the Dalits to cooperate with his Dalit uplift movement. Shri Madhavnath Shinde, Ramnathbuwa, Shri Bajrang Maharaj and many other saints followed him.

He was attracted towards Buddhism. He was at Aundha, but never entered the Nagnath temple for the purpose of worshipping the deity. He was against idol worship. He preached cleanliness and vegetarianism among his disciples. He propagated his thoughts through *bhajan* and *kirtan* throughout the erstwhile Nizam state.

He established Bhim ghat on the banks of the Godavari at Nanded in the year 1949. He started *Bhim Yajnya* at the ghat from 20 to 24 April 1949. He established the *Paduka* of Lord Buddha at the Bhim ghat. He was greatly helped in his activities by the leaders of the SCF, Shri Kadaknath Hatkar, Prabhakarrao Hingole, Laloji Sonkamble (Nanded), Shri Bajrang Maharaj, Kamal Babu (Hyderabad), Shri Jalbaji Shrungare (Mudhol) and many other persons.

Gopinath Maharaj died on 10 August 1951 at Aundha at the age of 69. He was loved and respected by the Dalits as well as non-Dalits in the Marathwada region.

GUJARATI, N.G[41]

Shri Narsinghdeo Gujarati was born in about 1920 in Mehtar community at Jodhpur in Rajasthan. His father Shri Ghisaram Gujarati was working as a sweeper in the Maharaja's palace at Jodhpur. Shri Narsinghdeo Gujarati had passed his seventh class from Arya Samaj Vidyalaya, Jodhpur.

He joined the Congress in 1942 and participated in the Quit India Movement and the struggle for independence of Jodhpur *Riasat*.

He was executive member of the Mehtar Sudhar Sabha at Jodhpur city in 1945. The Sabha was founded to remove certain

---

[41]. Source of Information: :
Personal Interview with the leader Shri Narsingdeo Gujarati.
117, Govindpuri, Sodala, Jaipur (Rajasthan) on 8.11.1989

evils prevailing in those days in the Depressed Classes, such as beef-eating, wearing the clothes of corpses, drinking, idol worship, etc. Shri Narsinghdeo had very actively organized the masses and propagated against all the social evils in the society. It had a positive effect on the untouchables.

He was nominated on the Committee for Grievances of Harijan Employees of Jodhpur Municipality, by the Maharaja of Jodhpur in the year 1946. He utilized this opportunity for the benefit of his brethren.

He led the strike of the municipal workers in 1946 and 1950 as a result of which their salary was increased, they got the right to avail certain holidays and moreover they received uniforms. In the year 1950, he was imprisoned for having led the strike of the municipal workers for a period of three months.

During 1951 to 1963 he was Secretary of Rajasthan Harijan Sevak Sangh District Unit, Jodhpur. He led Temple Entry movement and Hotel Entry movement in Jodhpur district, and became successful in his efforts. The barbers and the washermen also agreed to extend their services to the untouchables due to his relentless efforts.

He was a member of the Scheduled Castes Welfare Advisory Committee organized by the Government of Rajasthan, during 1954-56. He was elected member of Jodhpur Municipal Council from 1958-62. He was President of Rajasthan Safai Majdoor Sangh during 1957-59. He became Vice-president of All India Safai Majdoor Congress in 1959.

In order to bring about socio-political awareness amongst the untouchables he started one fortnightly, named *Dalit Awaj* in the year 1963. He started another paper *Samajik Azadi,* a monthly in 1963 and it continued till 1968. In the year 1985 he started *Atmik Azadi,* a monthly. However, it was in existence only for a year.

Shri Ram Sarvate Roopchand Chawaria and Shri Achalu Ram cooperated with him in all his activities.

In his early life he came under the influence of Arya Samaj. When he observed the spirit of casteism in the Arya Samaj, he left it. In the year 1974 he converted to Christianity.

He married Ramjyoti in 1943. He has a son and a daughter. Now, he is, despite his 74 years of age, active in social and literary work.

GURRAM JASHUA[42] (1895-1971)

Shri Gurram Jashua was born on 28 September 1895 at Missamma Thota (Vinukonda), Guntur district in Andhra Pradesh. His father's name was Gurram Veerayya.

Shri Jashua had completed teachers' training course from Bapatla. He was a teacher for some time. He was Publicity Officer under the Government of Madras from 1942-45. He served as producer in AIR at Madras from 1956-60. He was a prolific writer and poet. He wrote *Piradhousi, Swapnakatha, Gabbilamu, Nethaji, Swayamvaram, Kotha Lokam, Christ Charitha, NaKatha, Musafarlu, Kandiseekudu, Bapuji, Rastrapuja, Nagarjunsagar, Khandkavyas.* All these books are in Telugu. Of all the books his *Gabbilamu* earned him great fame. Gabbilamu is a creature which wanders in the closed darkness. Jashua depicted in his work the miserable condition of the untouchables.

His books reveal the pathetic plight of this section. Once he himself experienced the misery of untouchability. He was not allowed to sit with the caste Hindus in a theatre where he had gone to see a drama. Though he belonged to Christianity, he had to suffer from the handicap of being a member of untouchable Panchama community.

He was a nominated member of Andhra Pradesh Legislative Council from 1965 to the end of his life.

However, in recognition of his great contribution to Telugu Dalit literature of high literary value, the Kendra Sahitya Academy honoured him. He was honoured by the prestigious award of Padmabhushan in the year 1970.

He died in 1971 at the age of 76.

---

42. Source of Information:

Mr and Mrs Lavanam (Leader's son-in-law and daughter) Nastika Kendram Patamata, Viyayawada. AP.

GURU BALAKDAS (1830-1870) AND HIS SUCCESSORS[43]

Shri Guru Balakdas was born in about 1830 at Bhandar, Raipur district in Madhya Pradesh. His father Shri Guru Ghasidas was a great leader of the untouchables and the founder of the Satnami sect. Shri Guru Balakdas had no formal education. After the death of Guru Ghasidas in the year 1850, his son Guru Balakdas became the head of the Satnami sect.

Guru Balakdas propagated the teachings of the Satnami sect throughout his life. He tried to raise the confidence of his brethren. Being a Satnami, he was against the idol worship, sacrificing animals, meat-eating, drinking and uncleanliness. He advised his brethren to remain united, help each other and educate the children. He stood for equality and social justice. He advised his brethren to maintain cleanliness and high moral standard in the family.

In order to make the Satnami sect strong and financially self-sufficient he purchased land at Telasi, Bhandarpuri, Khapri and Girodhpuri villages in Raipur. He purchased an elephant for the purpose of carrying on the propaganda of the sect. He moved from place to place in the Chhattisgarh region of Madhya Pradesh which included the districts of Raipur, Bilaspur and Durg.

When he was on propaganda tour, the reactionary high caste people killed him in about 1870.

After the death of Balakdas his son became successor of the sect for a short period. He died without issue. Therefore the line of succession shifted at his death to his brother Guru Agardas. Shri Agardas was succeeded by his son Guru Agamdas. Agamdas had a brother named Muktawandas, who died in 1966.

Guru Agamdas had actively supported the national independence movement. He was a member of Constituent Assembly and the Provisional Parliament from 1946 to 1952.

When Agamdas was involved in a murder case in which he was awarded the death sentence, at the instance of Shri L.N.

---

43. Source of Information:
Michael Mahar (ed.). The *Untouchables tn Contemporary India.*

Hardas, Dr Babasaheb Ambedkar appeared in the High Court of Nagpur in the defence of Agamdas and saved his life. He got elected to the Lok Sabha in 1952. He died soon after his election, therefore, his wife Smt Minimuta succeeded him.

Guru Balakdas propagated Satnami Protest sect and thereby preached the principle of equality of human beings. The sect is still in vogue.

GURUSWAMI, L.K.[44] (1885-1966)

Shri Guruswami was born in 1885 in Madras. He was a son of Shri Kottappa. Shri Guruswami had his early education in Madras.

He was determined to lift up the untouchables from their backwardness. He thought that education could be the best means to resort to. Hence he established two night schools in Mylapur area of Madras in the year 1921. He started schools in Pudupettai, Koyyathope, Royapuram, Mylapore, Periamet and other places.

He obtained land for colonizing the people in places like Puliyanthope. He also secured amenities like lights, roads, water-supply, etc, in those localities.

Since 1920 to 1930 he was elected member of Madras Legislative Assembly. He had been an honorary Magistrate for 20 years. He was conferred with the title of Rao Bahadur in 1927. He was a member of the Madras University Senate in 1929. He was also a member of the Madras City Corporation. He struggled for abolition of untouchability.

HARDAS L.N.[45] (1904-1939)

Shri Hardas was born on 6 January 1904 in Mahar community at Kamathi, Nagpur in Maharashtra. His father Shri Laxmanrao Nagrare was a clerk in the Railway Department. Shri

---

44. Source of Information:

A.S. Ulakanathan, *Messengers of Equality*, Madras (1990).

45. Source of Information:

Bhanudas N. Meshram, *Babu Hardas Yanche Jeevan Charitra*, Kamathi. Nagpur.

Babu Hardas passed his matriculation in 1920 from Patwardhan High School, Nagpur. He studied Sanskrit from Swami Brahmanand, Arya Samaj, Nagpur.

In the year 1921, he started a weekly *Maharatha* from Nagpur with a view to spreading social awareness among the Dalits.

In order to avoid exploitation of the *beedi* workers, he started the *beedi* work on cooperative basis. It became successful. He opened a Mahila Ashram at Nagpur with a view to imparting training to Dalit women in household activities.

He founded the Mahar Samaj organization in 1922 to rally his brethren under one banner. He was Secretary of that organization. He also formed one Mahar Sevak Pathak to organize the decentralized youth force to protect the Dalits against atrocities and to maintain discipline in the society. It was to act as volunteer corps. He sincerely endeavoured to remove the sub-caste barrier from among the Depressed Classes. He used to invite the members of all sub-castes among the Depressed Classes to the community dinner arranged on the occasion of death anniversary of the great saint Shri Chokhamela in the temple of Chokhamela at Nagpur. The people usually gave a very nice response to the same.

In 1923 he appealed to the Governor of CP and Berar to nominate members from among the Depressed Classes to the Legislative Council, District Local Boards and Municipalities. The Governor, however, assured that he would consider the demands sympathetically.

On behalf of Mahar Samaj he started night schools at Bail Bazar, Kamsari Bazar and Naya Bazar Kamathi in the year 1924. There were reportedly 86 boys and 22 girls in the schools. At the same time he opened one Sant Chokhamela library at Kamathi.

He was against all the irrational, immoral and superstitious habits of the society. In order to arouse the opinion of the people against the evils of the society he wrote a book named *Mandai Mahatme* in October 1924. He distributed the copies of the book free of cost among the Dalits. It proved to be very effective. After reading the contents of the book, the Dalit women and men who used to go to witness the *Mandai* or *Krishna Leela* which was obscene, abandoned this practice.

He wrote a play named *Veer Balak* through the performance of which he tried to bring a new awareness among the people. The play also proved to be effective.

He was against idol worship. He organized a meeting of his brethren at Ramtek near Nagpur in 1927 under the presidentship of Kisan Faguji Bansod. Shri Babu Hardas exhorted his brethren to stop worshipping at the steps of the temple at Ramtek and to stop bathing in the dirty Ambada tank.

He, however, sent a group of his brethren under the leadership of one Shankar Mukunda Bele to participate in the Temple Entry Satyagraha at Nasik, which was going to be offered on 2 March 1930.

He was one of the main organizers of the Conference of the Depressed Classes at Nagpur on 8 August 1930. It was presided over by Dr Babasaheb Ambedkar. The conference resolved to have separate electorate for the Depressed Classes. The conference formed the All India Depressed Classes Federation under the presidentship of Rao Saheb Muniswamy Pillai (Madras). Babu Hardas was elected as its Joint Secretary.

Babu Hardasji founded Madhya Pradesh Bidi Majdoor Sangh in 1930. Shri Ramchandra Phule, MLC was its President and Babu Hardasji was its Secretary.

The second conference of the All India Depressed Classes was held at Kamathi on 7 May 1932. It was presided over by Muniswamy Pillai. Babu Hardasji was President of the reception committee. On 8 May 1932 the national executive body of the All India Depressed Classes Federation was elected, which included Muniswamy Pillai (Madras) as President, M.B. Mullick (Bengal) as Vice-president, Shri L.N. Hardas as Secretary and Shri Swami Achutanand (Lucknow) as its Joint Secretary.

Babu Hardas became Secretary of the CP and Berar branch of ILP in the year 1936. He contested the assembly election in 1937 from Nagpur-Kamathi (R) constituency and got elected. In the year 1938, he was nominated President of the CP and Berar branch of ILP.

It was he who started the practice of exchanging the greeting *Jaibhim* as a mark of friendly gesture in the year 1937.

He married Sahubai in 1920.

Babu Hardasji expired on 12 January 1939 at the early age of 35.

ISHWARIBAI, J. (1920-1991)

Smt J. Ishwaribai was born on 1 December 1920 in Hyderabad. She belonged to the Mala caste. Her father Shri Balleppu Balaram was an active social worker and a member of Adi-Hindu Jatiyonnati Sabha. She passed her B.A. and devoted herself to social service.

She joined the Scheduled Castes Federation from the very beginning. After the formation of the Republican Party of India, she joined it. After the death of Shri D.A. Katti, the then President of RPI, in 1986, Smt J. Ishwaribai was unanimously elected President of RPI.

She contested as SCF candidate in 1952 from Huzurabad (R) constituency, in 1957 from Jangaon (R) constituency, in 1962 from Yellareddy (R) constituency, for the Andhra Pradesh Legislative Assembly, but could not get elected in all the three elections.

She contested on RPI from Yellareddy (R) constituency for assembly seat in 1967 and got elected. Again, she got elected in 1972 from the same constituency.

She contested in 1978 (from Jukkal), in 1983 (from Andolej and in 1985 (from Andole) but without success. She had contested for the Lok Sabha in 1977 from Amalapuram constituency but met with failure.

She was a staunch Ambedkarite and a strong and uncompromising leader of RPI, throughout her life. She tried her best to spread Ambedkarite movement in Andhra Pradesh. She got very sincere co-workers in Shri B.V. Ramanaiah from Amalapuram and P.V. Manohar from Hyderabad.

She died on 24 February 1991 at the age of 71.

IYAKANNU, I.N.[46] (1875-1955)

Shri Ichiputtur Iyakannu was born on 8 October 1875 at Ichipattur, Arakonam Taluka, North Arcot district, Tamil Nadu. He was an Adi-Dravida. His father Ichiputtur Narayana Swamy was a small farmer. Shri I.N. Iyakannu acquired his Pandit degree in Tamil in 1910 from Madras. He worked as a Tamil teacher in a Buddhist school at Marikuppam from 1907 to 1942.

Shri I.N. Iyakannu Pulavar was a social worker to the core. In order to liberate his brethren he used to exhort them to live hygienically, to leave drinking and beef-eating and educate their children. At the instance of Pandit C. Iyodhi Dass, Buddhist preacher named M. Raghavan came to Marikuppam. Shri I.N. Iyakannu Pulavar was very much impressed by him. Consequently, he converted to Buddhism in 1900. Since then he started preaching and propagating Buddhism to the untouchables.

In order to spread education among the untouchables, he along with others founded the Buddhist Primary School at Marikuppam, KGF in the year 1907. He himself worked there as a teacher.

He was instrumental in starting the Buddhist Society of India at Marikuppam in 1907. The Society was working under the guidance of Pandit C. Iyodhi Dass, a Buddhist missionary at Madras.He was editor of *Tamizhan* weekly newspaper from 1932 to 1935. He was a renowned author and poet. He had written *Bhagavathiana Bakti Rasa Kirthanaigal* (1912); *Thiru Pasurakothu* (1912); *Buddha Charitra Pa* (1912); *Bhagavat Thotir Panmani Maloia* (1912); and *Mysore State History* (1930). His book on the history of Mysore is "considered original throwing fresh insights into the forgotten eras of the State's history." Therefore, the Maharaja of Mysore honoured him.

He was a staunch supporter of Dr Babasaheb Ambedkar in his demand of separate electorate for the Scheduled Castes. He

---

46. Source of Information:

Personal interview with his son. I. Loganathan. 4, Sarojini Compound, Marikuppam. KGF (Karnataka) on 6-6-1989.

also believed that conversion was a must for the salvation of the so-called untouchables.

He married Smt Ammai Ammal in 1920 and he had one daughter and one son. Presently, his son I. Loganathan is the President of the Buddhist Society of India.

Shri I.N. Iyakannu Pulavar died on 26 September 1955 at the age of 75.

JADHAV, RAIBHAN[47] (1888-1969)

Shri Raibhan Jadhav was born on 1 January 1888 at Chikhali, Buldhana district in Maharashtra. His father Shri Punaji Jadhav was an agriculturist. Shri Raibhan Jadhav could not reach up to the matric level. He was in service in the Forest Department. He retired from service in 1941 and since then he worked for the uplift of his community.

Previously, he was attracted towards Satya Shodhak Samaj. Even in service, he served his community. He advised them to abandon beef-eating, maintain cleanliness and educate their children. In 1938, he started a boarding institute for the Scheduled Caste students at Chikhali at his own expense. There were 15-20 students in the hostel. It was in existence for near about five years. It produced students like Maroti Kamaloji Jadhav, who became District Collector, Shri Sakharam Dagaduji Mhaske, who also became a District Collector and even Commissioner, and Narayan Banduji Jadhav, who became a Class One Officer in Madhya Pradesh.

In 1942, he joined the Scheduled Castes Federation. Later, he worked as President of its Buldhana district unit, till 1952. He contested in 1946 for the CP and Berar Legislative Assembly as an SCF candidate and got elected. The Congress candidate Shri L.S. Bhatkar was defeated. Shri Raibhan Punaji Jadhav had the unique honour of being elected to the Legislative Assembly on SCF ticket in 1946. He was the second candidate to get elected on SCF ticket in 1946 in India.

---

47. Source of Information:

Personal Interview with his wife, Smt Janakabai Jadhav, Ward No. 13, Bhimnagar, Chikhali Dist. Buldhana (Maharashtra) on 23.4.1989.

He participated in the satyagraha for political rights at Nagpur in 1946. He started a hotel for the untouchables as they were not allowed to enter the hotels. He built one Hanuman temple for his brethren as they were not allowed to enter the Hindu temple.

Shri Baliram Devaji Borde (1907-68) and Gopalrao Sakharamji Jadhav (1924), both from Buldhana, were his companions and co-workers. They also worked hard for the betterment of the community.

His brother Shri Rambhaji Punaji Jadhav was also an active social worker.

Previously he was a Hindu Mahar. However, he converted to Buddhism in 1956 and propagated Buddhism in his district.

He married Janakabai and later married Bheemabai. He had a son and four daughters.

He died on 22 October 1969 at the age of 81.

JATAVAVEER, MANIKCHAND[48] (1897-1956)

Shri Manikchand Jatavaveer was born in 1897 at Rajamandi, Agra in Uttar Pradesh. His father's name was Bholanath. Shri Manikchand was educated in Saint John's School, Agra.

Shri Manikchand had an innate urge for social work. Untouchability in its severe form prevailed in those days. Hence he decided to wage a war against it. He started his social life as a member of the Arya Mitra Sabha in 1914. He was appointed as a teacher in a school run by the Arya Samaj, where the untouchable students were allowed admission.

In the year 1917 he founded the Jatav Maha Sabha for uplifting the Jatav community. In this venture he was assisted by Pandit Sundarlal Sagar, Khemchand Bohare, Prabhu Dayal Vyas, Chhedilal Kaushik, Babu Ram Prasad, Babu Nandkishore and others.

---

48. Source of Information:

Interview with his grandson Shri Rajkumar Vaidya 31/149 Kataghar. Dr. Manikchand Road, Rajamandi, Agra on 9-6-1991 and Shri Nathilal Shastry 75 RPS Colony, New Delhi.

He worked very hard for providing medical aid and solace to the persons who were affected by widespread plague in Agra city and surrounding villages in the year 1918. Subsequently, he was appointed as incharge of the epidemic preventive section in the Municipal Hospital, Agra.

In the year 1923, he formed Jatav Swayam Sevak Mandal. He left for Kota in Rajasthan in 1929 for one year for serving the untouchables there. He visited several places in Rajasthan, Madhya Pradesh and Gujarat, especially the princely states and tried to bring a new socio-political awareness among the Depressed Classes.

In order to bring awareness to his brethren, he started a journal by name *Jivan* from Agra in 1936. In this venture he was actively assisted by Nathilal Shastry and Ramnarayan Yadvendu of Agra.

In the elections held in 1937, he was elected to the UP Legislative Assembly from Agra as an independent candidate. He was very active and assertive in the Assembly where the problems of Dalits were concerned. He tried to vent the grievances of Dalits and to get them solved.

In the year 1937-38, with the assistance of his coworkers Shri Nathilal Shastry and Ramnarayan Yadvendu, he formed one Jatav Veer Institute for the uplift of the Dalits. He started a hostel, library and schools. The hostel which is still in existence at Khatena in Agra is named after him.

He organized a conference of the Scheduled Castes at Agra in the presence of Dr Babasaheb Ambedkar, the then Labour Member in the Viceroy's Executive Council. The UP branch of Scheduled Castes Federation was formed in the conference. Dr Manikchand led the famous satyagraha at Lucknow in 1946. As such he was arrested and kept in jail at Allahabad. Subsequently, the Scheduled Castes offered satyagraha at many places in UP.

During the Second World War he cooperated with the British. He called upon his brethren to join the military and defend the country at any cost. It was because of his efforts that the Jatav Battalion was formed, but it was disbanded after the war was over. It was because of his cooperation with the British

Government during the war, that he was honoured with the title of Rao Saheb and membership of the UP War Committee.

In the first general elections held in 1952 he contested from Bharatpur (Rajasthan) parliamentary constituency (R) and got elected. He was a very active member of the Parliament.

He was a selfless and fearless leader of the Scheduled Castes. He was not addicted to any bad habit. He used to come to help the Dalits whenever they were subjected to atrocities. He relentlessly tried to uplift the Dalits throughout his life.

He married Vishatra Devi and had a son. He used to practise Ayurvedic medicine. He died on 28 December 1956 at the age of 59. He was popularly known as *Jatav-veer.*

JATIA, H.G.[49]

Shri Harichand Jatia was born on 22 November 1919 at Hyderabad in Sindh (now in Pakistan). His father Shri Gangaram Jatia was a painter. Shri Harichand Jatia passed his matriculation in 1936 from Sindh. Thereafter, he started a factory for manufacturing colour for leather. After partition his family migrated to India in 1947 and settled at Ajmer in 1949.

He came under the influence of one Swami Krishnanad of Arya Samaj in 1939, and he joined the Arya Samaj. When he realized that the high caste did not treat the low caste on an equal footing even in the Arya Samaj, he left it in 1941.

He tried to reform the society. He advised his brethren to stop carrying dead animals and eating beef. He advised them to maintain cleanliness and high moral standard in the family.

He joined Congress in 1937. He participated in the Quit India Movement in 1942, for which he was jailed for six months. After partition he came to India and settled at Ajmer. He started his social uplift activities at Ajmer and other parts of Rajasthan. He tried to see that the untouchables were properly rehabilitated in India. He was a member of the committee appointed by the

---

49. Source of Information:

Personal Interview with the leader Shri Harichand Jatia House No.609/25. Pahad Ganj, Gandhi Nagar, Ajmer. Rajasthan on 10-11-1989.

Government to assist and supervise the rehabilitation work. He cooperated with the refugees belonging to the Scheduled Castes.

He was elected four times as a member of the Municipality, Ajmer, namely in 1952, 1957, 1963 and 1972. He contested for Rajasthan Legislative Assembly in 1962 from Binai (R) constituency as Congress candidate, but could not get elected. Again, he contested from the same constituency in 1967, but met with failure.

In the year 1977 he joined the Janata Party under the leadership of Babu Jagjivan Ram.

He was of the opinion that Dr Babasaheb Ambedkar should get elected from Bombay in 1952 with the full support of all the Scheduled Castes. Therefore, he came to Bombay along with two other friends before the nominations were finalized to convince Shri N.S. Kajrolkar, the opponent of Babasaheb Ambedkar, to withdraw from the contest, but in vain. He had high regards for Babasaheb Ambedkar and Babu Jagjivan Ram.

His elder brother Shri Parasram Jatia is also a social worker and political leader. He also worked for the uplift of the Dalits.

He married Sundaridevi in 1933. He has four sons and six daughters.

Even at the age of 75 he is working as President of Jatia Panchayat, leading the Merchants Association and ready to come to the help of the Dalits.

JAYANAND BHARATI[49(a)] (1881-1952)

Shri Jayanand Bharati was born on 2 October 1881 in a Shilpkar Caste among the Depressed Classes, at Arkandai in Poudi Gadhwal district in Uttarakhand. His parents were Raveli and Chhavilal. In order to get rid of discrimination based on caste, he embraced Arya Samaj.

49(a). Source of Information :
Bharat Mein Dalit Jagaran Aur Usake Agradoot, by Mata Prasad, Samyak Prakashan (2010).

Later he joined British Army in 1918 and participated in the first World War. Later, he started social service. He participated in the independence struggle also. Consequently he was imprisoned in April 1930, February 1932 and in 1942.

He became active in the upliftment of the depressed classes from their low social status. He led the famous 'Dola-Palki' movement during 1923 to 1941. In the Gadhwal region, the Depressed Classes were not allowed to take out the procession of their wedding couple in Dola-Palki on the ground of their so called low caste and untouchability. Therefore he organized the movement of his breathren against that practice imposed by the caste Hindus. In 1929 he organized a march against it. In 1941 even they declared to abandon the meeting of the Congress party. The Arya Samaj was against the said practice of the Caste Hindus. Even the then Congress Govt, had declared the Dola-Palki Caste practice as unlawful. It was but a great victory to Jayanand Bharati and his followers.

He breathed his last on 9 December 1952.

JAYASEELAN, M.[50]

Shri Jayaseelan was born on 20 December 1912 in Cantonment area, Bangalore. His father Shri Manickum was a businessman. When Shri Jayaseelan was studying in SSLC in 1930, he left the school and plunged into politics.

Shri Jayaseelan was a born Buddhist. His father was converted to Buddhism. His father-in-law Shri Swami Pillai, who was serving in the Police Department of Burmese Government at Rangoon was also a Buddhist. Before conversion they were treated as untouchables.

Shri Jayaseelan came in contact with Brahmachari T. Ramchandra, a Brahmin social worker. Shri Jayaseelan worked in cooperation with T. Ramchandra in his social activities. Shri Jayaseelan used to advise his untouchable brethren to maintain cleanliness, to educate their children, to abandon drinking and to

---

50. Source of Information:
Personal Interview with Shri M. Jayaseelan
89/1 Dickenson Road. Bangalore on 5-6-1989.

discard beef-eating. He used to conduct Buddhist prayers and the *Panchsheela* and tried to attract his brethren towards Buddhism.

He started a hostel for the Scheduled Caste students, where students like L. Shivalingiah who rose to the position of Chief Executive Engineer of Karnataka State was a boarder.

He started one weekly in English, by name *Panch Sheela,* in the year 1956, which continued for a period of about three years. He wrote a book, entitled *Poona Pact.*

He took an active part in the national independence movement as well as in the Mysore State independence movement. He was jailed four times, in 1930 for 15 days, in 1937 for four and a half months, in 1942 for six months and in 1947 for one month. Thus, he put altogether one year in jail for the cause of independence. Hence, he was honoured as a freedom fighter by the Union and State Governments. He started his political career by joining the Congress in the year 1930. He was nominated as a member to the Municipality of Bangalore cantonment during 1945-49. In the year 1951-52 he was elected Deputy Mayor of Bangalore city and cantonment.

He was nominated as a member of All India Prohibition Council, in the year 1971, and still he is a member of the same.

He married Rukmini. He got two daughters. Presently, he is busy in reading and writing.

JENARAJU[51]

Shri Jenaraju was born on 5 April 1915 at Perambur, Madras. His father Nayanapallayam was a contractor at KGF. His mother Gouriamma was a teacher in a primary school at Buddha Vihar, Perambur. Shri Nayanapallayam and Smt Gouriamma converted to Buddhism at the instance of Pandit C. Iyodhi Dass. Hence, Shri Jenaraju is an 'original' Buddhist. He passed his matriculation in 1930 from Egmore High School, Madras. He

---

51. Source of Information:
Personal Interview with Shri N. Jenaraju
19, Kanna Biran Kovll Street. Perambur, Madras on 31-5-1989.

served as Chief Examiner from 1931-74 in Bukingham Carnatic Mills Ltd., Perambur.

He joined South Indian Buddhist Association and later became its General Secretary in 1946. He is still General Secretary of the said organization. He tried to propagate Buddhism among his untouchable brethren.

He founded Young Men's Buddhist Association at Madras in 1946 and tried to organize young Buddhists under one banner. He urged them to maintain high moral and cultural standard.

He joined Madras Labour Union in 1938. He was a member of the executive body of the trade union from 1938-43. Later, he became its General Secretary from 1943-46. He tried to unite the labour force and tried to solve their problems.

He married Yasodhara, daughter of Krishnaswamy. Shri Krishnaswamy was chief guard in South Central Railway at Hubli. He converted to Buddhism and became an active member of South Indian Buddhist Association, Hubli.

Shri N. Jenaraju is still active in preaching and propagating Buddhism among the masses even at the age of 79.

KAEN KARANSINGH[52] (1898-1990)

Shri Karansingh Kaen was born in Jatav community in 1898 at village Nagala Bhavani Singh, Agra Sadar, in Agra district (Uttar Pradesh). His father's name was Shri Niruthamdas Kaen. Shri Karan Singh Kaen passed his B.A. in 1926 from Agra College, Agra.

He joined the Congress and took active part in the freedom movement. He contested in 1937 to the UP State Assembly on Congress ticket from Agra city constituency and got elected. Later he was nominated as Parliamentary Secretary to the Minister of Education, Uttar Pradesh.

He came in contact with Dr Babasaheb Ambedkar and accepted his leadership. When Babasaheb Ambedkar was

---

52. Source of Information:
Personal interview with his son Shri Narendra Kumar
37/18, Bundu Katra, Gwalior Road. Agra, UP. on 8-6-1991.

writing the book, *What Congress and Gandhi have done to the Untouchables* Shri Karan Singh Kaen helped him by supplying relevant statistical information.

Shri Kaen joined SCF in about 1944. He contested in 1946 for the UP Legislative Assembly on SCF ticket from Agra, but could not get elected.

After independence in 1947, he was appointed as Rehabilitation Officer and he continued to be in service till his retirement in 1959.

After his retirement, he joined the Republican Party of India. He contested in 1962 for the UP Legislative Assembly on RPI ticket from Agra, but could not get elected. He was a dedicated social worker and a staunch Ambedkarite.

He married Smt Rameshwari and got two sons and two daughters.

He expired on 12 January 1990 at the age of 92.

KAKKAN, P.[53] (1908-1981)

Shri Kakkan was born on 18 June 1908 at village Thumpai Patti, in Melur Taluka, Madurai district, Tamil Nadu. His father was a worshipper of a community deity, hence he was named as Poojari. Shri Kakkan was a student of Christian High School at Madurai. He left the school in 1922 when he failed in the SSLC examination.

Thereafter, he served as a teacher for a period of four years and later turned to social work. He led the Satyagraha for Temple Entry at Meenakshi temple, Madurai in 1925. He was the first untouchable satyagrahi to enter the temple.

He joined Congress and took part in the national freedom movement. He became Secretary of the Taluka Congress Committee and later became Treasurer of Madurai District Congress Committee.

---

53. Source of Information:

Personal interview with his son Shri Kasivishwanathan, IPS Commandant V Btn. T.N. Sp. Pollce, Avadl, Madras on 31-5-1989.

Shri P. Kakkan was a member of the Constituent Assembly during 1946 to 1950 and a member of the Provisional Parliament. As a member of the Constituent Assembly, he rendered his services to the people in general and the Scheduled Castes in particular. He strongly stood for reservation of appointments, especially in police and military services.

In the first general elections held in 1952, he contested as a Congress candidate from Madurai (G and SC) Lok Sabha constituency and got elected. Thereafter, he concentrated on State politics. He became President of the Madras Congress Committee in 1954. In the second general elections held in 1957, he contested as Congress candidate from Melur (G and SC) assembly constituency and got elected. During this period he became Minister for PWD and SC Welfare, Madras Government. Again he was elected for the Madras Assembly from Samayanallur (R) constituency in 1962. He again contested as Congress nominee in the year 1967 from Melur (SC) assembly constituency, but was defeated by DMK candidate.

He led a very simple life. He was known for his high moral and incorruptible character. He was honoured as freedom fighter for his active association with the freedom movement.

He married Smt Parvati and had five sons and one daughter. He died on 23 December 1981 at the age of 73.

KAMBLE, SHIVRAM JANBA[54] (1875-1940)

Shri Shivram Kamble was born in 1875 at Pune. His father Shri Janba Kamble left his ancestral village Bhamburde and came to Pune for a livelihood. He was serving as a butler with the Europeans. He secured the same service for his son also. Due to poverty Shri Shivram Kamble could not take any formal education. However, he learned to read and write. He was very much impressed by the European culture and civilization. He

---

54. Source of Information:
Harishchandra Narayanrao Navalkar.
S.J. Kamble Yatiche Charitra, (biography) Pune.

was influenced by the thoughts and mission of Mahatma Phule and Lokhitwadi. The overall condition of the untouchables was very pitiable. Therefore, he decided to liberate his brethren from untouchability and casteism.

At first he started to bring about social awareness among the untouchables. He wrote an article in *Maratha Deenbandhu* being published from Kolhapur, in the year 1902 through which he urged his brethren to educate their children and exhorted the government to recruit the untouchables in the police and military services. He wrote one *Soochi Patra* in 1903, got it printed on his own and distributed the copies among his brothers in the villages. In order to bring sociopolitical awareness among his brethren, he started publishing a monthly journal named *Samvanshiya Mitra* from Pune on 1 July 1908. It continued till 1 June 1910.

Since 1896, the recruitment of Mahars in the British military was stopped. Like Subedar Ramji Ambedkar and Gopalbaba Walangkar, he intended to take up the question of recruitment of the Mahars in the military. Therefore, he called a meeting of his brethren living in the vicinity of Pune, at Saswad near Pune in the year 1904. The main objective of the meeting was to demand for recruitment of the Mahars in the martial services. The meeting was continued for two days. It was attended by persons from 51 villages. They, however, decided to submit the petition of their demands to the Bombay Government. Accordingly, he submitted the petition to the Governor of Bombay, with the signatures of 1,588 people. It contained the following demands:

1. To appoint the untouchables in the lower services.
2. To allow them to serve in the police department.
3. To recruit them in the Indian Army.
4. To allow the untouchable students to take admission in the public schools.

When he did not get a positive response from the Bombay Government, he submitted a petition of the same demands to the Indian Government in June 1905, but in vain, therefore, he submitted the petition to the Secretary of State for India, on 10 December 1910.

He, however, became successful in his efforts. On 6 February 1917 when the First World War was at its height, the British Government decided to recruit the Mahars in the Army.

In order to raise the strength of his movement, he founded an organization of his brethren, named Shrishankar Prasadik Somvanshiya Hitchintak Mitra Samaj on 1 August 1904 at Pune. The main objectives of the organization as stated therein, were:

1. To organize the untouchables for their own development.
2. To start a school exclusively for the untouchable students.
3. To start one library.
4. To arrange lectures and discourses for bringing social awareness among the untouchables.

He, however, started a school and a library, but due to spread of plague in Pune, he had to close both the institutions.

He was against all those superstitions and such customs which were humiliating to the untouchables. Therefore, he started a movement against the Devadasi system which was prevailing among the Mahars and Mangs in the Bombay Presidency. In the conference of the Somvanshiya Mitra Samaj, held at Jejuri near Pune, on 5 April 1910, he exhorted his brethren to propagate against those bad customs. It was addressed by a great social reformer Shri Vithal Ramji Shinde and Subedar Bahadur Gangaram Krishnaji Ghatge. At the initiative of Shri Shivram J. Kamble, Shivubai Laxman Jadhav, a Devadasi was married to Ganpatrao Hanmantrao Gaikwad. His thoughts and deeds had greatly influenced the society in abandoning such inhuman customs. After having seen the active interest of Shri S.J. Kamble in social reformation, the Maharaja of Baroda, Shri Sayajirao Gaikwad invited him to Baroda on 11 September 1908 and honoured him in appreciation of his efforts.

He used to advise his brethren to abandon the superstitious system of sacrificing animals like male buffaloes, bulls and goats before the fictitious deity. He advised them not to eat beef and not to take spurious drinks. He advised his brethren to maintain cleanliness and cultural standard in the family.

He founded a new organization called The Depressed Classes Committee, on 16 April 1921. The Committee appealed to the Education Minister that education should be made compulsory, teachers should be drawn from among the untouchables, scholarships should be given to the students and at least one hostel in each district should be opened for the untouchable students. The then Education Minister Shri Pranjape assured the deputation of the Committee that scholarships would be granted and a hostel opened in Pune. The last measure was carried out in the year 1922.

The first International Congress held at Geneva in 1925 decided to find out as to how the health of children could be ensured. In response to that, the Government of India desired to know the views on the issue from various places. From Pune, the views of Shri S.J. Kamble were sought. Accordingly, he gave a detailed account of the causes of ill- health of the children in India and the measures to be taken for improving the same. He attributed premature death and illness, among others, to superstitions, ignorance and poverty. His views in this respect are still very much relevant.

At the initiative of Shri G.R. Hingnekar, an editor of *Dnyan Prakash,* a meeting of leaders of different castes was convened at Pune in 1922. It was presided over by Shri S.J. Kamble. Shri N.C. Kelkar, editor of *Kesari,* was the chief guest on the occasion. In this meeting Shri S.J. Kamble appealed to the conscience of the high caste people to treat the so-called untouchables on an equal footing and allow them to enter the temples.

In order to assert their religious right, the untouchables decided to enter the Parvati temple, at Pune. They formed one satyagraha committee in September 1929. Shri S. J. Kamble was its President and Shri P.N. Rajbhoj was its General Secretary. They gave a notice to that effect on 2 October 1929 to the trustees of the temple. They met the Collector of Pune on 9 October 1929 and urged him to allow them to exercise their legitimate right and avert any untoward incident on the occasion. However, the trustees stated that the temple was not a public place of worship and there was no custom as such to allow the untouchables to enter the temple. Consequently the untouchables decided to offer satyagraha at the temple on 13 October 1929. Accordingly a mob of 250 satyagrahis started their march raising slogans for victory to Shivaji Maharaj and to Chokhamela. They were divided into five groups; first consisted of N.V. Gadgil, P.N. Rajbhoj, Vinayakrao Bhuskute and others; second consisted of S.J. Kamble, Mrs Tanubai S. Kamble, Miss Shevantibai Kamble and others; third group comprised Shri Landge, Kothalekar, Swami Yoganand and others; those led by Shri Ishwara, Bhau Waghchoure and Mrs Kothalekar made up the fourth group; the satyagrahis under Shri Ranade and Shri Deshdas formed the fifth. The temple was deliberately locked. Some miscreants hurled stones on the satyagrahis. Shri P.N.Rajbhoj was injured and taken to hospital. The satyagraha was again offered on 15 November 1929. In a meeting held on 16 November 1927 at Damodar Thakarsay Hall, Bombay under the presidentship of Dr Babasaheb Ambedkar, it was unanimously resolved to support Shri S.J. Kamble and the satyagrahis, in their bid to enter the Parvati temple. However, due to the apathetic and antagonistic attitude of the caste Hindus, the satyagraha committee unanimously decided to postpone the satyagraha for the time being.

He attended the All India Depressed Classes Conference held in 1920 at Nagpur. He, however, said in the conference that the British Government was of no help in ameliorating the miseries of the untouchables. Therefore, they would abolish the caste system and develop on their own.

When the issue of separate electorate or joint electorate was being discussed on large scale, a meeting of the Depressed Classes was called at Pune on 11 October 1931, under the presidentship of Shri S.J. Kamble. The meeting reposed confidence in the leadership of Dr Babasaheb Ambedkar and supported the demand of separate electorate. The meeting unanimously condemned the policy pursued by Mahatma Gandhi and Pandit Malaviya at the Round Table Conference.

He married Tanubai and had a daughter. He died in about 1940 at the age of 65.

KARDAK, BHIMRAO[55] (1904-1990)

Shri Bhimrao Kardak was born on 11 November 1904 at Kasabe Sukene, in Niphad Taluka, Nasik district in Maharashtra in a Mahar family. His father's name was Shri Dhondiba Kardak. He studied up to fifth standard in a night school in Bombay.

Due to poverty he came to Bombay in search of a job. He got the job of Goods' painter in a tramway company. Once he attended the speech of Babasaheb Ambedkar in 1924 at Damodar Hall, Bombay which had a great influence on him. He remained faithful to him throughout his life. For some time he served in the Security Press, Nasik and then he got service in the Central Railway where he continued till his retirement.

He participated in the famous Kalaram Temple Satyagraha in 1930. On 26 October 1930 he formed at Nasik one organization named Yuvak Sangeet Jalsa Sangh under the auspices of which he performed *Jalsa* (folk-song and drama) in Nasik district and tried to propagate the message of Dr Babasaheb Ambedkar.

He used to present his *Jalsa* with *Bhimstavan.* He wrote *Satyagraha Jalsa, Maharaki, Sanatani Brahman, Dharmantar, Congress Bhakti,* etc. During 1931 to 1945 he presented near about 378 programmes of his *Jalsa.* He earned public appreciation and money. He presented a silver sword of 80 *tolas* to Dr Babasaheb Ambedkar as a token of his tribute to him.

Later, *Shahir* Wamandada Kardak (1922) continued the tradition of propagating the thoughts of Babasaheb Ambedkar through his songs.

It was due to these *shahirs* that thoughts of Babasaheb Ambedkar could reach the masses in the countryside. They moved the people through their songs and the impact on their minds remained intact.

Shri Bhimrao Kardak wrote a book entitled *Ambedkari Jalse: Swarup ani Karya* in 1978.

He died in about 1990 at the age of 86.

---

55. Source of Information:
Bhimrao Kardak. Ambedkari Jalse : Swarup ani Karya, 1978.

KHANDALE, R.G.[56]

Shri Ramachandra Khandale was born on 21 May 1913 at village Kurkumbh, Dound Taluka in Pune district. He belonged to Mang caste. His father Shri Genuji Khandale was a poor agricultural labourer. Shri Ramchandra Khandale passed fourth standard in English Medium from Saints High School, Dound in 1931.

Shri R.G. Khandale was dedicated to the Goddess as Potraj. However, one Ambedkarite worker from his community Shri Baba Waghmare from Dound convinced Shri Khandale that worshipping the Goddess as Potraj was futile. He further convinced him to cut his hair and discontinue worshipping any Hindu deity, thereupon Shri Khandale had his hair cut in 1930. Once he happened to see the *Jalsa* staged by Ramachandra Hari Bansode at Indapur in Pune district. Since the *Jalsa* was based on social problems, it very much influenced him. Therefore, Shri R.G. Khandale decided to strive for the uplift of the untouchables under the leadership of Dr Babasaheb Ambedkar.

In 1932 Shri Ramchandra G. Khandale founded All India Matang Seva Samaj and started organizing his brethren under its banner and spreading among them a new awareness.

He organized Bombay Provincial Matang Parishad in 1934 at Dound. Shri P.N. Rajbhoj presided over the conference and Shri B.K. Gaikwad addressed it as a chief guest. The conference, however, resolved to follow Dr Babasaheb Ambedkar. In 1936, he invited Dr Babasaheb Ambedkar to Dound to advise the Dalits. The Matang Parishad was active up to 1944.

Being a true follower of Babasaheb Ambedkar, he believed that separate electorate was necessary for the Dalits to ensure their real representation in the legislatures.

He tried to unite the Mahar and Mang communities among the Scheduled Castes in Maharashtra. He advised his brethren to

---

56. Source of Information:
Personal Interview with Shri R.G. Khandale RPI Office, Dound, Dist Pune on 5-5-1989.

avoid beef-eating, worshipping idols and taking drinks. He was against the tradition of dedicating persons to the Goddess as Potraj, Devdasi and Murali. He sincerely thought that those traditions brought indignity to the society. He was against Maharaki and Mangaki, the two hereditary services respectively, performed by the Mahars and Mangs for Baluta and Crumbs (Baluta is involuntary servitude because of which the hereditary servants were getting crumbs of bread as reward).

Shri Khandale joined the Independent Labour Party in 1937, the Scheduled Castes Federation in 1942 and the Republican Party of India in 1957. He actively participated in all the programmes of those parties. He was elected as Joint Secretary of the Maharashtra RPI unit in 1960.

He was sent to assist the leaders in Marathwada in organizing the satyagraha of landless people in the year 1953. He was imprisoned at Aurangabad for one and a half month for having participated in the satyagraha. He took part in the satyagraha for land at Kalamba in Kolhapur in 1956 for which he was awarded the punishment of imprisonment for 15 days.

He was also involved in the satyagrahas held at Rahuri (Nagar district) in 1959 and Dound in 1964-65.

In 1939, he was elected to the District Local Board, Pune. In the first general elections held in 1952 he contested from Pune-Haveli (R) assembly constituency on SCF ticket, but could not get elected. In the elections held in 1957 he could not contest on reserved seat as, being a Buddhist, he was then not entitled to do. In the general elections held in 1962 he contested from Barsi (G) assembly seat, but lost. Again he contested in 1972 from Dound assembly seat as RPI candidate but could not get elected.

He founded Nav Jeevan Vidyarthi Vasatigrih (hostel) at Dound in 1959 for the SC boys and remained busy in looking after its affairs throughout his life.

He was converted to Buddhism on Vijayadashmi day, 14 October 1956 at Nagpur by Dr Babasaheb Ambedkar. He tried to propagate Buddhism among the Scheduled Castes.

He married Lalubai. He had a daughter. His wife expired in 1958 when he was out for social work.

In recognition of his dedicated services to society and the Ambedkarite movement, the RPI, Pune unit honoured him on 21 May 1987 at Pune under the Presidentship of Smt J. Ishwaribai, the President of RPI. Shri Khandale was presented with a purse of ₹ 15,051.00.

KHANDARE JANOJI[57] (1830-1903)

Shri Janoji was born in about 1830, at Paras, Belapur Tulaka in Akola district. His father Kacharuji Khandare was a rich and respectable person of Mahar community.

Shri Janoji Khandare rightly thought that education was a must for the poor untouchables for their progress. However, there was no hostel at Akola for the students coming from remote places. Therefore, he acquired some land from the government for charitable purposes near Kholeshwar temple at Akola and constructed a hostel for the untouchable students at his own expense in the year 1895. It was the first ever hostel meant for the untouchable students, where initially 20-25 students were admitted.

Though he was illiterate, he tried to educate his brethren. He also had to undergo humiliation on the ground of untouchability. Hence he wanted the abolition of this system.

He died in 1903 at the age of 73 at Akola. After his death, Shri Janoji Free Boarding was run by his son Keshavarao Khandare, and now it is being run by Someshwar Khandare, his great grandson.

KHANDARE, S.A.[58] (1885-1958)

Shri Sambhuji Khandare was born in about 1885 at village Paras in Taluka Belapur, Akola district in Maharashtra. He

---

57. Source of Information:

Interview with his great grandson Shri Someshwar Bhalchandra Khandare at Shri Janoji Free Boarding. Akola on 18-10-1988. and other sources.

58. Source of information:

Personal interview with his daughter-in-law

Smt. Kalavatibal S.Khandare

Bhimnagar, Akola on 18-10-1988.

belonged to the Mahar community. His father was an agriculturist. Shri Sambhuji Khandare was educated up to the seventh standard.

His economic condition was quite good. For some time he worked as a petition writer. Later, he became commission agent of cotton in about 1913. In 1920, he became Superintendent of Janoji Free Boarding at Akola. Subsequently, he decided to strive to uplift the untouchables. He advised them to abandon beef-eating, drinking and idol worship.

In 1919 he became a member of Berar Watandar Mahar Association. In 1926 he formed the Varad Asprushya Samaj Sudharak Seva Mandal at Akola and strove to organize his brethren throughout the Berar region. The main objectives of the Mandal were to reconvert the SC Muslims to Hinduism, especially the women who were forced to convert to Islam; to spread education; to start technical institutes for imparting technical training to the Depressed Classes students; and to strive to throw open the wells and temples for the Depressed Classes. The Mandal tried to fulfil its objectives.

He convened a conference of the leaders of the Depressed Classes at Sudam theatre, Amravati in erstwhile Berar Province on 25 December 1932 under the presidentship of Babu L.N.Hardas. It was well attended. Shri S A.Khandare was elected as President of the Berar Provincial Depressed Classes Federation in the same convention. He organized a conference of the said organization at Shriram theatre, Akola on 16-17 June 1935.

During 1936 to 1938 he was a member of Municipal Council, Akola.

He joined the Independent Labour Party (ILP) and contested in 1937 as its candidate from Akola-Belapur Rural constituency, but could not get elected.

In 1942, he joined the Scheduled Castes Federation founded by Babasaheb Ambedkar. He was elected President of SCF unit of Berar region. He actively participated in the satyagraha under the banner of SCF in 1946. He contested for CP and Berar Legislative Assembly in 1946 from Akola constituency but could not get elected.

Shri L.K. Ogale, D.K. Bhagat, D.Z Palaspagar Zabuji. Shirsat and Shri Deenbandhu Shegaonkar were his coworkers. They led the Dalit liberation movement very heroically.

Shri S.A. Khandare was a staunch supporter of Babasaheb Ambedkar. He supported the demand of separate electorate and the proposal of conversion. Ultimately, he was converted to Buddhism on 14 October 1956 at Nagpur by Babasaheb Ambedkar.

Shri S.A. Khandare married Tanabai. He had a son, named Shankarrao Khandare (1926-1984). He was also a prominent Dalit leader.

Shri Sambhuji Khandare died on 7 June 1958 at the age of 73 at Akola.

KHANDEKAR, H.J.[59] (1902-1952)

Shri Hemchandra Khandekar was born in 1902 at village Wakodi, Taluka Savaner in Nagpur district in Maharashtra. His father Shri Jagoba Khandekar was *Kotwal* (village Mahar servant) at Wakodi. Shri Hemchandra Khandekar passed his intermediate from Hislop College, Nagpur in 1924. He was well versed in English and Sanskrit apart from Marathi.

After completion of his education, he joined in Nagpur Municipality as sanitary inspector. He left the service in 1930 and plunged into political activities.

Shri Hemchandra was influenced by his uncle who had embraced the Mahanubhav sect, a liberal Hindu denomination. He also embraced the same sect as a protest against orthodox Hinduism. He was strictly vegetarian. He observed all the rules and regulations of the Mahanubhav sect.

He started his social career as a Secretary of the Madhya Prantiya Tarun Mahar Sangh formed at Nagpur in the year 1926 under the leadership of Shri Raghvendrarao Borkar. The Sangh

---

59. Source of information:
Personal Interview with his son Dr Pandit H. Khandekar
Opp. Tidake Vidyalaya, Katol Road, Nagpur on 23-10-1988.

was a social organization which undertook several reforms in the Mahar community. The Tarun Mahar Sangh was against conversion of the Mahars to any other religion. They were instrumental in reconverting near about 25 Mahar girls who converted to Islam and they were married in the community and well settled.

He was a strong supporter of Dr Babasaheb Ambedkar. A meeting was called by the Tarun Maha Sangh at Indora, Nagpur on 25 October 1930 to support their leader Dr Babasaheb Ambedkar. However, he joined the All India Depressed Classes Association under the leadership of Shri G.A.Gawai, M.C.Rajah and others in the year 1930. He attended the conference of the Depressed Classes Association held at New Delhi under the presidentship of Shri M.C. Rajah. The conference supported the Rajah-Moonje Pact which accepted joint electorate and deplored the demand of separate electorate for which Dr Babasaheb Ambedkar was trying his best.

Shri Hemchandra Khandekar was against the conversion of the Depressed Classes to any other religion.

He contested for the CP and Berar Legislative Assembly in the by-election held on 25 March 1939 as an independent candidate from Kamathi-Nagpur seat. It was a contest between Congress candidate Shri T.C. Sakhare, ILP candidate Shri G.T. Meshram and Shri H.J. Khandekar. Shri Khandekar. however, got elected in the election. He was very popular among the *bidi* workers, for whom he worked.

He left all India Depressed Classes Association in 1942 and joined the Congress. He took part in the Quit India Movement in 1942. He was elected to the CP and Berar Legislative Assembly in the elections held in 1945 from the Nagpur-Kamathi seat. He was elected to the Constituent Assembly in the year 1946. He was a very active member of the Constituent Assembly. He strongly advocated reservations for the Scheduled Castes. He justified reservations "as a compensation for the atrocities" they suffered. He did not think that it was any 'favour' to them. He pleaded that reservations must be continued for more than ten years. He presided over the 13th session of the All India Depressed Classes League held at Nagpur on 4 June 1950. He was however denied party nomination in the first general elections by the Congress high command due to his social commitment and strong policy. He contested in 1952 from Bhandara (G and SC) Parliamentary constituency as an independent but he was defeated by the Congress candidate Shri T.C. Sakhare.

He married Parvatibai, after whose death he married Shantabai, daughter of Shri Pandurang Nandram Bhatkar, a Dalit leader from Amravati. Shri Hemchandra Khandekar is survived by one son and one daughter, both are well settled in life.

Shri Hemchandra Khandekar died on 25 May 1952 at Nagpur at the age of 50.

KHOBARAGADE, D.B.[60] (1900-1966)

Shri Dewaji Khobaragade was born on 2 January 1900 at Chandrapur in Maharashtra. He belonged to the Mahar community. His parents Shri Bhiwaji Khobaragade and Shrimati Paikabai were agriculturists. Shri Dewaji had his primary education in Municipal School at Chandrapur. He, however, failed in High School Certificate examination in 1917.

After leaving school in 1917, he worked as time keeper in Mahakali Collieries. He started a handloom thread shop for weavers in 1923. He started brokership firm in agricultural produce since 1931. Since 1942 he started managing a timber stall at Ballarpur. He was an industrious and a hard worker. He was economically well-to-do.

He was active in social and political field since his youth. He led the movement of Dalit liberation in Chandrapur district. He was Chairman of the Reception Committee of Conference of the CP Dalit Congress held at Chandrapur under the presidentship of Shri Tularam Sakhare, on 29 June 1932. He was member of Jury in Chandrapur Court from 1937 to 1942.

He was close to Babasaheb Ambedkar since 1928. In the provincial assembly elections held in 1937, he contested as

---

60. Source of Information:

Interview with his nephew Dr Jamanadas P. Khobaragade, F.R.C.S. Mahatma Gandhi Road, Chandrapur on 14-4-1990.

Independent Labour Party candidate from Brahmpuri (Chandrapur district) (R) seat and get elected defeating his rival Congress candidate Shri Tularam Sakhare.

He was elected President of Municipal Notified Area Committee of Ballarshah from 1946 to 1947.

He presided over the conference of the Scheduled Castes of Mahakosal region at Chindwada on 26 and 27 May 1940.

He organized and presided over the mass conversion to Buddhism ceremony where Babasaheb Ambedkar had officiated at Chandrapur on 16 October 1956. About two lakhs of people embraced Buddhism. This was the second and last conversion ceremony conducted by Dr Babasaheb Ambedkar.

He married Indirabai in 1915. He had five sons and two daughters. His elder son Shri Bhaurao alias Rajabhau Khobaragade, Bar-at-Law (1925-1984) was a renowned leader of the Scheduled Castes in the post Ambedkar era. He led the Dalit liberation movement from 1950 till his death in 1984.

Shri D.B. Khobaragade got full support and inspiration in his social activities from his elder brother Shri Patruji Khobaragade.

Shri Dewaji Khobaragade died on 28 June 1966 at the age of 66.

KONADA SURYAPRAKASHRAO[61]

Shri Konada Suryaprakshrao was born on 13 February 1913 at Peda-Palaparra, Taluka Gudiwada in Krishna district in Andhra pradesh. He belonged to the Adi-Andhra community. His father Konada Yarkaiah was a small shopkeeper. Shri K. Suryaprakashrao passed his matric in 1930 from Gudiwada and Intermediate in 1934 from P.R.College, Kakinada.

He took part in Adi-Andhra movement from 1936 onwards. From 1941-43 he was President of Agricultural Labourers Union under the auspices of the Communist Party. The annual conference of the Krishna District Agricultural Labourers' Union

---

61. Source of Information:
Personal Interview with Shri Konada Suryaprakashrao
Arundelpeta, Sanjivaya Colony, Vijayawada. on 28-5-1989.

was held at Nidumolu under his presidentship on 25-26 April 1943. However, the leaders of the union moved a resolution in the said conference to support the Muslim league and not to support the SCF which was allegedly a communal organization. The President of the conference, Shri K. Suryaprakashrao asked for an explanation, which was given but did not satisfy him. Therefore, he left the Communist Party and joined the Scheduled Castes Federation in September 1944.

He started his social work under the leadership of Shri N. Hari and P. Gopalakrishnan who were respectively General Secretary and President of the SCF of Andhra Pradesh. Shri N. Hari and his co-workers successfully arranged the tour of Dr Babasaheb Ambedkar at several places in Andhra region. This brought about mass awakening in the region.

He contested in April 1946 on SCF ticket for Madras Legislative Assembly from Krishna (East) (R) constituency, but he was defeated by the Congress candidate Shri Vemula Kurmayya. He contested in the first general elections in 1952 as SCF nominee from Kankipadu (G) constituency but did not achieve success in the election. Again, he contested in the 1962 elections as an Independent from Vijayawada (North) constituency for Andhra Pradesh Legislative Assembly but he was defeated.

Presently, he is leading a happy family life with his wife Kamalabai, and three sons and two daughters at Vijayawada. Now, he is Vice-president of the Republican Party of India, Andhra Pradesh branch and still busy with socio-political activities.

KRISHNASWAMY[62] (1916-1973)

Shri Krishnaswamy was born on 1 June 1916 at Pallikonda, Vellore, in North Arcot district (Ambedkar district) in Tamil Nadu. He was an Adi-Dravida. His father Murugan was an

---

62. Source of Information:

Interview with his son Shri P.K. Manokaran

28 Thalapathi Krishnaswamy Nagar. Pallikonda (N.A.) Ambedkar district, Tamil Nadu on 30-9-1989.

agricultural labourer. Shri M. Krishnaswamy had passed his SSLC in 1933 from Weseley College, Royapettah, Madras.

Shri Krishnaswamy was influenced and inspired by Rao Bahadur N. Shivaraj. He decided to work for Dalit uplift under his leadership.

In the year 1934 when Mahatma Gandhi was about to enter the Ranganath temple at Pallikonda during his Madras State tour, Shri Krishnaswamy boldly came forward and told him that the untouchables were not allowed to enter the temple and they were subjected to discrimination in the schools and other public places. Thereupon, Mahatma Gandhi urged the caste Hindus to allow the untouchables to enter the temple first. He said that he would enter the temple only when the untouchables would be allowed to do so. His appeal, however, could not evoke favourable response from the caste Hindus. Hence, Gandhiji went back without entering the temple. Afterwards, Shri Krishnaswamy led a procession of thousands of people to claim religious equality and to enter the temple. Ultimately the temple authorities yielded to the demand of the Depressed Classes.

He joined the Scheduled Castes Federation in 1942 itself and organized its branches in Tamil Nadu and Karnataka. He organized the Scheduled Castes Students Federation in Tamil Nadu in the year 1947 under the presidentship of then student Shri A. Padmanabhan, who became an IAS officer later on. After the formation of the Republican Party of India, Shri Krishnaswamy was elected as president of RPI Tamil Nadu unit. He actively participated in almost all the activities of the RPI. He, however, led the satyagraha of the landless agricultural labourers in the year 1964 as per the decision of the Central Committee of the RPI. He was, therefore, awarded the punishment of imprisonment for a period of 15 days. He was put in Central Jail, Vellore.

He took an active part in the election politics also. In the year 1946 he contested as SCF candidate for the Madras Assembly from Tiruvannamali constituency, but in vain. He contested in the first general election in 1952 for Lok Sabha from Vellore

(G and SC) constituency but in vain. He contested from Gudiyattam (Assembly seat) in the by-elections held in 1955, but he was not elected. He again contested in the 1957 general elections for Lok Sabha from Vellore (G and SC) constituency as well as for Madras Legislative Assembly from Gudiyattam (R) constituency but without success. Again, he contested in 1962 from Vellore (G and SC) Lok Sabha constituency, but he could not get elected. He finally contested in 1967 for Lok Sabha from Vellore (G) as RPI candidate, but he failed.

He was a member of the North Arcot district Adi-Dravida Education Society, Vellore. He ran a free hostel at Pallikonda for the poor Scheduled Caste students coming from far off places.

He was co-editor of *Udhayu Surian,* a Tamil fortnightly, from 1940 to 1947 and editor and publisher of *Samathuva Sanghu,* a Tamil fortnightly, from 1947 to 1951 and from 1954 to 1962. Both were the mouthpieces of SCF and RPI.

He preached and propagated the philosophy of Dr Babasaheb Ambedkar throughout his life. He did not yield to the undue allurements and promises given by the Congress. He was a selfless servant of the society. Therefore, the Scheduled Castes people fondly called him, *Thalapathi* or the lieutenant of the Dalit movement.

He expired on 30 September 1973 at the age of 57. He is survived by two sons and one daughter.

KUREEL, PIARELALL[63] (1916-1984)

Shri Piarelall Kureel was born on 27 December 1916 at Ghatampur, tahsil Purwa, Unnao district in Uttar Pradesh. His father Shri Manuva Ram Kureel was in the British Army and retired as Subedar Major. Shri Manuva Ram Kureel (Imperial Service Order) was a brave military officer. After his retirement he came to his native place Ghatampur, but he could not feel

---

63. Source of Information:

Personal interview with his younger brother Shri Niranjanlall Kureel, Shiv Sadan, Motinagar, Lucknow. UP on 11.6.1991.

content there so, he came to Lucknow and settled there. He felt insulted at his village where there was acute untouchability. In those days the Scheduled Castes women were not allowed to wear silver or golden ornaments. Shri Manuva Ram protested against this unjust system and became successful in it. He could raise the morale of his brethren against the caste Hindus. Even after coming to Lucknow he was always in contact with his brethren at his village and other places.

Shri Piarelall Kureel was well-educated. He was M.A., LL.B. Soon after his education he continued the mission of social service which his father had started. At first, he started his campaign against Brahmanism. He used to tell his people about how Brahmanism had ruined the Scheduled Castes.

He started his campaign against the Choudhary system in the community. The Choudharies or elites who were adjudicating the cases between community members were exploiting the community. On the other hand the *Bhaktas* or the priests among the Scheduled Castes were also taking advantage of the community. They considered themselves to be superior to the *Jagtas* or the laymen. Therefore, he exhorted his brethren to abolish Choudhary system of adjudication and the Bhakta system. He was against sanskritization of the society. He was against *Bhakti.* He favoured *Shakti.* He preached against vegetarianism and traditionalism, which were growing fast in the society and dividing it into two groups. He taught them to unite, earn strength and give a decisive fight to Brahmanism.

He thought that the Scheduled Castes should educate their children. He started Manuva Ram Primary School and a hostel at Unnao in about 1940.

He was very active in politics. He was elected member of the Working Committee of the All India Scheduled Castes Federation founded in 1942 under the leadership of Dr Babasaheb Ambedkar. He became President of the SCF of UP branch. He convened several meetings and conferences of the party and propagated the message of the party throughout UP. He was mainly responsible in spreading party activities in UP.

When Babasaheb Ambedkar became Labour Member in the Viceroy's Executive Council, Shri Piarelall was nominated as a member of the Central Assembly in which capacity he remained from 1942 to 1946. He contested for the UP Legislative Assembly in 1946 from Kanpur city constituency on SCF ticket, but he could not get elected. In the first general elections held in 1952, he contested from Banda district cum-Fatehpur (G and SC) Lok Sabha seat as Congress candidate and got elected. He was elected as member of Rajya Sabha in 1962.

He submitted a memorandum of Demands to the Parliamentary delegation on 5 February 1946. He thought, "The Scheduled Castes deserve far greater political protection than any other minority in India." He was of the view that the Scheduled Castes ought to be recognized as a separate entity and their representation should be by separate electorate.

During 1940-41 he ran a weekly *The Untouchable* with the help of his brother Shri Niranjanlal Kureel. Piarelall Kureel had written *Navai-Sherosh, Surir-e-Khama* and *Nala*-e-Dard in Urdu and *What about the sixty millions*?'

He married Krishna Devi and had three sons and six daughters. Mrs Krishna Piarelall Kureel was also an active socio-political worker. She was Municipal Commissioner of Unnao in 1946.

His whole family was active in the social life. His eldest brother Shri Mohanlall Kureel (1910-1980) was in INA under the leadership of Subhas Chandra Bose. His younger brother Shri Niranjanlall Kureel (1920) cooperated with him in his social activities.

Shri Piarelall Kureel breathed his last on 27 December 1984 at the age of 68.

KUSUM DHARMANNA[64] (1898-1948)

Shri Kusum Dharmanna was born in about 1898 at Rajahmundri in Andhra Pradesh. He was a great poet. His

---

64. Source of Information:

Andhra Pradesh State Harijan Conference Souvenir (1976). Hyderabad.

poems were published under the title *Nalladothanamu* (Brown Bureaucracy).

He wrote *Harijan Sathakam,* based on the socio-economic life of the Scheduled Castes. He was an Ambedkarite thinker, poet and activist. In order to propagate the thoughts of Dr Babasaheb Ambedkar, he started one Telugu weekly *Jayabheri.*

He was popular throughout Andhra Pradesh including the erstwhile Hyderabad State. His poems were very popular in those days. Therefore he was popularly known as 'Modern Vemanna'.

On 29 September 1936 he was invited to Hyderabad by the Youth League of Ambedkarites and an address was presented to him in his honour by Shri P.R. Venkataswamy, a great writer and activist, in the presence of Rao Saheb, B.S. Venkatrao.

Shri Kusum Dharmanna, being a true follower of Babasaheb Ambedkar, was of the view that there was no salvation for the Scheduled Castes unless and until they change their religion based on Varna and caste system.

He was of the view that the so-called untouchables were the original inhabitants of this country; as such they ought to gain an honourable place as a separate entity. He was a pioneer of Adi-Andhra movement in the Andhra region. He presided over many Adi-Andhra conferences in Andhra region. He tried to bring about a new awareness amongst the Scheduled Castes in Andhra Pradesh.

He died in 1948 at the age of 50.

LALINGKAR, P.L. (1902-1974)

Shri Punaji Lalingkar was born in about 1902 at village Laling near Dhulia in Maharashtra. He belonged to Mahar community. His father Shri Lingaji Lalingkar was a supplier of grass grown in the jungles of Khandesh. Shri Punaji Lalingkar was educated up to fourth standard.

He took an active part in Kalaram Temple Entry Satyagraha from 1930-35. In 1930, he protected Babasaheb Ambedkar when the opponents of the said satyagraha pelted stones on the satyagrahis at Nasik. During those days he organized a volunteer corps of 100 young social workers to combat the forces of the orthodox caste Hindus in probable attacks on Dalits.

He, with the help of his volunteers fetched water from a public well at Laling, for which the caste Hindus boycotted the Dalits. The boycott continued for one year. He tried to unite the Mahars, Mangs and Bhangis for the social cause.

When Dr Babasaheb Ambedkar came to Dhulia on 31 July 1937 in connection with court work, Mr Lalingkar organized a meeting of the Depressed Classes at Gajanan theatre, Dhulia. Dr Babasaheb Ambedkar exhorted the meeting to spread education among the Dalits, and if possible to start their own schools. Taking inspiration from his mentor's advice Shri Lalingkar founded Paschim Khandesh Dalit Shikshan Prasarak Mandal, an educational institution at Dhule in June 1939. On its behalf he established a hostel for the Dalit students at Nandurbar, a remote town in Dhule district. He continued the hostel without the aid of the government for three years. He would collect the necessary grains from his brethren and feed 10 to 15 boarders in the hostel. After his death, Shri Raosaheb Nilay (1924-1986), President of the institute, developed the institute.

Mr Lalingkar joined the ILP in 1936 and SCF in 1942. He contested for the Bombay Legislative Assembly in the first general elections held in 1952 from East Shahada-Sindkheda-Nandurbar constituency, but in vain.

He converted to Buddhism in 1956 itself at the instance of Babasaheb Ambedkar at Nagpur. He was present at the time of formation of RPI at Nagpur in 1957. He was executive member of All India Samata Sainik Dal which was constituted under the presidentship of Baba Awode in 1957. Shri D.Y. Bagale, Ashok Niley and Shri Sane were his co-workers.

He married Smt Bhagirathibai. They got three sons and two daughters. He died in about 1974 at Dhulia.

LASKAR, N.C.[65] (1908–1987)

Shri Nibaran Chandra Laskar was born in February 1908 at village Nizphubari, Cachar district in Assam. His father's name was Ratan Moni Laskar. Shri Nibaran Chandra Laskar had passed his matriculation from Haila-Kandi H.E. High School, B.A. from M.C. College, Sylhet, and M.A. in Sanskrit from Dacca University in 1931. He was appointed as Professor of Sanskrit and Bengali at G.C. College, Silchar in 1935 and continued to be so till 1945. Thereafter, he joined Congress and participated into national freedom movement and Dalit liberation movement.

He started his political career as a member of Silchar Municipal Board from 1946 and continued to be so till 1949. He was elected member of Assam Legislative Assembly in 1947. Subsequently, he was elected to the Constituent Assembly in August 1947. He was a member of the Constituent Assembly from 1947 to 1950. Later, he was inducted in the Ministry of Assam as Deputy Minister, Department of Relief and Rehabilitation in 1951.

In the first general elections held in 1952 he contested from Cachar-Lushai Hills (G and SC) Lok Sabha constituency and got elected. In the second general elections held in 1957, he was elected unopposed from the same Lok Sabha constituency.

He worked for the abolition of untouchability and for securing the legitimate rights for the welfare of the Scheduled Castes in Assam. He was of the view that the Scheduled Castes would have no future in Pakistan.

He breathed his last on 25 June 1987.

MAHARSHI BALINATHJI[66] (1867-1925)

Shri Balinathji was born in 1867 at Mandavari, tahsil Lalsot, Jaipur district in Rajasthan. He belonged to the Bairava caste. His

---

65. Source of Information:

Shri Nihar Ranjan Laskar. Phulbari (Shiilongpatti) P.O. Silchar Dist. Cachar, Assam.

66. Source of Information:

Shivprasad Marmat (ed.), *Batrawa Jyoti* (Jan, 1989), Bairawa Ashram, New Delhi,

parents were Shri Kisanaram and Smt Sundaribai Bendval. Shri Hira Bharati was his Guru.

Shri Balinathji Maharaj was pained to see the pathetic condition of the untouchables in Rajasthan. He manifested his resentment against Hinduism by preaching *Manushdarma* to his brethren. He opposed casteism, untouchability and superstitions in the name of religion. He believed in the equality of all the human beings. Due to age-long oppression and suppression of the untouchables by the Brahmanic forces, the untouchables had lost all courage and vigour to oppose them. Shri Balinathji Maharaj tried his best to raise the morale of his brethren, by infusing a new vigour and confidence in them. He tried to liberate them from the most exploitative bonded labour system prevailing in those days. He tried to change the mental attitude of the untouchables and encouraged them to protest against Brahmanism. He advised them to maintain high moral and cultural standard.

Maharshi Balinathji Maharaj breathed his last in 1925.

MAJUMDAR, SARAT CHANDRA[67]

Shri Sarat Chandra Majumdar was born on 14 September 1897 at Poradanga, Jessore district (now in Bangladesh). His father Shri Darpa Narayan Majumdar was a rent-collector under the Chanchra Raj Estate, and his uncle late Raicharan Majumdar was a popular Dalit leader. He belonged to Namasudra caste.

Shri Sarat Chandra Majumdar was born with cataracts in both his eyes. However, he passed his matriculation in 1920 from Panjia H.E. School, Jessore. He passed his B.A. from Daulatpur Hindu Academy, Calcutta in 1925. He passed his B.L. from Calcutta University in the year 1937.

For some time he worked as a teacher at Mashihati H.E. School founded by his uncle Raicharan Majumdar. In the

---

67. Source of Information:

Shri Sarat Chandra Majumdar, Village Dogachia, P.O. Monomohanpur, Dist. North Pargana, W.B. on 22.11.1988

meantime, he was elected President of Kultia Union Board and nominated as a member of Jessore Sadar Local Board and the District Board.

In 1933, he was elected Assistant Secretary of All Bengal Namasudra Association, and Vice-president of Namasudra Association, Calcutta.

He took part in the satyagraha in support of the demand for one-third share to the landowners and two-thirds share of the yield to the tenants.

He opposed the Muslim Mullahs in their attempts to convert the Namasudras of Sylhet in Assam to Islam. He took an active part in the movement for rescuing Hindu women, including the Dalit women abducted by the Muslims in those days. He wrote many articles in *Amrit Bazar Patrika* and tried to raise mass opinion against the Muslim atrocities on the Hindus.

He joined the Indian National Congress in 1935. He was elected member of the Bengal Provisional Congress Executive Committee in 1946.

However, after the partition of India in August 1947, he stayed in East Pakistan (now Bangladesh). In 1954, he was elected to the East Pakistan Legislative Assembly as a candidate of the Pakistan National Congress. He became a Minister to the Government of East Pakistan from 1955 to 1958. He earned wide popularity as a minister for his honesty, integrity and ability. After the imposition of martial law in East Pakistan, he left his homeland with a heavy heart and came to West Bengal on 28 June 1961. He left all the ancestral property in Bangladesh. He settled down at Dogachia near Bongaon in North 24 Parganas district of West Bengal.

Since his arrival in India, Shri Majumdar had been agitating for the cause of the Hindus and the Scheduled Castes left in Bangladesh.

Shri Majumdar is a good writer. He wrote *Panch Kath,* a collection of short stories in 1959, *Palwal,* a collection of verses in 1961, *Patra-Mukutika,* a novel in 1981 and *Raicharan Charit,* a biography of Raicharan in 1983. He was a member of Sahitya Sangh, Jessore.

Shri Rasiklal Biswas, Anant Kumar Biswas, Phani Bhusan Roy and others were his co-workers.

He has two daughters and one son. Even at this age he takes interest in the uplift of the Dalits.

MAKESAR, V.D.[68] (1878-1968)

Shri Vithal Makesar was born in 1878 at Shendurjana Dashasar, Taluka Chandur in Amaravati district. His father Shri Dashrath Makesar was a village *Kotwal*. Shri Vithal Makesar did not come up to matric level. He belonged to the Mahar community.

Shri V.D. Makesar decided to serve the untouchable community. He chose Yeotmal. He was a member of Mahar Sudharak Mandal founded in 1910. Shri V.D. Makesar visited many villages in Amravati and Yeotmal districts and preached for unity among the sub-castes of the Scheduled Castes. He advised his brethren to maintain high moral and cultural standard, educate their children and not to drink.

In 1925, Shri V.D. Makesar started Shri Chokhamela free boarding at Yeotmal for the Scheduled Castes students. It is still in existence. It was his great contribution to the welfare of his brethren.

He participated in the Temple Entry Satyagraha at Amravati and Pune in 1929.

He got the honour of being appointed as the honorary Magistrate for Yeotmal. He was Vice-president of Berar Depressed Classes Federation in 1932. He presided over the Conference of the Untouchables at Dhanora in Buldhana district held on 30-31 January 1934. He joined ILP in 1937, SCF in 1942 and RPI in 1957.

---

68. Source of Information:

Personal Interview with his son Shri Madhukar Makesar

Shri Chokhamela Free Boarding Yeotmal (Maharashtra) on 31-10-1988.

He converted to Buddhism at the instance of Babasaheb Ambedkar and tried to propagate Buddhism in Yeotmal and Buldhana districts.

He took part in election politics, but could not achieve success.

He married Smt Banabai and had two sons and three daughters. He was selfless social worker throughout his life. He died on 29 July 1956 at the age of 90.

MANDAL, J.N[69] (1904-1968)

Shri Jogendra Nath Mandal was born on 29 January 1904 at village Maister Kandi, Barisal district in Bengal. He was a Namasudra. His father's name was Shri Ramdayal Mandal and mother's name was Smt Sandhya Devi. Shri Ramdayal Mandal was a farmer. Shri Jogendra Nath Mandal was admitted in primary school at the age of eight. He passed his entrance examination in first division in 1924. He completed his B.A. from B.M. College Barisal in 1929. He sought admission for M.A. and law course in Dacca University in 1930. He, however, left Dhaka due to financial and political reasons and came to Calcutta, where he passed his B.L. in 1934.

He thought that the Scheduled Castes would not attain emancipation unless they get a due share in political power. He strove throughout his life for securing political power for the Scheduled Castes. In the elections held in 1937 for the Bengal Legislative Assembly, he contested as an independent candidate against a mighty zamindar Congress candidate and got elected. He was leader of the Independent Scheduled Castes Party consisting of a group of 20 legislators of the Scheduled Castes. He was elected Secretary and Shri Hemchandra Naskar was President of the Independent Scheduled Castes legislative party. Their group was well united and strong. They could secure 15 per cent reservation in the services for the Scheduled Castes.

---

69. Source of Information:
Personal Interview with his son Shri Jagadish Chandra Mandal 28/12 Nakuleswar Bhattacharya Lane, Calcutta on 28-10-1988.

He was honourably inducted in the ministry of Bengal in April 1943. He worked under the leadership of the then Chief Minister of United Bengal, Shri Khwaja Nazimuddin. In his ministry, there were three Scheduled Caste ministers. Shri Mandal accepted the ministership to serve the poor Scheduled Castes from inside the government.

In the meantime Shri Mandal joined the Scheduled Castes Federation under the leadership of Dr Babasaheb Ambedkar and formed the Bengal Provincial Scheduled Castes Federation. He started one weekly paper, *Jagaran* through which he tried to make people politically conscious.

In March 1945, the Nazimuddin ministry was defeated. In the elections held in 1946 for the Bengal Legislative Assembly Shri Mandal successfully contested from Bakarganj South West (Rural) General Constituency as a candidate of the Scheduled Castes Federation. Thereafter, H.S. Surahvardy, the leader of Muslim League formed the ministry in Bengal in April 1946 and he included Shri J.N. Mandal in his ministry.

According to the Cabinet Mission Plan, the Interim Government was formed in August 1946 under the leadership of Pandit Nehru. The Congress included Shri Jagjivan Ram in the ministry. The Muslim League joined the Interim ministry in October 1946. The Muslim League, however, included Shri J.N. Mandal in the ministry. He got the portfolio of Law. Thereafter, the SCF in its convention held in the last week of October 1946 at Agra under the presidentship of Shri P.N. Rajbhoj, passed a resolution congratulating Shri Mandal on his induction in the Interim ministry. Shri Mandal joined the cabinet on 1 November 1946.

The meeting of the Working Committee of the SCF was held at Rajgriha, Bombay on 16 January 1947, in which the memorandum to be submitted to the Constituent Assembly was approved. Both, Dr Babasaheb Ambedkar and Shri J.N. Mandal were present at the meeting.

When Dr Babasaheb Ambedkar found that there was no possibility of getting elected to the Constituent Assembly from Bombay due to lack of supporters, Shri J.N. Mandal came to his help. Shri Mandal on the strength of the SC MLAs and Muslim

League, got him elected from Bengal Legislature. Thus, it was because of Mandal's cooperation that Babasaheb Ambedkar entered the Constituent Assembly in 1946. However, due to partition he lost the seat. Then, he got elected from Bombay Legislature in 1947.

In the All India SC Students Conference held at Nagpur on 26 December 1946, Shri Mandal made it clear that, "We have no quarrel with any party. We demand our legitimate rights and we look upon those who accept our demand as our friends." Further, he said, "the Congress is not prepared to give anything to the Scheduled Castes, but if any other party gives out of its share some concessions to us the Congress leaders feel enraged. How can we accept the Congress assurance about the future of our community under the new Constitution?"

When Pakistan came into existence on 14 August 1947 under the Indian Independence Act, 1947, Shri J.N. Mandal opted to remain in Pakistan. Moreover, he was inducted in the first ministry formed under the leadership of Premier Liaquat Ali Khan as a Minister of Law and Labour. He had the unique honour of presiding over the first meeting of the Pakistan Constituent Assembly on 10 August 1947. However, due to severe differences with the leaders of Pakistan on the issue of protecting the interests of the Scheduled Castes, he submitted his resignation from the ministership and presidentship of the Constituent Assembly on 8 October 1950. Subsequently, he left Pakistan and came to India. He settled in Calcutta and resumed his service of his community.

Due to his dedicated services to his community he was called *Mahapran* J.N. Mandal.

Shri J.N. Mandal was against the partition of Bengal. On 21 April 1947 he said very categorically, "The present communal trouble was a temporary phase, which could not last long and that division of the province was not solution to the problem. It was not in the interests of Hindus to divide the province and the Scheduled Castes were definitely opposed to partition." Again, in a meeting held under the auspices of the Bengal Provincial

Scheduled Castes Federation at the Indian Association Hall, Calcutta on 16 May 1947 under the presidentship of R.B. Anukul Chandra Prasad, "a resolution expressing the determination of the Scheduled Castes to oppose the demand for partition was passed." He was, however, "disillusioned" to see "the resolution passed by the Working Committee of the Bengal Provincial Congress Committee supporting the proposal of partition." It. could presumably be said that he previously opted to go to Pakistan only with the intention to protect the interest of the Scheduled Castes who remained in the territory of Pakistan believing in the assurances given by the Muslim League. When he realized that it was difficult to carry out his intentions he had no other option but to return to India.

In order to educate his brethren, he started *Jagaran,* a weekly journal from Calcutta in 1943. It was, however, discontinued. Thereafter, he started *The People's Herald,* a weekly paper from Calcutta in the first week of January 1945. Dr Babasaheb Ambedkar was present at the inaugural function of the said paper.

He contested from Barasat Lok Sabha constituency (G) (West Bengal) as a candidate of Republican Party of India in the general elections held in 1967, but could not get elected.

He died on 5 October 1968 at the age of 64 at Calcutta.

MANE. R.K.[70] (1917–2002)

Shri Revansiddh Krishnath Mane was born in 1917 at village Bembli in Osmanabad district, Maharashtra. He belonged to the Mahar caste. He passed his matriculation in 1940 from Vivek Vardhini High School, Hyderabad. He joined intermediate, but could not complete it. During his student life, he was one of the organizers of the Depressed Classes Students Union at Hyderabad.

---

70. Source of Information:
Personal interview with R.K. Mane
Bembli, Osmanabad on 9-5-1989.

He joined the Depressed Classes Association led by B.S. Venkatrao. However, he left that organization in 1946 and joined the Scheduled Castes Federation led by J.H. Subbiah. He became Joint Secretary of the SCF, Hyderabad State branch and continued to be so till 1954. When Shri J.H. Subbiah merged his group with the Congress in 1954, he also joined the Congress.

He had tried to awaken and organize the Dalits in Osmanabad district. After the police action in Hyderabad, he was nominated as member of the Scheduled Castes Trust Fund established by the Nizam for the welfare of the Scheduled Castes in the Nizam State.

The Scheduled Castes Federation at the initiative of Dr Babasaheb Ambedkar had decided to launch a massive satyagraha for securing wasteland and *gairan* to the landless people in the Marathwada region. Accordingly, the satyagraha was launched in Marathwada in the year 1953. Shri Mane led the satyagraha very successfully.

He contested for the Hyderabad Legislative Assembly in 1952 general elections from Ibrahimpatnam reserved constituency on SCF ticket, but was defeated by Congress nominee Shri M.B. Goutam. He contested in 1957 on Congress ticket from Kalam (Osmanabad) reserved constituency for Maharashtra Legislative Assembly and got success. In the 1962 general elections, he contested for Lok Sabha from Osmanabad (G) as an independent, but in vain.

Now, he was leading a happy family life with his wife, Parvatibai and six sons. He breathed his last on 1 July 2002.

MANE, S.N.[71]

Shri Shantaram Mane was born in 1908 at Kondi, in Chikodi Taluka, Belgaum district in Karnataka. He belonged to the Mahar community. His father Shri Nanasaheb Mane was an

---

71. Source of Information:
Personal Interview with Barrister S.N. Mane
Jawahar Nagar, Kolhapur on 6-5-1989.

agriculturist. Shri Shantaram Mane passed his B.A. from Rajaram College, Kolhapur and Bar-at Law from Middle Temple, London.

After having seen the wretched condition of the untouchables, he decided to strive for their uplift. He advised his brethren to abstain from eating beef, not to drink liquor, not to beg Baluta from the Caste Hindus; not to act as sweepers, not to dedicate women as Jogati and not to worship idols. He advised them to educate their children and maintain cleanliness in houses.

When the Third Conference of the Bombay Presidency Depressed Classes was held at Nipani on 11-12 April 1925, Shri S.N. Mane supervised the volunteers' work. When Dr Babasaheb Ambedkar was busy in the Round Table Conferences in London, Shri Mane sent telegrams to the British Government supporting the demand of separate electorate and reposing faith in the leadership of Babasaheb Ambedkar.

The Maharaja of Kolhapur appointed Shri Dadasaheb Survey as Prime Minister of Kolhapur on 1 June 1947. Shri Dadasaheb Survey included Barrister S.N. Mane in his five member council of ministers. During his ministership Barrister S.N. Mane convinced the Maharaja to distribute uncultivated land to the landless people.

Barrister Mane got the honour of being a member of the Constituent Assembly of India. He became a member of the Steering Committee of the Constituent Assembly. He vehemently argued for providing special provisions for the benefit of the Scheduled Castes.

In the general election held in 1952, barrister S.N. Mane contested for Lok Sabha from Kolhapur-cum-Satara (G and R) seat as Peasants and Workers Party (PWP) candidate, but he was defeated. In 1967 he contested from Chikodi (R) Lok Sabha constituency on RPI ticket, but could not get success in the election

He married Housabai and has two sons and three daughters.

MARIAPPA, M.K.[72] (1907-1989)

Shri Mottayan Mariappa was born in 1907 at village Pappireddipatty, in Harur Taluka, Dharmapuri district in Tamil Nadu in Adi-Dravida community. His father Shri Mottayan Konan was a small farmer. Shri M.K. Mariappa completed his primary eduction in 1913 at primary school Pappireddipatty.

He entered politics at the age of 18. He joined the Congress and started serving the community as well as the nation. However, he joined Adi-Dravida movement prevalent in the erstwhile Madras state. He was elected President of Dharmapuri District Adi-Dravida Welfare Association.

He fought for regaining the civil rights of the so-called untouchables. In the year 1942 he entered, along with thousands of people, the temple of Theerthgiri Iswara, Theerthmalai. It was a very successful event.

He joined the Scheduled Castes Federation in 1942 itself, he was very much influenced by the thoughts and mission of Dr Babasaheb Ambedkar and Shri N. Shivaraj, the President of SCF. He rose to the presidentship of District branch of the SCF.

In the first general elections held in 1952 he contested as SCF candidate for the Madras Legislative Assembly from Harur (R) constituency, but he could not get elected. In the elections held in 1957 he contested as a Congress nominee from Harur(R) constituency and got elected to the Legislative Assembly of Madras State. Again he contested from the same constituency in 1967, but without success.

He was a trustee of the Teerthgiri temple, teerthmalai during 1957-1962, where once upon a time he had to force his entry for claiming equality and religious freedom.

He started the Sheep Growers Co-operative Society at his native place with the cooperation of the Animal Husbandry Department of Government of Tamil Nadu in the year 1977. He was its President till his last.

---

72. Source of Information:

Personal interview with his son, Shri M.Venu

Pappireddipatty, Taluka Harur, Dist. Dharmapuri, Tamil Nadu. on 2-6-1989.

He married Chinnamma and then Chinnakka. He had two sons and one daughter. He died on 28 January 1989 at the age of 82.

MESHRAM, G.T.[73] (1895-1953)

Shri Govindrao Meshram was born on 30 September 1895 at Indora, Nagpur. His father Tukaram Meshram was working in a soda factory at Nagpur. He was a Mahar by caste.

Shri Govindrao T. Meshram had passed his matriculation from Roman Catholic High School, Nagpur in the year 1915. Thereafter, he joined the Indian Army. He left the service and became a member of the Municipality, Nagpur.

When Dr Babasaheb Ambedkar declared his intention to discard Hinduism at Yeola in 1935, Shri G.T. Meshram strongly supported him. When a seat in the CP and Berar Legislative Assembly became vacant due to the sad demise of Shri L.N. Hardas, an ILP member, on 12 January 1939, Shri G.T. Meshram was given party ticket to contest the Kamathi-Nagpur reserve seat. However, he was defeated by Shri Hemachandra Khandekar, an independent candidate, in the by-election held in February 1939.

Shri G.T. Meshram was elected as Chairman of the reception committee of the All India Depressed Classes Conference held at Nagpur on 18, 19 and 20 July 1942. In this conference the All India Scheduled Castes Federation, the first national level political organization of the Dalits, was formed at the initiative of Dr Babasaheb Ambedkar. Shri Rao Bahadur N. Shivaraj was elected as its President. When the state branch of SCF was formed on 2 January 1943, Shri G.T. Meshram was elected as its President. Soon he joined the Government of India service as Estate Officer as desired by Babasaheb Ambedkar who was then Labour Member in the Viceroy's Executive Council. On account of his commendable services as Estate Officer, he was given an honorary title of Rai Saheb by the Governor-General.

---

73. Source of Information:

Personal Interview with the leader's daughter Mrs Kamal Uke and son-in-law. Mr N.G.Uke. 1217 Pocket A, Sector A. Vasant Kunj. New Delhi on 20-3-1990.

He was associated with Dr Babasaheb Ambedkar in his educational activities. Shri G.T. Meshram was one of the founding members and trustee of the People's Education Society, established by Babasaheb Ambedkar on 8 July 1945. He was also responsible for procuring Albert and Menkawa buildings at a reduced price for the People's Education Society, Bombay where Siddharth College was located. After his retirement as Estate Officer in the year 1951, he joined People's Education Society's Milind College at Aurangabad as Registrar. It is due to his efficient management that the magnificent college building was constructed in a short while.

In the first general elections held in 1952, he contested from Nanded double member constituency as an SCF nominee, but could not achieve success.

He married Smt Sarubai and had one son and two daughters. He was a man with untiring energies devoted to public cause and endowed with uncommon organizing capacity. He breathed his last on 10 April 1953 at the age of 57 at Aurangabad.

MHASDE, SHANKARRAO[74] (1893-1977)

Shri Shankarrao Mhasde was born on 24 December 1893 at Mhow, near Indore in Madhya pradesh, in a Mahar family. His father Shri Ramaji Mhasde was an ostler in the British Army. Shri Shankarrao Mhasde was educated up to the fourth standard.

Shri Shankarrao Mhasde was a good photographer. He owned a sports shop also. He was against idol worship and all the superstitions prevailing in the untouchable community. He was instrumental in abolishing the system of *Zamara* prevailing in the vicinity of Indore. According to this custom the young or newly married Balai untouchable women were asked to carry throughout the village on their heads a pot filled with dirt, on the next day after Holi festival. It was adding insult to the injury of untouchability. Therefore, he moved from place to place and convinced the untouchable masses that they should stop that

---

74. Source of Information:
Personal Interview with his daughter. Smt Gangutai Mhade
ESI Hospital, Nanda Nagar, Indore (MP) on 13-9-1989.

ugly system. There was stiff opposition to the awakened untouchables, which was followed by boycott and atrocities but he ultimately became successful in abolishing that abominable system. He advised the untouchables to abandon beef-eating and intoxication. He had no faith in Hindu deities.

Shri Mhasde used to go to teach the sweepers' boys at night. Shri Gangaramji Dhuldhoye and Sajjansinh Vishnar were his main supporters.

Shri Mhasde formed one Ambedkar Ashram at Mhow. He travelled through western Madhya Pradesh and eastern Rajasthan, propagating Ambedkarism. He became the Secretary of the Scheduled Castes Federation's branch of Indore, Princely State in 1942. He was in SCF till 1970. He participated in the satyagraha for political demands in the year 1946 under the banner of SCF, for which he was imprisoned for two days.

He was a Nathpanthi, but on 14 October 1956 he embraced Buddhism at Nagpur. Since then he was propagating Buddhism in the vicinity of Indore.

He married Smt Vithabai and had two sons and five daughters.

Shri Shankarrao Mhasde died on 3 March 1977 at the age of 84.

MINIMATA[75] (1916-1973)

Smt Minimata was born on 15 August 1916 at Salnabagan, Nawagaon district in Assam. Her father's name was Shri Budhari Dass Mahant.

Smt Minimata married Guru Agamdas on 2 June 1930. Shri Guru Agamdas was son of Agardas and was head of Satnami sect at Bhandarpur in Raipur district of Madhya Pradesh. Shri Guru Agamdas was elected to the CP and Berar Legislative Assembly in 1930. He was a member of Constituent Assembly and of Provisional Parliament from 1946 to 1952. In the first general elections held in 1952 he contested from Bilaspur-Durg-Raipur (G and SC) Lok Sabha Constituency on Congress ticket

---

75. Source of Information:
Who's Who in Parliament.

and got elected. He died in 1954. Thereafter Smt Minimata contested the by-election held on 10 February 1955 from the same constituency on Congress ticket and won. She contested in 1957 from Baloda Bazar (G and SC) Lok Sabha constituency and got elected. In the election held in 1962 she successfully contested from the same constituency. She got elected for Lok Sabha from Janjgir (SC) constituency in 1967 and in 1971. Thus she was Member of Parliament from 1955 to 1973.

Smt Minimata was President of Guru Bhavji Seva Sangh and member of Bharatiya Depressed Classes League of Madhya Pradesh unit.

She propagated the principles of Satnami sect throughout her life. She was against casteism, untouchability, child marriage, drinks and dowry. She was popular among her disciples.

She died in 1973 at the age of 57.

MONDAL, SITANATH[76] (1885-1926)

Shri Sitanath Mondal was born in 1885 at Hurka in Khulna district, now in Bangladesh. His father Shri Laxman Mondal was a landlord. Shri Sitanath Mondal passed his L.M.F and started medical practice in 1908. He belonged to the Namasudra community.

Shri Sitanath Mondal himself was subjected to untouchability during his student life at Calcutta. He rightly thought during his student life at Calcutta that there was no hope for the untouchables unless they educate their children. In 1908, he started a school at his village for the untouchable students.

He was member of District Local Board, Khulna. He used to help the poor whenever they were in need. Hence he was known as *Danvir.* He managed to construct a hostel for the untouchable students at Bagerhat. He used to propagate the importance of education and inspired the people to send their children to the schools.

---

76. Source of information:
Dr K.L. Majumdar
19, Baganbari Road, Santoshpur, Calcutta-75 Date: 24-11-1988.

He expired in 1926 at the age of 42 only. He was survived by his wife and a son. He was highly appreciated by the people for his selfless service.

MOON, VITHOBA RAOJI[77] (1864-1924)

Shri Vithoba Raoji Moon-Pande was born in 1864 at Hinganghat, Wardha district. Later on, he came to Nagpur and settled at Shanivar Peth. He started cotton business at Nagpur. His financial position was sound. He was a Guru of the Mahar community. He studied the Hindu religious scriptures. He tried to awaken the Dalits by *Bhajan-Kirtan.* He advised his brethren to observe cleanliness, not to eat carrion and meat of the cows, and to develop religious attitude.

In the year 1903 he resecured the right from the temple committee of Shrikshetra Ramtek in Nagpur district, to take holy bath at Ambala tank on the occasion of Kartik Poornima festival. He constructed a *Shivalaya* in 1907 at Ramtek solely for the Dalits.

He founded Antyaj Samaj Committee in 1906. Obviously, the purpose of that committee was to organize the untouchables at various villages and to instil in them an awareness of their own rights. He was the President of that organization.

In order to bring more vigour to the organization, he founded the Mahar Sabha on 18 December 1912 at Nagpur. He was Secretary of the Sabha. Almost all the big leaders of the Dalits in Vidarbha region as well as persons from Pune and Pandharpur were its members. The Sabha propagated the importance of education and organization, for securing due place to the untouchables in the society. He worked for the welfare of the labourers also.

He had good relations with the Christian missionaries and officers. His co-workers were Shri Karunaji V. Malgujár, Jairam Paiku Gaikwad, Kalicharan Nandagawali and many others.

---

77. Source of Information:
Interview with his grandson Shri Vasant Moon
Govt. Colony, Bandra (East), Bombay
On 14.7.1981

He was well to do and happily lived with his wife, six sons and two daughters. He worked for the socio-religious uplift of the Scheduled Castes.

MORE, B.S.[78] (1915-1995)

Shri Balkrishna alias Bhausaheb More was born in 1915 at Kannad in Aurangabad district of Maharashtra. He belonged to the Mahar community. His father Shri Shivramji More was a prominent person at Kannad.

After completing education up to the intermediate level, he joined the Nizam's service as Propaganda Officer. In those days the condition of the Dalits was very much pitiable due to which they were induced to convert to Islam. This, of course, melted the heart of young B.S. More. He met Dr Babasaheb Ambedkar and appraised him of the situation in Nizam State. He requested Babasaheb Ambedkar to visit Aurangabad and address the people. Dr Babasaheb Ambedkar agreed to visit Aurangabad, but due to restrictions on public meetings in the Nizam State, it was arranged at Makranpur in Jalgaon district, adjacent to the boundary of Kannad. It was attended by a large gathering of the Dalits in Aurangabad district. The Chairman of the reception committee of the conference was Shri Shyamrao Bhikaji Jadhav, a Dalit leader in Kannad. It was the first address of Dr Babasaheb Ambedkar to the Dalits in Nizam State.

Shri Bhausaheb More became an accredited leader of the Dalits in Aurangabad. He advised his brethren not to convert to Islam and not to be in favour of Nizam. He kept liaison with the freedom fighters on the boundary of Aurangabad district. Therefore, a warrant was issued against him. He left the service and devoted himself to social service.

He advised his brethren to abandon carrion or beef- eating. He was to beat those people who disregarded his advice, engaged themselves in filthy occupation, continued beef-eating and evil customs. He created a terror in the society for the good

---

78. Source of Information:
Personal interview with Shri B.S. More,
Bhoiwada, Aurangabad on 25-12-1988.

cause. He launched reconversion of those Dalits who had converted to Islam

In his political career, he joined the Scheduled Castes Federation under the leadership of B.S. Venkatrao, B. Shyamsundar and later on Shri J.H. Subbia. He became full time social and political leader from 1945 onwards. He organized SCF throughout the Marathwada region.

At the time of police action in Hyderabad State in September 1948, he could save many Dalits, who were allegedly supporters of the *Razakars* (Muslim volunteers supporting Nizam of Hyderabad) from the wrath of Hindus and the army of the Indian Government, by stating that such persons were the members of the SCF and not of the *Razakars*.

In the first general elections held in 1952 he contested on SCF ticket for the erstwhile Hyderabad Legislative Assembly from Bhokardan constituency, but lost to the INC.

On the advice of Dr Babasaheb Ambedkar, the SCF in Marathwada under the leadership of B.S. More launched a massive and successful satyagraha of the landless workers in the year 1953. Another satyagraha was successfully launched in 1959 and in 1964.

He converted to Buddhism in 1956 itself. He participated in the process of formation of the Republican Party of India, at Nagpur in 1957.

He could very successfully organize the second conference of the Republican Party of India at Aurangabad in the year 1959. It was addressed by Dadasaheb Gaikwad, Barrister Khobragade and other top leaders of the party.

He contested for the Lok Sabha on RPI ticket from Aurangabad general seat in the year 1962, but without success.

In acknowledgement of his services to the Dalits and the freedom movement, the Maharashtra Government honoured him with "Dalit Mitra" in 1975 and "Freedom Fighter" in 1976.

He married Smt Sundarbai. He has six sons and two daughters.

He breathed his last on 16-5-1995.

MORE, HANMANTRAO[79] (1901-1993)

Shri Hanmantrao More was born in 1901 at Fort Nanded in Maharashtra, in Mahar community. His father's name was Shri Dharmaji More. Shri Hanmantrao More completed his education only up to the fourth standard. His elder brother was in the military.

As a protest against Hinduism which was based on the caste system, he embraced Arya Samaj in the year 1930, as it was propagating for equality. As a true Arya Samaji he gave up meat-eating and observed all the principles of Arya Samaj. He tried to preach the principles of the Arya Samaj to his brethren.

In 1933, he launched a satyagraha along with his followers for entry into the temple of Hanuman, at Nanded. He, along with the satyagrahis, entered the temple without any restriction.

Later on, he came under the influence of Rao Saheb B.S. Venkatrao, a great leader of Dalits in the Nizam State. In 1935 he met Dr Babasaheb Ambedkar at Bombay and narrated the tale of woes of the Dalits in Nizam State. He was encouraged and advised by Babasaheb Ambedkar to struggle against the humiliating and exploiting tradition being observed by both the Hindus and the Muslims.

Shri More organized Panchayat Committees in the Dalit localities to deal with their affairs and started *Akhadas* to counteract the anti-Dalit forces.

Shri More was one of the prominent organizers of the Depressed Classes Association in Nanded District. Ganpatrao Waghmare was his companion, among others. His other companions named Shri Kadaknath Hatkar and Prabhakarrao Hingole had organized the Hyderabad State Scheduled Castes Federation, under the leadership of Shri Bh. Subbiah and P.V. Manohar in the year 1945. After the accession of Hyderabad in 1948, both the organizations came under one banner.

---

79. Source of Information:
Personal Interview with Shri Hanmantrao More
Milind Hostel, Anand Nagar, Nanded on 23-10-1989.

Shri More led the land satyagraha in 1953 along with his companions and made it successful. He converted to Buddhism in 1956 itself. He was one of the prominent organizers of mass conversion to Buddhism at Nanded in the year 1958. That time Shri Prabhakarrao Hingole was President and Shri Sambhajirao Jondhle was Secretary of the Boudha Maha Sabha, Nanded district.

He started Milind Hostel at Anand Nagar, Nanded in 1965 and Milind Primary Scixool at Naik. Nagar, Nanded in 1966.

He married Smt Hirabai. He had six sons and four daughters. He died on 8 January 1993 at the age of 92.

MORE, R.B.[80] (1902-1972)

Shri Ramachandra More was born on 10 June 1902 at Dasgaon, Taluka Mahad, Raigad district in Maharashtra. He was a Mahar by caste. His father Shri Babaji More was an agricultural labourer. He had purchased some land out of his hard-earned savings. However, the *Khot* of his village prepared a forged document, by which he snatched the agricultural land bought by Shri Babaji More. Therefore, he became helpless in his old age and died in frustration in the year 1915.

Thereafter, Shri Ramachandra More went along with his mother Bhimabai to his maternal uncle at Ladvali in Mahad. Shri R.B. More entered the Anglo-Vernacular School at Mahad. He discontinued his education due to acute poverty.

He went to Bombay and then to Pune to earn his livelihood as a coolie. He came into contact with Babasaheb Ambedkar and other leaders at Bombay. Having seen the pitiable socio-economic condition of the untouchables, he decided to work for the liberation of his toiling brethren.

Babasaheb Ambedkar decided to hold the Kolaba District Depressed Classes Conference at Mahad. He entrusted the responsibility of making necessary arrangements to Sambhaji Tukaram Gaikwad, Subedar Sawadkar and Ramachandra Babaji

---

80. Source of Information:
B.S. Hate, *Jithe Pani Petale* (1977) Bombay.

More. They could successfully arrange the conference on 19-20 March 1927. Shri R.B. More actively participated in the Mahad satyagraha.

He organized many conferences of the Depressed Classes in Kolaba district and tried to bring about mass awareness. He organized the agricultural labourers and small farmers conference at Ratnagiri in 1931. His organization Kolaba Peasants Union was banned by the government. Hence, he joined Tarun Mazdoor Sangh, Bombay where he came in contact with communist leaders like Jagannath Adhikari. During these days he started one weekly named *Avhan,* but after some time it was discontinued. During these days he came in contact with Shri Deshpande and Comrade Ranadive. Shri More was one of the founding members of Lalbavata Girani Kamgar Union founded in 1932. He was one of the leaders of the strike organized in 1933 by the said union. Therefore, he was sentenced to imprisonment for a period of one and a half months. In 1937, he led a movement against the *Khot* of Chari in Kolaba district for the settlement of which Shri Morarji Desai, the then minister in the Bombay Government had to come to Chari.

During 1940 to 1943 when Second World War was going on, he was working underground as there was a warrant against him.

He was included in the delegation under the leadership of N.M. Joshi to represent the Indian labour class at the International Labour Organization held at Paris in the year 1946.

He resolved to fight not only against untouchability and casteism but also against landlords and capitalism. He tried to unite the Dalit and non-Dalit labourers and peasants on some issues of common interests. He, however, could not get much success in it.

When at first the birthday of Dr Babasaheb Ambedkar was celebrated at Dilide Road, Bombay on 14 April 1933, Shri More called him by the appellation of "Babasaheb". Thereafter Dr B.R. Ambedkar became popularly known as "Babasaheb" Ambedkar.

Shri R.B. More thought that the Buddhist converts should not be called Nav Boudha, but as Nav Deekshit Boudha. He believed in Buddhism, as it has no faith in God, soul, hell or heaven.

He expired on 11 May 1927 at Goregaon, Bombay at the age of 70.

MULLICK, M.B.[81] (1888–1974)

Shri Mukunda Behari Mullick was born on 27 December 1888 at village Kharasambal, Bagerhat Sub-Division, Khulna district (now in Bangladesh). He was a Namasudra. His father Shri Prasanna Kumar Mullick was a big landlord. Shri Mukund Behari Mullick started his education at the age of six in his own house under a teacher Kuver Chandra Ghosh. In 1893, Mukunda Behari was admitted into the Bagerhat High School. He completed his entrance in 1905; and intermediate in 1907 and his B.A. in 1909 from Presidency College, Calcutta. He passed his M.A. in Pali in 1913 and his B.L. in 1914 from Calcutta University.

On 20 April 1914 he enrolled as lawyer in the High Court at Calcutta. From 1914 to 1974 he was in legal profession, excluding the period of his ministership during 1937-41. Simultaneously, he was a lecturer in Pali in Calcutta University from 1914-1937. During this period he served as a part time lecturer in Law in Calcutta University.

He started his social service in 1912 when he apprised the Governor of the miseries of his community. In order to muster the strength of his brethren, he founded the Bengal Namasudra Association in the year 1912. Under the banner of this organization he held many meetings and conferences at several places like Dhaka, Khulna, Jessore, Calcutta, Cuttack and Lucknow, through which a new strength was infused in the Dalit masses. He tried to boost up the morale of the people and tried to raise their confidence.

Shri Mukund Behari was an educationist. He was a professor, fellow and senate member of Calcutta University during 1914-1937. He started a hostel, named Bani Bhavan Hostel

---

81. Information furnished by his son:
Shri Suniti Prasanna Mullick, IFS (Retd)
17, Ritchie Road, P.O. Ballygunge Calcutta on 19-12-1988.

for college students at Calcutta. He encouraged the Scheduled Castes students to seek higher education.

He intended to use his political power to serve the people in a better way. At first, he contested for Bengal Legislative Assembly in 1921 from Khulna constituency as an independent candidate, but he was defeated by a high caste candidate. Again he contested from the same constituency in 1925, but in vain. However, he was nominated by the government as a member of the Legislative Council. He continued to be so till 1936. In the elections held under the Act of 1935 in the year 1937, he contested from Khulna Assembly constituency (R) and got elected. Again he was elected in 1946 as a member of Legislative Assembly of Bengal.

Many a time he represented the grievances of the untouchables to the authorities for getting redressal. He made it clear to the governor in an appeal, submitted in December 1918 that "a vociferous and small band of organized castes could not pretend to represent the interests of the down-trodden."As President of All-Bengal Namasudra Association, he submitted a memorandum to the Indian Statutory Commission headed by Sir John Simon, in 1929 in which he stated, "Franchise should be based on population and not on any property or educational qualification." He supported the demand of separate electorate made by Babasaheb Ambedkar during the Round Table Conferences. Shri M.B. Mullick participated in the Second All India Depressed Classes Congress at Kamptee, near Nagpur on 7-8 May 1932 and denounced the Rajah-Moonje Pact in a resolution. He appeared before the Lothian Committee and demanded increase in seats for the Depressed Classes.

Shri M B. Mullick served as a minister in charge of co-operative credit and rural indebtedness in the first Fazlul Huq cabinet of Bengal from 1937 to 1941.

During 1942-47 he was Chairman of Coal Mines Stowing Board under the Government of Bengal.

After the partition of India, he was elected as a member of the Constituent Assembly of India.

After 1947 he resumed his legal practice in the Calcutta High Court and continued to be so till his last.

He worked for the liberation of the untouchables throughout his life. He was, however, not attached to any political party. Being a dedicated leader, he was very popular among the Depressed Classes. They addressed him by the respectful appellation of *Jananayaka.*

He was felicitated by the Bar Association of Calcutta High Court in April 1964 for having completed 50 years of legal practice in the High Court.

He married Smt Haripriya in 1914. He had five sons. His younger brothers Shri Nirod Behari Mullick (1894-1934) and Shri Pulin Behari Mullick (1901-1975) were also well- educated and leaders of the Dalit liberation movement in Bengal.

Shri M.B. Mullick died on 4 August 1974 at the age of 86 at Calcutta.

MURTHY, B.S.

Shri Bayya Suryanarayan Murthy was born on 29 October 1906 at Nagaram, Taluka Razole, East Godavari district in Andhra Pradesh. His father's name was Shri Bayya Nagayya. Shri B.S. Murthy was educated at Rajahmundri and at Madras. He was B.A., B.Ed.

He was elected Secretary of the Andhra Pradesh Harijan Sevak Sangh in 1935. Later, he was its President from 1940- 49. He was elected as a member of the Madras Legislative Assembly in 1937. Again, he was elected in 1935. He was Minister for Industries and Labour of the then Madras Government from 1937-39 and from 1946-47.

He contested in 1952 general elections for the Lok Sabha from Eluru (G and SC) constituency as a candidate of Kisan Mazdoor Praja Party and got elected. In 1957, he contested from Kakinada (G and SC) Lok Sabha constituency on Congress ticket and won. He got elected from Amalapuram (SC) constituency in 1962, 1967 and 1971 to the Lok Sabha.

He was Deputy Minister for Health and Family Planning from 1962-67 in the Union Government.

He led the temple entry satyagraha at Tirupati Hills demanding entry of the untouchables in the famous

Venkateshwara temple in the year 1947, and succeeded in his objective.

He founded M.C. Rajah hostel for the Scheduled Caste college students in Madras.

He took part in national freedom movement. He offered individual satyagraha in 1940, for which he was sentenced to rigorous imprisonment (RI) for nine months and a fine of ₹ 300. He took part in the Quit India Movement in 1942 and as such he was sentenced to one year RI and a fine of ₹ 100.

He was a thinker and a writer. He wrote *Revolt of Six Crores, Depressed* and *Oppressed forever in Agony* and *The Glimmer in darkness.*

He married Smt Adilakshmi in 1927. He had three sons and two daughters.

MURUGESAN, M.Y.[82] (1856-1921)

Shri Mount Murugesan was born in 1856 at Kolar Gold Field. His father Mount Yagambara was in the British Army and rose to the position of subedar Major. Shri M.Y. Murugesan completed his Intermediate from Christian college, Madras. Later, he was appointed as an ordinary employee in Marikuppam Gold Mines, but was promoted as Assistant Pay Roll Officer. He was converted to Buddhism in 1902. Since then he strove for the uplift of his untouchable brethren by converting them to Buddhism. He himself was a vegetarian and exhorted the people to abandon meat-eating and drinking.

He became a member of the South Indian Sakya Buddhist Association established in 1900 by Pandit C. Iyodhi Dass. Shri M.Y. Murugesan started a branch of the said Association at Marikuppam. He built a palatial hall for the Association. Previously, they were running one Sivakesavadvaida Sirtsabar Sabha at Marikuppam. However, they converted the same association into a Buddhist Association in the year 1907.

---

82. Source of Information:

Personal Interview with his son-in-law Shri M.Y. Gurunathan 421 MKN Road. Alandur. Madras on 31-5-1989

He was instrumental in converting 1,000 workers and their families to Buddhism. The conversion ceremony was performed by an Irish monk, *Bhikshu* U. Visudha.

He was instrumental in opening the branches of the South Indian Buddhist Association at Champion Reefs, KGF, Bangalore and Hubli in Karnataka and in Pallikonda and Tirupattur in Tamil Nadu.

In order to spread education among the untouchables and Buddhists, he started a primary school named South India Buddhist School, at Marikuppam in the year 1932. Now it imparts education up to the seventh class.

In all his social and religious activities, Shri R.L. Umapathi was with him.

He married Krishnamal. His family consisted of three sons and four daughters. He breathed his last on 27 June 1921 at the age of 65.

MUTTHU, SATIYAVANI[82(a)] (1923-1999)

Smt. Satiyavani Mutthu was born on 15 February 1923 in a Adi-Dravida family at Chengalpet in Tamil Nadu. She was educated at Teresa Convent Ernakulam (Kerala) and Presidency High School, Egmore, Madras. She served as Registered Homeopathic Practioner till 1957.

She was active in 'Self-Respect Movement' which was in vogue in those days. She joined the Scheduled Caste Federation founded by Dr. Babasaheb Ambedkar in 1942 whose President was R.B.N. Shivaraj. Mrs. N. Meenamble Shivaraj was also active in the Dalit upliftment movement and in SCF. Mrs. Satiyavani Mutthu became the president of the SCF Women's Wing of Madras branch in 1943 and remained in that position till 1949.

Satiyavani Mutthu became a member of Indian Rationalist Association in 1945 and its president from 1975-76. She was one

---

82(a). Source of Information :

1. *Hame Jin Par Garva Hae* by Smt. Dropati
Harit Sahitya, Prakashan Nanakpur, New Delhi. (1992).
2. Shri Manokaran, Vellor (T.N.).

of the founding members of Dravid Munnetra Kazhagam in 1973.

Later, she formed her own party, named Thazhthappattoor (Depressed Classes) Munneta Kazhagam. She was a member of Madras Legislative Assembly from 1957 to 1962. She was minister in the DMK Government under the Leadership of Aringar Anna and K. Karunavidhi during 1967 to 1974.

Later on she joined AIADMK (All India Anna Dravid Munnetra Kalhgam) in 1977. She was member of Legislative Council from December 1977 to April 1978. She was member of Rajya Sabha from 1978 to 1984. During this period she served as a member of Parliamentary Committee for the Scheduled Castes and Scheduled Tribes. Even she became minister for social welfare in the Union Ministry formed by Choudhari Charan Singh from 19th August 1976 to 23rd December 1976.

She had the honour of being included in several organizations and delegations and to participate in the national and international conferences.

In 1986 again she joined DMK Party. She wrote "Erikkappattal", "Joan of Arc", "My Agitation" and "Enathu Porattum".

She married to M.S. Mutthu in 1943 and led a happy family life even in such a hectic social and political activities.

She breathed her last on 11 November 1999.

NAGAPPA, S.[83]

Shri Sardar Nagappa was born on 6 October 1911 at Kurnool in Andhra Pradesh. He belonged to the Mala community. His father Sardar Buchayya was in the domestic service of a British officer. Shri Nagappa had completed his education up to matric level in 1932 from a local municipal high school, Kurnool. From 1933-36 he used to weave Khadi and stitch it and thus earned his livelihood.

---

83. Source of Information:
Personal Interview with Shri Sardar Nagappa
Fort Kurnool, AP on 24-11-1988.

He joined the Congress in 1930. In order to bring awareness and unity among the untouchables, he inspired the people to arrange *Bhajans* in every locality. His teacher Shri Vaidyanath Aiyyer gave him one bicycle to move from place to place and educate the people in cleanliness and morality. Shri Nagappa started a free hostel for the Scheduled Castes students at Kurnool in 1938. He used to collect foodgrains and his wife used to cook for the students.

He was elected to the erstwhile Madras State Legislative Assembly in 1937 from Kurnool constituency. Again he was elected on Congress ticket from the same constituency in the year 1946. He got the great honour of being elected to the Constituent Assembly from Madras Legislative Council in the year 1947. In the first general elections held in 1952 he contested as KMPP (Kisan Mazdoor Praja Party} candidate from Nandyal (G) Lok Sabha constituency, but he was defeated in the election. In 1967 he contested for Andhra Pradesh Legislative Assembly as a Congress nominee from Alur (SC) constituency, but he was defeated.

He took an active part in the national freedom struggle. He participated in the Quit India Movement in 1942, for which he was detained for one year and six months. His wife Mrs S. Amravati Devi also participated in the Quit India Movement, for which she was detained in jail along with her infant son. Both of them offered satyagraha and courted arrest for several times.

His contribution to the Constituent Assembly is of great importance. He was convenor of the SC members. During that period he was residing near the residence of Dr Babasaheb Ambedkar. Babasaheb Ambedkar used to invite him for informal discussions in the night. At the instance of Babasaheb Ambedkar, Sardar Nagappa moved an important resolution in the Constituent Assembly regarding "qualified joint electorate" for the Scheduled Castes. He stated that the SC candidate, before he is declared to have been elected to the seat reserved, shall have secured not less than 35 per cent of the votes polled by the Scheduled Castes in the election, and the highest votes polled by the general voters. However, the motion was not accepted by the members of the Constituent Assembly.

Both Shri and Smt S. Nagappa were honoured as freedom fighters, and as such they got 30 acres of land for their livelihood.

Shri Nagappa very proudly claims to be the 18th or 19th generation of his dynasty which heroically fought against the Raja of Kurnool under the command of Abdul Wahab who was serving under the Sultan of Bijapur, in about and won the battle. Therefore, his ancestor got the honorific title of 'Sardar' and the house site near the Fort at Kurnool where Nagappa presently resides with his three sons. He claims with pleasure that Shri D. Sanjivayya, the first SC Chief Minister of Andhra Pradesh had received his early education under the former's parental care. Even now he comes to help the poor and needy people.

NAIK, S.G.[84] (1884-1969)

Shri Sampatrao Naik was born in Mahar community in 1884 at Kolhapuri Gate, Amravati in Maharashtra. His father's name was Shri Ganpatrao Naik. Shri Sampatrao Naik was educated up to seventh at Amravati.

He plunged into the social uplift movement of the Depressed Classes. He was one of the organizers of the Mahar Parishad in Vidarbha. In the third meeting of the Vidarbha Mahar Parishad held at Brahmanvada, Amravati on 25-26 March 1923, he was a prominent figure. He attended the Depressed Classes Association, Berar branch 'conference held at Amravati on 13 February 1929. He was elected Vice-president of the Berar provincial Depressed Classes Federation. He presided over the Daryapur Taluka Vatandar Mahar Parishad held at Amravati on 15 April 1934. He was Chairman of the reception committee of the conference of the Depressed Classes held at Amravati on 29 December 1935 under the presidentship of Patitpavan Das. The

---

84. Source of Information:
Personal Interview with his son Shri Manohar S. Naik,
Rukmini Nagar, Amravati on 19-10-1988.

conference through a resolution supported the declaration of conversion made by Dr Babasaheb Ambedkar at Yeola on 13 October 1935.

He was one of the important leaders of the satyagraha at the temple of Ambadevi at Amravati. A meeting in that respect was held at Amravati under the presidentship of Dr Babasaheb Ambedkar on 13 November 1927. It was attended by Dr Punjabrao Deshmukh, G.A. Gawai, K.B. Deshmukh, Deorao Naik, R.D. Kowly, D.V. Pradhan among others. He was a devout supporter of Babasaheb Ambedkar's move for religious conversion in Vidarbha region. He converted to Buddhism at Nagpur at the historic mass conversion on Vijaya Dashmi day in 1956.

Shri S.G. Naik worked as a member of the Legislative Assembly of CP and Berar from 1929 to 1936. He contested the election to the assembly in 1937 on behalf of Independent Labour Party from Elichpur-Daryapur constituency but without success.

Shri Naik started one Adarsh hostel and a school at Belpura locality of Amravati. His wife Mrs Laxmibai Naik also worked along with him. Even, she herself had to teach in the school. She was an active social worker. She also converted to Buddhism in 1956 itself and later on she became a *Bhikshuni* and preached Buddhism throughout her life.

Shri S.G. Naik had three sons and three daughters. He expired on 21 September 1969 at the age of 85.

NANDAGAVALI, KALICHARAN[85] (1860-1962)

Shri Kalicharan Nandagavali was born in 1860 at village Bothali, in Balaghat district in the then CP and Berar. He was a

---

85. Source of Information:
Personal Interview with
Smt. Devinibai Paramanand Nandagavali (Daughter-in-law)
Krishnapura Ward. Gondia, Dist. Bhandara
on 30.10.1988
and other sources.

Mahar. His father Shri Ganuji Nandagavali was a rich and respectable person in society. He owned near about 100 acres of agricultural land. Later on he came to Gondia in Bhandura district and settled there.

Kalicharan was educated up to the eighth class. Having seen the pitiable and poor condition of his brethren he turned to Social Service. He was Mahanubav Panthi by birth, as such he was a vegetarian and a teetotaller, and inclined towards spiritualism.

He rightly thought that unless the Dalits get education there cannot be remarkable change in their lives. In order to enable the girls to take education, he built a school at his own expense at Gondia in the year 1910. In 1914 he became member of the Municipality of Gondia and in 1916 he became its Chairman. In the same year he established one Bharatiya Mahar Panchayat for solving the problems of the Mahars; and convened a conference on the issue of untouchability.

During the First World War he appealed to the government to recruit Dalits in the army. He gave evidence before the Southborough Franchise Committee and appealed for representation for the Dalits in the legislature. He was nominated on CP and Berar legislative Assembly in 1920 for a period of three years. He was Chairman of the reception committee of the first All India Depressed Classes Conference held in 1920 at Nagpur. Chhatrapati Shahu Maharaj of Kolhapur was the President of the Conference and Dr Babasaheb Ambedkar was the chief guest.

Kalicharan Nandagavali moved an important resolution in the Assembly on 16 March 1921, through which he proposed that a committee be set up to inquire into the condition of the Depressed Classes, with special reference to their employment in the government services: their education; their rights as *Kotwal;* boycotts in the villages and separate settlements for the Dalits. The Assembly passed this resolution. Accordingly, the government of CP and Berar appointed a seven-member "Depressed Classes Inquiry Committee" in June 1921. The committee completed its work in 1922. Shri Kalicharan Nandagavali was one of its members along with Ganesh Akkaji Gawai. He moved another resolution on 13 August 1923 seeking civil rights for the untouchables, such as right to access to public wells, bathing ghats and such other public places. It was passed by the legislature; but it remained a mere resolution.

In the year 1926, he formed Madhya Prant Tarun Mahar Sangh. Shri Patitpavan Das, Revaram Kawade, Dashrath Patil, G.T. Meshram, Hemchandra Khandekar, Tularam Sakhare and L.N. Hardas were its prominent members. The Sangh was active till 1930. The said organization was in favour of the demand of separate electorate for the Depressed Classes, made by Dr Babasaheb Ambedkar. The Sangh appealed to the Simon Commission to grant this demand.

Kalicharan Nandagavali arranged community dinner at the residence of Vishramji Savaitul in 1929 which was attended by prominent persons including Pandit Jawaharlal Nehru, Subhas Chandra Bose, Sir Bhavani shankar Niyogi and many others.

He thought that India should be free from British imperialism. Therefore, he supported the Indian National Congress. He supported non-cooperation movement and participated in the Salt Satyagraha also. However, his activities were not acceptable to the other Dalit leaders. Therefore, he was not allowed to read his welcome address at the All India Depressed Classes Conference, held at Nagpur in 1930.

Later on, he participated in the second conference of the Depressed Classes Congress held at Nagpur on 7 and 8 May 1932. Dr Babasaheb Ambedkar addressed the conference. In the Conference, Kalicharan Nandagavali was elected as President of the CP and Berar branch of the Depressed Classes Congress. However, he resigned from his post on 7 July 1933. Thereafter he left politics.

He led a happy family life at Gondia with his wife Baija and his adopted son Paramanand. He died on 7 March 1962 at the age of 102.

NAYAK, MOHAN[85(a)] (1921-1983)

Shri Mohan Nayak was born on June 3, 1921 at Berhampur, Dist. Ganjam in Orissa. His father's name was Shri Bijuli Nayak. Shri Mohan Nayak was educated upto ninth class at Behrampur.

He started his social life as Secretary of Ganjam District Harijan Sevak from 1938. During 1945-53 he was a member of Ganjam District Board. In 1952 he was elected member of Municipality, Behrampur. In 1954 he became President of Depressed Classes League, Ganjam. He founded Thakar Bappa Ashram at Nimakhandi on November 11, 1952.

He worked for the abolition of untouchability. He led a Satyagraha for entry into the temple of Jagannatha at Puri in the year 1938. He offered Satyagraha in 1940 and 1941 for the independence of the Country. He participated in the Quit India Movement in 1942 for which he was imprisoned.

He was elected member of Orissa Legislative Assembly during 1953-1957. He got elected from Behrampur. In the second general elections held in 1957, he contested on Congress ticket for Lok Sabha from Ganjam (G + SC) Constituency and got elected. Again he contested in 1962 from Bhanjnagar (SC) Loksabha Constituency and got elected.

He started *'Sevaka'* a monthly from 1947 for the propogation of removal of untouchability. He wrote two books in Oriya - (1) *Kalanko Mochano,* and (2) *Asprusyata Mochano.*

He married Anapurna Devi in 1921. He had three sons and two daughters. He expired on September 27, 1983 at the age of sixty three.

NIDHADAK, CHARANDAS[85(b)] (1901-1990)

Shri Charan Das Nidhadak was a very devoted and well determined disciple of Dr. Babasaheb Ambedkar. He was born in

---

85(a) Source of Information :

Son of the Leader, Shri Dayanand M. Nayak,

Behrampur, Dist. Ganjam, Orissa on 20-08-1991.

85(b). Source of Information :

1. *Ambedkari Andolan Main Punjabiyoka Role* (1976) by K.C. Leel
2. Advocate Santokh Lai Virdhi, Fagwara, Punjab.

1901 in a poor Ad-Dharmi (Chamar) Community at Fagwada in Punjab. He was not highly educated but he had political understanding and zeal to work hard for the uplift of the scheduled castes. He became a staunch member of the Scheduled Castes Federation.

He used to participate in Ravidas Mela every year. However, once some miscreants were attempting to commit some mischief in the Mela and disturbing its performance. Charan Das could not tolerate it and gave beating to them with the help of his party. Therefore almost all the miscreants had to run away from the Mela. Therefore, Shri Charan Das was called as 'Nidhadak' (fearless).

He was strictly against superstitions and blind faith. Advocate Santokhlal Virdhi and others were his strong supporters.

He met Babasaheb Ambedkar in Jan. 1948 alongwith Sadhu Ram, Mota Singh Lyallpuri, Mr. Kartara Ram Midhas at his residence of 1 Hardings Avenue New Delhi.

After the sad demise of Dr. Babasaheb Ambedkar, he took his movement to the masses, especially the rural masses. He organized a grand mass Deeksha Programme on 17 June 1958.

He was a great poet and singer in Punjabi. He was known for his style of satirical speeches and reciting self composed Punjabi poems, thereby moved the people.

He had a son by name Balvir chand.

He breathed his last on 13 Feb. 1990 at Fagwada at the age of eight nine years.

PAMPADY JOHN JOSEPH[86] (1887-1940)

Shri Pampady Joseph was born in 1887 at Pampady, Kottayam district in Kerala. His father's name was Shri Pampady

---

86. Source of Information:

T.H.P. Chentharassery, *Pampady John Joseph* (Malayalam), Trivandrum (1989).

John. Shri Pampady Joseph was educated up to the sixth standard at Trukkakara Mission School. He came to Kottayam in 1910 and then to Trivandrum in 1918. For some time he served as a teacher.

Shri Pampady John Joseph was a Catholic Christian. His father converted to Christianity from his original Pulaya untouchable caste. Shri Pampady Joseph changed the name of Pulaya caste to *Cheramar* which means the people of Kerala.

Shri Pampady Joseph also had to suffer untouchability. The Syrian Christians were not treating the untouchable Christians on terms of equality. In order to show his non-acceptance of the traditional attitude and customs of the caste Hindus and caste Hindu converts, he founded an organization called, Cheramar Mahajan Sabha on 14 January 1921. In this Sabha the Christians as well as untouchable Hindus were allowed to be members. He was of the view that the Cheramars were the original inhabitants of Kerala, and as such they should not be suppressed in their own land. He thought that they should struggle against the Hindu mentality and obtain their lost rights under the banner of the Sabha.

In order to awaken his brethren he started one magazine *Sadhujan Dootan* in 1919. He wrote thought-inspiring articles in the magazine. It was in existence up to 1924.

He wrote a book *Cheruma Boy* and attacked the Syrian Christians' apathetic and discriminatory attitude towards the untouchable Christians.

On 8 June 1931, he was appointed as a member of the Shri Moolam Legislative Assembly, Travancore. He submitted a memorandum to the British Parliament on 24 April 1935 and requested it to accord all the civil rights on a par with the others.

When he observed that his brethren were not getting equal treatment in the Church, he advised them to build their own churches and temples.

He was associated with Shri Ayyan Kali, the pioneer of Dalit liberation movement in Kerala. He also acquired some land and distributed the same for agricultural purposes amongst his brethren.

He married Smt Saara in 1915. He had two sons and a daughter. Shri Pampady John Joseph died in July 1940 at the age of 56.

PANDIT GOPALANAND MAHARAJ[87] (1905-1982)

Shri Gopalanand Maharaj was born on 1 July 1905 at Jodhpur in Rajasthan. His father Shri Pandit Sanwalram was a sweeper. Shri Pandit Gopalanand completed his intermediate from Hyderabad (Sindh) now in Pakistan.

Shri Pandit Gopalanand came into contact with Shri Swami Sachidanandji of Arya Samaj in 1925. He accepted Arya Samaj and started preaching the same to his brethren. He studied Vedanta from Pandit Bodhanandji.

He started his campaign against untouchability, casteism and traditionalism from 1930 onwards, through the medium of religion. He was a saint-poet and singer of devotional songs. His *kirtan* in the *satsang* was influential and effective. He tried his best to root out the bad habits prevailing in the society, such as drinking, playing cards, beef-eating, uncleanliness, sub-casteism and involvement in disputes. He waged a war against all these evil habits among his brethren and inculcated virtues in them. He asked his brethren to maintain cleanliness and high moral standard in the society. He himself was a true follower of Arya Samaj, as such he was vegetarian, a teetotaller and a real pious man.

In the year 1937, he formed Harijan Hitaishi Veer Sabha at a huge conference of his brethren at Bombay. The main objectives of the Sabha were to unite the untouchables, especially the sweepers under one banner, to struggle for their legitimate rights and to boost their morale and confidence, so that they might have an honourable and respectable status in society.

---

87. Source of Information:
Smt Krishnabai Maharaj
81. Masuria Harijan Colony. Jodhpur (Rajasthan) on 4-8-1991.

He was a nominated member of All India Charkha Sangh and Baroda Harijan Sevak Sangh.

His talks on various religious and social subjects were relayed on All India Radio, Baroda, many a time from 1949 to 1955.

He moved almost throughout India for the propagation of good moral habits among his brethren. He visited places like Hyderabad (Sindh), Karachi, Delhi, Ajmer, Bombay, Baroda, Calcutta, etc. He was well conversant with 11 languages including Hindi, Urdu, Bangla, Marwari, Punjabi, Gujarati, Marathi, Parsi, English and Sanskrit.

He was invited by Shriram Sarvate and Narsinhdeo Gujarati, the leaders of the sweepers community at Jodhpur to inaugurate the Outer Rajputana Harijan Sammelan. It was well attended.

He wrote *Shri Gopal Bhajanuali* in 1933 and *Harijan Hitaishi Bhajanavali.*

He married Santoshibai and Krishnabai. He had three sons.

He breathed his last on 6 January 1982 at the age of 77.

PANDIT PALANISWAMI[88] (1870-1941)

Shri Palaniswami was born in 1870 at Madras in a Pariah family. His father's name was Thiru Madurai Pillai. Shri Palaniswami was well versed in Vedas and knew astrology.

He was influenced by his teacher Shri Gangadhara Navalar, with whom he worked till 1900 in Tiruppani-K-Kuttam, a religious organization. Thereafter, he constructed his own temple named, Balsubramanyam Swamy temple in Madras.

In order to spread education among the Depressed Classes, he started a school in 1917 for them. In 1921, he started a hostel for the students of the Depressed Classes. He started Dravidian Youth Society for bringing a new social awareness among the untouchables. In 1929, he organized an exhibition where the

---

88. Source of Information:
A.S. Ulakanathan, *Messengers of Equality,* Madras 1990.

handicrafts made by the Depressed Classes were displayed. In the year 1931 he contested for the Madras City Council, but lost. He was a member of Justice Party.

He was honoured by the Shankaracharya of Kanchikamkothi with a golden-laced shawl in 1923 in appreciation of his socio-religious activities.

He worked in cooperation with Shri M.C. Rajah in the socio-political field. Throughout his life he tried to awaken and uplift his brethren.

He expired in 1941 at the age of 71. His son P. Shivasankaran, who also served the community.

PANDIT PATRAMSINH[89] (1900-1972)

Shri Patramsinh Jatav was born in 1900 at Mehrauli, New Delhi. His father Shri Doulatramji Jatav was manager of a small shoe factory. Shri Patramsinh was educated up to the seventh standard in a mission school in New Delhi. He was well-versed in Sanskrit and English apart from Hindi.

He came under the influence of Shri Ramachandra Dehloi. a member of the Arya Samaj. Shri Patramsinh accepted Arya Samaj. He was against idol worship, strictly vegetarian and performed all the rituals of Arya Samaj.

After having seen the adverse condition in which his brethren were living, he resolved to work for them. He was inspired by Devisinh Jatav and Swami Achhutanand, who were the supporters of Babasaheb Ambedkar. Shri Patramsinh was in favour of separate electorate for the Scheduled Castes.

He, however, had no faith in Gandhism. He opposed the appellation 'Harijan' given by Mahatma Gandhi to the untouchables. He asked Gandhiji that if the untouchables were Harijan, then were other people Chandal?

Shri Patramsinh joined the Scheduled Castes Federation at its inception itself. Later on he became Secretary of the Delhi unit of

---

89. Source of Information:
Personal interview with his son Shri Dharamvir Jatav
Teliwada, Mandal Sadar, Delhi-10006 on 15-3-1990.

Scheduled Castes Federation. In the year 1951 he became its President. He tried to spread the message of Babasaheb Ambedkar in Delhi and the nearby area.

In the first general elections held in 1952 he contested as a candidate of Jan Sangh for the Lok Sabha seat from outer Delhi (G and SC) constituency. He was, however, defeated by Congress candidate Shri Naval Prabhakar.

Shri Patramsinh was a great poet and author of many books. He composed a good number of devotional songs on Dalit uplift. His books are *Jati Upadesh, Sangathan Yukti; Achhut Bharat; Bhakta Ravidas Chalisa; Dr. B.R. Ambedkar ji ka Jeevan Charitra (1951) etc;* His books are thought provoking and inspiring.

He married Ratna Devi. He got one son and nine daughters. He breathed his last on 14 May 1972 at the age of 72.

PARMAR G.T.[89(a)]

Shri Govind Taba Parmar was one of the Leaders of the Depressed Classes of Gujarat. He became a member of the executive committee of Bahishkrit Hitkarini Sabha founded by Dr.Babasaheb Ambedkar in a meeting held at Damodar Hall, Mumbai on 9 March 1924. He has engaged himself in the upliftment of the Scheduled Castes and the improvement of labourers. In order to give a impetus to election propoganda in 1945, the provincial conference of SCF was held at Ahmedabad on 29-30, November, 1945 in a Specious Pendal called Boudhanagar, on the bank of Sabarmati in Ahmedabad. Govind Parmar had the privilege of presiding over the conference. Dr.Babasaheb Ambedkar addressed the conference as Chief-Guest.

He was member of the Governing Body of the people's Education Society founded by Dr. Babasaheb Ambedkar (On 8th July 1945) from the year 1954 and graciously elected as its Chairman from 1969 to 1970.

89(a). Source of Information :

1. Milind College Magazine 1970-71.
2. Prabuddha Bharat, 26-01-1957.
3. Dr. Babasaheb Ambedkar Biography Vol. 2 by C.B. Khairmode.

After the sudden death of Dr. Babasaheb Ambedkar on 6th December 1956 his Lieutenants convened a meeting of the executive committee of the Scheduled Castes Federation to think over the emergent situation on 31 December 1956. They, however decided to form a Presidium consisting of eleven members under the presidentship of Barrister Rajabhau Khobragade. The Presidium was to work in place of Babasaheb Ambedkar till the formation of a new body. G.T. Parmar was one amongst them. In the convention held at Nagpur on 3rd October 1957 he took part in the formation of Republican Party of India.

When a Special Committee of the party was formed under the Presidentship of Dadasaheb Gaikwad to get the demands of The Bidi Workers sanctioned, he was appointed as one of its members.

Shri G.T. Parmar serving the cause of the upliftment of the Scheduled Castes expired on 2 May 1970 at his home town Amreli, Saurashtra, Gujarat.

PARMAR, V.T.[90]

Shri Vishrambhai Parmar was born in 1910 at Sojitra in Taluka Petlad, Kheda district of Gujarat. He belonged to Rohit (Chamar) caste. His father Shri Tishabhai Parmar was an agricultural labourer. Shri Vishrambhai Parmar had completed his education up to matric level from Baroda High School, Baroda.

He came in contact with Shri Lallubhai Makwana who started Mahagujarat Dalit Navyuvak Mandal in 1930. Shri Vishrambhai Parmar joined the organization and became its General Secretary in 1940. He went to Nagpur to attend the convention of the Dalits held in 1942, in which the Scheduled Castes Federation was formed at the initiative of Dr Babasaheb Ambedkar. He organized the Gujarat State unit of SCF. Shri Gangaram Pitamber Parmar was its President and Shri Vishrambhai Parmar was its General Secretary.

---

90. Source of Information:

Personal interview with Shri V.T. Parmar

Velanuvas, Behind Pratap Cinema, Dr. Ambedkar Road. Ahmedabad on 6-11-1989.

He led the Bus Entry Satyagraha at Ahmedabad, Naroda and Kaloon. He participated in the famous Temple Entry Satyagraha at Swaminarayan temple, Ahmedabad, in the year 1948.

He founded one Sweepers Association at Ahmedabad. Dr Babasaheb Ambedkar was its President and Shri Vishrambhai Parmar was its General Secretary.

He was with Babasaheb Ambedkar in the Dalit liberation movement. He embraced Buddhism and tried to spread it in Gujarat. He led the satyagraha of landless labourers in Gujarat in 1964.

He started a monthly journal named *Samanata* in Gujarati from Ahmedabad, which was devoted to bringing about a new awareness under the leadership of Dr Babasaheb Ambedkar. The journal was in existence from 1951 to 1955.

In the first general elections held in 1952, he contested for the Bombay Legislative Assembly from Ahmedabad city constituency on SCF ticket, but could not achieve success in the election.

He devoted his whole life for the cause of his brethren. He remained unmarried. Shri Shivarambhai Motilal Parmar of Mehsana, Ranchodbhai M. Parmar, Shri Sundarlal Patel (Baroda), Bhavanjibhai Master, Mohanlal D. Ambedkarvadi and many others were his companions in his socio-political activities.

PASWAN, BHOLA[91] (1914-1984)

Shri Bhola Paswan was born in 1914 at Bairgachhi, Purnea district in Bihar. He passed his 'Shastri' examination of Kashi Vidyapeeth, Banaras. He belonged to Pasi community.

He started his career as a member of the District Board of Purnea. He was its member from 1939 to 1941. He started taking part in the independence struggle under the banner of Congress.

---

91. Source of Information:
Who's Who, 1983.

He participated in the Quit India Movement in 1942, for which he was imprisoned for 21 months.

He was the champion of the downtrodden communities in Bihar. He tried to elevate their position.

He was elected to Bihar Legislative Assembly in 1946. He became Parliamentary Secretary to Minister for Local Self Government in 1952. During 1952-53 he was Cabinet Minister in Bihar Government. He got elected from Banmankhi (R) Assembly constituency in 1957 and 1962.

In the general elections held in 1967 he successfully contested from Korha (R) Assembly constituency. However, he left the Congress and formed his own party named Lok Tantric Congress in 1968. He became Chief Minister of Bihar in 1968 and continued to be so till June 1969. Again he became Chief Minister for one year during 1971-72. He joined the Congress in 1972.

In the year 1972 he was elected to the Rajya Sabha and continued as member of Rajya Sabha till his last. He was Union Minister for Works and Housing during 1973-74 under the Prime Ministership of Indira Gandhi.

He was appointed as Chairman of the newly formed Scheduled Castes and Scheduled Tribes Commission, in August 1978. The Commission had submitted its first Report for 1978-79 on 8 February 1980, and second report for 1979-80 on 25 May 1981 under his chairmanship.

He started a weekly in Hindi, named *Rashtra-Sandesh.* He was assistant editor of *Rashtra Vani,* Patna.

He died on 10 September 1984 at the age of 70.

PILLAI, MADURAI[92] (1858-1913)

Shri Madurai Pillai was born in 1858 at Madras. He was son of Markandan Pillai. He had his early education in SPG School, Vepery in Madras, St.Paul's High School, Rangoon and Christian College, Madras.

---

92. Source of Information:

A.S. Ulakanathan, *Messengers of Equality,* Madras (1990).

For some time he served as a writer in the office of the Governor of Madras, Lord Buckingham. Later, he served in a steel company at Rangoon. He started his own business and successfully engaged in import-export business. In that connection he extensively toured the foreign countries such as England, Scotland, Wales, Germany, Denmark, France, Norway, Italy, Egypt, etc.

He set apart a portion of his income for charitable purposes. He built one high school on his own for the spread of education among the Depressed Classes, at Madras.

He had been Rangoon Municipality Commissioner from 1885 to 1900. For 25 years he was an honorary magistrate.

He was a great philanthropist and a great lover of knowledge. Many poets composed their poems in his praise. These poems are collected in a book form called *Madurai Pillai Prabandham.* He was introduced to King George V as a leader of the downtrodden community. This speaks volumes of his greatness.

He died in 1913 at the age of 55.

PILLAI MUNISWAMY V.I.[92(a)] (1889-1953)

Rao Saheb V. I. Muniswamy Pillai was born in a poor Scheduled Caste family in Ootacamund, Dist.: Nilgiri, Tamil Nadu in 1889. Due to his adverse financial condition he had to take up a job as a clerk at the age of twenty. Later in 1925 he set up his own busines and started taking part in social upliftment movement.

He was nominated to the Madras Legislative Council in 1926. He became a member of the Madras Legislative Assembly

---

92(a) · Source of Information :

1. *Dr. B.R. Ambedkar : Framing of Indian Constitution* (2015) by Dr. S.N. Busi (Hyderabad).

2. *Vidarbhatil Dalit Chalvalicha Itihas* by H.L. Kosare. (Nagpur) 1984.

in 1937. He got the unique opportunity to serve as Minister of Agricuture and Rural Development in the Ministry of C. Rajagopala Chari from 1937 -1939. Later he was elected to the Constituent Assembly from Madras in 1946. He was very much active in the working of the Constituent Assembly. Later on he contested in the first general elections from Tindivanam as a Congress Candidate, but he was defeated.

From the very beginning of his political career he supported congress, but he had fascination for Dalit upliftment and inner attachment to Ambedkarte movement. In order to enlist is support to Parvati Temple Entry Satyagrah at Pune, he organized a meeting of Madras on 22 October 1929 alongwith R.B. N.Shivaraj. He presided over the convention of All India Depressed Classes Congress, held at Nagpur on 7-8 May 1932. It was addressed, among others by Dr. Babasaheb Ambedkar. Muniswami Pillai in his Presidential address admired the role played by Dr. Babasaheb Ambedkar and R.B.R. Srinivasan in the Round table conferences held in London during 1930-32 and expressed his support to their demands as they were in the interests of the Scheduled Castes.

He called the provision of political safeguards in the Constitution of India as "Magna Charta" for the Scheduled Castes. He opined that, " I am one of those who believe in political power for the elevation of the weaker sections of our land."

He died on 14 December 1953 at the age of 63 years.

PILLAI, SHIVASHANMUGHAM[93]

Shri Shivashanmugham Pillai was born on 24 February 1901 in Madras. He was an Adi-Dravida. His father Pillai Jagnathan was a steward. Shri Pillai J. Shivashanmugham graduated from

---

93. Source of Information:

Dictionary of National Biography (Vol. III) Institute of Historical Studies Calcutta (1974).

Loyola College, Madras. Further, he passed his M.A. (privately) from Madras University.

He was elected member of Madras Corporation from 1930 to 1938. In the year 1938-39 he got a unique opportunity of being elected Mayor of the Madras Corporation. He was the first member of the Scheduled Caste to be Mayor of Madras.

He was an active member of Congress. He got elected to the Madras State Assembly in 1937. He was again elected as a member of the Madras Legislative Assembly in the year 1946. From 1946 to 1955 he was the Speaker of the Madras Legislative Assembly.

From 1955 to 1961 he was a member of the Union Public Service Commission. He was a nominated member of the Rajya Sabha from 1962 to 1968,

He presided over the 26th Orcot District Madras Harijan Conference and over the All India Scheduled Castes Parliamentarians and Legislators' Conference held at Nagpur in 1950.

He gave evidence on behalf of the Depressed Classes before the Whitley Commission, the Simon Commission, the Lothian Commission, etc.

He was a firm supporter of the Parliamentary system of government. Though he belonged to the Congress Party, he did not fully believe in Gandhism. He was a staunch nationalist. He condemned the rise of fissiparous tendencies in India.

He criticised the demand of Dravidstan made by the Dravid Kazagam.

He firmly believed that casteism and untouchability must be abolished. He condemned *Murichittu,* an agricultural bonded labour system prevailing in the South which virtually enslaved the Scheduled Castes.

He was a good speaker and writer. He had written *The History of the Adi-Dravidas; Life, Select Writings and Speeches of Rao Bahadur M.C. Rajah* and *Legislative protection of the Cultivating Tenant Labourers.*

He married Smt Chandra in 1937 and had three sons and one daughter.

PIPAL, GOPI CHANDRA[94] (1901-1989)

Shri Gopichandra Pipal was born on 1 June 1901 at Yelanganj, Kanpur in Uttar Pradesh. His father's name was Shri Mangli Prasad Pipal, who belonged to the Jatav caste. Shri Mangli Prasad Pipal came to Agra with his family in 1905 and started a shoe factory there. Shri Gopichandra Pipal, after his matriculation, completed a course named. Scientific Shoe Fitting and Salesman Course conducted by a London based institute at Bombay, in the year 1940. Thereafter, he started his own shoe manufacturing factory at Agra in 1940.

He was very much perturbed to see a ghastly incident in which one untouchable student named Hiralal Jatav was killed as he happened to touch the water pot in a school in Hing Ki Mandi at Agra in 1914. This incident led him to wage an organized war against Brahmanism. In 1918, he joined the All India Jatav Mahasabha.

He met Babasaheb Ambedkar in 1931 at Bombay. He got a new inspiration from him. He became a strong supporter of separate electorate for the Scheduled Castes.

He led the satyagraha at Agra and Lucknow to press his demand for abolition of sales tax on the shoes manufactured by the shoemakers.

He joined the Scheduled Castes Federation in 1942. He was elected General Secretary of the Agra district branch. He led the satyagraha for political demands as per SCF programme at Agra in 1946. He was imprisoned for three months for the same. In 1949, he was elected as President of the Uttar Pradesh SCF. Later on, he joined the Republican Party of India. He could enlist strength for RPI in Uttar Pradesh.

---

94. Source of Information:
Personal interview with his son Shri Prakash Chandra Pipal, 7/5 Oliya Road, Chhipi Tola, Agra, UP on 7-6-1991.

He put up RPI candidates in the election to the Municipal Corporation, Agra, in 1959 and got 17 candidates elected with one Deputy Mayor, out of 54 seats.

The Ravidas Mission, Agra presented an address to him on 18 March 1980.

He married Parvatibai and had seven sons and three daughters. Shri Pipal died on 27 July 1989 at the age of 88.

POWAR, D.S.[95] (1896-1970)

Shri Dattatraya Powar was born in 1896 at Kolhapur in Maharashtra. He belonged to the Chambhar caste. His father Shri Santram Powar was engaged in the business of leather. Shri Dattatraya Powar was educated up to the matric level.

He was appointed as *Nazar* at Civil Court at Kolhapur. After the succession of princely state of Kolhapur, he was appointed as *Mahalkari* at Raibag in Ratnagiri district. He was in service till 1951.

He was benefited and influenced by the benevolent and liberal attitude of Chhatrapati Shahu Maharaj of Kolhapur. He met Babasaheb Ambedkar in 1917 itself. Shri Dattatraya Powar introduced Babasaheb Ambedkar to Chhatrapati Shahu Maharaj in 1919. Subsequently, Babasaheb Ambedkar came in closer contact with the Maharaj.

A conference of the untouchables was organized at Mangaon, near Kolhapur in 1920. Shri D.S. Powar was one of the organizers of the conference. Babasaheb Ambedkar was the President, and Chhatrapati Shahu Maharaj was the chief guest at the conference.

Shri Powar attended the conference of the Depressed Classes at Nagpur on 30-31 May, 1920. He moved a resolution in a conference that the non-Brahmins should be recruited on a large scale in the education department in the interest of the

---

[95] Source of Information:
Personal interview with his son. Dr Raghunath Powar
2407. "A" ward, Shivaji Peth, Kolhapur (Maharashtra) on 6-5-1989.

educational development of the backward communities. It was passed in the conference.

He started Maharani Indumati Boarding at Kolhapur in 1924 for the untouchable students. Babasaheb Ambedkar expressed his satisfaction over the working of the said boarding when he visited the same in 1929.

He was a very trusted companion of Dr Babasaheb Ambedkar. However, he joined the Congress in 1951. He contested in the first general elections in 1952 from Hatkanangale (R) assembly constituency on Congress ticket and gave successful fight to his nearest rival Shri Shirke of the SCF. He contested in 1957 also from the same constituency but was defeated.

He married Vithabai. He had four sons and three daughters. He breathed his last on 22 May 1970 at the age of 74.

POYKAYIL YOHANNAN[96] (1879-1939)

Shri Poykayil Yohannan was born on 17 February 1879 at Eraviperoor village, Pathanamthitta district in Kerala State. His father Shri Kandan and mother Smt Kunjulechy were serfs of a Christian landlord. When Poykayil's parents worked in the paddy fields of the master, he used to graze the cattle. He did not get formal education due to his low caste and heavy burden of work. However, an astrologer had taught him secretly and a Christian missionary gave him the Bible for reading.

Shri Poykayil Yohannan was a Christian, but not by conversion. His master was a Christian, hence he had to profess the same religion. In those days the masters owned the serfs who were to follow the former. His previous name given by his parents was Kumaran, but his Christian master named him as Yohannan.

Shri Yohannan became a member of the Marthoma Sabha, a prominent Christian denomination of Central Travancore. He studied the Bible and tried his best to convert the downtrodden

---

96. Source of Information:
Shri V.K. Raman President:
PRDS Eraviperoor, Taluka Tiruvalla. Pathanamthitta district. Kerala dt. 5-8-1991.

people to Christianity by giving discourses on the subject matter of the Bible. Even though he served Christianity, he was treated as an untouchable. He observed that casteism was in existence among Christians also. There were separate churches for the Depressed Classes who embraced Christianity. Even the cemetries were not common.

A very pathetic incident took place only on the ground of untouchability at Pularikad near his village, where the dead body of a Christian which was buried in a high caste Christian cemetry was deliberately unearthed and buried in a nearby wasteland. This incident had a great impact on Yohannan. He asked his people, "How can we get entrance to heaven if this is the situation in this mortal earth?" Thereafter, he left the Marthoma Sabha along with his brethren and joined a new sect of Christian faith called Brothers Mission. Even in this sect, he found acute untouchability. When Shri Yohannan helped to bring about the marriage of one Daniel, an untouchable with a high caste Christian lady named Mariamma, the high caste Christians became furious and attempted to beat Poykayil Yohannan and the couple.

After having seen the discrimination against the Depressed Classes in the Christian religion, he was very frustrated and disappointed. He came to the conclusion that Christianity was not a solution on the problem of the untouchables. He, therefore, founded a new faith named Pratyaksha Raksha Deiva Sabha (PRDS) in the year 1910. He was renamed as Poykayil Sree Kumara Devan. He tried to convince his Hindu and Christian brothers to be members of PRDS. He persuaded them to leave superstitious beliefs, and to stop practising black magic and sacrificing the animals. He taught them to observe cleanliness and lead a life of high moral standard. He evolved a common prayer in the name of the incarnate God. His followers prayed in separate prayer halls.

He could successfully convince the majority of his brethren to abandon Christianity and embrace PRDS. According to him the Bible was nothing but a historical account of the Jews. Hence he argued that, "the Bible is not meant for this generation and it shall not provide any solution for the problems of the Depressed Classes." His learned and thought-provocating lectures had a magic impact on the people, belonging to different sub-castes among the Depressed Classes. They accepted his thoughts and observed them in their lives.

He purchased approximately 125 acres of land in different parts of Travancore for the use of PRDS. There are 7.5 acres of land at Eraviperoor where the head office of his organization is situated. He purchased 5.5 acres of land at Madapally in Changanacherry, Pathanamthitta district and 13.5 acres of land at Neyyattinkara in Trivandrum district.

He established schools and industrial training centres at different places in addition to buildings constructed for religious ceremonies and public functions.

Having considered his leadership calibre, zeal for social reforms and strength of his followers, Yohannan was twice nominated to the Sreemoolam Praja Sabha - the Legislative Council of the princely State of Travancore in the years 1921 and 1931.

His main demands in the legislature were on education and employment for the Depressed Classes. In those days the Christian community was considered as a single unit. There was no separate census of the Depressed Classes converted to Christianity. Therefore, it was not possible to identify them for the concessions, if any. Consequently, on 1 March 1921 he submitted that, "it is wrong to consider Christian community as one society as there was no intermarriage and inter-dining between the upper class Christian and those belonging to downtrodden caste Christians." He said very categorically that the people of Paraiyar, Pulayar, Marvar and Kuravar castes who had embraced Christianity were not treated as equal to the upper class Christians. Therefore, those children, among these castes who studied up to fourth to seventh classes should be given appointments as peons, clerks and police constables. He said that fee concession should be given to those students who continued their studies beyond fifth class.

On 3 March 1921 he argued for getting wasteland to the extent of at least two acres to each of the untouchable families. On 31 March 1931 he argued in the Praja Sabha that special scholarships be granted to the students belonging to the Depressed Classes.

He started schools with the assistance of the government to spread education among the untouchables. He sought emancipation of the Dalits through religion and education..

He married Janamma in 1910. He had two sons. Shri Poyakayil Yohannan breathed his last on 29 June 1939 at the age of 61.

PRAGILAL

Shri Pragilal was born in March 1898 at Sekhapur, Sitapur district in Uttar Pradesh. His father's name was Lachhman Prasad.

He joined the Congress. He became President of UP Depressed Classes League. In the elections held in 1937, he got elected on Congress ticket from Sitapur district (North-west) constituency for the Legislative Assembly of the United Provinces.

Again he got elected as a Congress candidate in 1946 from the same constituency. Subsequently, he was elected to the Constituent Assembly from the UP Legislative Assembly in 1946.

He was elected to the first Parliament in 1952 from Sitapur district-cum-Kheri district (West) on reserved seat. He was elected in 1957 and 1962 (Akbarpur) elections to the Parliament. However, in the 1967 Lok Sabha elections, he was defeated by R. J. Ram on Republican Party of India.

He married Kamala Devi and had a son and a daughter.

PRASHANT, GAYA PRASAD[96(a)] (1925-1998)

Gaya Prasad 'Prashant' was a great Leader of the Dalit emancipation movement in U.P. He was born on 9 May 1925 at Shyamabudhi village in Maliabad tahsil of Lucknow district, in Uttar Pradesh. He belonged to Jatav Community. He was

---

96(a). Source of Information :

1. Kanoji Lal Boudha his Grandson Hathikhana, Fatehgad, Dist. Farrukhabad U.P. on 23-02-1992, and

2. Uttar Pradesh Mein Dalit Andolan - by Dr. Angnelal and Raj (2011) Goutam Book Centre, Hardeopuri, Shahdara, Delhi.

educated in Maliabad and in Lucknow. His father's name was Bihari Lai.

For sometime Gaya Prasad Prashant was employed in the Rly Department as Collection Inspector and later in the Municipal Commission Office in Lucknow. However, he left the service and joined the Dalit Movement.

He and his companions invited Dr. Babasaheb Ambedkar to Lucknow to address the Dalits. Babasaheb came to Lucknow and addressed his brethren thereat, this event gave a boost to the movement in U.P.

There were statewise agitations of the Scheduled Castes Federation in 1945-46 for certain demands, including the separate electorates. There were public meetings, rallies and demonstrations of Dalits through out the state. During the agitations many of the participants courted arrest in furtherence of their demands. Gaya Prasad led the agitation in U.P.

After the formation of Republican Party of India, under the leadership of N. Shivaraj and other leaders at Nagpur in 1957, Gaya Prasad started RPI branch in U.P. The R.P.I. U.P. branch participated in the 1962 general election and won three seats for the Lok Sabha.

Later, the RPI launched a nationwide land Satyagraha alongwith other demands in 1964-65. RPI UP branch under the leadership of Gaya Prasad took active part in the Satyagraha.

Gaya Prasad Prashant had embraced Buddhism at the time of Dhamma Deeksha Ceremony held at Nagpur on the day of Vijayadashmi on 14th Oct. 1956.

Subsequently, Gayaprasad under the able leadership of Bhadant Bodhanand (Lucknow) launched Dhamma propagation programme in U.P.

Gaya Prasadji was a prolific writer. He wrote certain books on Dalit movement and Buddhism. They were, *Bhim Geetavali, Mool Vansh Katha, Babasaheb Ambedkar Ka Jeevan Sangharsha,* etc.

He had a daughter and three sons.

He breathed his last on 6 August 1998 at the age of seventy three years.

PURANCHAND[97] (1900-1970)

Shri Puranchand was born in August 1900 at Agra, in Jatav community. His father, Shri Sundarlal was a building contractor. Shri Puranchand completed his education up to the matric level. He was employed in the Department of Public Works under the Government of India. He became very much experienced in construction work.

Shri Swami Shraddhanandji successfully convinced him to accept Arya Samaj. Shri Puranchand agreed to do so as he had felt that there was equality in Arya Samaj. Thereafter, he became a strict vegetarian, and observed all the rules of the Arya Samaj.

He used to preach the tenets of the Arya Samaj to his untouchable brothers. He taught them to observe the rules of sanitation, vegetarianism and temperance. He taught them to live a life of high moral standard.

When Dr Babasaheb Ambedkar was holding the charge of the Department of Labour, as well as of Public Works and Construction, Shri Puranchand came into contact with the former. Shri Puranchand was very much influenced by the mission of Babasaheb Ambedkar and thereby became a true follower of the latter.

At that time a crack in the Taj Mahal was observed. The British engineers tried their best to patch up the crack, but in vain. Thereafter, Shri Puranchand accepted the challenge and succeeded in the task. Dr Babasaheb Ambedkar felt great pleasure and pride on seeing the skill of an untouchable mason who could do wonders. He recommended the name of Puranchand for promotion as an Assistant Engineer and for the award of Raisaheb. The Governor General also gladly accepted the recommendation and acted accordingly.

Raisaheb Puranchand started a school at Agra in 1947. Later, it was handed over to the Agra Municipal Corporation.

---

97. Source of Information:
Personal Interview with his son Shri Vishva Mitra, Retd. Civil Engineer, 16 Hanuman Road, Near Regal Cinema. New Delhi, on 19-3-1990.

He was elected Vice-president of the Delhi Scheduled Castes Association and the Ambedkar Bhavan on 2 January 1947.

He married Ganga Devi. He had a son and three daughters.

Shri Puranchand died on 10 February 1970 at the age of 70 years.

PRASAD, MAHADEO

Shri Mahadeo prasad was born in August 1901 at Sariya Sardarnagar, Gorakhpur district in Uttar Pradesh. His father's name was Jaimangal Prasad. Shri Mahadeo Prasad was educated at Government Middle School at Dumari Koti.

He started his social life as a member of Gorakhpur District Board in 1930. He was President of Adi-Hindu Depressed Classes Association for three years, through which he tried to bring a new consciousness to the people under the leadership of Swami Achhutanandji.

He was elected member of the UP legislative Assembly from 1952-57. He got elected as a member of the Lok Sabha from Gorakhpur (R) constituency as Congress candidate in 1957. In 1962, he got elected to the Lok Sabha from Bansgaon (SC) but in 1967 he was defeated by Shri Molahu of SSP. Again in 1980 Shri Mahadeo Prasad was elected from Bansgaon as Congress candidate to the Lok Sabha.

He married Anuragi and had three sons and seven daughters.

RAJAH, M.C.[98] (1883-1947)

Shri M.C. Rajah was born in 1883 at St.Thomas Mount, Madras. His father, Shri Chinna Thambi Pillai, was manager of the Lawrence Asylum Press, Madras. Shri M.C. Rajah was educated at Wesley Mission High School, Royapettah and Christian College, Madras. He belonged to the Pariah caste.

---

98. Source of Information:

Dictionary of National Biography, Vol. Ill, Institute of Historical Studies. Calcutta (1974)..

Shri M.C. Rajah started his career as a teacher in 1906. In 1917 he was nominated to the Elementary Education Committee and in 1924 to the Madras University Senate. He was appointed as a member of the Chinglepet District Elementary Education Committee, the Secondary Education Reorganization Committee, and the Advisory Committee on Education, Madras. He started Dravidian School at Nungambakkam in 1936. He was of the view that education should be properly oriented so as to infuse in the students the spirit of social uplift and patriotism.

Shri M.C. Rajah took a very active part in organizing and uplifting the Depressed Classes. He became Secretary of the State Adi-Dravida Mahajan Sabha in 1916. He was a propounder of free and compulsory education to the Depressed Classes. He advised the people of those classes to educate their children. He considered Britian as the liberator of the lower classes in India. He had the honour of presiding over the conference of the All India Depressed Classes Association established in 1928. He was its elected President and Shri G.A. Gawai was its Secretary.

He was nominated as a member of the Madras Legislative Council in 1920. He continued to be its member till 1926. Then he was nominated as a member of the Indian legislative Assembly in the year 1927. He continued as a member of Indian Legislative Assembly till 1937.

When the demand of separate electorate for the Depressed Classes was put forward by Dr Babasaheb Ambedkar and R. Srinivasan at the Round Table Conference (RTC) 1930, Shri M.C. Rajah supported the said demand. Speaking as President of the ninth All India Depressed Classes Conference held at Gurgaon in Punjab on 31 October 1931 he vehemently criticized Mahatma Gandhi and the Congress. He congratulated Dr Babasaheb Ambedkar for his brilliant arguments in favour of separate electorate.

However, he entered into a pact for joint electorate and reserved seats, with Dr Moonje, the leader of the Hindu Mahasabha. Shri M.C. Rajah was one of the signatories of the Poona Pact.

He, however, realized the futility of the electorate arrangement under the Poona Pact. He confessed very explicitly that "our entering the joint electorate with the Caste Hindus under the leadership of the Congress, far from helping us, has enabled the Congress led by Caste Hindus to destroy our independence and to use us to cut our own throats." Ultimately he again accepted the leadership of Dr Babasaheb Ambedkar. He was one of the participants in the meeting called by Dr Babasaheb Ambedkar at New Delhi on 30-31 March 1942 for discussing the Cripps proposals. All the prominent Dalit leaders including Shri Rajah condemned the Cripps proposals as they were not in the interests of the Scheduled Castes.

In 1928 he visited Sri Lanka, and England in 1929. He was a member of several committees appointed by the government. He served as a member of the Advisory Committee to the Simon Commission.

He was presented with the title of Rao Bahadur in the year 1922.

He died in 1947 at the age of 64.

RAJAMANI DEVI (1920-1985)

Smt J.M. Rajamani Devi was born on 10 February 1920 at Hyderabad in Andhra Pradesh. Her father's name was Shri Kante Muthayya. She married Shri J.H. Krishnamurthy, a social and political leader at Hyderabad. She was the sister of Kante Prem Kumar, an honest and sincere worker of the Scheduled Castes Federation. Thus, she got a legacy of social service from both the sides, that is from her brother and her husband. She belonged to the Mala community.

She had great inclination towards social service of her community. She got the honour of becoming a Joint Secretary of the SCF Hyderabad on 16 July 1944. Later on, she was elevated to the position of President of Women Section of the SCF.

In the first general elections held in 1952 she had successfully contested for the Hyderabad Legislative Assembly on SCF ticket from Sircilla constituency against Shri S.R. Babiah of Congress. Later on she joined the Indian National Congress. She was Congress candidate in the same constituency in 1957, but could not get elected. She contested in 1967 as an independent candidate, but in vain. She was a member of Legislative Council in 1969.

Her husband, Shri J.H. Krishnamurthy was a great leader of the community. He was brother of a great Dalit leader Shri J.H. Subbiah. Rajamani Devi had two sons.

She died on 6 June 1985 at the age of 65.

RAJBHOJ, P.N.[99] (1905-1984)

Shri Pandurang Rajbhoj was born on 15 March 1905 at Kanashi, Nasik district in Maharashtra. He belonged to the Chambhar community. His father's name was Shrinathuji Rajbhoj. Shri Pandurang Rajbhoj was educated at Nutan Marathi Vidayalaya and Maharashtra Education Society's High School, Pune. After his high school education he joined government service. However, he left the service due to casteism in the office.

He started his social life as a member of the Bahishkrit Hitkarini Sabha, Pune unit. At the instance of Dr Babasaheb Ambedkar he convened the first conference of Dhor and Chambhar castes among the untouchables at Pune in the year 1926. He participated in the satyagraha at Mahad Choudar Tank on 19-20 March 1927 under the leadership of Dr Babasaheb Ambedkar. It was he who proposed to make a bonfire of the *Manusmriti* at Mahad on 25 March 1927. The proposal was unanimously approved, and it was actually burnt by Shri Bapusaheb Sahastrebuddhe, a Brahmin social worker. On 7 October 1928 he led the temple entry satyagraha in front of Parvati Mandir, Pune. He was severely beaten up by the caste Hindus. He participated in Kalaram Mandir satyagraha at Nasik on 2 March 1930 under the leadership of Babasaheb Ambedkar.

On 20 December 1931 he presided over the conference of the Depressed Classes Association, Pune unit, in which it was decided to support the proposal of joint electorate for the Depressed Classes under the Rajah-Moonje Pact, 1931. Due to his

---

99. Source of Information:

Personal Interview with his son, Shri Keshav Pandurang Rajbhoj, 207. Ghorpade Peth. Pune-2 and biography of Bapusaheb Rajbhoj (In Marathi) by Bhalchandra Phadke (Pune).

stand on the issue of separate electorate as proposed by Babasaheb Ambedkar at the RTC, he was not allowed to take part in the All India Depressed Classes Congress Conference held at Nagpur on May 1932. When Babasaheb Ambedkar and Mahatma Gandhi agreed upon the joint electorate and the Poona pact was signed between the two parties, Shri Rajbhoj also was one of the signatories of the said Pact. On 4 January 1936 a meeting of the Working committee of All India Depressed Classes League was held at Lucknow under the presidentship of R.L. Biswas, in which it was proposed to oppose the conversion move taken by Babasaheb Ambedkar. Shri P.N. Rajbhoj and Babu Jagjivan Ram were secretaries of the League in those days.

Shri P.N. Rajbhoj, however, changed his views in 1936 and came to the side of Babasaheb Ambedkar. On 6 June 1941, he spoke in support of Dr Babasaheb Ambedkar in the Conference of the Bidi Workers held at Bhandara under the presidentship of Shri D.G. Jadhav. He participated in the conference of the Depressed Classes held at Nagpur on 7, 8 and 9 July 1942 in which All India Scheduled Castes Federation was formed at the instance of Dr Babasaheb Ambedkar. Shri N. Shivaraj was elected as its President and Shri P.N. Rajbhoj was elected as its General Secretary. He led the nationwide satyagraha for political rights, launched by the SCF in July 1946. He visited Lucknow (UP) and Raipur (MP) in early 1947 for seeking information about the ill treatment meted out to the satyagrahis. He was, however, sent to jail at both the places.

He actively participated in the election politics. He was a member of Poona Municipality from 1927-30 and Poona district Local Board from 1929-32. He contested for Maharashtra legislative Assembly in 1937 from Bombay as an Independent but he was defeated by Dr Babasaheb Ambedkar, an ILP candidate.

In the first general elections held in 1952, he contested for Lok Sabha seat from Solapur (G and SC) constituency as a SCF nominee and he got elected. Due to differences with Babasaheb Ambedkar he left SCF on 11 April 1955. After the death of Babasaheb Ambedkar in 1956, he joined the Congress. The Congress government nominated him as a member of Rajya

Sabha. He was a member of the Rajya Sabha from 1957 to 1968. He contested for the highest office of President of India, held on 2 February 1966, but he was defeated by the Congress candidate Dr Zakir Hussain. Later, in August 1974 he was nominated as a member of Maharashtra Legislative Council for a period of six years.

Previously, he was against conversion of the Scheduled Castes to any other religion. However, he became inclined towards Buddhism at the later stage. On 15 May 1950 he participated in the World Buddhist Conference held at Colombo in Sri Lanka, along with Dr Babasaheb Ambedkar. He embraced Buddhism at Bangkok in Thailand on 17 May 1957 in the next World Buddhist Conference. He was a very staunch, devout and active Buddhist till his end. He founded Indian Buddhist Council for strengthening Buddhist movement in India. From the very beginning he demanded all the constitutional and statutory facilities to the Neo-Buddhists at par with the Scheduled Castes. He went on hunger strike from 9 December to 18 December 1966 in front of Parliament for granting facilities to the Neo-Buddhists. Again he observed hunger strike for the same demand from 19 November to 25 November 1977 at New Delhi. He presented a memorandum to Smt Indira Gandhi, the then Prime Minister of India and urged her to grant the facilities to the Neo-Buddhist on a par with the Scheduled Castes, on 16 July 1982 at New Delhi. He consistently pursued the demand of facilities for the Neo-Buddhists till his last. He participated in the first World Buddhist Conference held in Ceylon, second World Buddhist Conference held in Tokyo in 1952 and fifth World Buddhist Conference held in Thailand in 1958.

He founded the Bharat Dalit Sevak Sangh at Pune on 15 April 1955. The main objective of this organization was to unite all the Dalits under one banner of the Sangh for getting redressal of their grievances. He submitted memorandums to the President and Prime Minister of India many times on the problems of the Scheduled Castes and the Neo-Buddhists. On 13 May 1962, he arranged a march in New Delhi for a period of seven days in order to attract the attention of the government to the ill condition of the hutment dwellers in the country. He repeated the same on 14 November 1964 for a period of ten days for the same demand. In order to attract the attention of the government to the problems of the Scheduled Castes, including the problems of atrocities, he started his fast for a period of 12 days on 16 June 1966 at New Delhi. Again he went on fast from 6 October to 12 October 1969, from 6 December to 15 December 1970 (at Pune), from 1 July to 11 July 1977 (at New Delhi), from 19 November to 25 November 1977 and on 21 December 1981 at Pune. He was put behind the bars many times. But all the while he gave a tough fight to the government on the issues of the Scheduled Castes and the Neo-Buddhists.

On behalf of the Bharat Dalit Sevak Sangh, he started Mahatma Phule hostel at Malinagar, Pune in 1959 for the boys and Kamala Nehru Hostel at Hingne, Pune in 1963 for the girls.

He was quite aware of the role of journals in any movement. Therefore, he started *Dalit Bandhu* in 1928, *Samata* in 1954 and *Dharma Jyoti* in 1960.

He was mainly responsible for popularizing the Scheduled Castes Federation among the Scheduled Castes masses, almost throughout India. He extensively toured the country to spread Dalit liberation movement under the leadership of Dr Babasaheb Ambedkar. However, after the death of Babasaheb Ambedkar he drifted away from the organization started by the latter, but he fought throughout his life for achieving the objectives of Dalit liberation movement led by Babasaheb Ambedkar.

He stood for renaming of Marathwada University (Aurangabad) as Dr Babasaheb Ambedkar University.

He visited many countries like England, Switzerland, France, Germany, USA, Japan, Sri Lanka and Thailand.

He was very popular among all the castes and sub-castes of the Scheduled Castes. He was popularly known as Babusaheb Rajbhoj.

He married Rukminidevi. He had two sons.

He breathed his last on 22 July 1984 at the age of 79.

RAMCHANDRA[100] (1908–2004)

Shri Ramchandra was born in 1908 at Humanabad, Bidar district, in Karnataka. His father's name was Veerappa. Shri Ramchandra could complete his education up to seventh class from Humanabad.

Shri Ramchandra accepted Arya Samaj and he was leading his life strictly according to the tenets of this organization. He joined the Congress and participated in its activities. He was against the Nizam's domination. He participated in the Hyderabad State independence movement under the banner of Congress. During those days the *Razakar* movement was proving to be fatal to the interest of the society in general and the Scheduled Castes in particular. Due to undue influence of *Razakars* many untouchables were accepting Islam. Thus on the one hand the majority caste Hindus, and on the other, the Muslims were exploiting the Scheduled Castes. Therefore, the untouchables were caught in a very precarious and bewildered conditions. In that situation Shri Ramchandra came to their rescue. He could give them courage to face the situation and thus raised their confidence.

He participated in the Quit India Movement in 1942 under the leadership of Pandit Shivacharanji. He participated in the Hyderabad independence movement.

He got involved in the election politics. In the general elections held in 1957 he contested for Mysore (Karnataka) Legislative Assembly from Aland (G and SC) constituency as a Congress candidate and won. In the elections held in 1962 he contested for Lok Sabha from Gulbarga (SC) constituency and got elected. In 1967 he contested from Bidar (SC) constituency with success. In the elections held in 1971 he contested as a candidate of National Congress (Organization) from Bidar (SC) Lok Sabha seat, but without success. In the elections held in 1977

---

100. Source of Information:
Shri Ramchandra Veerappa
Humanabad. Dist. Bidar (Karnataka) on 31.1.1990.

he contested for the Lok Sabha from Bidar (SC) constituency as a candidate of Bharatiya Lok Dal, but could not get elected. In the elections held in 1983 he contested for Karnataka Legislative Assembly on Congress ticket from Hulsoor (SC) constituency and emerged victorious this time. Again, he contested from the same constituency in 1985 but met with failure. He contested in the elections held in 1991 as BJP candidate and got elected.

Shri Ramchandra has got four sons and four daughters. Even at the age of 87 he was active in public life. He expired on 19-7-2004 at the age of 96.

RAM BABU MILKHI[100(a)] (1926-1989)

Babu Milkhi Ram was born on 14 June 1926 at Jammu City in Jammu and Kashmir. He belonged to Chamar Caste. He completed his matriculation from Jammu, B.A. from Kashmir University and LL.B. from Delhi University.

Babu Milkhi Ram started his legal practice and social service also. He was associated with All Jammu and Kashmir Ravidas Sabha. He firstly met Dr. Babasaheb Ambedkar in 1951 at Ludhiana Rest House (East Punjab) when he was on his mission in Punjab. Eventually he was attracted towards Dr. Babasaheb Ambedkar's Movement.

It was in November 1956, the Constitution of Jammu and Kashmir came into implementation and the elections were firstly held in 1957. Babu Milkhi Ram contested for Jammu and Kashmir Assembly and got elected.

He participated in the Convention of Republican Party of India held at Aligarh in U.P. in 1961. He moved the resolution in the convention stating that the state of J & K. should extend all the facilities under the Indian Constitution to the Scheduled

---

[100(a)]. Source of Information :

1. Kuldip Kumar, Sarangal Editor, Subah-i-Jammu, Urdu Weekly, 138, Kanji House, Jammu Tawi. (1987, 1989)

2. Daily Excelsior, dated July 5, 1984.

3. Article by T.R. Azad in Dalit Voice, Oct 16-31, 1989.

Castes in J & K. It was passed in the said Convention. He was included in the executive committee of RPI in the convention. It is, obviously because of his persuasion the Schedule Castes in J & K were entitled to get all the constitutional facilities.

He was appointed by the State Govt, as Vice-Chairman of State Scheduled Castes Advisory Board having status of State Minister in 1982. However, he resigned his post on 3 July 1984 when Dr. Farooq Abdulla's Ministry was toppled down on moral ground.

He embraced Buddhism and tried to propogate Buddhism among his brethren in Jammu and Kashmir. He gave a strong moral support to the community in protection of their self respect and development.

He married Ishri Devi. They got a son by name Kuldip Kumar Sarangal.

Babu Milkhi Ram breathed his last on 8 May 1989 at Jammu.

RAM, CHANDRIKA

Shri Chandrika Ram was born in 1918 at Saran, Saran district in Bihar. His father was a landlord. Shri Chandrika Ram passed his M.A., LL.B. from Patna university. He started his legal practice in 1945.

Shri Chandrika Ram became Secretary of the Bihar Provincial Depressed Classes League in the year 1942. He joined the Quit India Movement in 1942 and was sentenced to imprisonment for a period of two and half months.

He was elected to the Bihar Legislative Assembly in 1946. Subsequently, he was elected to the Constituent Assembly of India. He stated in the Constituent Assembly with regard to the provision of a period of ten years' limit for reservation of seats, that the said time limit was not reasonable. He thought that the Scheduled Castes would not be able to come to the level of other communities within such a short period.

In elections held in 1952 and 1957 he was elected to the Bihar Legislative Assembly. During 1952-57 he was General Secretary of the Bihar Congress Committee and Parliamentary Secretary to the Chief Minister. He was Deputy Minister of Bihar from 1957 to

1962. In the year 1962 he was elected to the Bihar Legislative Council from Assembly Constituency and remained so till 1971.

RAM, JAGJIVAN[101] (1908-1986)

Shri Babu Jagjivan Ram was born on 5 April 1908 at Chandwa, Ara district in Bihar. He came from a cultured family of Chamar caste. His father, Shri Shobhi Ram was an employee in a military hospital. Later on, he settled in Chandwa. Shri Shobhi Ram embraced the Shivnarayana sect. He used to sing devotional songs. Shri Shobhi Ram died when Jagjivan Ram was only six years old. Thereafter his mother, Smt Basanti Devi and his eldest brother took care of him.

Shri Jagjivan Ram entered the school run by a Brahmin teacher in his village in the year 1911. He passed his matriculation from Ara in 1926. He passed his intermediate from Banaras Hindu university, Banaras in 1928. Then he sought admission in Vidyasagar College, Calcutta and passed B.Sc. in 1931 from Calcutta University.

During his school days, Shri Jagiivan Ram was subjugated to discrimination on account of untouchability at several places. He was not allowed to take drinking-water from a common pot. The barber refused to cut his hair. The servants in the hostel at Banaras were not ready to clean his utensils. These bitter experiences of untouchability, naturally led him to struggle for the abolition of untouchability. He was inspired by one well-to-do untouchable named Nidhali Bhagat to take part in the Dalit uplift.

He met Pandit Madan Mohan Malviya in a conference of the students held at Banaras in 1926. He presented an address to Malviyaji at Patna on behalf of the Depressed Classes. After having seen the eloquence of this young student, Malviyaji was impressed and invited him to come to Banaras to prosecute his further education.

---

101. Source of Information:
Devendra Prasad Sharma. *Jagjivan Ram.*
Prabhakar Machave, *Babu Jagjivan Ram.*

In 1928 when he was studying at Calcutta, he established Ravidas Maha Sabha and tried to unite the untouchables under its banner. The main objective of this Sabha was to bring about social reforms. He urged his people to give up drinking and uncleanliness.

In 1930 he joined the Congress. He was attracted towards Gandhiji. However, he did not like the nomenclature of Harijan given by Mahatma Gandhi. He took exception to it. He expressed his resentment at the comparison of the untouchables with cows, saying that it was but "unfair". But when he came into contact with Dr Rajendra Prasad, he became a Gandhian.

He was one of the signatories of the Poona Pact in 1932. He took over as the Secretary of the Bihar unit of the Harijan Sevak Sangh in 1933.

In 1934, in the annual conference of Ravidas Maha Sabha at Calcutta, it was decided to establish the Depressed Classes League. In the year 1935, a conference of the Depressed Classes was organized at Kanpur. The conference declared the formal establishment of the Depressed Classes and elected Rasik Lal Biswas as its President and Jagjivan Ram and P.N. Rajbhoj as its Secretaries.

In the conference of Hindu Maha Sabha held under the Presidentship of Pandit Madan Mohan Malviya, at Pune on 29 December 1935, Jagjivan Ram moved a resolution to throw open the temples, watering places, schools, etc, for the Depressed Classes. Though there was opposition to the move from Shri Shankaracharya of Puri, it was passed due to Babuji's forceful insistence.

In the conference of the untouchables held at Lucknow on 22 May 1936, it was however decided at Babuji's initiative, that the mass conversion of the untouchables as proposed by Dr Babasaheb Ambedkar, be postponed for an indefinite period. It was presided over by Pandit Pavan Das and attended by many important leaders like Swami Achhutanand and others.

In the elections held in 1937, Jagjivan Ram was elected to the Bihar Provincial Assembly on Congress ticket.

Babu Jagjivan Ram took part in Quit India Movement in 1942. Therefore, he had to undergo imprisonment for a period of 14 months.

When an Interim Government was formed on 12 August 1946 under the leadership of Pandit Nehru, Babu Jagjivan Ram was inducted as Labour Minister. It was in this capacity that he had gone to Geneva to take part in the International Labour Conference held in September 1947. While coming back to India his plane crashed near the Sahara desert and most of the crewmen died. Babuji was injured. He was brought to India and admitted for treatment to Willingdon Hospital, New Delhi. Dr Babasaheb Ambedkar went to the hospital to see him. He was very much grieved over the incident.

Babu Jagjivan Ram was a member of the Constituent Assembly. He met Mahatma Gandhi along with other SC members of the Constituent Assembly and successfully persuaded him to provide for reservation for the Scheduled Castes.

He became Minister of Communication in the first ministry formed by Pandit Nehru in the post-constitution era, on 13 May 1952.

Babu Jagjivan Ram was an able administrator and shrewd statesman. He could very successfully handle the portfolios assigned to him. He handled the departments like labour, communication, railways, defence, food, agriculture and irrigation. He worked under Prime Minister Pandit Nehru, Lal Bahadur Shastri, Indira Gandhi and Morarji Desai. He was a Member of Parliament from 1946 to 1977.

He was with the Congress from 1930 to 1977. He left the Congress in 1977 on the eve of general elections after the Emergency and formed his own party named, the Congress for Democracy. This party was merged with Janata Party after the elections. He left Janata Party and formed Congress (J) on 5 August 1982. He was President of the party till his last.

Shri Jagjivan Ram married Indrani Devi. He had a son and a daughter.

Shri Jagjivan Ram breathed his last on 6 July, 1986 at the age of 78.

RAM, MANGU[102] (1886-1980)

Shri Babu Mangu Ram was born on 14 January 1886 at village Mugowal in Hoshiarpur, Punjab. His father Shri Hamamdas was a trader of tanned hides. Shri Mangu Ram was educated up to the seventh standard in a school at Mahilpur. He left the school in 1905 and helped his father in developing their leather trade. He belonged to the Chamar caste.

Shri Babu Mangu Ram went to the USA in 1909 for the purpose of business. He was employed in California in a sugar mill.

In 1913 Shri Mangu Ram joined the Gadar Party founded by a nationalist Shri Lal Hardayal. He worked at San Francisco under the leadership of Shri Sohan Singh Bhakna, a Gadar leader in America.

When the Ship Kama Gatamaru was prohibited from entering Calcutta port by the British authorities, the Gadar Party asked five Gadarites, including Shri Mangu Ram to carry smuggled weapons shipped from California to the Punjab. However, their ship was detained by the Japanese who handed the Gadarites to the British authorities. For that offence, they were awarded death punishment. Anyhow, they escaped from the detention. Shri Mangu Ram went to Manila and thereafter to the USA. Again he was employed there in an embroidery factory for six years.

Babu Mangu Ram came back to India in 1925. After his return he began teaching in a primary school at Mugowal. He constructed a well for drinking water for his brethren. After his return, he came to know the suffering of his brethren on account of the stigma of untouchability. At Meenakshi temple in Madurai, he was told not to touch an untouchable. After coming to Punjab he wrote to Gadar Party headquarters in San Francisco about the difficult condition of the Scheduled Castes in India, stating that their freedom was more important to him than that

---

102. Source of Information:

K.C. Leel Ambedkari Andolan Mein Punjabiyon Ka Role, and *Religious Rebels In the Punjab*

Mark Juergenmeyer Delhi (1988)., *The Social Vision of Untouchables.*

of the nation itself. He decided to struggle against untouchability instead of fighting against the British Government. Caste imperialism was more severe than the British variety. At first he decided to organize his brethren under one banner. In order to establish an organization of the Dalits, he convened a conference of his brethren at Mugowal on 11-12 June 1926. In the conference, Babu Mangu Ram proposed to start Ad Dharm Mandal for the uplift of the Dalits. The conference agreed to the proposal. Thus, the Ad Dharm Mandal was formed under the presidentship of Babu Mangu Ram. Its initial executive committee consisted of Thakar Chand, (Secretary), Hans Raj (Vice-president) and Swami Shudranand and Vasant Rai were members of the executive committee. The head office of the Ad Dharm Mandal was at Jullundur. He expressed that the untouchables should have three powers: community power (Qaumiat), a religious power (*Mazhab*) and organization *[Mazlis)*. Through the organization of Ad Dharma, he tried to bring a new awakening among the untouchable masses in Punjab. However, he finally closed the office of the Ad Dharma in June 1946. The headquarters of the movement at Jullundur were converted into Ravi Das high School which continues to exist even today.

Babu Mangu Ram was in favour of separate electorate for the Scheduled Castes. He sent telegrams "pledging" the Ad Dharm's support to Dr Babasaheb Ambedkar, the untouchables representative at the RTC and continued to stand behind him. When Mahatma Gandhi started his fast unto death against the separate electorate, at Pune, Shri Mangu Ram also declared his fast against the joint electorate. Babu Mangu Ram wrote a letter to King George in support of separate electorate.

He appealed to the government to take back the regulation which did not allow the Depressed Classes member to acquire agricultural land in the State of Punjab. He appealed for the abolition of the bonded labour system prevailing on large scale in Punjab. Moreover, he appealed to the government to give special facilities for educational development of the Scheduled Castes.

The Ad Dharm Mandal slowly spread throughout Punjab and gathered strength. The then British authorities had to take cognizance of the Ad Dharm Mandal and the leadership of Babu

Mangu Ram. Shri Babu Mangu Ram was nominated as a member of the District Board of Jullundur in the year 1940. He was elected in 1946 on the Punjab Legislative Assembly as a candidate of the Unionist Party led by Sikandar Hayat Khan.

He was honoured with the title Freedom Fighter by the government. Babu Mangu Ram passed away on 22 April 1980, at the age of 94.

RAMKRISHNAIAH, G.S.[103]

Shri Gowdagere Singri Ramkrishnaiah was born in 1905 at Village Gowagere in Mandya district in Karnataka. He belonged to the Adi-Karnataka caste. His father Shri Singri Sidappa was an agriculturist and also engaged in weaving. After completing his high school education in 1927 Ramkrishnaiah joined silk weaving factory and worked there up to 1947.

Shri G.S. Ramkrishnaiah strove to unite the labour force in the weaving factory as early as 1932. Simultaneously, he joined congress and enlisted the cooperation of the labourers with the national independence movement. He took part in the Quit India Movement in 1942.

He formed weavers cooperative society in 1947 at Mysore which was named as Adikarnataka Handloom Weavers Cooperative Society. He made efforts for the establishment of a housing colony for the weavers belonging to the Scheduled Caste where hundred tenements have come up at Mysore.

He was President of Adi-Karnataka Sangh, Mysore in 1930 and Shri M. Madish was its Secretary. He thought that the untouchables were the original inhabitants of this country.

Shri Ramkrishnaiah joined the Scheduled Castes Federation in 1950. He was SCF candidate from Mysore city South Assembly Constituency in the first general elections held in 1952. He was defeated by Congress candidate.

---

103. Source of Information:
Personal Interview with the leader Shri G.S. Ramkrishnaiah
62. Weavers Colony. Mysore on 4-6-1989.

He was elected as Vice-president of City Municipal Council, Mysore in 1957. He was Vice-president of Siddharth Education Trust (1965) which runs one high school and one hostel at Mysore.

He married Smt Puttamma in 1936. He got five sons and three daughters.

RAO AMBADAS[103(a)]

Shri Ambadas Rao alias Shivaji was born on 1 January 1924, at Bimalkheda in Taluka Zaheerabad in Medak district of then Hyderabad State. His father's name was Rukhmaji. He belonged to a Samgar (Chamar) Caste; but he accepted Arya Samaj faith. He passed his Hindi Kovid examination, and served for some time as a Hindi Teacher in a primary school.

In those days Arya Samaj organization founded in Hyderabad in 1892 was very active. It was actively busy in organizing the Hindus under one banner. It propagated for removal of untouchability. It propagated for entry for the untouchables in the Hindu Temples, hotels and organized inter-caste dining. Therefore the downtrodden people were being attracted towards Arya Samaj. Shri Ambadas Rao was also attracted towards Arya Samaj.

When the Arya Samaj organized mass Satyagraha for securing civil liberties, which were denied in the erstwhile Hyderabad State, in October 1938 Ambadas Rao also participated in the Satyagraha. Therefore he suffered R.I. from 26-12-1938 to 25-06-1939 and S.I. from 26-06-1939 to 04-07-1939 in the Central Jail at Hyderabad.

He worked underground during the Quit India movement, 1942. He was arrested thrice under the Arms Act for possessing arms and ammunition during the join Indian Union Movement 1947-1948 in the former Hyderabad State.

103(a). Source of Information :

Our struggle for Emancipation Vol. 2 by P R. Venkatswamy Hyderabad. (1955).

He was active in Dalit Jatiya Sangh. Shri Ambadas Rao and Shankar Deo were closely related to each other. After accession of Hyderabad to Indian Union, Ambadas Rao contested on Congress ticket from Yadigir (SC) Assembly Constituency in 1952 and got elected. He was a member of Hyderabad Legislative Assembly from 1952 to Oct. 31, 1956. Later he worked as Secretary of the Depressed Classes League of Telangana branch.

RAUT, BHOLA[104]

Shri Bhola Raut was born on 4 November 1914 at Bettiah, Champaran district in Bihar. His father's name was Shri Harihar Raut. He belonged to the Mehtar community. He could complete his education up to intermediate.

Shri Bhola Raut became Secretary of Depressed Classes League of Bihar State in 1938. He was elected as General Secretary of Mehtar Dom Sabha in 1939. Later he became organizer of Bihar State Mehtar Mazdoor Sangh in 1949. He became President of Bihar State Safai Mazdoor Sangh in 1950, and Vice-president of All India Mehtar Mazdoor Sangh in 1950.

Shri Bhola Raut became a member of the Champaran District Board in 1941. He was a member of the Provisional Parliament during 1950-52. He got elected to the Lok Sabha in 1952 from Saran-cum-Champaran, in 1957 from Champaran (SC) in 1962 from Bettiah, in 1967, 1971, 1980 and 1985 from Bagaha (SC) Constituency as Congress candidate.

He married Babani Devi in 1930 and had four sons and two daughters.

REV RATHNAM, JOHN[105] (1846-1942)

Rev. T. John Rathnam was born in an Adi-Dravida family in 1846 at Thousand Lights area of Madras city. He completed his school education at Madras. He could not endure the invidious miseries perpetrated by the caste system and untouchability on

---

104. Address: Jagjivan Nagar Bettiah. West Champaran District, Bihar

105. Source of Information:

A.S. Ulakanathan. *Messengers of Equality, Madras. (1990).*

him and his brethren. He came to the conclusion, that it was none but Hinduism, which was responsible for all those miseries. Hence, he decided to leave Hinduism and accept an egalitarian religion like Christianity. Eventually, he was baptized in Christianity in 1877. He proved to be a well-educated, influential and devoted missionary. However, he did not disassociate himself from his own brethren even after conversion.

He had an indomitable urge to uplift his fellow sufferers. In order to raise the social awareness of the Depressed Classes, he started a magazine named, *Dravidar Pandian* (Dravid King) in 1885. He tried to publish the cases of atrocities, and grievances of the Depressed Classes in his journal. He tried to preach the message of equality and self- help through his journal.

He believed that the untouchables were in need of technical and professional education for their economic uplift. Therefore, he established in 1886 a 'Model School' at Thousand Lights area in Madras, where technical and professional courses were conducted. In 1892 he opened at the same place a school for the untouchable boys and girls. Rev. John Rathnam himself worked as a teacher there. In 1899 he started a hostel for the untouchable boy students.

He has successfully secured 100 acres of barren land from the government, which he distributed among the landless untouchable cultivators.

In order to awaken the people he started an organization named Dravida Kazhagham in the year 1892. He was honoured by the Governor of Madras in 1887 by the title of Justice of Peace.

He breathed his last in 1942 at the age of 96.

ROHAM, P.J.[106] (1905-1991)

Shri Prabhakar Roham was born on 15 January 1905 at Akole, Ahmednagar district in Maharashtra. He was a Mahar by caste. His father, Shri Janardan Roham, was an agriculturist. Shri Prabhakar Roham was educated up to matric level at Nasik.

---

106. Source of Information:

Personal Interview with the leader Shri P.J. Roham at Pimparne, Sangamner Taluk Ahmadnagar District (Maharashtra) on 3.5.1989.

Shri P.J. Roham was obviously inspired by Dr Babasaheb Ambedkar. He took part in the famous Choudar Tank satyagraha at Mahad in 1927. He took part in Kalaram Temple Entry Satyagraha at Nasik. For some time he was the Secretary of the Kalaram Temple Entry Satyagraha Committee in 1931, when Shri B.K. alias Dadasaheb Gaikwad was imprisoned.

Shri Roham was General Secretary of the Youth League, Nasik from 1931 to 1934. He was nominated member of the Sangamner Municipality from 1934 to 1936. He was member of the District Local Board, Ahmadnagar since 1935.

He worked as Superintendent of Shri Shahu Chhatrapati Boarding, Nasik from 1929 to 1934. He started a Depressed Classes hostel at Sangamner and ran it from 1932-1935.

Shri P.J. Roham was present at the Untouchable Conference at Yeola in Nasik district on 13 October 1935 where Babasaheb Ambedkar declared his intention to quit Hinduism. He was also present at Nagpur on 14 October 1956 at the mass conversion ceremony where he converted to Buddhism. He propagated Buddhism in Ahmednagar, Pune and Nasik districts.

He served as a recruitment officer (honorary) from 1939 to 1945 for Nasik and Nagar districts.

He joined the Independent Labour Party in 1936 formed by Babasaheb Ambedkar. He was elected President of ILP of Ahmadnagar district unit. He contested in 1937 on ILP ticket for the Bombay Legislative assembly from Ahmadnagar (South) and got elected. In the elections held in 1946 and in 1952, hecontested from Rahuri assembly constituency but could not get elected. He took part in the satyagraha in 1964 launched by the Republican Party of India, under the leadership of Dadasaheb Gaikwad.

He married Meerabai in 1931. He had six sons and three daughters. He died on 21 February 1991, at the age of 86.

SABAK, PRABHATI RAM[107]

Shri Prabhati Ram Sabak was born in about 1918 in a Chamar family at Lahore, now in Pakistan. After partition he

---

107. Source of Information:
Personal Interview with the leader at Chandigarh on 18.3.1990.

migrated to India and settled at Sadar Thana, Amritsar in Punjab.

He joined SCF in 1948 and later the RPI. He was greatly impressed by Dr Babasaheb Ambedkar.

He was elected member of the Corporation of Amritsar from 1968 to 1972. He contested in 1967 for Punjab Legislative Assembly on RPI ticket from Veraka (Amritsar) constituency, but in vain. He led the satyagraha for land to the landless peasants launched by RPI in 1964 at Amritsar.

He married Ishwari Devi and got four sons and four daughters.

SADHU JITAU[108]

Shri Jitau Jeetbahadur was born on 2 January 1856 at village Sahijanpur, Lucknow district in Uttar Pradesh. He belonged to the Chamar caste. His father, Shri Kuberdasji was a railway employee. Shri Jitau Jeetbahadur had no formal education; but he could learn Hindi, Urdu and English.

Since his childhood Shri Jitau Jeetbahadur was very religious. He used to read *Ramayan* and *Geeta* and other religious books. He used to sing devotional songs. He practised meditation and kept himself aloof from mundane pleasures. At the age of 25 he became a disciple of Mahatma Mohandasji of Kamalpur who converted him to the Ravidas Panth. Since then he used to live in the company of Satsang sadhus and preached Ravidas Panth to his brethren.

Since 1926 he started taking part in national independence movement under the banner of Congress. He tried to enlist the active participation of the Depressed Classes in the independence struggle. He took part in the civil disobedience movement, for which he was imprisoned for a period of six months. During 1926 to 1933 he was active in independence struggle.

---

108. Source of Information:
Sadhu Jitau Jeetbahadur alias Maharshi Badal,
Shri Ravidas Satsang Sagar, Lucknow (1975).

Thereafter, he again turned to religious work. He got constructed the Ravidas temple at Belipur in Lucknow district. He got many disciples in the districts of Lucknow, Unnao, Kanpur, Faizabad and Hardoi.

He wrote the *Rahasya Yuktam, Shri Hare Ravi Bhajan mala, Shri Sadguruji ki Amrit Vani* and *Shri Ravidas Satsang Sagar.*

His books are based on the spiritual philosophy of Sant Ravidasji and reveal the rational thoughts of the author. He had stated in *Ravidas Satsang Sagar* that Brahm-Iswar-Onkar, all are myths. He had no faith in Theism. He thought that those who are passionless, virtuous and social are worthy of admiration. He thought that all the saints owe their root to Buddhism. He exhorted his brethren to observe cleanliness and to lead a life of high moral standard. He advised them to embrace Buddhism and strictly observe the Buddhist principles in their individual and social life. He advised them not to tolerate injustice any more. They should devote their energies to the liberation of their community.

Sadhu Jitau Jeetbahadur married Sukhadeyi Devi at the age of 20. He had a son and a daughter.

SAGAR, SUNDARLAL[109] (1886-1952)

Shri Sundarlal Sagar was born in 1886 at Agra in Uttar Pradesh. His father Shri Nathusinh Sagar was a petty contractor. Shri Sundarlal Sagar had no formal education. However, he learnt to read and write. He was a Jatav by caste.

He accepted the Arya Samaj as a protest against caste-based Hinduism. He strictly observed the rules of the Arya Samaj including vegetarianism and temperance.

He resolved to liberate the untouchables from their slavery imposed by Hinduism. In order to give a collective fight to orthodox Hinduism, he founded an organization named, the *Jatav Maha Sabha* at Agra and got it registered on 16 February 1918.

---

109. Source of Information:

Personal Interview with his grandson, Shri Arun Kumar Sagar, 30/201 Kidwai Park. Rajamandi, Agra, UP on 9.6.1991.

He preached against alcoholism, beef-eating and child-marriage. He tried to infuse a new blood in his brethren. He used to call his community as Jatav and the same has been accepted by the government on 8 November 1939.

He had knowledge of Sanskrit literature and comparative religions. He wrote *Jatav Jivan* in 1924.

He felt that the untouchables must get educated. He opened Jatav Pathshala, a primary school for the Jatav students at Agra.

He was a pioneering leader of the Depressed Classes in Agra. He was assisted by Dr Manikchand Jatav Veer and many others.

He married Dropadi Devi and had a son. He was popularly known as Pandit. He died on 16 January 1952 at the age of 66.

SALVE, LAHUJIBUWA[110] (1811-1881)

Shri Lahujibuwa Salve was born in about 1811 at village Peth near the fort of Purandar in Maharashtra. He belonged to the Mang caste. His father Shri Raghu Salve migrated to Pune to make his fortune. Shri Lahuji had no formal education, but got *Talim* from his father. He lived at Mith Ganj (now known as Mahatma Phule Peth) in Pune.

In those days the position of Dalits was very precarious. They were not treated as human beings, but as untouchables. Thereafter, Shri Lahuji decided to work for the uplift of the untouchables.

He opened one *Talimkhana* at Ganjpeth in Pune wherein even revolutionaries like Sadashivrao Paranjape, Moro Vithal Walvekar, Mahatma Jyotiba Phule, Vasudeo Balwant Phadke, Lokmanya B.G. Tilak were well trained in martial arts.

However, the acquaintance of Mahatma Phule turned into companionship in the cause of liberation of the Depressed

---

110. Source of Information:

Shahir Yogesh. *Guruvarya Lahuji Vastad,* Pune, 1990, and other sources.

Classes. He was with Mahatma Phule in his mission of spreading of education among the untouchables from 1850 onwards. Shri Lahuji Salve and Shri Ranoji Mahar's objective was to spread the message of Mahatma Phule in Pune stating the importance of education to their brethren. They also urged them to send their children to the schools started by Mahatma Phule.

Shri Lahujibuwa being a true friend and follower of Mahatma Phule, adhered to the philosophy of Satya Shodhak Samaj (Satya Dharma) founded by the Mahatma in 1873. Shri Lahujibuwa was against Brahmanism, superstitions and the scriptures. He stood for equality, human dignity and clean character. He was of the opinion that by maintaining human relations with all the people one can worship the *Nirmik* or the Creator. He tried to spread the principles of Satya Shodhak Samaj throughout his life.

He died at Pune on 17 February 1881 at the age of 70.

His contemporary and companion Shri Ranoji was his co-worker. They tried to spread the message of Mahatma Phule among the Mang and Maharas, the two major untouchable castes in Maharashtra. Both of them were great social reformers, but no detailed information about them is available.

SANT RAM[111] (1887-1988)

Shri Sant Ram was born on 14 February 1887 at Purani Bassi in Hoshiarpur district of Punjab. He was a Megh by caste. His father's name was Shri Ramdas Gohal and his mother's name was Malini Devi. He had passed his B.A. and thereafter he devoted himself to the uplift of his brethren.

He joined the Arya Samaj as a religious protest against inequality in Hinduism. He founded his own organization called Jat-pat Todak Mandal (Society for the abolition of caste system)

---

111. Source of Information:
Smt Gargi Chadha.
51 Navjiwan Vihar. New Delhi on 13.3.1990.

in 1922. The main objective of this organization was to attempt to abolish the caste system by arranging inter-caste marriages. He aimed to abolish caste system within the Depressed Classes. Initially the relations between the Jat-pat Todak Mandal and the Arya Samaj were very close. However, due to differences with the Arya Samaj, the Jat-pat Todak Mandal remained an independent organization.

Shri Sant Ram invited Dr Babasaheb Ambedkar to deliver his presidential address on the annual convention of the Jat-pat Todak Mandal to be held in the year 1936. However, the presidential address sent by Dr Babasaheb Ambedkar in advance was not acceptable to some of the members of the Jat- pat Todak Mandal, as such they requested him to make some amendments. Dr Babasaheb Ambedkar was, however, reluctant to do so. Hence the proposed programme was cancelled. Later, the said address was published under the caption *Annihilation of caste,* in 1936. Shri Sant Ram translated it into Hindi and published the same in *Kranti,* an Urdu monthly.

Shri Sant Ram led a strike of the sweepers in Jullundur in 1938. He joined the Congress in 1945. In 1946 he was elected to the Punjab Legislative Assembly and continued to serve it till 1962.

He was an author of many books including *Hamara Samaj; Mere Jeevan Anubhav*, etc. He worked as an editor of *Kranti* (Urdu) and *Yugantar* Hindi journals run on behalf of Jat-pat Todak Mandal.

He was honoured with the Mahatma Gandhi Prize for his commendable efforts in serving Hindi language by the Rashtra Bhashya Prachar Samiti, Wardha in 1958.

After the death of his first wife in 1929, he remarried a widow named Sundarabai from Maharashtra. He had a daughter.

He breathed his last on 5 June 1988 at the age of 101 at New Delhi.

SARDAR DEVISINGH[112] (1898-1966)

Shri Sardar Devisingh was born in 1898 at Pahar Ganj, New Delhi. His father Shri Netisingh used to carry goods by a bullock cart as a means of livelihood. Shri Devisingh had no formal education. He was a Jatav.

Shri Devisingh joined the Dalit uplift movement in 1922 at the instance of Swami Achhutanand, a Dalit leader from Uttar Pradesh. Shri Devidas Jatav and Swami Darshanand were both from Delhi.

Shri Devidas Jatav, G.A. Gawai and others decided to welcome the Emperor George V on his arrival at New Delhi in 1922. They wanted to arrange a huge procession in the honour of the Emperor and present a memorandum of demands on behalf of the Depressed Classes of India. They arranged a voluntary corps for maintaining discipline in the procession and rally near the India Gate under the leadership of Shri Devi Singh. Though it was his first involvement in the public activity, he became very successful in the same.

He worked as President of the Achhut Uddhar Sabha from 1922 to 1932. He was impressed by the discourses of Swami Achhutanand who preached and propagated the philosophy of Dr Babasaheb Ambedkar. He used to move from lane to lane in Delhi propagating the mission of Babasaheb Ambedkar. He asked his brethren to educate their children, especially the girls. He tried to organize his brethren in Delhi and nearby areas.

He joined the SCF in 1942 itself. After the formation of the Republican Party of India, he joined the same. He was of course in favour of separate electorate for the Scheduled Castes.

Shri Devisingh was an active supporter of the conversion move taken by Dr Babasaheb Ambedkar. When he observed that Babasaheb Ambedkar's inclination was towards Sikhism, he

---

112. Source of Information:
Personal Interview with his son Shri Kishan Singh, Bawa Tailoring. Pahar Ganj. New Delhi on 15.3.1990.

converted to Sikhism in the Shish Ganj Gurudwara, New Delhi along with a group of his followers. When Babasaheb Ambedkar declared his inclination towards Buddhism, he embraced Buddhism, the ceremony being personally conducted by the Dalai Lama, before the conversion of Babasaheb Ambedkar. He was Vice-president of the Buddhist Council of India, Delhi Unit and Swami Darshanand was its President.

He participated in the satyagraha for political rights launched by Babasaheb Ambedkar in 1946. He led the satyagraha at Delhi. He was chief of the Samata Sainik Dal of Delhi unit.

When the satyagraha of landless people for land was launched by the RPI under the leadership of Dadasaheb Gaikwad, Shri Devisingh, along with his wife and a good number of followers launched satyagraha at Lucknow. Therefore, he was imprisoned for 15 days.

He married Champa Rani. He had three sons and three daughters.

He breathed his last on 26 February, 1966 at the age of 68. After his death, his eldest son Shri Kishan Singh has been leading the Dalit movement in New Delhi.

SATHE, TUKARAM BHAU[113] (1920-1969)

Shri Tukaram Sathe was born on 1 August 1920 at Wategaon, Sangli district in Maharashtra. His father Shri Bhau Sathe was engaged in his ancestral occupation of rope making at his native place. On the one hand, his family was often subjected to harassment as it belonged to Mang caste, the so-called criminal class, and on the other hand, it could not endure abject poverty due to recurrence of famines in that area. Consequently, Shri Bhau Sathe migrated to Bombay in search of peace and bread, when Shri Tukaram Sathe was 11 years old. Shri Tukaram Sathe was also engaged in earning bread along with his father. Hence,

---

113. Source of Information:
Baburao Gurav, *Anna Bhau Sathe*, Bombay.

Shri Tukaram Sathe could not get any formal education. Later on, he could learn to read and write.

Later, Shri Tukaram alias Annabhau Sathe joined in a *Tamasha* managed by his near relative Shri Bapu Sathe. When the *Tamasha* was to give its performance at village Rather, the revolutionary activist Shri Kranti Sinh Nana Patil appeared on the stage and delivered a revolutionary speech against the British and feudal rulers. Shri Tukaram Sathe was very much influenced by the personality and philosophy of Nana Patil; as a result he was attracted towards the freedom movement.

Later on, he left the *Tamasha* and came to Bombay. He had to earn his daily livelihood by working in the Cotton Mills in Bombay, where he came into contact with labour leaders and communists. He was attracted towards communism. In about 1943 he wrote a *Powada* of Stalinguard (a heroic song of Stalinguard) which became very popular amongst the workers in those days. In 1944, he came in contact with Shahir Amar Shekha and Shahir Gavankar both revolutionary bards in a farmers' conference at Didwala.

Shri Tukaram alias Annabhau Sathe had decided to bring awareness among the masses against Brahminism which imposed untouchability and virtually compelled the deprived lot to take recourse to criminal and filthy occupations against the British Government which imposed the Criminal Tribes Act and subjected his community to harassment, and against the forces of feudalism and capitalism which exploited his community and made life unbearable. He, however, thought that the philosophy of communism would be helpful in liberating his brethren from untouchability and criminality. He used his art and poetic genius in educating the masses.

He formed his own organization named Lal Bavata in 1945. He composed revolutionary songs, and wrote plays and farcical dramas, and performed them very artistically and skillfully. Shahi Amar Shekh, Gavankar and Shahir Annabhau Sathe were his companions and co-workers.

He wrote a good number of novels, short stories and songs. His first book of songs, named *Shahir* was published in 1952. He wrote his first play *Inamdar* in 1958. He wrote a number of novels including *Fakira, Vaijayanta, Alguj, Mangala, Makadicha Mal,*

Fulpakharu, Roopa, Murthi, Aag, Tara, Ranganga, Chandan, Ran Boka, Agnidivya, etc. Some of his novels were selected for films.

His novel *Fakira* fetched him name and fame. In 1961, he was honoured by the Government of Maharashtra on his writing of *Fakira*. He was even invited to Soviet Russia under the auspices of the Indo-Soviet Cultural Association.

He was a revolutionary and rational thinker. He thought very rightly, that "This world is not based on the head of Shesha, the mythological snake God, but on the palms of the toiling masses." This implies that the real upholders of the world are the peasants and workers.

He had high regard for Dr Babasaheb Ambedkar. His famous novel *Fakira* was dedicated to the leader. Contrary to Marxists, he thought to destroy both the class and caste structure of the society. He even said very categorically that, '*Jag badal, ghaluni ghav, sangun gele, mala Bhimrao*'. In other words he said that it was the message of Dr Babasaheb Ambedkar that the so-called untouchables must give a decisive fight to change the traditional social order and restructure it on the principles of liberty, equality and fraternity.

He was loved and honoured by the people in Maharashtra. His books were translated in many Indian and foreign languages. However, his later life was not very happy. He lived in a hut at Chirangnagar slum area in abject poverty. He did not get cooperation from his friends and family members. Due to frustration, he was addicted to drinks. He married Kondubai. Later, he married Jayawantibai. He got a son from his first wife.

Shri Tukaram alias Annabhau Sathe could not sustain the burden of life and he passed away on 18 July 1969 at the age of 49 only.

SETH KISHAN DAS

Seth Kishan Das was born at Mohalla Ramdaspur, Boutan Mandi, Jullundur in Punjab. He belonged to Klare (Chamar) caste. He was a rich leather merchant and a social reformer.

First, he joined Ad Dharm Mandal, an organization founded by Shri Mangu Ram in 1926. He contributed a greater share to the construction of the Ad Dharm Bhavan, which has been presently converted into Guru Ravidas School, at Jullundur. However, he left the Mandal in about 1930. Later on he was attracted towards Ambedkarite movement.

Seth Kishan Das contested in 1937 from urban Jullundur constituency for the Punjab Legislative Assembly and defeated his Congress rival, Shri Guruvanta Singh who once upon a time happened to be his co-worker in Ad Dharm movement.

He was present at the formation of the Scheduled Castes Federation at Nagpur in 1942. He was elected member of the executive body of the All India Scheduled Castes Federation. He was President of the Punjab unit of SCF.

He was instrumental in arranging the tour of Dr Babasaheb Ambedkar in Punjab in October 1951. Shri Charan Das Nidhadak and Kartar Ram Midhas helped him in successfully arranging the tour. Babasaheb Ambedkar visited Amritsar, Ludhiana and Jullundur and addressed the Scheduled Castes meeting at several places.

Seth Kishan Das was obviously responsible in spreading the Ambedkarite movement in Punjab. He died on 16 September 1988.

SHIRKE, D.M.[114] (1901-1985)

Shri Dadasaheb Shirke was born in 1901 at village Shiye in Karvir, Kolhapur district in Maharashtra. His father, Shri Malharrao Shirke, was an agriculturist. He had 14 acres of land which was given to his ancestors by Chhatrapati Tararani for the bravery they had shown in a war. Shri Malharrao Shirke was in the Maharaja's service, and was known as *Hulswar*. Shri Dadasaheb Shirke was educated up to the matric level at Rajaram High School, Kolhapur. He was a Mahar.

---

114. Source of Information:

Personal interview with his son Shri Vasantrao Shirke

"C" Ward, H. No.2890/91, Siddhartha Nagar, Kolhapur (Maharashtra) on 7.5.1989.

Shri Dadasaheb Shirke was influenced by the Satya Shodhak movement. He was influenced by Chhatrapati Shahu Maharaj and Dr Babasaheb Ambedkar. Shri Shirke tried to improve the moral and cultural standard of the untouchables. He propagated against beef-eating, Devdasi and Mharaki systems in the princely state of Kolhapur and nearby areas.

In order to bring about a new awareness amongst the Dalits, and propagate the thoughts and mission of Babasaheb Ambedkar, he started a weekly named *Garud* from Kolhapur in the year 1926. He continued it despite many difficulties for a long period of 30 years. It was very popular in southern Maharashtra.

He was nominated member of Praja Paris had, the Council of Kolhapur State. He was member of the ILP and SCF. He became President of SCF Kolhapur State.

He contested in the first general elections held in 1952 from Hatkanangale (R) seat for the Bombay Legislative Assembly on behalf of SCF, but he could not get success in the elections. In 1957 also he contested from the same constituency and got elected to the Bombay Legislative Assembly. In the elections held in 1962, he contested for the Lok Sabha seat from Hatkanangle (SC) seat as RPI candidate, but failed. Again, he contested in 1967 from Hatkanangale (R) assembly constituency, but without success.

He converted to Buddhism on Vijaya Dashmi day, 14 October 1956 at Nagpur. He tried to propagate Buddhism in Kolhapur and nearby districts. He organized the mass conversion ceremony at Dhakale in Shahuvadi, Kolhapur district in the year 1957.

For some time he ran a school named Samata Vidyalaya in Bhangi locality at Kolhapur. He participated in the satyagraha launched by the SCF in 1946 and the RPI in 1964. Shri Gangaram Kamble, Limbaji Lingade and M.I. Kurane were his co-workers.

Shri D.M. Shirke was a thinker and writer. He wrote *English Satta Ani Dalit Janata* and *Kolhapurcha Rajyakar bhar* in about 1940.

It was because of his selfless social work, that he was honoured by the title of Dalit Mitra by the Government of Maharashtra in the year 1976.

He married Janabai and got two sons and a daughter. He expired on 26 December 1985 at the age of 86.

SHIVARAJ, MEENAMBAL[115] (1902-1992)

Shrimati Meenambal Shivaraj was born on 26 December 1902 at Rangoon in Burma. Her father, Shri Pillai Vasudeo Govindraju, a native of Vallore in Madras, was engaged in business in Burma. For some time he was a member of the Madras Corporation. He was nominated member of the Legislative Council of Madras from 1923 to 1926. Shrimati Meenambal passed her matriculation from Madurai Pillai High School, Rangoon founded by her father Vasudeo G. Pillai in about 1900. Then she completed her F.A. in 1917 from Rangoon College, Rangoon. She came back to Madras for her marriage with Shri N. Shivaraj which took place in 1918.

Smt Meenambal Shivaraj took active part in the Dalit uplift movement. She was born in a family of an Adi-Dravida social and political leader and married to a renowned Dalit leader N. Shivaraj.

She was the first among the Scheduled Caste women to receive the honour of being a member of Madras Corporation. She was elected by the University Senate to represent Madras University in the Corporation.

She was a very active and faithful member of the Scheduled Castes Federation formed in 1942. Both Mr and Mrs Shivaraj were trusted followers of Dr Babasaheb Ambedkar.

Smt Meenambal Shivaraj presided over the SCF Women's conference held at Madras on 23 September 1944 and which was attended by Dr Babasaheb Ambedkar. Later, she presided over the All India SCF Women's Conference held at Bombay on 6 May 1945. Dr Babasaheb Ambedkar, Shri N. Shivaraj and others addressed the conference. Smt Meenambal Shivaraj exhorted the women audience to actively take part in social uplift of the

---

115. Source of Information:
Personal Interview with Smt Meenambal Shivaraj,
7, Bronson Garden Street. Kelleyan. Madras-10 on 31.5.1989.

community. They should educate their children, improve their confidence and inculcate in them good moral culture. She advised them to struggle to liberate themselves from untouchability, casteism and oppression.

In the first general elections held in 1952 for the Madras Legislative Assembly she contested as SCF candidate from Madurantakam (G and SC) constituency but could not get success in the election. She was an SCF candidate for the Madras Legislative Council in 1952 from the constituency of State Legislative Assembly, but could not get elected. At last she contested for Madras Legislative Assembly as a Congress candidate from Thousand Lights (G) constituency in 1967, but she was defeated by DMK candidate.

Her son Shri Dayashankar, IPS, (Retd.) looked after her in her old age. She passed away on 30 November 1992 at the age of 92.

SHIVARAJ, N.[116] (1892-1964)

Shri N. Shivaraj was born on 29 September, 1892 at Cudappa (AP) in the erstwhile Madras State, where his father Shri Namoshivaya was serving as an Accounts Officer. His original native place was a village named Pondu Malli near Madras. Shri N. Shivaraj passed his matriculation in 1907. He passed his B.A. in 1911 from Presidency College, Madras and B.L. in 1915 from Madras University.

Thereafter, he started his legal practice at Madras High Court. He served for 13 years as a Professor of Law in Government Law College, Madras.

He started his political career as an active member of the Justice Party founded by Periyar Ramaswamy Naicker. He, however, decided to liberate his brethren from the thraldom of untouchability and casteism. He served the community people whenever they were in need.

---

[116] Source of Information:
Personal Interview with his wife. Shrimati Meenambal Shivaraj, 7 Bronson Garden Street. Kelieyan. Madras on 31.5.1989

On behalf of the Justice Party he was elected to the Madras Legislative Assembly in the year 1926. It was during those days that he came to know about the Dalit uplift movement being run by Dr Babasaheb Ambedkar. He also realized that Justice Party was of no use to the Dalits. Hence, he left Justice Party in 1928 and joined the Dalit uplift movement under the leadership of Dr Babasaheb Ambedkar.

He arranged a meeting at Madras on 22 October 1929 to support the temple entry satyagraha at Parvati Temple, Pune, launched by Babasaheb Ambedkar. He presided over the conference of the Depressed Classes held at Pune on 12-13 January 1936 in which it was decided to support the conversion move declared by Dr Babasaheb Ambedkar.

He presided over the Third All India Depressed Classes Conference held in the presence of Babasaheb Ambedkar, at Nagpur on 18-20 July 1942. In this conference, the Scheduled Castes Federation, the first national level political party of the Dalits was formed. Shri N. Shivaraj was elected as its President and Shri P.N. Rajbhoj was elected as its General Secretary. The Scheduled Castes Federation had played a very vital role in the politics of the community, as well as in the politics of the nation, from 1942 to 1956. Even after the formation of the Republican Party of India in October 1957, he was elected as its President and continued in this capacity till his death in 1964. This speaks volumes for his credibility in the society.

Dr Babasaheb Ambedkar was invited by the Pacific Relations Committee to participate in the conference to be held at Quebec in December 1942, but he could not go there due to his engagements. However, he deputed Shri N. Shivaraj to participate in the conference and present a paper on the problems of the untouchables on his behalf. N. Shivaraj had complied accordingly.

As the President of the Scheduled Castes Federation, he attended the Simla Conference held under the Wavell Plan in June 1945. He vehemently criticized the "obnoxious policy" of the government of not giving any share in the power.

He presided over the conference of the Scheduled Castes Federation held at Agra on 10 March 1946.

The Scheduled Castes Federation could not get any success in the general elections held in 1946. Dr Babasaheb Ambedkar had attributed its failure to the Poona Pact. He wanted to secure political rights to the Scheduled Castes as a separate group. Hence, he launched a nationwide satyagraha in 1946 for political rights.

He was one of the founding members of the Republican Party of India. He was elected President of the party from 1957 to 1964. He was member of the Madras Legislative Council from 1926 to 1937. In 1937, he was nominated as a member of the Indian Legislative Assembly and he continued to be so till 1945.

In the first general elections held in 1952, he contested for Lok Sabha seat from Thiruvallur (G and SC) constituency, but he could not get success in the election. In the second general elections held in 1957 he contested for the Lok Sabha seat for Chinglepet (G and SC) constituency and he got elected. Lastly, he contested from Vellore (G and SC) Lok Sabha seat in the year 1962, but met with failure. In the second Parliament, he however said very categorically that it was a fashion to talk on socialistic pattern of society without doing anything concrete. He thought the benefits of the plans and policies of the government could not reach the people. Hence, he suggested that Brahmanism should be abolished, otherwise there would not be equality.

He got a unique opportunity of being elected as Mayor of Madras city during 1945-46.

His father Shri Namoshivaya, an Adi-Dravida, was converted to Buddhism. So. N. Shivaraj was a born Buddhist. He used to advise his brethren to convert to Buddhism.

He helped the British Government in the Second World War. Hence, the Government of India honoured him with the title of Rao Bahadur.

He married Smt Meenambal in 1918. They had two sons and two daughters. All of them are well-settled.

He expired at New Delhi on 29 September 1964, when he went there to lead the famous satyagraha for land under the auspices of the Republican Party of India.

SHIVTARKAR, S.N.[117] (1891-1966)

Shri Sltaram Shivtarkar was born on 15 July 1891 at Kamathipura in Bombay. He belonged to the Chambhar community. His father Shri Namdeorao Shivtarkar was a teacher. Shri Sitaram Shivtarkar had passed his vernacular final in 1909. He was appointed as teacher in a Marathi school at Parel, Bombay. Later on he was promoted as Head Master in 1926 and thereafter as an educational supervisor. He retired in 1949.

Shri Sitaram Shivtarkar was a social worker, therefore, he came close to Dr Babasaheb Ambedkar as early as 1914. When Dr Babasaheb Ambedkar was in England for the pursuit of higher education, Shri D.D. Gholap and Shri Sitaram Shivtarkar were managing the affairs of *Mook Nayak* started by the former in 1920.

Shri Shivtarkar was Secretary of the Bahishkrit Hitkarini Sabha founded by Babasaheb Ambedkar on 20 July 1924. He was one of the organizers of the conference of the Depressed Classes at Mahad on 19 and 20 December 1927. It was presided over by Babasaheb Ambedkar. Shri S.N. Shivtarkar moved a resolution in the conference that, "all the men are born equal and ought to be treated equal." It was passed unanimously.

Shri Shivtarkar was Secretary and Treasurer of the Depressed Classes Education Society established by Babasaheb Ambedkar on 14 June 1928. Shri S.N. Shivtarkar had participated in the conference held at Nasik on 2 March 1930 for launching the temple entry satyagraha at Kalaram temple, Nasik. During the Round Table Conference, he strongly supported Dr Babasaheb Ambedkar. He was one of the signatories to the Poona Pact 1932.

Shri Shivtarkar presided over the CP and Berar Provincial Depressed Classes Conference held at Lokmanya theatre, Akola

---

[117] Source of Information:
Shankar Sitaram Shivtarkar, *Shri Sitaram Shivtarkar Master: Samarpit Pravas* (Marathi biography), Bombay.

on 6 and 7 May 1933. He presided over a conference of the cobblers in Berar held at Kapus Talni on 9 May 1933. In these conferences he strongly supported the views of Babasaheb Ambedkar. He opposed the fake and selfish leaders among the Dalits who were misguiding the people.

When Babasaheb Ambedkar declared at Yeola in 1935 his intention to renounce Hinduism, Shri Shivtarkar did not support him. He, however, yielded to the persuasive tactics of the Gandhian community leaders like N.S. Kajarolkar and others. He attended the pro-Congress meeting of the Dalit leaders held at Pune under the presidentship of A.D. Rankhambe of Nasik on 31 May 1940. Thereafter he joined Congress. He was inclined towards Arya Samaj.

In the first general elections held in 1952, he contested on behalf of the Congress for the Bombay Legislative Assembly against Shri R.D. Bhandare of SCF and got elected. He founded Rohidas Samaj Panchayat Sangh in 1952. He was its President from 1952 to 1963.

He married Vittabai in 1913 and Venubai in 1916. He expired on 29 March 1966 at the age of 75.

SHYAMSUNDAR, B.[118] (1908-1975)

Shri Baddula Shyamsundar was born on 8 December 1908. His father Baddula Manikam was a Railway head constable at Aurangabad. He passed his B. A. and LL.B. from Osmania University, Hyderabad. He belonged to the Mala caste.

At first he addressed the gathering at the inauguration of the Youth League of Ambedkarites, held at Hyderabad in 1936. He was elected to the presidentship of the Depressed Classes Students' Union in 1942.

He joined the Depressed Classes Association under the leadership of Raosaheb B.S. Venkatrao. He presided over the Depressed Classes Conference, Marathwada Unit held at

---

[118] Source of Information:

P.R. Venkataswamy, *Our Struggle for Emancipation,* Hyderabad (1955): V.T. Rajshekar, *Dalit Movement In Karnataka,* Madras (1978).

Parbhani on 30 May 1942. Raosaheb B.S. Venkatrao addressed the gathering as chief guest. B. Shyamsundar had participated in the All India Depressed Classes Conference held at Nagpur on 18-20 July 1942.

Shri B. Shyamsundar was elected President of the Depressed Classes Association in 1947 when Raosaheb B.S. Venkatrao became the Education Minister in the Nizam's government.

Shri B. Shyamsundar was a strong supporter of the alliance of the Depressed Classes with the Ittehadul Muslimeen in order to protect the former from the wrath of ruling Muslims.

During those days, there was a controversy over the problem of accession of Hyderabad with India. He thought that the Hyderabad State should remain independent. He issued a joint statement with Venkatrao supporting the *Firman* relating to the independence of Hyderabad. He felt that the interests of the Scheduled Castes would be safe in independent Hyderabad.

He opposed *Razakar* leader Kasim Razvi's move "to work in co-operation with the State Congress on parity in the interim ministry" saying that, "by this declaration Mr Razvi has stabbed the Depressed classes on their back and broken the pledges which were given to them on behalf of the Anjuman." He did not want that the Scheduled Castes be again at the mercy of the caste Hindus.

He was nominated member of the One Crore Scheduled Caste Welfare Fund for a period of three years. He was at one time the President of the Nizam Railway Employees Union.

Just before the police action, he was included in the delegation as a representative of the Scheduled Castes to represent the case of Hyderabad at the UN Security Council. However, in view of successful police action, the delegation was called back.

In the first general elections in 1952 he contested as a nominee of the Depressed Classes Association for the Hyderabad State Legislative Assembly from Nalgonda (G and SC) constituency as well as Malakpet (G) constituency. He was defeated in both the constituencies.

In the elections held in 1957 he contested as independent candidate for the Karnataka Legislative Assembly from Bhalki (G and SC) constituency in which he was elected. At the same time he had contested as an independent candidate for Lok Sabha from Gulbarga constituency, but he was defeated by the Congress.

In the general elections held in 1962 he contested as PSP candidate for Karnataka Legislative Assembly from two constituencies, namely, Santpur and Aland and lost in both the constituencies.

Again, he contested as an independent from Bidar (R) Lok Sabha constituency in 1967, in which he was defeated.

He had formed the Bhim Sena on 29 April 1968 in a big rally at Gulbarga in Karnataka. It was a volunteers corps for self defence. It was based on truth and justice. Its branches were opened at many places in Andhra, Karnataka and Maharashtra.

He propounded the theory that the Scheduled Castes and Scheduled tribes, Muslims, Christians, Anglo-Indians, Sikhs and Parsis are minorities in India, as such they should forge a united front against the caste Hindus and protect their fundamental rights.

He attempted to revive the All India Scheduled Castes Federation in a conference held at Nanded (Maharashtra) on 26 January 1968. In the conference, three important resolutions were unanimously passed. They were:

1. The Scheduled Castes should have separate settlement. In every Taluka, 30 per cent of the villages should be handed over to the Scheduled Castes. The government should take the responsibility of rehabilitation of the newly-settled Scheduled Castes as well as the affected caste Hindus.
2. The Scheduled Castes should be granted separate electorate so that they would be able to choose their true

representatives to the Parliament and the State legislatures.

3. They should have a separate university for their educational development. The university, which would be either at Bombay or Aurangabad be named after Dr Babasaheb Ambedkar.

Shri B. Shyamsundar had popularized five slogans. They were: "(i) We are Mool Bharatis, original sons of the soil;" (ii) "We are not Hindus, but Buddhists;" (iii) "We want people's raj, not Hindu Raj – democracy, not fascism;" (iv) "We need freedom to shape our social, economic and educational policies"; and (v) "We want to live in peace with all as equals, not as second rank citizens."

He was a great writer. He wrote *Diksha; Federation is a must for India's minorities; Zindagi Ek Safar* (novel)*; National integration and problems of minorities; The Menace of the Dragon; They Burn:* and *Mool Bharatis.* These books of course reveal his philosophical solutions to the problems of Dalits and minorities.

He was prosecuted by the State of Andhra Pradesh allegedly on the ground of "creating disharmony" between the communities, under section 153(A), 505(b) and (c) read with 34 of IPC in October 1968. He was, however, acquitted of the charge on 8 April 1971.

He breathed his last on 19 May 1975 at Hyderabad at the age of 68 years. He was a bachelor and a teetotaller. He was well versed in Urdu, English, Marathi and Kannada apart from Telugu. He moved the people by his forceful and thought-provoking speech. A fearless and selfless leader, he was well known to the leaders in India and outside for his distinguished character and leadership.

SIDDAYYA, S.M.[119]

Shri Siddayya was born on 15 August 1918 at Sosale in Narasipur Taluka, Mysore district in Karnataka. He belonged to

---

119. Source of Information:
Who's Who. 1971

Adi-Karnataka caste. His father's name was Shri M. Mariyappa. Shri Siddayya passed his B.Sc. from Maharaja's College, Mysore and LL.B. from Raja Lakham Gouda Law College, Belgaum. Thereafter he started his legal practice.

When he realized the despicable conditions to which his brethren were subjected he resolved to endeavour to ameliorate them. He started taking part in the Adi-Karnataka movement. He was Secretary of Mysore State Adi-Karnataka Abhivridhi Sangha during 1947-57. He was member of the District Board, Mysore from 1947-53. He started educational institutions for the spread of education among the downtrodden people. He was the founder President of Siddharth Education Society and Siddhartha High School, Mysore. He had been President of Adi-Karnataka Aided Hostel, Ashokpuram, Mysore and Shri Mallikarjuna Swamy Aided Hostel, Bettahalli.

In the year 1953, he joined the Kisan Mazdoor Party (KMP). Later, in 1956 he left it and joined the Congress party. He became executive committee member of the Bharatiya Depressed Classes League, New Delhi. He was member of the Central Silk Board from 1957-60. He worked as a member of the Central Harijan Welfare Board from 1962 to 1971.

He was elected to the Lok Sabha in 1957 from Mysore (G and SC) constituency and in 1962, 1967 and in 1971 from Chamrajanagar (R) constituency. In 1980 he had contested from the same constituency on Janata Party ticket for the Lok Sabha, but in vain.

His contribution as a member of the Committee on Untouchability etc, constituted by the Government of India in 1967 to investigate into the implementation of the constitutional safeguards for the Scheduled Castes under the presidentship of Shri L. Ellayaperumal deserves special mention. The said committee submitted its report in 1969.

He had translated *The Untouchables* and *Annihilation of Castes* by Dr Babasaheb Ambedkar into Kannada.

He married Mahadevamma in 1941. He had four sons and daughters.

SOLANKI, P.G.[120] (1876-1953)

Shri Purushottam Solanki was born on 19 December 1876 at Navasari in Surat district (Gujarat). His father Shri Govindji Solanki was a businessman. Shri Purushottam Solanki passed his matriculation in 1894 and then he completed L.M. and S. from Grant Medical College, Bombay. He had joined medical profession at Bombay. For some time he was in the service in Gujarat region. He belonged to Mahya Vanshi caste.

Being an untouchable, he had to undergo inhuman treatment at the hands of the caste Hindus. Hence, he left Hinduism and embraced Christianity on 11 April 1925 at Saint Andrews Church, Agripada, Bombay.

He came in contact with Sir Narayan Chandavarkar, a great social reformer and promoter of Prarthana Samaj. He was influenced by him.

Shri P.G. Solanki was the founder President of Mayawat Rajput Hitvardhak Sabha. The Sabha was working for the uplift of the Depressed Classes in Gujarat since 1909. He was a member of the Depressed Classes Mission and Servants of India Society since 1910.

Due to his keen interest in the uplift of his brethren, he was nominated by the Government of Bombay to the Legislative Council to represent the Depressed Classes, in the year 1927. Dr P.G. Solanki moved a resolution on 8 August 1928 in the Council that the government should appoint a committee to inquire into the social and economic condition of the Depressed Classes, and it was passed. Accordingly, a committee under the chairmanship of O.B.H. Start was formed on 5 November 1928. Among others. Dr P.G. Solanki and Dr Babasaheb Ambedkar were its members. The Start Committee submitted its report after due inquiry in March 1930, which stated that, the Depressed Classes were obliged "to live in a state of isolation which prevented social osmosis and resulted in servility." In order to improve their condition the committee suggested several

---

120. Source of Information:

Personal interview with his admirer Shri Devidas Kantharia, 14. Daruwalawadi, Lemington Road, Bombay on 29.6.1991 and other sources on Dalit movement.

measures such as common schools, increase in scholarship and hostels for the Depressed Classes students, due representation in village cooperative societies, recruitment of the Depressed Classes in the police and military services, the appointment of a special officer to look after the welfare of the Depressed Classes, etc.

Dr P.G. Solanki gave evidence before the Simon Commission on 23 October 1928. In his evidence he said categorically that he concurs "with the document submitted by Dr Ambedkar." Both of them were of the view that certain safeguards should be provided to the Scheduled Castes for their development.

When Dr Babasaheb Ambedkar was to leave for London to take part in the Round Table Conference, a rousing send off was given to him on 2 October 1930 under the presidentship of Dr P.G. Solanki.

He presided over the conference of the Depressed Classes of the CP and Berar held at Nagpur on 24 February, 1929.

Dr Solanki was renominated to the Bombay Legislative Council on 28 November 1930 for a period of three years.

He presided over the meeting at Nasik on 8 February 1931 which was called for working out the further plan of the Kalaram temple satyagraha. It was, however, decided in the meeting to reactivate the satyagraha with all vigour.

Dr P.G. Solanki presided over the meeting on 29 January 1932 held at Bombay in which Dr Babasaheb Ambedkar was profusely felicitated on behalf of the 114 organizations for his successful representation in the Round Table Conference. Dr Solanki was one of the signatories of the Poona Pact 1932.

In the elections held in 1937, Dr Solanki contested for the Bombay Legislative Assembly from Surat constituency and he became successful in the election. Subsequently, he joined the Independent Labour Party founded by Babasaheb Ambedkar. However, he left the ILP in 1940, but continued working for Dalit uplift.

He died in 1953 at the age of 77.

SRINIVASAN, R.[121] (1859-1945)

Shri Srinivasan was born on 7 July 1859 at village Kozhialam in Madhauranthagam Taluka, Chengalpet district in Tamil Nadu. His father Rattamalai was a poor Adi-Dravida farmer. Srinivasan had keen interest in painting, as such he was sent to Government Arts College, Coimbatore for his further education. There he became well-versed in arts and painting.

He got the service on Hill Station of Nilgiri district. There he happened to meet Colonel Olcott and Madam Blatvastky. He came to Madras in 1890.

He was, however, perturbed to see the abundant miseries of the so-called untouchables in those days. He decided to fight against injustice perpetrated on his brethren. In order to organize them, he founded Adi-Dravida Mahajan Sabha in the year 1891. He organized the first conference of the untouchables on 23 December 1893 and declared his "open war" on untouchability, caste system and religious myths. In order to bring a new awakening to the masses, he started one magazine named *Parayan* in 1893. He convened the next conference of the untouchables on 7 October 1895 at Victoria Hall in Madras.

He entered the service of the South African Government as a translator in the courts, in the year 1904. He was in South Africa up to 1920. In South Africa he found that there were severe discriminations against the Blacks by Whites or British people on the ground of mere colour or race. An untouchable in India was again treated as untouchable in South Africa. During those days, he was acquainted with Mahatma Gandhi, who was an advocate for the Indian merchants in South Africa. Mahatma Gandhi learnt Tamil from R. Srinivasan.

---

121. Source of Information:

Dictionary of National Biography Vol. IV, Institute of Historical Studies, Calcutta (1974).

Mrs Nirmala Arulprakash 76,V.M. Street, Mylapore, Madras.

Shri R. Srinivasan came back to India in 1920. Thereafter, he was nominated to the Madras Legislative Council as a representative of the Depressed Classes in 1923. He was a member of the Legislature from 1923 to 1935. During his membership he was instrumental in securing several amenities and educational facilities for the Depressed Classes.

He had a unique opportunity of being nominated as a representative of the Depressed Classes in India to the Round Table Conferences held during 1930-32 in London, along with Dr Babasaheb Ambedkar. A true follower of Dr Babasaheb Ambedkar, Shri R. Srinivasan also believed that, "The removal of untouchability depends upon the vesting of political power in the Depressed Classes... I find that there is no alternative but that we should be bestowed with political power." Further he explained that, "our object is to have adult suffrage and to have separate electorate only as a temporary measure. We want reservations of seats on a population basis with sufficient weightage to enable us to withstand the majority in the Council." Dr Babasaheb Ambedkar and R. Srinivasan could argue their point very staunchly and ultimately they became successful in convincing the Prime Minister of England and other members of the Conferences. However, Mahatma Gandhi opposed the demand of separate electorate tooth and nail. Eventually he undertook a fast unto death to oppose the separate electorate; as a result the Poona Pact was signed in 1932 between the two parties.

However, Shri R. Srinivasan was not in support of conversion move of Dr Babasaheb Ambedkar taken in 1935. Therefore, he drifted away from the latter. Later, he remained aloof from the Dalit political movement.

For the selfless services which he rendered for the nation as well as for the community, the British Government bestowed the honour of Dewan Bahadur on him.

He married Ranganyakkimma in 1887.

He breathed his last in September 1945 at the age of 86.

SUBHANANDA GURUDEVAN[122] (1882-1950)

Shri Subhananda Gurudevan was born on 1 May 1882 at village Venpala in Chengannur Taluka, Allapuzha district in Kerala State. His original name was Pappan. His father's name was Shri Ittyathi. He was engaged in basket making. Shri Pappan, popularly known as Subhananda Gurudevan, had no formal education, but he was well conversant with Malayalam. He was a Pariah.

He was a religious minded man. He tried to uplift his brethren, especially in Central Kerala through religion. He founded a spiritual organization called, Atma Bodhodaya Sangham and tried to unite the untouchables under that banner. He advised his brethren to maintain a high moral and cultural standard. He preached equality. He was against idol worship and superstitions.

He remained a bachelor throughout his life. He was purely vegetarian and teetotaller. He was a saintly man and a proponent of righteous conduct.

He died on 27 July 1950 at the age of 68.

SWAMI ACHHUTANAND[123] (1879-1933)

Swami Achhutanand was born in 1879 at Umari, Tehsil Sirasaganj, Mainpuri District in Uttar Pradesh. His parents originally belonged to village Sourikh, Tehsil Chhivramau, Farukhabad district in Uttar Pradesh. However, they left the original place due to dispute with the caste Hindus and migrated to a new place in Manipuri district. Thereafter, his uncle Shri Mathura Prasad joined the British Army and was elevated to the

---

[122] Source of Information:

Shrl T.H.P. Chentharassery, a biographer of Dalit heroes, Trivandrum.

[123] Source of Information:

Chandrika Prasad Jigyasu, *Shri 108 Swami Achhutanandji* Harihar, Lucknow (1960).

position of Subedar. Therefore, his whole family started living in Devali Cantonment.

The original name of Shri Achhutanandji was Hiralal. He got education in the Camp School, where he studied Urdu, English, Punjabi, Sanskrit and philosophy of religion. At the age of 14 he joined the group of sadhus who left for a pilgrimage. He was in their company till the age of 24. Thereafter, he came under the influence of Swami Sachitanandji of Arya Samaj which he joined. After joining the Arya Samaj, his name Hiralal was changed to Swami Hariharanand. He later on lost his faith in the Arya Samaj. He thought that Arya Samaj was meant to save Hinduism by introducing certain minor reforms in the Hindu society. It could not change the society radically. Hence, he left Arya Samaj and started Adi-Hindu movement for the uplift of the Depressed Classes. In the philosophical discussion (*Shastrarth*) arranged on 22 October 1921 at Delhi, he defeated Pandit Akhilanandji. He rightly came to the conclusion that unless the untouchables secured political rights, there would be no salvation for them. His name Swami Hariharanand was again changed to Swami Achhutanand.

Swami Achhutanandji is known as the pioneer of Adi-Hindu movement in Uttar Pradesh. He thought that the untouchables were the original inhabitants of India. The Hindus were not original inhabitants of India. The main principles of Adi Hindu movement could be epitomized as under:

1. There is one God, who is attributeless.
2. The religion of Saints is the true religion of India.
3. All human beings are equal. To treat someone as high and another as low is wrong.
4. All the gods enunciated by Brahmanism are not true. They ought to be discarded.
5. The so-called untouchables are the original inhabitants of Bharat.
6. People should be away from all passions, greed, pride and malice.
7. Their glorious culture and civilization should be restored and developed.

The main centre of the Adi-Hindu movement was at Kanpur in Uttar Pradesh. Therefrom, he propagated the principles of Adi-Hindu movement in India.

Swami Achhutanand was a great rationalist of his times. He viewed any principle and policy from utility point of view. He tried to eradicate irrationalism, sub-casteism and superstitions from among the Depressed Classes. He advised his brethren that the caste system had been purposely imposed by the foreign conquerers on India. Therefore, it should be given up. The Depressed Classes should not accept such an ugly system, which differentiates man from man. He felt that the main objective of the untouchables was to attain emancipation, which could be possible only by their involvement in gainful politics. They should be free from the yoke of casteism. They should unitedly struggle for their human rights. In order to abolish sub-casteism among the Dalits, he invariably used to take every alternate meal with a man of different caste. He exhorted them to abolish sub-casteism by inter sub-caste marriages. He used to tell his people to seek help from Christians or Muslims if needed. They should take the help of Christian missionaries in educating the people.

Previously, his own brethren were reluctant to accept his thoughts. When he was in Agra for the purpose of his mission, he was driven out by the men of his own community. Later on, he became very popular among the Depressed Classes and attracted many persons towards his movement.

When the Prince of Wales was to arrive in India in 1922, the Congress decided to boycott him. However, Swami Achhutanand and his followers decided to accord a grand welcome to him on the occasion of his visit to Delhi. Therefore, a huge rally was arranged at Delhi and the demands of the Dalits were submitted for the sympathetic consideration of the British authorities on 17 February 1922. Thereupon the Prince replied that, "I thank you very warmly for the very kind and enthusiastic welcome which you have given me on two occasions at Delhi. I much value your good wishes. I wish the communities whom you represent all prosperity and well being". (Walker David, *The Prince of India,* 1923, p. 289).

Swami Achhutanand contemplated full Swaraj or freedom to all; and not just to few castes. He thought that the communities so far deprived of human rights were really the claimants of Swaraj. The Swaraj, in which the untouchables had no place, was meaningless.

He was against landlordism. He criticized the government for its policy of conferring honours on the landlords who exploit the untouchables, kill their kith and kin and attack the chastity of their womenfolk.

He appealed to the government to pass land reform laws and thereby abolish landlordism and fuedalism in the society.

A special session of the Depressed Classes representatives from all over India was convened at New Delhi in December 1927 to discuss the question of reforms in view of the arrival of the Simon Commission. Swami Achhutanand was Chairman of the Reception Committee of the convention. Shri M. C. Rajah presided over the convention. The convention, however, demanded separate electorate and increased seats in the legislatures for the Depressed Classes.

Swami Achhutanand supported the demand of separate electorate made by Babasaheb Ambedkar in the Round Table Conferences. Swamiji was against the Rajah-Moonje Pact. He moved from place to place and propagated against the pact. He very strongly opposed the nomenclature of *Harijan* given by Mahatma Gandhi.

In order to bring a new awareness among the Depressed Classes, he started *Achhut,* a monthly paper in 1922 from Delhi. It was soon discontinued. Again, he started *Prachin Hindu,* a monthly. This continued for one and a half year during 1922-23. He started *Adi-Hindu Journal* from Kanpur in 1924, and it continued up to 1932.

He was a philosopher-poet and a playwright. He wrote *Shambuk Muni Balidan or Ram Rajya Nyaya Natak. Mayanand*

Balidan Natak and *Adi Vansh ka Danka* – a collection of devotional songs. He was a singer. He used to sing his own poems or songs of new spirit which were very influential.

He married Durgabai. He had three daughters.

Swami Achhutanand breathed his last on 20 July 1933 at Kanpur at the age of 54.

SWAMI PRABHUTANAND VYAS[124] (1877-1950)

Shri Prabhu Dayal *alias* Swami Prabhutanand Vyas was born in 1877 at Bhogipura, Agra in Uttar Pradesh. His father's name was Navalsing Dayal and mother's name was Sukhdevi. He had no formal education, but he was well versed in Hindi, Urdu and Sanskrit. He was a Jatav.

The untouchables in those days were living in a very bad condition. Shri Prabhu Dayal thought to improve their social condition. He used to preach to his brethren to maintain cleanliness and moral and cultural standard. He was against beef-eating and removing skin of the dead animals. He used to preach them to behave on right way and according to religious norms. He was against untouchability, casteism and even against idol worship.

He was one of the founders of the *Jatav Maha Sabha* in 1917. They wanted to unite their brethren under one organization, for giving fight against untouchability.

In order to protest against Hinduism, he accepted Arya Samaj, a more liberal cult. The ceremony was conducted on 28 February 1938 by Swami Swarupanandji Saraswati, in a ceremony at Agra. Since then he was known as Swami Prabhutanand Vyas.

---

124. Source of Information:
Personal Interview with his grandson Shri Ishwarlal Deepchand Dayal H.No. 8/300 Opp. Shahganj Police Thana, Bhogipura, Agra, on 8-6-1991.

He was a great thinker, social reformer and a writer. He wrote a book entitled *Brahmadi Bodh* in Hindi in 1939. It was published by Dr Manikchand Jatav Veer of Agra.

He married Ladho Devi and had two sons. After 1938 he became an ascetic. He died in about 1950 at the age of 73.

SWAMI SAHJANANDAR[125] (1881-1959)

Swami A.S. Sahajanandar was born in 1881 in Madras. He studied Sanskrit and Vedas. He was a good religious speaker.

He had an urge to uplift the so-called untouchable community. In 1910, he opened a school in Madras for the untouchable students. He built a separate temple, named Nandnar temple.

In 1917 he organized a satyagraha to touch the water of the sacred tank of Omekalam, for which he was prosecuted.

He attended the conference of the All India Depressed Classes Federation held at Kamathi, Nagpur on 7-8 May 1932. It was presided over by Dr Babasaheb Ambedkar.

He was nominated as MLC of the Madras Legislative Council from 1929 to 1936. He was elected to the Legislative Assembly in 1937 from Chidambaram (R) constituency. In the first general elections held in 1952 he contested on Congress ticket for Madras Legislative Assembly from Chidambaram constituency and got elected, defeating his nearest rival Shri Kuppuswamy of the SCF. Again, he got elected from the same constituency to the Madras Legislative Assembly in 1957.

He died on 19 October 1959 at the age of 78.

TAGADI KESHWAN SHASTRI[126] (1907-1962)

Shri Tagadi Keshwan Shastri was born on 23 April 1907 at Aranmula, in Tiruvalla Taluka, Patanamtitta district in Kerala. He was a Pulaya by caste. His father Shri Tagadi Thevan and

---

125. Source of Information:

A. S. Ulakanathan, *Messengers of Equality*, Madras (1990).

126. Source of Information:

Personal interview with his son-in-law, Shri K. Chinmayan Poonilav. Statues. Uppalam Road. Trivandrum on 22.4.1991.

mother Thali were labourers in the field of a landlord. On the inspiration of Vallikara Chothi, a Dalit leader, he joined a school at Tiruvalla. The caste Hindus could not tolerate an untouchable's entry in the school and they burnt the school. Thereafter, Shri Keshwan, at the instance of Shri Narayana Guru, a great social reformer of Kerala, entered Adavait Ashram, a Sanskrit school at Alwaye founded by the Guru himself and passed his Shastri (Sanskrit) examination in 1929.

For some time he was a teacher at Kalliassery Chenganoor. He came in contact with Vallikara Choti, Ayyan Kali, Kurumban Deivatan and Sri Narayana Guru. Inspired by them, he entered the movement of Dalit liberation. He strove to secure the right to walk along public roads and enter the schools.

In order to organize his brethren and infuse a new blood in them, he founded an organization called, The Pulayar Mahasabha. He opened the branches of this new organization at several places in erstwhile Travancore.

For the spread of education among the untouchables, he started several night schools. He constructed a housing colony for the untouchables in Trivandrum.

Shri T.T. Keshwan Shastri joined Congress and thereby took active part in freedom movement.

He started *Karyadarsh,* a weekly in Malayalam from Trivandrum. It continued for 2-4 years. He wrote *Bhagwad Doott,* a collection of his poems. He was a good singer. He sang devotional songs aimed at bringing awareness among the untouchables.

He married Thankamma, daughter of a famous Kerala Dalit leader, Shri Ayyan Kali. He had four sons and four daughters.

He expired on 1 November 1962 at the age of 55.

THAKUR, HARICHAND[127] (1811-1879)

Shri Harichand Thakur was born in 1811 at Orakhandi, Faridpur district, now in Bangladesh. He belonged to the Namasudra community.

---

127. Source of Information:
The Oppressed Indian, July 1982 and April 1983.

In those days the condition of the so-called untouchables was very precarious. In order to get rid of the oppression by the case Hindus, they were getting converted to either Christianity or Islam. The reformist Brahmo Samaj movement could not reach to the untouchables. Therefore, Shri Harichand Thakur, whose heart was moved by the agony of his brethren, decided to work for their liberation.

He founded a new sect called *Matua* sect to liberate his brethren from orthodox oppressive Hinduism. He told his brethren that they need not enter the temples of the caste Hindus for worship. They should worship only Shri Hari for their spiritual satisfaction. They need not worship the idols. They should not accept the superiority and priesthood of Brahmins. They should lead highly moral and cultural life.

He propagated the new philosophy to his brethren in the erstwhile Bengal. It had a great impact on the moral and cultural life of the untouchables, especially the Namasudras in Bengal.

Shri Harichand Thakur died in 1879 at the age of 68.

Thereafter, his son Shri Guru Chand Thakur successfully continued the Dalit liberation movement.

THAWARE, G.M.[128] (1902-1952)

Shri Gangaramji Thaware was born on 23 April 1902 at Jamb, in Bhandara district in Maharashtra. His father's name was Mathaji Thaware and mother's name was Kautukabai Thaware. He was a Mahar by caste.

Shri Gangaramji Thaware had completed his primary education at Jamb in 1912. Then he was sent to Tumsar for higher education. After passing fourth standard English medium, he came to Nagpur in 1916 for further education. However, he discontinued his education in 1918, when he was in sixth standard English medium.

He married Champa in 1918 and after her death he married Mainavati. Thaware had a son by name Nana Thaware.

---

128. Source of Information:

N.R. Shende. *Shri G.M. Thaware-Charitra Ani Chyaritrya,* Nagpur (1968).

Shri G.M. Thaware was a staunch Mahanubhava Panthi, as such he was strict vegetarian and teetotaller throughout his life.

It is said that he got inspiration from the thoughts and deeds of Kisan Fagu Bansod and plunged into social service. Shri Thaware thought that all the sub-castes among the untouchables should not observe casteism amongst themselves. They should encourage inter-dining and inter-sub-caste marriages. They should discard all the old traditions and superstitions. They should get education and unite on common cause.

In the year 1920 he opened one primary school and one library in Nagpur. In the year 1922 he founded an educational institution named The Central Provinces and Berar Depressed Classes Education Society at Nagpur with an objective to spread education among the Depressed Classes. He started Depressed Classes Night School at Sadar Bazar, Nagpur in 1920; Rajaram Library, Sadar Bazar, Nagpur in 1921, Depressed Girls School, Sadar Bazar. Nagpur in 1921; Depressed Clases Night School at Tumsar, Bhandara district in 1923, Sweepers' Boys School, Bhadarpura, Nagpur in 1923; Depressed Classes Girls School, Indora, Nagpur in 1924; Reading Room for *bidi* workers, Tumsar in 1929 and Depressed Classes students hostel at Bhandara in 1929.

He was nominated member of the Nagpur District Council in the year 1928-29. He was Honorary Magistrate during 1934-38 and 1940-44. He worked as District Assistant Recruiting Officer in 1941-42, and helped the British Government in the Second World War. Therefore, the British Government awarded him the honorary title of Rao Saheb.

He gave evidence before the Simon Commission, on 15 November 1928 at New Delhi and requested the British Government to improve the educational level of the Depressed Classes. He advocated compulsory education for the boys and girls of the Depressed Classes. In 1929, he submitted a memorandum to the Statutory Commission, through which he appealed to the government that, there should only be communal representation and no class representation till at least 1950, strictly in proportion to their population. He also stated that "different communities should have proportionate representation in all kinds of public services, that is, (a) Police,

(b) Judiciary, (c) Executive and (d) Administrative." He submitted in a memorandum to the hon'ble Sir Arthur Nelson. President, Provincial Franchise Committee, Central Provinces, Nagpur, on 17 February 1932 that, "Separate electorate and number of seats in legislatures to their numerical strength will serve the cause of Depressed classes in the new Constitution."

For some time he was associated with Hindu Mahasabha. He was elected Vice-president of the reception committee of the All India Hindu Mahasabha Conference held in 1938 at Nagpur. He was in the executive council of the Central Provinces Hindu Mahasabha in 1941.

In a letter to Mahatma Gandhi on 14 January 1933, he wrote that a separate University, at Wardha should be established for the students belonging to the Scheduled Castes. Mahatma Gandhi, of course, did not favour this idea. Further, he attracted the attention of Mahatma Gandhi towards the denial of admission in the Mahanubhav temples to the untouchable converts to Mahanubhav. He was opposed to the use of the nomenclature Harijan and suggested the use of the word Scheduled Castes. The Government of CP and Berar, ultimately accepted the proposal in 1941.

From 1926 to 1944 he was Secretary of All India Depressed Classes Association. However, after the death of Shri M.C. Rajah, its President, the Association virtually came to an end. Thereafter, Shri G.M. Thaware joined the Scheduled Castes Federation founded by Dr Babasaheb Ambedkar. He was in SCF from 1945 to 1949.

Thereafter, he tried to organize the labourers working in PWD, Railway, textile industries and *bidi* factories. He became President of the CP Cotton and Textile Workers Union. He joined the Congress in 1950.

He contested the election for the Legislative Assembly of the CP and Berar in 1937 from the Bhandara-Sakoli reserved seat, but he was defeated by the ILP candidate Raghobaji Ghodichor. He was to contest for the first Lok Sabha from Bhandara constituency but his nomination was rejected. However, he was elected to Rajya Sabha in 1952. He died at New Delhi on 16 August 1952 at the age of 50 only.

THYKAD AYYAVU SWAMY[129] (1817-1909)

Shri Thykad Ayyavu Swamy was born in about 1817. He was originally from Thanjavur (Tamil Nadu), but migrated to Trivandrum in his youth. He could not get any formal education. However, he was well versed in Malayalam and Sanskrit apart from Tamil, his mother tongue. He was a great musician, saint, philosopher and social reformer, belonging to the Pariah caste.

Swamy Thykad was strictly vegetarian. He worshipped the deity named Subramanya. He wanted to reform the Hindu society which believes in caste and untouchability. He felt that the so-called untouchables should live an ideal life. They should live hygienically clean and religious life.

He moved from place to place and brought new awareness among the people. He taught that there was only one God and all the human beings are equal. He used to educate the people in his thoughts through *Bhajans* or *kirtans.* He was a poet. He composed hundreds of *stotrams* or holy hymns and used to recite them.

The then Maharaja of Travancore, Shri Mulam Tirunal came to know about the Swamy. He invited the Swamy and offered him the post of Superintendent of Government Guest House at Trivandrum. The Maharaja was so impressed by the Swamy's knowledge of music that he accepted the Swamy as his teacher in music. Further, the Maharaja used to seek his advice on the matters of religion and philosophy.

Shri Thykad Ayyavu Swamy was respected by Shri Ayyan Kali, the famous Dalit leader in Kerala as well as Shri Narayana Guru, the famous leader of the Ezhava community in Kerala. They were very much influenced by Thykad Ayyavu Swamy's philosophy of "one caste, one religion and one God".

Though the King of Travancore honoured him, the high caste Hindus contemptuously called him Pariah Swamy instead of Thykad Ayyavu Swamy.

---

129. Source of Information:

Personal interview with a great historian and biographer of Dalit leaders. Shri T.H.P. Chentharassery T.C. 3/1925 near Sevagirikatta Kendram T.K.D. Road, Pattom, Trivandrum on 22.4.1991.

Thykad Ayyavu Swamy had a son named Loganath. Swamy died on 18 July 1909 at the age of 92.

UMAID RAMJI MAHARAJ[130]

Shri Umaid Ramji Maharaj was born in 1808 at Jodhpur in Rajasthan in a *Bhangi* family. His father's name was Gendaramji and mother's name was Sugnabai. In his childhood Shri Umaid Ramji used to meet one saint Bana Nathji Maharaj at Mertiagate of Jodhpur. Shri Bana Nathji Maharaj taught him meditation and metaphysical knowledge.

Afterwards, Shri Umaid Ram founded his own panth or sect. The principles of his sect were :

1. The Bhangis should refrain from eating the meat of any animal.
2. They should not accept any bride price for their daughters at the time of marriage.
3. They should obey the advice of their parents.
4. They should lead a life based on the moral and spiritual sanctions of their society.
5. They should educate their children.

Shri Umaid Ramji preached the tenets of his sect to his brethren in the Jodhpur region of Rajasthan and tried to uplift them till the end of his life.

VAISHYA, MULDAS[131] (1894-1977)

Shri Muldas Vaishya was born on 16 August 1894 at village Umta, in Taluka Visnagar, Mehsana district in Gujarat. He belonged to the Vankur caste. His father Shri Bhudardas Vaishya was engaged in weaving. Shri Muldas Vaishya could not complete his matriculation. He left the school at the age of 21.

---

130. Source of Information:

Shyamlal, *The Bhangi - A Sweeper Caste –Its Socio-economic portraits*, Popular Prakashan, Bombay. 1992.

131. Source of Information:

Personal Interview with his son. Prof Brahmadatta M. Vaishya, Suttariya Society. Shahpur, Ahmedabad on 7.11.1989.

He, being an untouchable, had to undergo many difficulties. When he sought admission to the eighth standard in Government School, Baroda, the caste Hindu students boycotted the school to protest against an untouchable's admission. However, they reached a compromise by which Muldas was allowed to enter only by backdoor and sit at the backside of the class room. This grieved him. At the same time he decided to fight against the untouchability at any cost.

During his student life he met a school inspector by name Pandit Atmaramji, who was an Arya Samaji. Influenced by Pandit Atmaramji, Shri Muldas Vaishya embraced the Arya Samaj. He strictly observed all the rules of Arya Samaj. He was purely vegetarian and teetotaller. His family migrated to Ahmedabad in 1921.

He attended the conference of the Depressed Classes held at Ahmedabad in 1921 under the auspices of Labour Welfare Association. Smt Anusayaben Sarabhai was its chief. The conference was addressed among others by Mahatma Gandhi. Shri Muldas Vaishya was impressed by the conference. He had an occasion to meet Gandhiji for the first time, by whom he was very much influenced. He remained an ardent admirer of Gandhiji throughout his life.

Later, Shri Muldas was appointed as a teacher in a Sanskrit School at Ahmedabad in 1921. He started a hostel, where initially there was only one boarder. Later, the number of boarders increased to 50. He served as hostel Superintendent from 1921-51. He was Superintendent of a girls' hostel started by Shri Shankarlal Banker in the year 1927.

He led satyagrahas to assert the right to enter the buses, hostels and temples. In his activities Shri Keshavaji Vaghela and Viraji Bhagat helped him.

Shri Muldas Vaishya founded an organization named Maha Gujarat Dalit Harijan Samaj in a convention of his brethren held at Ahmedabad on 14-15 March 1936. The main objectives of the Samaj were to organize Dalit communities of Gujarat, to revive traditional occupations like tanning and weaving to improve their economic conditions, to remove untouchability within Dalits, to take steps to obtain political rights, to take advantages of indigenous games for physical development, to give ethical education to the Dalits, to give equal treatment to women and to oppose conversion to other religion.

He launched the famous satyagraha for entering the temple of Swaminarayan at Ahmedabad in the year 1948. Thereupon one Shastri Yagnapurushdasji along with other Satsangis or the members of the Swaminarayan sect filed a suit in the Court at Ahmedabad on 12 January 1948 for issuing injunctions directing the Mahants of the said temple to take steps to prevent Shri Muldas Vaishya and other non- Satsangi Dalits from entering the temple. The Trial Court passed the decree in favour of the appellant Shri Yagnapurushdasji on 24 September 1951. The respondent Shri Muldas Vaishya challenged the decision in the High Court of Bombay under the provision of the Bombay Harijan Temple Entry Act, 1947, the Untouchability Offences Act, 1955 and the Bombay Hindu Places of Public Worship (Entry Authorization Act), 1956. The case was sent back to the Trial Court, on 25 March 1957 for recording the finding in view of the legal abolition of untouchability. The Trial Court, however, came to the conclusion that the Swaminarayan temple was a Hindu religious institution within the meaning of Article 25 (2) (b) of the Constitution. The finding was recorded on 24 March 1958. Again, the case came to the High Court for hearing. The High Court held that the Swaminarayan Sect form a part of Hindu community and as such it was within the purview of the Act. Then, the case came in appeal before the Supreme Court. Finally, the case was decided in favour of Shri Muldas Vaishya on 14 January 1966. Thus, from 12 January 1948 to 14 January 1966 that is, for a long period of 18 years he gave a legal fight, asserting the religious right of the Scheduled Castes and finally he emerged successful.

He was active in the political field also. At first he was nominated member of the erstwhile Baroda State Assembly from 1925 to 1928. He became Member of the Parliament in 1951, filling a vacant seat which existed due to the death of Sardar Patel. In the first general election held in 1952, he contested as a Congress candidate from Ahmedabad (G and SC) Lok Sabha seat and got elected. Again he contested on behalf of Congress from the same constituency in 1957, but he was defeated by SCF candidate, Shri K.U. Parmar. He contested in 1962 also for the Lok Sabha from the same constituency on Congress ticket and got elected.

He married Smt Ambabahen and got two sons and two daughters.

He breathed his last on 1 August 1977 at the age of 83.

VALLON, K.P.[132] (1894-1940)

Shri Kolote Vallon was born on 2 September 1894 at Mulavukad, a small island village in Taluka Kanayanur, Ernakulam district in Kerala State. His father Shri Kolote Pizhangan was a native physician. Shri Kolote P. Vallon had no formal education, but learnt to read and write.

He had an "intense desire" to raise his Pulaya community to the level of caste Hindus. He came under the influence of Pandit Karuppan. Shri Vallon formed in 1912 Pulaya Maha Sabha of Cochin State; he served as the Secretary and subsequently as President of the Sabha till his last.

During those days, the Dalits were denied the right to walk along the main street in the capital of Ernakulam. Shri Vallon organized the untouchable youths from various nearby villages and organized a satyagraha for regaining that right. It was highly successful. He took part in the Vaikom satyagraha also.

Taking into account his social aptitude, the then Maharaja of Cochin nominated him as a Member of the Cochin Legislative Assembly first in 1931 and again in 1939. In the Assembly he fought for the cause of the untouchables and labourers. He demanded minimum wages and better conditions of work.

He used to move from place to place to propagate the importance of education. He succeeded in getting a Government Hostel established at Ernakulam in 1938. It proved to be very useful to the Dalit students.

---

132. Source of Information:

Interview with his son, Shri K.V. Kumaran, Retd. Member of KPSC, Tharam, Perukada, Trivandrum on 15.11.1991.

He was against caste inequality and exploitation of the Dalits. It was his firm conviction that this situation existed only because of Hinduism. Therefore, he converted to egalitarian Buddhism in the year 1935. He tried to propagate Buddhism among his brethren.

In 1936 he started publishing a journal called *Adhakridhan* (the Depressed Classes) which was subsequently renamed as *Harijan.*

He married Thara and had two sons and one daughter. Though by profession he was a mason, he was not less than a missionary for the Dalits.

It was while working among the Dalits of Mala village which was infested with smallpox, he himself became a victim of this disease. He died on 14 April 1940 at the age of 46.

VARALE, B.H.[133] (1900-1977)

Shri Balwantrao Varale was born in a Mahar family in 1900 at Benadi, Taluka Chikodi, Belgaum district in Karnataka. His father Hanmantrao Varale was a tobacco merchant at Benadi. Shri Balwantrao Varale had passed his intermediate from Rajaram College, Kolhapur in 1924.

He was attracted towards social work. He attended the conference of the untouchables held at Mangaon in the presence of Chhatrapati Shahu Maharaj and Dr Babasaheb Ambedkar, in the year 1920. Shri B.H. Varale and Barrister S.N. Mane worked as volunteers in the third conference of the untouchables held at Nipani on 11-12 April 1925. It was presided over by Dr Babasaheb Ambedkar. Shri Varale participated in the famous Mahad satyagraha in 1927. He was appointed as the first honorary Superintendent of the Depressed Classes hostel started by Dr Babasaheb Ambedkar at Dharwad in the year 1929. Thereafter he was appointed as Secretary of the Backward Class District Committee, Dharwad by Mr Starte.

---

133. Source of Information:

Personal interview with his wife Mrs Radhabai B. Varale.

Nipani, Belgam district. Karnataka on 18.1.1989 and the leader 's autobiography.

When Dr Babasaheb Ambedkar left India for London to participate in the first Round Table Conference in 1930, Ramabai Ambedkar and all the other members of Ambedkar family were at Dharwad with Shri B.H. Varale. This indicated that he was a close and trusted follower of Babasaheb Ambedkar. He supported the demand of separate electorate and declaration of quitting Hinduism, made by Babasaheb Ambedkar.

He joined the Independent Labour Party founded by Babasaheb Ambedkar in the year 1936. In the elections held in 1937 he contested as ILP candidate for Bombay Provincial Legislative Assembly from Nipani (R) constituency and got elected. He gave a tough but successful fight to Congress candidate Sambrani and Independent candidate Raosaheb T.J. Papanna. However, in the wake of outbreak of the Second World War in 1939, the provincial governments were dissolved. Thereafter, he was appointed as a Recruiting Officer.

On the advice of Dr Babasaheb Ambedkar the untouchables launched a satyagraha in November 1941 against the oppressive system of *Judi* prevalent in the region of Maharaja of Miraj. Shri B.H. Varale and Shri D.M. Shirke of Kolhapur had successfully led the satyagraha.

When the All India Scheduled Castes Federation was founded in 1942 by Dr Babasaheb Ambedkar, Shri B.H. Varale joined it. He tried to spread its branches at several places in the then Bombay Province.

He was appointed as Labour Officer in November 1943 at Dehu road, Nasik in which position he continued till 1945.

In the general elections held in 1946, he contested on SCF ticket for the Bombay Legislative Assembly from Belgaum (North) constituency, but he could not achieve success in the election.

On the advice of Dr Babasaheb Ambedkar, the satyagraha for political rights was launched in 1946 almost throughout the country. Shri B.H. Varale participated in that satyagraha at Pune, along with his wife Mrs Radhabai Varale. Both of them along with others were awarded imprisonment for a period of one month.

From 1946 to 1951 he was again busy with his tobacco business and Dalit uplift movement. He contested in the first general elections held in 1952 on SCF ticket from Chikodi(R) constituency for the Bombay Legislative Assembly but he was defeated.

In 1953, he was appointed as Registrar of Milind Mahavidyalaya, Aurangabad, run by the People's Education Society, Bombay, founded by Dr Babasaheb Ambedkar. He strove hard for the overall development of the college. In 1957 he became a member of the People's Education Society, Bombay, and left the service of Registrar. He was elected as Chairman of the PES Bombay on 11 January 1975, which position he graced till his last.

In the meantime he joined the Republican Party of India and contested on its behalf for Lok Sabha from Chikodi (G) constituency in the year 1962. He was defeated in the election.

He embraced Buddhism at Nagpur on 14 October 1956. The ceremony was personally conducted by Babasaheb Ambedkar. When Babasaheb Ambedkar went to participate in the World Buddhist Conference held at Kathmandu in Nepal on 14 November 1956, Shri B.H. Varale accompanied him along with Principal M.B. Chitnis and Mrs Maisheb Ambedkar.

Shri B.H. Varale breathed last on 8 August 1977 at the age of 76. He is survived by three sons and one daughter.

VEERASWAMY, K.R.[134]

Shri Kartikela Veeraswamy was born on 23 December 1919 at Secunderabad, Andhra Pradesh. His father Katikela Rama swamy was serving as an accountant in a local mill and before that he served in the military for six years. He belonged to the Mala caste.

---

[134]. Source of Information:

Personal Interview with Shri K.R. Veeraswamy.

6-1-338. Padmarao Nagar, Venkatapuram Colony. Secunderabad on 23.11.1988/9.7.1991.

Shri Veeraswamy received his primary education in a Scheduled Caste school, named Sir William Barton Middle School in Secunderabad, founded by late Shri M.L. Audiah, the first Scheduled Caste engineer in Hyderabad. He completed his B.A. in 1943 from Nizam College. Hyderabad. He passed his M.A. in 1947 from Madras University. He was the first postgraduate from the Scheduled Castes community in the erstwhile State of Hyderabad. Thereafter, he was selected for a lecturer's post in Siddhatha College, Bombay, founded by Dr Babasaheb Ambedkar, but he could not continue in it, allegedly because of the unfavourable attitude of Shri Chitre, the then Registrar of the college. Later on, he plunged into politics.

He was inspired by Rao Bahadur B.S.Venkatrao, J.H. Subbiah and Dr Babasaheb Ambedkar. He got a unique opportunity of residing with Dr Babasaheb Ambedkar for 13 days at New Delhi in June 1947.

He got an honour of inaugurating the sixth session of the Scheduled Castes Educational Conference held on 8 June 1947 at Adi-Hindu Bhavan, Hyderabad.

He joined Scheduled Castes Federation under J.H. Subbiah. Soon he became the organizing Secretary of the Federation. He was entrusted with the task of opening branches of the Federation all over the State. However, due to differences with J.H. Subbiah, he left SCF in January 1949 and joined Dalit Jatiya Sangh. Later on he became Vice-president of the Sangh under the leadership of Arigay Ramaswamy. However, he left the Sangh due to differences with S.R. Babiah, its nominated President.

Later on he joined the All India Depressed Classes League. He became President of the Hyderabad State Depressed Classes League, in its convention held on 8 November 1950.

He stood for responsible government in the State. He was of the opinion that, "The hobnobbing of the Depressed Classes leaders with the *Ittehad,* will not bear absolutely any fruit for the Depressed Classes."

In June 1948, a secret political delegation headed by J.M. Subbiah, President of the SC Federation and Shri K.R.

Veeraswamy, Organizing Secretary of the SCF flew to Delhi and met Babasaheb Ambedkar, the then Law Minister, Sardar Patel, Deputy Prime Minister and Home Minister, and Gopalaswamy Iyengar, State Minister, and told them about the atrocities committed on the community in general and the Scheduled Castes in particular. The delegation impressed upon them the need to launch police action on Hyderabad to save its people from nightmare of atrocities perpetrated by the *Razakars.* Ultimately, Dr Babasaheb Ambedkar convinced Sardar Patel to take action expeditiously. Thus the Dalit leaders could impress upon the Sardar the urgent necessity to launch the police action in September 1948.

Shri Veeraswamy was involved in the national independence movement also. He wore Khadi, and he was once suspended from the college for refusing to give up his Gandhi cap. He participated in the Vande Mataram and Quit India Movement.

He was nominated on the Board of Trustee of the Sir William Barton High School, Secunderabad. In 1961, he was appointed as honorary Secretary of the school. He got it renamed after M.L. Audiah under the Chairmanship of late D. Sanjeeviah, the first Scheduled Caste Chief Minister of Andhra Pradesh.

After accession of Hyderabad State with India, he was a nominated member of the Scheduled Caste Trust Fund from 1948-57.

Shri Veeraswamy contested as an independent candidate from one of the Secunderabad wards on reserved seat in the Municipal elections in 1950 but he was defeated by Smt J. Ishwari Bai, his own sister-in-law and an independent candidate.

In 1948 he joined the Congress party. He contested as Congress nominee in the first general elections held in 1952 from Kalvakurthi (G and SC) for the Hyderabad State Legislative Assembly. He won in the election. Again he contested for the AP Legislative Assembly in 1957 from Kamareddy (G and SC) as a candidate of Peasants and Workers Party but was defeated by T.N. Sadalaxmi of Congress.

He contested as an independent candidate from Mahbubnagar Lok Sabha constituency in 1962 and in 1969, but in vain.

He has written two books. *Glimpses into our Problems* in 1950 and *Hyderabad in Retrospect.*

He married Manikbai. He has two sons and a daughter. Even at the age of 74 he comes to the help of the poor and needy people.

VELAYUDHAN DAKSHAYANI[135] (1912-1978)

Smt Dakshayani was born on 4 May 1912 at Mulavukad, Ernakulam district in Kerala. Her father Shri Kunjan was a school teacher and engaged in growing coconut trees in his one acre land. Smt Dakshayani was admitted to the school at the age of six. She passed her B.A. in 1935 and teacher's training (L.T.) in 1938 from Madras University. She got scholarship for her education from the Cochin State Government. She belonged to the Pulaya Caste.

Smt Dakshayani was appointed as a teacher under the Cochin Government service. From 1935 to 1942, she served in the Government High School at Perigothikara, Trichur, and from 1942 to 1945 at Tripunithura. She got bitter experience of untouchability when she was a teacher. She, however, faced it with courage and confidence.

She thought to struggle against the inhuman institution of untouchability and liberate the Depressed Classes. She thought that politics could be a useful means to serve the community and the nation. She urged the Cochin Government to give her an opportunity to serve as a member of the Legislature and her demand was conceded. Thereupon, she resigned her job of teacher. She was nominated by the erstwhile Cochin

---

135. Source of Information:
The daughter of the leader Dr Meera Velayudhan
BH-6, DDA Flats, Munirka, New Delhi.

Government to the Cochin Legislative Council in 1945. Later on, she was elected to the Constituent Assembly by the Cochin Legislative Council. She was member of Constituent Assembly and the Provisional Parliament of India from 1946 to 1952. She was, of course, the only Dalit woman member of the Constituent Assembly.

She was President of the Depressed Classes Youths Fine Arts Club, Madras from 1946-49.

She was founder President of Bharatiya Mahila Jagriti Parishad, a Dalit Women's group in Delhi in 1978.

She was Managing Editor of *The Common Man,* an English weekly started from Madras from 1946-49.

Smt Dakshayani married Shri R. Velayudhan (1912- 1974), a prominent Dalit leader in Kerala. Her marriage was performed in Sevagram at Wardha in the presence of Mahatma Gandhi and Kasturba Gandhi. Shri and Smt Velayudhan had four sons and one daughter.

Shri R. Velayudhan was elected to the Provisional Parliament in June 1950. He, however, resigned from the Congress protesting against repression of the people in Travancore-Cochin. Thus, the wife and husband were in two opposite camps in the Parliament.

Shri R. Velayudhan contested from Quilon-cum-Mavelikara (G and SC) Lok Sabha constituency in 1952 as an independent candidate and got elected. Again he contested in the second general elections in 1957 from Kottayam (G) Lok Sabha constituency as a PSP candidate but could not get elected.

Smt Dakshayani Velayudhan contested in 1971 for Lok Sabha from Adoor (SC) constituency as an independent but she was defeated by the CPI candidate.

Her elder brother, Shri K.P.Vallon was also a great Dalit leader in Kerala.

Smt Dakshayani Velayudhan died on 20 July 1978 at the age of 66.

VELLIKKARA CHOTHI[136] (1878-1927)

Shri Vellikkara Chothi was born on 29 January 1878 at village Puramattom, Taluka Thiruvalla, Pathanamthitta district in Kerala. His father's name was Deivathan. Shri Chothi was educated up to the sixth standard. For some time he worked as a shepherd with the landlord whom his father served as a serf. He was a Pulaya.

After having seen inequality, discrimination, exploitation and ill-treatment in Hinduism, he protested against it by converting to Christianity with his whole family. He was renamed as Mathai after his conversion. He was popularly known as Vellikkara Mathai Asan among his Christian brethren.

Subsequently, he felt that even in Christian faith there was no equality so far as the members of the Depressed Classes were concerned. The converts were wantonly treated separately by the high caste converts. Therefore, he reconverted to Hinduism. He changed his name from Mathai to Chothi.

Shri Chothi came under the influence of Shri Ayyan Kali, a famous Dalit leader in Kerala. Shri Chothi became member of Sadhujan Paripalan Yogam founded by Shri Ayyan Kali in the year 1905. Under the leadership of Shri Ayyan Kali he started taking part in Dalit uplift movement.

Taking into account his active interest in public life, the Maharaja of Travancore nominated him as a member of Sri Moolam Popular Assembly in the year 1914.

In order to humble the caste Hindus who opposed the Civil rights of the Dalits, Shri Vellikkara Chothi, Shri Aninchan (1878-1968) and P.K. Chothi (1905-1989) learnt martial art and guerrilla tactics of war and gave fight whenever there were clashes between the caste Hindus and the untouchables.

Shri Vellikkara Chothi died on 23 January 1927 at the age of 49. After his death, Shri P.K. Chothi, son of Shri Vellikkara Chothi's younger brother came forward to lead the movement.

---

136. Source of Information:

Interview with his niece Smt P.K. Leela (Retd. Add. Secretary. Government of Kerala), 'Poornima', Perukada, Trivandrum on 22.4.1991.

VEMULA KURMAYYA[137] (1903-1970)

Shri Kurmayya Vemula was born in 1903 at Mallavaram, Taluka Gudivada, Krishna district in Andhra Pradesh. His father's name was Vengalayya. Shri Kurmayya passed his B. A. from the Andhra University and LL.B. from the Banaras Hindu University. Shri Ayyadevara Kaleshwar Rao Pantulu helped him during his student life.

He had actively participated in the Adi-Hindu movement. When the eighth conference of the Adi-Andhra Mahasabha was held in 1929 at Vijayawada under the presidentship of Prattipati Audinarayana, Shri Vemula Kurmayya was Chairman of the reception committee of the conference. The eleventh conference of the Adi-Hindu Mahasabha was held in 1936 at Vijayanagaram under the presidentship of Vemula Kurmayya. The conference was inaugurated by the pioneering leader of the movement Shri Bhagnareddy Varma of Hyderabad.

Shri Vemula Kurmayya was elected Joint Secretary of the Andhra Pradesh Provincial Harijan Sevak Sangh in November 1932. Its President was the famous social reformer in Andhra, Shri Desodharak K. Nageswara Rao Pantulu.

He took part in the national freedom movement. He participated in Salt Satyagraha in 1930. He participated in an individual satyagraha in 1940 for which he was sentenced to imprisonment for a period of six months.

Shri Vemula Kurmayya got elected in 1937 to the Madras Legislative Assembly on Congress ticket. He was elected in 1946 also.

He was Harijan Welfare Minister in the Prakasam Ministry from 1946-49.

He contested for the AP Legislative Assembly on INC ticket in 1955 from Gudivada (SC) constituency and got elected. Again, he contested from the same constituency in 1962, but without success. He, however, got elected in 1967 from Tiruvur (SC) Assembly constituency.

He expired on 5 June 1970 at the age of 67.

---

137. Source of Information:
Andhra Pradesh State Harijan Conference Souvenir, 1976.

VENKATRAO B.S.[138] (1896–1953)

Shri Bathula Venkatrao was born in October 1896 at Ghasmandi, Hyderabad. He was a Mala. His father Bathula Sayanna was in the domestic service of the Europeans.

Shri B.S. Venkatrao had completed his education up to ninth class. However, he was well versed in English, Urdu, Persian and Marathi, apart from Telugu.

During 1914-18 he worked as a sculptor in Poona. Then he joined the Public Works Department of the Nizam's Government as an overseer. After some time he was appointed as an Assistant Recruiting Officer at the Nizamsagar Project.

After having seen the civil effects of untouchability on the Depressed Classes, he determined to eradicate it. He formed The Adi-Dravida Sangham in 1922 with the assistance of M. Govindrajulu and M. Venkataswamy. Its main objective was to remove the Devadasi system and unite the Dalits. Later on, he formed The Adi-Hindu Mahasabha in April 1927. The Working Committee consisted of Arigay Ramaswamy, B.S. Venkatrao, C.S. Ethirajan, K. Ramaswamy, M. Venkataswamy and others. He tried to bring a new awakening among the untouchable masses, especially in Nizam State.

He constructed some houses in the Ghasmandi area and named it Audia Nagar. He constructed 18 temples in Hyderabad for the use of the untouchables. He constructed a library in the Ghasmandi area.

He led a delegation to the Maharashtra Asprishya Youth's Conference, Poona in January 1936 which was presided over by N. Shivaraj and addressed by Dr Babasaheb Ambedkar. Later on, at the initiative of P.R. Venkataswamy The Youth League of Ambedkarites was formed. B.S. Venkatrao was its President and P.R. Venkataswamy was its Secretary.

In recognition of Raosaheb B.S. Venkatrao's contribution to the Dalit uplift in Hyderabad, Dr Babasaheb Ambedkar invited

---

138. Source of Information:

Personal interview with his wife. Smt Nalini Devi.

6-1-292. New Boiguda. Venkatrao Nagar, Secunderabad on 22-11-1988 and other sources.

him to preside over the Bombay Presidency Mahar Conference held on 30 May 1936, at Bombay. The conference was attended by 10,000 people. The conference unanimously resolved to support the conversion move initiated by Dr Babasaheb Ambedkar.

Shri Venkatrao was nominated by the Nizam government to the Hyderabad Municipal Corporation in October 1937. The general body meeting of Youth League of Ambedkarites was convened on 29 May 1938 in Jamshed Hall, under the presidentship of Rao Saheb B.S. Venkatrao. In the meeting the League of Ambedkarites was renamed as the Hyderabad State Depressed Classes Association. In its meeting on 31 October 1938 Shri B.S. Venkatrao was elected as its President and K. Jagannathan as its Secretary.

Shri B.S. Venkatrao participated in the All India Depressed Classes Conference held at Nagpur on 18, 19 and 20 July 1942.

He was nominated to the Defence Council of Nizam in 1942. He was nominated by the Nizam to the Secunderabad Municipal Committee in 1945. He was elected unopposed from the local bodies constituency to the Nizam's Legislative Assembly, in December 1946.

On 1 April 1947, the Assembly debated on the resolution moved by Palayam Pillai, recommending to the President-in-Council for a grant of twenty lakh rupees for the uplift of the Depressed Classes of the State. Shri Venkatrao moved an amendment to the resolution raising the grant to one crore rupees. The House agreed to recommend to the Prime Minister for the grant of one crore to the fund. Accordingly, the Nizam constituted the Depressed Classes Welfare Fund and sanctioned one crore rupees for the same.

Shri B.S. Venkatrao was offered an enviable seat in the Interim Ministry with the portfolio of Education, under the leadership of Prime Minister Mir Laik Ali on 17 December 1947.

He formed an alliance with the Majlis Ittehadul Musalimeen in order to protect the untouchables from the inhuman treatment and exploitation by the caste Hindus as well as from the undue pressure by the Muslims. In order to protect his brethren from the menace of both the Hindus and the Muslims he founded The

Depressed Classes Volunteer Corps in April 1948. (It should be borne in mind that even the Lingayats also formed an alliance with the Ittehadul and joined the coalition government).

The Government of India, in its bid to integrate India, successfully launched Police Action on the Nizam's State in September 1948. The Military government formed after the police action, put Shri B.S. Venkatrao in preventive detention in September 1948. However, he was released honourably.

In the first general elections in 1952 he contested as an independent candidate for the Hyderabad State Legislative Assembly from Secunderabad constituency, but could not get elected. However, he was elected to the Rajya Sabha by the State Legislative Assembly.

He married Shanta Devi and later on Nalini Devi. He had one daughter from his first wife and one son from his second wife.

He was a very staunch, courageous, generous and selfless leader of the community. In recognition of his meritorious services to the public at large in Hyderabad State, his Exalted Highness, the Nizam honoured him by awarding the title of Khusru-E-Deccan. He was popularly known by the Depressed Classes people as Rao Saheb.

He expired on 4 November 1953, at the age of 57.

VISHNAR, SAJJANSINH[139] (1918-1988)

Shri Sajjansinh Vishnar was born in Balmiki family in 1918 at Indore in Madhya Pradesh. His father's name was Shri Kanhayalal Vishnar. Shri Sajjansinh was a graduate from Indore.

He took active interest in the Dalit liberation movement. His grandmother was working as housemaid with the British officer. She was influenced by the British manners and thoughts. She

---

139. Source of Information:
Personal interview with his son Shri Rajansinh Vishnar.
82 Indrapuri, Indore. MP, on 13.9.19S9

used to teach them to Shri Sajjansinh. Shri Sajjansinh was influenced by Shri Shankarrao Mhasde and Gangaramji Dhuldhoye, both social workers from Indore. They were Ambedkarites.

Shri Sajjansinh later on joined the Congress. In the first general elections held in 1952 he contested for the Madhya Pradesh Legislative Assembly from Depalpur (R) constituency and got elected. He was elected in 1957 from the same constituency and in 1962 from Sawer (R) constituency. He was minister in Madhya Pradesh Government from 1952 to 1967.

He married Parvatibai and had six sons. He died on 4 June 1988 at the age of 70.

WAGHMARE, GANPATRAO[140] (1916-1986)

Shri Ganpatrao Waghmare was born in a Chambhar family in 1916 at village Manjram, Taluka Biloli, Nanded district. His father's name was Manikrao Waghamare. His father had agricultural land extending up to 22 acres in the village, but he came to Nanded for the education of his son. Shri Ganpatrao completed his education up to ninth standard. After having seen the oppression of the untouchables, he got involved in social activities.

He started working in the Harijan Sevak Sangh. However, he left it in 1939 and joined the Depressed Classes Association led by Rao Saheb B.S. Venkatrao in the erstwhile Nizam State. Shri Hanmantrao *alias* Kakasaheb More was the President and Ganpatrao Waghmare was the Secretary of the Association. They organized the Marathwada regional level conference of the Depressed Classes Association at Parbhani in the year 1942, which was graciously addressed by B.S. Venkatrao and B. Shyamsunder of Hyderabad. It was decided in the conference that the untouchables should abandon all the old traditional activities and get freed from untouchability and caste system.

---

140. Source of Information:
Interview with his son Vasant Ganpatrao Waghmare,
283. Block No.21, Labour Colony, Nanded on 18.11.1988

Such conferences were held at Jintur (Parbhani), Sillod (Aurangabad) and many other places.

However, due to the rift between B.S. Venkatrao and Subbaiah a new organization named the Hyderabad State Scheduled Caste Federation was established at the initiative of the latter. Shri Kadaknath Hatkar, Prabhakarrao Hingole and other Dalit leaders at Nanded formed the new organization – SCF in 1945.

Taking into account his Dalit liberation activities, the Nizam government nominated him on the Legislative Assembly of Hyderabad on 17 January 1946. Like his mentor B.S. Venkatrao, he also stood in support of the Nizam. However, due to successful Police Action on 17 September 1947, he had to leave for Secunderabad for shelter. Eventually, the Depressed Classes Association was merged into the Scheduled Castes Federation.

Later, Shri Ganpatrao Waghmare joined the Dalit Jatiya Sangh under the leadership of M. Laxmiah Arigay Ramaswamy and K.R. Veeraswamy.

In the first general elections held in 1952, he contested the SC reserved seat from Degloor in Nanded district on Congress ticket and got elected to the Hyderabad State Assembly.

He contested for the Lok Sabha seat in 1962 and in 1967 from Nanded (G) constituency as an independent candidate, but in vain.

When B. Shyamsundar rejuvenated the All India Scheduled Castes Federation in 1968, he joined it. The conference of the said party was held at Nanded in Maharashtra on 26 January, 1968. The conference demanded separate settlement for the Scheduled Castes, a due share in the political power through proper representation by separate electorate and a separate university for the Dalits either at Bombay or at Aurangabad. They organized the Bhim Sena to protect the Dalits from the atrocities and safeguard their interests.

He was of the view that he was a "born Buddhist". He discarded Hinduism.

He married Shewantabai. He got six sons and a daughter. He died on 3 December 1986 at Nanded at the age of 70. He was respected by all the Dalits, irrespective of their caste or sub-castes.

WALANGKAR, GOPALBABA[141] (1840-1900)

Shri Gopalbaba Walangkar was born at village Walang, Taluka Mahad, Kolaba district, most probably in 1840. His father's name was Vithalnak Salve Walangkar. After completing normal school education, Shri Gopalbaba joined the British Army and retired as Havaldar in 1886. He was influenced by Ramanand Panth when he was in the British Army. He studied Sanskrit and the religious texts. He was a Mahar by caste.

After retirement from military he started his social and literary work. He tried to uplift the untouchable masses by bringing a new awareness among them. In order to vent the grievances of the untouchables, he used to write for *Deenbandhu* and *Sudharak,* the Marathi journals. He wrote *Vitalvidhvanson,* a book in Marathi, in 1888. It was published on 1 August 1889. He stated in his book that "It is absolutely wrong to say that the caste system and untouchability are created by the God." He said that 'caste' was an instrument to keep certain castes perpetually lower and poor and others higher and well-off. He rightly observed that, "We tolerated injustice, hence the Hindus imposed injustice". Hence Depressed Classes should not tolerate injustice.

In order to organize the depressed and oppressed masses under one banner and to make them aware of their human rights, he established a social organization named Anarya Dosh Parihar Mandali in the year 1890 at Dapoli. When the British Government decided to abandon recruitment of the untouchables in the army, he prepared a petition in Marathi, requesting the British authorities to continue to recruit the Parwaris (Mahar), Mochi or Chamar and Mang in the British Army. However, the petition was neither translated in English

---

141. Source of Information:
Gangadhar Pantawane,
Vadatanche Vanshaj, Kolhapur. 1982. and other sources.

nor was it presented to the British Government. Later, Gopalbaba Walangkar and Subedar Ramji prepared a draft to be submitted to the British authorities requesting them to continue the recruitment of the untouchables in the army and after seeking expert advice from Justice M.G. Ranade, they made certain amendments in the petition and submitted the same to the British authorities in March 1895. However, the British authorities did not give positive response to their petition.

In the year 1895 he was respectfully nominated as a member of the Local Board, Mahad. However, the other high caste members of the Board did not like an untouchable being appointed as a member.

He, being a true follower of Mahatma Phule, adhered to the principles of Satya Shodhak Samaj. However, after the demise of Mahatma Phule, the then members of the Satya Shodhak Samaj changed their egalitarian attitude. They did not allow the members of the untouchable castes to attend the meeting of the Samaj arranged at Novelty theatre, Bhavani Peth, Pune, on 15 September 1895. Gopalbaba Walangkar did not go to attend it, but felt that the attitude of the caste Hindus was wrong.

In those days the Indian National Congress was inclined more towards political reforms than to social reforms. Gopalbaba Walangkar stated in that respect, in 1897 that "unless social reforms were brought about, political reforms cannot be demanded".

He was a great writer and active reformer. Apart from *Vital Vidhawansan* he wrote *Hindu Dharma Darpan* in 1894. He composed many *Abhangas* or poems.

He sincerely served to bring unity among all the subcastes of the untouchables and worked for all of them. He thought that military service would be beneficial for them. He thought that they could bring their salvation through education.

After retirement he settled at Ravandhal in Dapoli. Shri Walangkar had a daughter named Yamunabai and a son Shantaram. He died in the year 1900.

YADAV, SHYAMLAL[142] (1894-1959)

Raisaheb Shyamlal Yadav was born on 12 February 1894 at Allahabad in Uttar Pradesh. His father, Shri Sukkhaji Yadav, was a poor washerman. (SC). Shyamlalji was admitted in the primary school at the age of six. He could complete his education up to middle school only. He had to discontinue the education due to the death of his father. Thereafter, he started a laundry to earn his livelihood.

After having observed and experienced the ugly and exploitative untouchability he resolved to work for its abolition. At the age of 20 he started his social mission of organizing the untouchables and teaching them to abandon all the caste customs and sub-casteism. He was elected Secretary of Dhobi Samaj, Allahabad. In the year 1921, he convened an All India Dhobi Conference at Prayag. It became very successful.

He started taking an active part in politics since 1924 under the leadership of Swami Achhutanandji. Shri Shyamlalji Yadav became a very active leader of Adi-Hindu movement. He dedicated for the spread of Adi-Hindu movement in almost every district of Uttar Pradesh. In 1927 he organized the All India Adi-Hindu Depressed Classes Conference at Myohal, Allahabad district. The Conference was attended by the Adi-Hindu leaders from different parts of the country. Babu Baldev Prasad Jaiswar and Rai Saheb Nanakchand Dhusia helped him a lot in organizing the conference. They were his companions in all his sociopolitical activities.

Shri Shyamlalji appeared before almost all the commissions appointed by the British Government and gave his evidence on behalf of the untouchables. Taking into account his helping nature, missionary zeal and cooperation with the government, the British Government honoured him with the prestigious title of Rai Saheb.

---

142. Source of Information:
Son of the leader Shri Choudhary Chunnilal, Ex-Member UP PSC, Advocate, 5 B/1, Bellogaon, Allahabad (UP) dated 1.8.1991.

In the elections held in 1937 he contested for UP Legislative Assembly from Allahabad constituency. He was, however, defeated in the election by one Shri Hari Jaiswar, who was a servant of Pandit Nehru. People in the name of Pandit Nehru voted for Shri Jaiswar. They did not take into account the missionary contribution of Rai Saheb Choudhary Shyamlalji.

Rai Saheb Choudhary Shyamlalji joined the Scheduled Castes Federation under the leadership of Dr Babasaheb Ambedkar. He was a member in the executive body of the All India Scheduled Castes Federation constituted under Rao Bahadur N. Shivaraj of Madras.

Rai Saheb Choudhary Shyamlalji again contested the election for the UP Legislative Assembly from Allahabad (R) constituency on the ticket of SCF, but in vain.

He was, however, elected in the elections held in 1952 for the UP Legislative Assembly.

He advised his brethren to educate and organize. It was because of his inspiration that many people were well educated and could achieve important posts in the administration.

He was a good singer. He used to sing *Birah, Kajari* and *Lavari Ragas.* He participated in many singing competitions and won prizes and praises.

He had two wives and two sons and one daughter.

He expired on 5 June 1959 at Allahabad at the age of 65.

YADAVENDU, RAMNARAYAN[143] (1909-1951)

Shri Ramnarayan Yadavendu was born in a Jatav family in 1909 at Agra in Uttar Pradesh. His father Shri Dalchand Yadavendu was engaged in construction work. Shri Ramnarayan Yadavendu completed his B.A. and LL.B. from Agra University. Later, he started his legal practice.

---

143 Source of Information:
Interview with the wife of leader, Smt Savita Devi Yadavendu 30/174, Kidwal Park, "Narendra Bhavan", Rajamandi, Agra, UP, on 9-6-1991.

He accepted the Arya Samaj and strictly observed all the rules and rites of Arya Samaj. He inherited the tradition of social service from his grandfather, who had established a school for Depressed Classes students at Agra. Shri Ramnarayan Yadavendu tried to root out bad habits of the people, like meat-eating, drinking, child marriage, etc.

He was a close associate of Dr Manikchand Jatav Veer. They invited Dr Babasaheb Ambedkar to address a conference of the Scheduled Castes at Agra. For some time Shri Yadavendu worked as editor of *Vishwamitra,* a monthly started by one Seth Moolchand from Calcutta. Shri Ramnarayan Yadavendu and Nathilal Shastry helped Dr Manikchand in the formation of Jatav Veer Institute in 1937- 38.

He was very close to Dr Babasaheb Ambedkar, the then Labour Member and Law Minister of India, because of whom he was appointed first as 'Public Officer' in 1945 and second as Resettlement Officer after the partition of India.

Shri Yadavendu was a prolific writer. He wrote a number of books in Hindi. They were *Bharatiya Sanskriti Aur Nagarik Jeevan; Bharatiya Shasan Aur Nagarik Jeevan; Bharatiya Neeti Vidnyan; Gramya Swarajya; Manav Jeevan (1950); Vishwa Dnyan Bharati (1950); Rashtra Sangh Aur Vishwa Shanti: Bharat Ka Dalit Samaj; Yadu Vansh ka Ithias; and Antarrashtriya Dnyan Kosh.*

He married Savita Devi in 1935. She served as a teacher till her retirement. They got three sons and a daughter.

Shri Yadavendu breathed his last on 26 September 1951 at the age of 42.

CONCLUSION

During the period under study several Dalit leaders tried to uplift their brethren. Here, efforts had been made to include the socio-political profiles of as many notable Dalit leaders as possible. However, it was not possible to include some of the notable leaders in the list due to want of adequate information about them.

Table 6.1: Gives the State-wise and Period-wise Number of Dalit Leaders Included in the Study

SI. No	States	Number of Leaders						Total
		I		II		III		
		1857–1890		1891–1918		1919–1956		
		Male	Female	Male	Female	Male	Female	
1.	Andhra Pradesh			1		8		9
	Telangana			2		6	3	11
2.	Assam					2		2
3.	Bihar			1		5		6
4.	Jammu-Kashmir					1		1
5.	Karnataka			1		6		7
6.	Kerala	1		5		3	1	10
7.	Madhya Pradesh			2		1		3
	Chattisgarh	1					1	2
8.	Maharashtra	2		5		39	4	50
	Gujarat					6		6
9.	Orissa					2		2
10.	Punjab			2		5		7
	Himachal Pradesh					2		2
11.	Rajasthan	1		1		4		6
12.	Tamil Nadu	1		8		9	2	20
12.	Uttar Pradesh	2		5		12		19
	Uttrakhand					1		1
14.	West Bengal	1		1		5		7
15.	Delhi					3		3
		9		34		120	11	174

The history of Dalit liberation movement could be divided into three phases. The first phase which roughly begins from 1857, ends with the death of Mahatma Phule in 1890. The second phase begins from 1891 and comes to an end in 1918. The third and final phase begins from 1919 coinciding the inquiry by the Southborough Committee and ends in 1956 with the mass conversion to Buddhism (Tables 6.1 and 6.2).

Table 6.2 : Gives the State-wise and Caste-wise Number of Dalit Leaders Included in the Study

Sl. No.	States	Principal Leaders	Total
1.	Andhra Pradesh	Adi-An 5, ML 2, Pan 1, UN 1	9
	Telangana	ML 10, CR 1	11
2.	Assam	UN 2	2
3.	Bihar	RJK 1, MEH 1, PAS 2, CR 2	6
4.	Jammu-Kashmir	CR 1	1
5.	Karnataka	Adi–K3, Budh 2, MRI Arya 1	7
6.	Kerala	PUL 6, Pariah 2, UN 1, Chvt 1	10
7.	Madhya Pradesh	MR 1, Wal 1, Mochi 1	3
	Chattisgarh	SAT 2	2
8.	Maharashtra	MR 40, CR 6, Mang 4	50
	Gujarat	UNK 2, CR 1, Mahy 1, UN 2	6
9.	Orissa	UN 2	2
10.	Punjab	ADD 4, CR 1, MZ B1, Ary 1	7
	Himachal Pradesh	Bal 1, UN 1	2
11.	Rajasthan	Meg 1, MEH 1, Bair 1, Bhangi 1 Arya 2	6
12.	Tamil Nadu	ADDR 9, Budh 3, Pariah 2, UN 6	20
13.	Uttar Pradesh	NSD 1, BAL 1, Jatav 9, DHB 1, CR 2	19
		KU 1, Adi-Hindu 2, Arya 1, UN 1	
	Uttrakhand	Shilp 1	1
14.	West Bengal	NMS 6, RJB 1	7
15.	Delhi	Jatav 3	3
			174

Note: ML = Mala, AA = Adi-Adhva, PAN = Panchama, UN = Unknown, CR = Chambar or Chamar, MO = Mochi, ADK = Adi- Karnataka, MR = Mahar, PUL = Pulaya, PAR = Pariah, SAT = Satnami, BAL = Balmiki, RJK = Rajak, MG = Mang, MAH = Mahyavanshi, VAN = Vankar, MEG = Megh or Meghwal, MEHT = Mehtar, BRWA = Bairawa, SWP = Sweeper, NSD = Nishad, SON = Sonkar, KU = Kureel, DHB = Dhobi, NMS = Namasudra, RJB = Rajbanshi, Shilp = Shilpkar.

Of all the 174 leaders included in the present study, a few of them were national level leaders, some of them were state level leaders and a majority of them were local level leaders.

Thus, the Dalit liberation movement was led by several leaders belonging to almost all the regions and almost all the major castes or sub-castes among the untouchables. The number of Dalit leaders in Maharashtra is somewhat more than other states. It indicates how the movement was widespread and strong in Maharashtra. This could be attributed to several factors including the military history of Mahars and their success in the abolition of Peshwa rule in 1818, the social reforms movement run by Mahatma Phule and his Satya Shodhak Samaj, the spread of new education, and industrialization especially in Bombay and Nagpur and the dynamic and deep-rooted Ambedkarite movement. The movement was quite strong in Tamil Nadu, Uttar Pradesh and Andhra Pradesh. The movement in erstwhile Bengal was popular, but it became weak after the partition in 1947. In Kerala also the movement was quite deep-rooted. It seems that wherever the movement was self dependent and change oriented, it gathered strength.

7

Dalit Movement in Various States

Untouchability was practised, more or less, throughout the country. Therefore, the movement to abolish it came into existence in almost all parts of the country. However, neither was it started at a time, nor was it equally strong throughout the country. Its growth, intensity and effectiveness depended on the quality of the leadership and the surrounding socio-political situation.

Though the Dalit liberation movement was steadily gathering momentum from 1857 onwards, it was firstly reflected in the Indian Legislative Council when Shri M.B. Dadabhoy moved a resolution for the abolition of untouchability, on 16 March 1916. However, it was not passed due to the apathetic attitude of the Congress towards social reforms.

Later on, the Congress which intended to capture power under the Montague-Chelmsford Reforms (August 1917) decided to win over the Depressed Classes. However, the two Depressed Classes conferences held in November 1917 under the presidentship of Sir Narayan Chandavarkar, Chairman of the Depressed Classes Mission, and Bapuji Namdeo Bagade, a non-Brahmin leader, respectively exercised great influence on the Congress. Therefore, the Congress in its annual session held-under the presidentship of Mrs Annie Besant at Calcutta passed a resolution against untouchability, on 26 December 1917.[1]

---

1. Dr B.R. Ambedkar *What Congress and Gandhi have done to the Untouchables*, pp. 1-18. 1990 Edition.

After the implementation of the Montague-Chelmsford Reforms, Shri M.C. Rajah, an untouchable leader from Madras was nominated as a member of the Indian Legislative Assembly in 1927. After the conclusion of Poona Pact in 1932, the Dalit Movement gained momentum. The Depressed Classes were recognized at the first as a separate significant entity in Indian politics. Dr Babasaheb Ambedkar and Mahatma Gandhi, both the top leaders of the two opposite camps mustered their strength to intensify their efforts in ameliorating the socio-political condition of the Dalits. On 24 March 1933 Shri Ranga Iyer introduced the Temple Entry Bill in the Indian Legislative Council, but due to the apathetic attitude of the Congress, it was not passed.

In 1942 Dr Babasaheb Ambedkar was nominated as Labour Member in the Viceroy's Executive Council. It was because of his efforts in 1943 that the Scheduled Castes got 8.33 per cent reservations in the government services. In 1946 the percentage of reserved seats was raised to 12 per cent and in the 1947 it was raised to 16⅔ per cent in respect of the posts to be filled otherwise than by open competition. Moreover, the scheme of post-matric scholarships was also sanctioned. It proved to be a sort of boon to the Scheduled Castes.

The Constituent Assembly which came into existence on 9 December 1946, constituted a Drafting Committee on 29 August 1947 under the chairmanship of Dr Babasaheb Ambedkar. who was already included in the Cabinet of Pandit Nehru on 3 August 1947 as Law Minister.

On 29 April 1947 the Constituent Assembly resolved to abolish untouchability tooth and nail. Articles 11 of the Draft of the Constitution was passed on 29 November 1948 and it formed Article 17 of the Constitution which came into implementation on 26 January 1950. The Parliament of India empowered under Article 35(a)(ii) to pass a law prescribing punishment for the "offence" of untouchability under Article 17 of the Constitution, passed The Protection of Civil Rights (PCR) Act, 1955. It has been in implementation since 1 June 1955.

With the abolition of untouchability, all the avenues of development were thrown open to the Depressed Classes. Certain measures under Article 15 (4), 16 (4) and 46 of the Constitution were taken to improve the educational and economic level of the Dalits. In order to ensure political participation of the Dalits, the provision for reservation in the Central and State Legislatures was made under Articles 330 and 332 of the Constitution. Thus the Constitution envisages justice —social, economic and political—to all the people including the Dalits.

Now, it is proposed to have a bird's eye view over the profile of the movement in various states.

ANDHRA PRADESH (ANDHRA AND TELANGANA)

It was formed on 1 November 1956, consisting of two parts, the Andhra region which was carved out from the erstwhile Madras State in 1953 itself, and the Telangana region that is the Telugu speaking part of erstwhile Hyderabad State which was added to the Andhra region under the State's Reorganization Act, 1956.

The Christian missionaries were active in Andhra region as early as 1877. The number of Christian converts during 1891 to 1921 rose from 172,319 to 431,324. In the Telangana region during 1896 to 1920 the number of Christian converts from the untouchables rose from 3,991 to 37.000.[2] Naturally, the Hindus with a view to protecting their religion started working for the amelioration and assimilation of the Depressed Classes into their fold.

Among the caste-Hindu social reformers in Andhra region, Shri Kandukuri Veeresalingam Pantulu (1848 -1919) was the first and foremost social reformer. He started a school for the Panchama children with the aid of a liberal financial grant of

2. Dr Sarojini Regani "Social Reformers of Andhra Pradesh in the Cause of Harijans upliftment" Andhra Pradesh Harijan Conference Souvenir, Hyderabad, p. 140. 1976.

₹ 70,000 from the Maharaja of Pithapuram. The Prarthana Samaj was established at Rajahmundry in 1878 by Veeresalingam. Another branch of the Samaj was opened at Kakinada in 1888. It was changed into Brahmo Samaj in 1910. It undertook social reforms activities in Andhra region.

The Maharaja of Pithapuram, Shri Rao Venkata Mahipate Surya Bahadur (1885-1965) established two hostels for the boys and girls of the Depressed Classes at Pithapuram. He established four primary schools for the children of the Depressed Classes.

The social reformers like Chilakamarti Lakshmi Narasimhan (1867-1945), R.Venkatratnam Naidu (1862-1939), Shri Nallapati Hanumanth Rao, Shri Vellanki Krishna Murthi and many others contributed their might for the uplift of the Depressed Classes.[3]

In the Telangana region, the Arya Samaj played a notable part in preventing conversion of the untouchables to Christianity and Islam. The notable social reformers in the region were Rai Balmukund, Baji Krishna Rao, Justice Keshav Rao and Vaman Rao Naik. The Brahmo Samaj was also active at Hyderabad.

The first conference of the Depressed Classes was held at Vijayawada in November 1917 under the presidentship of Shri Bhagya Reddy Varma, the pioneer of Dalit movement in Andhra Pradesh. They resolved to call themselves as Adi-Hindus. Thereafter, several conferences were held, the second at Gudivada in 1922, the third at Eluru in 1922, the fourth at Guntur in 1924, and the last (13th) conference in this series was held in 1938.

The Depressed Classes conferences were also held in the Telangana region. The first was held in 1921, second in 1922, third in 1923, fourth in 1924, and the last in this series in 1931, all at Hyderabad.

In all these conferences the resolutions *inter alia,* were unanimously passed urging the concerned government to

---

3. M.B. Goutam *"The Untouchables Movement In Andhra Pradesh"*. APSH Conference Souvenir pp. 65-76. 1976.

reserve adequate seats in the decision-making bodies and to throw open the schools for the Depressed Classes.[4]

Thereafter, the Harijan Sevak Sangh under the leadership of Mahatma Gandhi and the Scheduled Caste organizations under the leadership of Dr Babasaheb Ambedkar spread their network, as in other states, in Andhra Pradesh also.

In 1923, the then Government of Madras opened a separate department namely the Labour Department to look after the welfare of the untouchables, including the educational development.

In the Telangana region which was being ruled by the Nizam, Shri B.S. Venkatrao, the accredited leader of the Depressed Classes was nominated as Minister of Education in 1946. Thereafter, the Depressed Classes members of the Hyderabad Legislature under the leadership of Hon'ble B.S. Venkatrao tried their best to convince the Nizam government to constitute one crore trust fund for the welfare of the Depressed Classes in the State. The said fund was utilized for various welfare activities including the educational betterment of the Dalits.[5]

In the Andhra region Dalit leaders like Shri Gurram Josheva (Guntur), Gottipati Brahmayya (Masulipattanam), Kusum Dharmanna (Rajahmundry), Vemula Kurmayya (Vijayawada), B.S. Murthy (East Godavari), Sardar Nagappa (Kurnool), Geddala Brahmaiah (East Godavari), Konada Suryaprakashrao (Vijayawada), V.C. Keshav Rao (Krishna), Damodaram Sanjivayya (Kurnool), Ravuri Ekambaram (Vijayawada), Nandanar Harishchandra (West Godavari), Bojja Appalswamy (Amalapuram), Mangalgiri Nanadas (Nellore), B.V. Ramanayya (East Godavari) and many others worked for the uplift of their brethren.

---

4. *Ibid.* pp. 65-76.

5. P.R. Venkataswamy, *Our struggle for emancipation.* Vol. II. p. 478-79 and 546-47. No. 40 Ghasmandi Rd. Secunderabad, 1955.

In the Telangana region, Dalit leaders like Shri M.L. Audiah (Secunderabad), Arigay Ramaswamy (Hyderabad), M.V. Bhagya Reddy Varma (Hyderabad), Rao Saheb B.S. Venkatrao (Hyderabad), Eswari Malliah (Golkonda), Puli Ramaswamy (Secunderabad), Bollepali Premdas (Hyderabad), B. Shyamsundar (Hyderabad), Butti Rajaram (Karimnagar), M.B. Goutam (Hyderabad), Smt B. Sumitra Devi (Hyderabad), K.R. Veeraswamy (Secunderabad), Smt Rajamani Devi (Secunderabad), Smt J. Ishwaribai (Secunderabad), G. Venkataswamy (Hyderabad), B.Machandar Rao (Secunderabad), Ambadas Rao (Medak), M.R. Krishna (Hyderabad), D. Rajaiah (Hyderabad), Vemula Yadgiri Rao (Hyderabad), Edla Gopiah (Nalgonda), Smt Leelavathi Natham (Hyderabad), Acharya Somdeva Shastri (Secunderabad), S.R. Lakshmaiah (Secunderabad), Suthrapu Babiah (Hyderabad), S. Palanivelu (Hyderabad), Mudigonda Laxmiah (Hyderabad), K. Antiah (Medak), J.H. Subbiah (Secunderabad), Sunkum Achalu (Nalgonda), Gangaram (Adilabad), Pandit Prem Kumar (Secunderabad), J.H. Krishna Murthy (Secunderabad), and many others had endeavoured for the uplift of the Dalits.

It was because of the efforts of the leaders of the Dalit liberation movement, the process of the eradication of untouchability had started in the State. The erstwhile Madras State passed the Social Disabilities Removal Act in 1938 and the Madras Temple Entry Act in 1948. These Acts were in application in Andhra region..

The erstwhile Hyderabad State, after the Police Action, passed The Hyderabad Harijan Temple Entry Regulation in 1358 F, and 'The Hyderabad Harijan (Removal of Social Disabilities) Regulation in 1358 F. These Acts and Regulations were in implementation in Telangana region.

Shri M.V. Bhagya Reddy Varma (1888-1939) was the pioneering leader of the Dalit movement in entire Andhra Pradesh. He led the Adi-Hindu movement, through which he could bring about a new awakening among the Dalits in Telangana as well as Andhra region. He was one of the important leaders of the Adi-Hindu movement at the national level.

ASSAM

It was made a separate province of British India under a Chief Commissioner in 1874. In 1921, it became a full-fledged province. In 1947, the Muslim majority part of Assam was ceded to Pakistan (now Bangladesh).

At first. Rev. Brown (1807-1886) and Brouson (1812- 1883) of the American Baptist Mission took up the cause of the suffering people. Shri Gunabhiram Barua started his social reforms movement, especially in respect of widow remarriages. He wrote a book titled *Ram Navami* on the problem of widows, in 1857. The Ramkrishna Mission also started social reforms in Assam. The Maharaja of Manipur Shri Churachand Singh encouraged the young non-tribal Manipuris to get higher education in British India.

Due to conspicuous presence of the tribal population, there was no severe form of untouchability in Assam. Therefore, the Dalit movement was not so strong. The first All Assam Depressed Classes Conference which was held in Shillong on 6 January 1929 was presided over by Senapati Sonadhar Das. The conference raised the demand for separate electorate for the Depressed Classes.[6]

The leaders like Beli Ram Das, Ramnath Das, G. Namasudra and Prof Nibaran Chandra Laskar (Cachar district) were the important leaders who worked for the uplift of their brethren. The Dalit movement in Assam was more under the influence of Congress party than that of the Scheduled Castes Federation.

BIHAR AND JHARKHAND

Previously Bihar formed a part of Bengal. On 1 April 1912 Bihar, Chotanagpur and Orissa were separated from Bengal and

---

6. Bhakta Das. A *Glimpse of Scheduled Castes in Assam,* p. 26, 1986.

made a separate province. Later on 1 April 1936 Orissa was constituted as a separate state. Presently, Bihar consists of North Bihar, Santhal Pargana and Chotanagpur.

The Christian missionaries were the pioneers of the new awakening. The German missionaries started schools in Bihar as early as in 1840. Bishop Hartman established a Church on 23 September 1849 at Bankimpore. In 1854, St.Michael's School for boys was established at Kurjit near Patna. In 1872 a girls school was opened at Bettiah.

The first branch of Brahmo Samaj was opened at Bhagalpur in 1863. In 1867 two branches, one each at Patna and Monghyr were opened. Shri Nibaran Chandra Mukherjee, Prakash Chandra Roy and Mrs Roy were responsible for the spread of Brahmo Samaj in Bihar. The Arya Samaj also started its activities in Bihar from 1878.

The Kayasthas started their organization in 1877. The Kshatriya Mahasabha was founded in 1891. The Bhumihar Brahmin Mahasabha came into existence in 1896. The Ahirs also formed their organization in 1912.[7]

The Depressed Classes in Bihar were the worst sufferers of untouchability and casteism. Leaders among the Dalits like Choudhary Jaglal (Saran), Bhagat Har Govind, Babu Jagjivan Ram (Bhojpur), Bhola Paswan Shastri (Pumea), Bhola Raut (Champaran), Nayantara Das (Monghyr), Chandrika Ram (Saran), Somar Ram (Ranchi), Mushahar Kirai and many others strove for the uplift of their brethren. In Bihar the Dalit liberation movement was not so strong and it was obviously under the influence and control of the Congress.

The Government of Bihar passed Bihar Harijan (Removal of Civil Disabilities) Act, 1946, which was in implementation till the implementation of the PCR Act 1955.

---

7. Jamuna Nag. *Social Reform Movements in Nineteenth Century* India, 1988.

JAMMU AND KASHMIR

The erstwhile princely State of Jammu and Kashmir became an integral part of India when the Maharaja signed the Instrument of Accession on 26 October 1947.

The movement for the liberation of Dalits was initiated by Babu Milkhi Ram (1926-1989) from Jammu in Jammu and Kashmir. He was a staunch Ambedkarite and active social and political leader of the community. Shri Shivram Motan and Omprakash Bhagat (Jammu) also worked for the uplift of the Dalits.

KARNATAKA

Previously, it was known as Mysore State, which came into existence in 1956. It consisted of Kannada speaking part of erstwhile Hyderabad State, the Kannada speaking part of Bombay State, and Mysore State. The State was renamed as Karnataka State in 1973.

The Christian missionaries were the pioneers in the social reforms in the State. The London Mission established the first Kannada School for girls in 1840. The Maharaja Chamraja Wodeyar of the erstwhile Mysore State was quite liberal in social reforms. He started a girls school at Mysore. During 1869-70 there were 33 schools where 2,071 girls were studying. The Maharaja started a free boarding for the untouchable students at Mysore, where nearly 50 students were admitted. The Maharaja had passed the order to admit the untouchable students in the schools of the State.[8]

The Secretary of Brahmo Samaj at Mangalore, Shri K. Ranga Rao started a school for the Depressed Classes in 1897.[9] Later, the school was taken over by the Depressed Classes Mission in the year 1906. During the 1920s an organization named Civil and Social Progressive Association was in vogue. It was headed by

---

8. V.R. Shinde, *Bharatiya Asprushatecha Prashna* (Marathi), p.240. 1976.

9. *Ibid.* p. 235.

Sir Kanti Rao Narsinhraj Wodeyar, the brother of the Maharaja himself.[10]

In Karnataka State, the Dalit movement was led by Dalit leaders like Rao Saheb T.J. Papanna (Belgaum), Yellappa Awappa Hongal (Dharwad), D.Y. Sambrani and M.D. Ghodke (Hubli), M.Y. Murugesam (Marikuppam), R.L. Umpathi (KGF), G. Appaduraiyar (KGF), M. Madaiah (Mandiya), M. Chikkalingaiah (Mandiya), B.H. Varale (Nipani, Belgaon), G.S. Ramkrishnaiah (Mandiya), Revappa Somappa Kale (Bijapur), Gabbur Mallappa Shettappa (Hubli), Ramchandra Veerappa (Bidar), M. Jayaseelan (Bangalore), S.M. Siddayya (Mysore), Datta Appa Katti (Belgaum), Shankar Deo Vedalankar (Bidar), P.M. Swamidorai (KGF), B. Shankaranand (Belgaum), C.M. Arumugham (KGF), B. Basavalingappa and many others.

The Removal of Civil Disabilities Act, 1943 and The Mysore Temple Entry Authorization Act, 1948 were in implementation before the PCR Act, 1955.

The Dalit liberation movement in Karnataka was more under the influence of Dr Babasaheb Ambedkar than that of Mahatma Gandhi. The conversion to Buddhism took place at Kolar Gold Field even before the historic mass conversion to Buddhism at Nagpur, in 1956. Pandit Iyodhi Dass was the pioneering leader in converting the Depressed Classes to Buddhism. Marikuppam, Bangalore and Hubli were centres of South Indian Buddhist Association, founded by Pandit Iyodhi Dass at Madras.

KERALA

Kerala State which was formed under the States Reorganization Act (SRA), 1956, comprised Travancore, Cochin and Malabar district of old Madras State.

In Kerala State the socio-economic condition of the Dalits was very precarious. However, it has a long history of social reforms. The Christian missionaries were the 'fountain-head' of the cultural renaissance in Kerala. The Basel Mission had the

---

10. *Ibid.* p. 240.

credit of spreading education in Malabar. Special schools were opened for the education of Panchamas from 1893. According to the 1901 census, there were 22 primary schools for the Panchamas with 908 pupils in Malabar.

The first and foremost social reformer in Kerala from among the backward classes was Shri Narayana Guru (1856-1928). He belonged to a numerous backward Ezhava community. They were not supposed to enter within a distance of 12 feet from the *savarnas,* lest they were to cause pollution to them. Therefore, he resolved to strive for the uplift of the Depressed Classes, including the Ezhavas. For undertaking socio-religious reforms, he founded an organization, named Sree Narayana Dharma Paripalana Yogam (SNDP) in 1903.[11] Dr Palpu (1863-1950) was its first Secretary and after him Kumaran Asan (1873-1924) became its second Secretary. Both of them were devoted leaders of the SNDP.

In Kerala, the Ezhavas and the castes lower than them were denied entry into Hindu temples. They were even forbidden to walk along the public roads adjoining the temples. Hence, Sree Narayana Guru opened separate temples for his brethren. He was opposed to drinks and sacrifices of animals in the name of worship.

The Ezhavas who were quite numerous but divided into Thiyyas, Chovans, Thandans, etc, were united under the banner of SNDP Yogam. Sree Narayana Guru gave utmost importance to education as well as economic development of the community.

Sree Narayana Guru organized a conference of religions at which Hindu, Muslim, Buddhist and Parsi thinkers had participated. The object of the conference was "to know and to make known, not to argue and to vanquish". It was held at the Adwaita Ashram at Alwaye in 1924.[12]

---

11. Murkot Kunhappa, *Sree Narayana Guru,* pp. 51-52. (National Book Trust. India, New Delhi. 1982).

12. *Ibid.* p. 43.

Sree Narayana Guru's contribution to the philosophical literature is of immense importance. He wrote *Darsan mala* (the garland of Darsana); *Self-knowledge; Atmopadesa Satkam;* (Hundred verses) and *Daiva Dasakam* (prayer to God). He preached Adwait philosophy through his literature.

In the words of T.K. Ravindran, "Sree Narayana Guru believed that caste was the main obstacle in the way of social economic and political emancipation of the country. He wanted the rule of Dharma and not the law of varna to guide the lives of the people.[13] The temples which he established for his brethren were the centres of his philosophy. It was because of his philosophy and the movement that the downtrodden masses, especially the Ezhavas were enlightened and elevated to the level of the so-called upper castes.

Shri Changaram Kumarath Krishnan (1867-1938) was associated with the SNDP Yogam. He protested against Hinduism by embracing and preaching Buddhism in Kerala. He published a Malayalam journal *Mitavadi* from 1913 to 1938.

Dr Palpu, Kumaran Asan, Ayyappan Sahodaran, Bahuleyan, T.K. Madhavan (1886-1930), R. Sugathan (1902-1970), I.K. Kumaran, G. Kesavan, Kelappan, Natarajan, Sadhu Shivprasad, N. Kumaran and Swami Anand Thirth had endeavoured for the uplift of the untouchables. Swami Anand Thirth started a school named *Narayana Vidyalaya* for the untouchable students at Payyanur in 1932. He led the temple entry movement at several temples in Kerala.[14]

From among the untouchables, several leaders came forward to emancipate their brethren from untouchability and caste-based exploitation. They included Krishnati Asan (Ernakulam). T.T. Keshavan Shastri (Pattanamtitha), R. Velayudhan

---

13. T.K. Ravindran, *Vaikom Satyagraha and Gandhi,* pp. 12, (Trichur, 1975)..

14. A.M. Ayrookuzhiel, Abraham *Swami Anand Thirth,* pp. 92-108.

(Kottayam), K.P. Kuruppan (Ernakulam), Soloman Markose and P.K. Chatan Master (Trichur).

In the history of social reforms in Kerala, the Vaikom Satyagraha was an important milestone. The SNDP Yogam in its annual meeting held on 13 May 1920 passed a resolution saying that, "All Public temples belonging to the Government should be open to all Hindus regardless of Caste."[15] In the same meeting T.K. Madhavan moved the resolution that if the Hindu temples are not thrown open to all the Hindus regardless of their caste, they would embrace Christianity *en masse.*[16] Thereafter, the All India Congress Committee in its conference held at Kakinada in 1923, recognized the right of lower caste Hindus to enter the Hindu temples. As a result, the Kerala Pradesh Congress Committee met at Ernakulam on 20 January 1924, formed a special committee for the eradication of untouchability under the chairmanship of Shri Kelappan. This committee organized the historic Vaikom Satyagraha which demanded for the lower castes, the right to use public roads adjoining the temple. The satyagraha was launched under the leadership of Shri Kelappan, T.K. Madhavan, T.R. Krishnaswamy, Swami Anand Tirth, K.P. Kesava Menon and others. Even Thanthai Periyar E.V. Ramasami of Justice Party (Madras) participated in the satyagraha at Vaikom. The satyagraha was launched in 1932 for the right to enter the temple of Krishna at Guruvayur in Ponnani Malabar. Shri Kelappan commenced his fast on 20 September 1932, but in vain.

In view of the growing mass support to the temple entry satyagrahas and the threat given by the SNDP Yogam to convert to Christianity, the Maharaja of Travancore Sir Bala Rama Varma declared on 12 November 1936 that subject to certain rules and conditions, as may be laid down, there shall be no restriction on any Hindu entering and worshipping at the temples controlled by the government.

---

15. *Ibid.* p. 20.
16. *Ibid.* p. 20.

The Madras Government passed The Madras Removal of Civil Disabilities Act, 1938 which was in implementation in that region which was a part of Madras State. The Travancore Cochin Removal of Disabilities Act, 1125 ME, and the Travancore Cochin Temple Entry (Removal of Disabilities) Act, 1950 were in implementation in the rest of Kerala.

Of all the Dalit leaders in Kerala Shri Ayyan Kali (1863-1941) was the pioneering leader of the Dalit movement. The Dalit leaders in Kerala, who converted to Christianity, including Poykayil Yohannan were not satisfied with Christianity due to caste-based churches. The Ezhavas are no more treated as untouchables. The Dalit leaders protested against the Hindu social system, but they were not united. They were divided into several sects or organizations of their own.

MADHYA PRADESH (MADHYA PRADESH AND CHHATTISGARH)

Madhya Pradesh was formed on 1 November 1956, consisting of old Madhya Bharat, Bhopal, Vindhya Pradesh and Mahakosal and Chhattisgarh.

Madhya Pradesh had no significant history of social reforms, especially of the non-Dalits. However, the Maharaja of Indore Sir Sawai Tukoji Holkar was somewhat interested in eradication of untouchability.

There was Dalit movement in Mahakosal and Chhattisgarh. Guru Ghasi Das (1756-1850) was pioneer of the Dalit liberation movement. He founded the Satnami sect as a protest against inequality in Hinduism and tried to spread the principles of his new organization in the eastern part of the State. After his death his son Guru Balak Das led the movement. The disciples of the movement are found in Raipur, Bilaspur and Durg districts of Chhattisgarh region of Madhya Pradesh.

The other leaders of the movement in the State were Shri Gangaramji Dhuldhoye (Indore), Shankarrao Ramji Majade (Indore), Sajjan Singh Vishnar (Indore), Smt Minimata (Raipur), Parashramji Bhardwaj (Bilaspur), Bansilal Ramteke (Raipur),

N.L. Khobragade (Balaghat), R.L. Jangde (Raipur), Agnibhoj, Sitaram Sadhu (Khargaon), G.R. Jambhulkar (Chhindwara), Smt Sahodarabai Rai (Sagar), Nakul Didhi (Raipur) and others.

In Madhya Bharat region, The Central Provinces and Berar Scheduled Castes (Removal of Civil Disabilities) Act, 1947 and the Central Province and Berar Temple Entry Authorization Act, 1947 and in other parts the Madhya Pradesh Harijan Ayogata Nivaran Vidhan, 1949 were in implementation before the PCR Act, 1955 came into implementation.

MAHARASHTRA STATE (BOMBAY AND GUJARAT)

The Bombay State including Vidarbha region of erstwhile CP and Berar and Marathwada region of the erstwhile Hyderabad State and excluding the Kannada speaking region was formed on 1 November 1956. Gujarat remained a part of the Bombay State till 1960. The Vidarbha region ruled by Bhosale dynasty from Nagpur was taken over by the British East India Company in 1853 and made a separate province in 1861 with Nagpur as its capital. In 1956 it was attached to the Bombay State on a linguistic basis.

Maharashtra State especially the Bombay and Vidarbha region had a very long history of Dalit liberation movement. The Christian missionaries, could not evoke much more response in the State. The American mission sent the missionaries at Ahmadnagar in 1831. Dr John Wilson of the Church of Scotland founded Wilson College in Bombay. The Bombay Native Education Society was founded by Elphinston in 1822. The Bombay University was established in 1857.

The social reformers like Balshastri Jambhekar (1812-1846), Dadoba Pandurang (1814-1882), Vishnubuwa Brahmchari (1825-1871), Lokhit Vadi (1823-1892), Mahatma Phule (1827-1890), Gopal Ganesh Agarkar and Karmveer Bhaurao Patil (1887-1959), M.G. Ranade (1842-1901), G.K. Gokhale (1866-1915), V.R. Shinde (1873-1944), V.D. Savarkar (1883-1966) and many others endeavoured to awaken the people in the Bombay Presidency. Gadge Maharaj (1876-1956), Dr B.S. Moonje (1872-1948),

Dr Punjabrao Deshmukh and many others had tried to bring a new awakening in the society in Vidarbha region.

The Press also had contributed to a great extent in bringing about a new awareness in Bombay Presidency. The papers like *Darpan* (1831), *Dnyanodaya* (1842), *Kesari* (1881) and *Sudharak* (1888) were prominent in this respect.

The cotton mills at Bombay and Nagpur could attract many poor untouchables from the rural areas. The concentration of those people gave rise to strong organizations and awakening. The means of communications also proved to be very useful in bringing about exchange of thoughts and views.

The Maharaja of Kolhapur, Chhatrapati Shahu Maharaj was a great leader of the non-Brahmin movement and a great benefactor of the Depressed Classes.

The social reforms movement led by Mahatma Phule needs a special mention. Mahatma Phule wrote thought provoking books such as *Brahmanche Kasab* (Priest Craft exposed) 1869; *Gulamgiri (Slavery)* 1873; *Shetkaryancha Asud* (Cultivators Whip-cord) 1883; *Satsar* (The Essence of Truth) 1885; *Sarvajanik Satya Dharma Pustika,* 1891; *Akhandadi Kavyarachana; Trutiya Ratna* (a play).

Mahatma Phule was against all sorts of exploitation. He was a great sympathizer of the peasants and workers. He used to criticize Brahmanism and capitalism scathingly.

Mahatma Phule thought that the British Government could bring about at least some social reforms. He founded Satya Shodhak Samaj (1873) and preached Satya dharma to the people. He could unite and organize the truth loving people under one banner. He visualized an ideal state, named Balisthan wherein the workers and the peasants would be happy. The people of Maharashtra cannot forget his legacy of progressive thoughts and the social reforms.

Maharishi Vithal Ramji Shinde (1873-1944) was a great social reformer of Maharashtra. He founded 'Depressed Classes Mission' with its headquarters at Bombay in 1906. He tried to spread education among the Depressed Classes and tried to teach them new professions. The branches of the DC Mission worked in various parts of the country.

Maharashtra had a rich tradition of saints. Among all the modern saints Shri Gadge Baba (1876-1956) was prominent one. He tried to eradicate untouchability and superstitions prevalent in the society. He tried to remove illiteracy and ignorance from society.

The Brahmo Samaj and Arya Samaj were not deeply rooted in Maharashtra. The Prarthana Samaj worked as a branch of Brahmo Samaj in Maharashtra. There were only 136 persons who returned themselves as Brahmos in 1911. In the Bombay Presidency there were 578 Arya Samajis in 1911 and 1,512 in 1921. In Central Provinces and Berar there were 974 Arya Samajis in 1911. In Marathwada, the Arya Samaj became popular at certain places, but that too in the later period.

The untouchables, especially the Mahars in Maharashtra had a bright history of serving in the military of the British Government. By virtue of their military service, they could learn discipline, decent living and knowledge. After retirement they were disseminating the sense of self pride in the society.

Among the galaxy of Dalit leaders Lahujibuwa Salve (Pune), Subedar Ramji Maloji Sakpal (Ratnagiri) Sampatrao Ganpatrao Naik (Amravati), V.D. Makesar (Yeotmal), Ramchandra Domaji Wasnik (Nagpur), Sambhu Ansu Khandare (Akola), Gopinath Narsingrao Kamble Maharaj (Parbhani), Keshavrao Raoji Ingle (Amravati), Pandurang Nandram Bhatkar (Amravati), Kakasaheb Zabuji Shirsat (Akola), Revajibuwa Dagadu Dolas (Bombay), Fattuji Bapuji Shende (Nagpur), Balkrishna Janoji Deorukhkar (Pune), Smt Jaibai Choudhari (Nagpur), Sardar Amarsing Dhar (Bhandara), Narayan Sadoba Kajrolkar (Bombay), Sakharam Narayan Kajrolkar (Bombay), Balu Babaji Palavankar (Bombay), Swarupbuwa Atmaram Kamble (Satara), Shidu Laxman Savakhande (Sangli), Smt Ratibai Puranik (Wardha), G.T. Meshram (Nagpur), Kadaknath Hatkar (Nanded), Devaji Bhivaji Khobragade (Chandrapur), Tukaram

Ambadas Purohit (Wardha), Gangaram Krishnaji Bhatankar (Bombay), Baburao Mahadeo Waghmare (Pune), Pandit Revaram Kavade (Nagpur), D.K. Bhagat (Akola), T.C. Sakhare (Nagpur), Vishram, Gangadhar Sawadkar (Kolaba), Rambhau Somaji Mandavdhare (Amravati), Dadasaheb Malharrao Shirke (Kolhapur), M.G. Meshram (Amravati), Laxman Shravanji Bhatkar (Buldhana, Amravati), Laxman Krishnaji Ogale (Amravati), Shantaram Anaji Upsham Guruji (Bombay), Pralhad Tukadoji Kamble (Nagpur), L.N. Hardas (Nagpur), K.S. Sawant (Satara), R.R. Patil (Nagpur), V.J. Arak (Beed), P.L. Lalingkar (Dhulia), Dashrath Laxman Patil (Nagpur), G.R. Ghatge (Ratnagiri), Ganpatrao Krishnaji Shinde (Nasik), Shankarrao Khanderao Dighe (Kolhapur), Purushottam Martandrao Choure (Pune), Sitaram Gangaram Gangurde (Nasik), S.D. Manake (Nagpur), C.N. Mohite Guruji (Bombay), Dadasaheb Lingappa Londhe (Sangli), Sopanrao Dhanave (Beed), Bhausaheb More (Aurangabad), Shyamrao Jadhav (Aurangabad), Abaji Suburao Gawali (Kolhapur), Nasikrao Tirpude (Bhandara). K.B. More (Nasik), G.K. Mane (Satara), Sowlaram Tribhuvan (Aurangabad), Shahir Annabhau Sathe (Bombay), B.C. Kamble (Bombay), D.M. Khairkar (Nagpur), Namdeo Vatkar (Kolhapur), K.K. Sakat (Pune) Amrutrao Rankhambe (Nasik), B.K. Tembhurne (Yeotmal), Sambhaji Laxmanrao Jondhale (Nanded), K.B. Talwatkar (Bombay), Surajmal N. Choudhary (Parbhani), Ganeshacharya (Kolhapur), R.B. Chandorkar (Kolaba), Smt Sulochanabai Dongre (Amravati), Tanaji Ganpatrao Gaikwad (Kolaba), Dr Sanatkumar V. Ramteke (Nagpur), V.B. Godbole (Nagpur), M.I. Kurane (Kolhapur), M.D. Nerlikar (Parbhani), Pandurang P. Tajane (Amravati), K.V. Umare (Nagpur), Sawaleram Hanmantrao Gaikwad (Nagar), Deenbabdhu Shegaonkar (Akola), Shahir Wamandada Kardak (Nasik), N.D. Pagare (Aurangabad), Hariharrao Sonule (Nanded), Tukaram Gade (Parbhani), Tukaram Shivram Borkar (Nagpur), R.S. Nikalje (Satara), B.C. Babhale (Wardha), N.S. Kamble (Solapur), A.G. Pawar (Nasik), Baliram Borde (Buldhana), K.M. Jumade (Akola), and many others were active in the movement.

Dalit movement could gather momentum in Maharashtra. The movement for the recruitment of Mahars in the military became ultimately successful. Gopalbaba Walangkar, Shivaram Janba Kamble, Subedar Ramji Ambedkar and Dr Babasaheb Ambedkar led the said movement.

Dr Ambedkar's advocacy for political safeguards, including separate electorate for the Dalits at the Round Table Conference from 1930-32 and conclusion of the Poona Pact in 1932 gave a new impetus to the movement. His contribution as Chairman of the Drafting Committee of the Constitution of India was of immense importance. He gave the Constitution a new social order based on liberty, equality and fraternity. Eventually, he gave Buddhism to his brethren, a true religion based on rationalism and morality.

The movement under the leadership of Dr Babasaheb Ambedkar was undoubtedly spread almost throughout the country. In Maharashtra, especially it could reach to the grass-root level.

Before 1960, Gujarat formed a part of the Bombay State. In 1848 Kinloch Forbes (an Assistant Judge at Ahmedabad) founded the Vernacular Society at Ahmedabad, which started a fortnightly namely *Buddhiprakas* in 1850. In 1878 a Temperance Society was formed in Surat. Its Secretary was a Roman and his assistant was one Mahipatram Rupram. A branch of Prarthana Samaj was formed in Gujarat on 17 December 1871. The Arya Samaj opened its branch in Ahmedabad in 1876.

The Maharaja of Baroda, Sayajirao Gaikwad supported social reformation. The Maharaja himself sponsored the Infant Marriage Prevention Act of 1904 and the Civil Marriage Act of 1908. He favoured free and compulsory education in Amreli district in North Gujarat. He opened a separate department for the education of the untouchables in his State and started special schools for the untouchable children from 1883. The number of such schools were 7 in 1884 and 10 in 1891 [17]

---

17. V.R. Shinde *Bhartiya Asprushyancha Prashna* (Marathi), pp. 233-34.

From among the Dalits Dr Purushottam Govindji Solanki (Surat), Muldas Bhundardas Vaishya (Mehsana), V.T. Parmar (Kheda), Khemchandbhai S. Chavda (Mehsana), Lekhalal Vaghela (Ahmedabad), Mohanlal Dundarlal Ambedkarvadi (Ahmedabad), Shivrambhai Motilal Parmar (Mehsana), Sundarlal Muljibhai Patel (Baroda), Bhaijibhai Ukabhai Vaghela (Ahmedabad), Bhavanjibhai U.Chouhan (Ahmedabad), Somchandbhai Jasabhai Makwana (Ahmedabad), Balabhai V. Movadia (Mehsana), Vasantlal Tulsidas Chauhan (Mehsana), Hirajibhai K.Patel (Surat), G.T. Parmar (Amreli) and many others endeavoured for the uplift of their brethren in Gujarat.

The temple entry satyagraha at the Swami Narayan Temple, Ahmedabad led by Muldas B. Vaishya in 1948 was a notable event. The caste Hindus instituted a suit against Shri M.B. Vaishya which was finally settled by the Supreme Court in 1966 in favour of the Scheduled Castes right to enter the temple.

In the Bombay Presidency including Gujarat, The Bombay Harijan Removal of Social Disabilities Act, 1946 and The Bombay Harijan Temple Entry Act, 1947 were in implementation till the PCR Act, 1955. In other parts, the Saurashtra Harijan Removal of Social Disabilities Ordinance of 1949 was in force till the PCR Act, 1955.

ORISSA

The Orissa State was constituted into a separate State on 1 April 1936. Previously it was a part of Bihar. All the princely states in Orissa were merged with India by 1949 and became part of Orissa.

During 1880-90 branches of the Brahmo Samaj were opened at several places in Orissa. In this State, Oriya social reformers like Bairagi Charan Mishra and Govind Chandra Misra condemned the dowry system, supported inter-caste marriages and fought for abolition of untouchability.[18]

---

18. Jamuna Nag. *Social Reforms Movement in Nineteenth Century India,* p. 75.

Dalit leaders like Santanu Kumar Das (Jeypore), Kanhu Charan Jena (Balasore), Mohan Nayak (Berhampur), Baishnab Charan Mullick (Cuttuck), Chaitanya Sethi (Balasore) had worked for the uplift of their brethren.

The Orissa Civil Disabilities Act, 1946 and the Orissa Temple Entry Act, 1948 were in operation in Orissa State till the passage of the PCR Act, 1955.

PUNJAB (PUNJAB, HARYANA AND HIMACHAL PRADESH)

The Punjab was annexed to British India in 1848 after the Second Sikh war. In 1859, it became a Lieutenant Governors province. In 1947 the Punjab was partitioned into India and Pakistan. On 1 November 1956 the erstwhile States of Punjab, Patiala and the East Punjab States Union (PEPSU) were integrated. On 1 November 1966 under the Punjab Reorganization Act, the Hindi speaking part was formed into a separate state namely Haryana, and Shimla was merged with Himachal Pradesh.

The Punjab had a bright history of social reforms. The Christian missionaries were actively engaged in proselytization activities in Punjab. American missionaries started their activities at Jullundur in 1846, Ambala in 1848, Lahore in 1849 and Sialkot in 1855. In 1911 there were 163,994 Christians in Punjab. One Chet Ram (1835-1894) converted to Christianity in 1870 and started preaching the tenets of this religion in the society. His followers are known as Chet Ramis.

Some people were also attracted towards Islam. After the formation of Ahmadia sect in 1879 by a Sufi saint Mirza Ghulam Ahmed (1838-1908) in Gurdaspur district of the Punjab, several persons, especially the Dalits were attracted towards it.

The. Arya Samaj was founded in 1875 by Swami Dayanand Saraswati. The Arya Samaj believed that there is one God and he alone should be worshipped spiritually. The Samaj was opposed to idolatry. It accepted the superiority of Vedas. Hence, it preached 'back to Vedas'. However, it preached for social equality and a strong Hindu organization.

The Arya Samaj undertook *shuddhi* (purification) of the converts to other religions and tried to assimilate them with the Hindu fold. According to Choudhari Ram Bhaj Dutt, the President of All India Shuddhi Sabha, the total number of persons purified or raised socially during the year 1901-10 in the province of Punjab was about 60,000-70,000.[19]

In 1887 the Arya Samaj opened Dayanand Anglo-Vedic College at Lahore. It started Gurukul educational institutions at several places in the country.

The Arya Samaj was opposed to untouchability. Therefore, several untouchables were attracted towards it. The caste Hindus were against the *shuddhi* of the untouchables. Even some of the untouchable leaders were against the Shuddhi movement. Shri Puranchand, a freedom fighter of Gurdaspur district and a Dumna or Mahashe by caste believed that, "it was a tricky method devised by the Arya Samaj to deal with the threat posed by Christianity. The untouchables were converting to other religions to find a new identity, respect and social status, which they could not find in Hindu social system."[20] Whatever might be the motive behind the Shuddhi movement launched by the Arya Samaj, its contribution to the uplift of the untouchables, be it little, cannot be ignored.

The two other sects, one, the Radha Soami Satsang founded by Radha Soami in 1861, and other, the Dev Samaj founded by Siva Narayan Agnihotri in 1887 were spread in Punjab and among others, attracted the Dalits also. They tried to reform the Hindu society.

A good number of untouchables were attracted towards Sikhism as it opposed the caste system, idol worship and

---

19. S.K. Gupta, *The Scheduled Castes in Modern Indian Politics*, p. 134,

20. Satish Kumar Sharma, ***Social** Movements and Social Change*, p. 105. (B.R. Publishing Corporation, Delhi, 1985).

superstitions. The untouchables converted to Sikhism were called Mazhabis. However, the Sikh converts could not get equal status with the high caste Sikhs. The Hindu caste customs were not fully given up by them. The Udasi cult also attracted several persons in Punjab.

Dalit movement in Punjab was quite strong. Dalit leaders like Sant Brahma Das (Ludhiana), Santram (Hoshiarpur), Swami Shudranand (Jullundur), Thakar Chand (Jullundur), Prithvi Sing Azad (Ambala), Prabhati Ram (Amritsar), Kartar Chand Sulekh (Jullundur), Mihan Singh (Patiala), Nanak chand Rattu (Hoshiarpur), Keharsing Choturam Gondi (Rohtak), Charan Sing (Shimla), Chanan Ram (Shimla), Chand Ram (Rohtak), Prabharam Boudh (Panipat) and many others endeavoured for the uplift of their brethren.

In Punjab most of the leaders were Ambedkarites. The Ad Dharm movement was locally powerful but at the national level it was affiliated to Ambedkarite movement.

The East Punjab (Removal of Religions and Social Disabilities) Act, 1948 was in operation in Punjab till the passage of PCR Act, 1955.

RAJASTHAN

It was formed on 1 November 1956; it comprised the erstwhile states of Ajmer, some parts of Madhya Bharat, and erstwhile princely states in that region.

Swami Dayanand Saraswati himself tried to spread the teachings of the Arya Samaj in Rajasthan. He was in close touch with some of the native princes in Rajputana. The Maharana of Udaipur Shri Sajjan Singh accepted his discipleship. He became the President of the Paropakarini Sabha in 1883, which aimed at the propagation of the principles of the Arya Samaj throughout India. After the death of Maharana Sajjan Singh, the office of the Paropakarini Sabha was shifted to Ajmer in 1894, and Maharaja Mahar Singh of Shahpura was chosen as the President of the Paropakarini Sabha. The Arya Samaj tried to eradicate evil practices of the Hindus and undertook *shuddhi* of the untouchables who converted to Islam and Christianity.

It was because of the favourable atmosphere, that the Commissioner of Ajmer, on 20 September 1887, proclaimed in Ajmer-Merwara that child marriage would be a punishable offence.[21] At the initiative of Colonel Walter, the Agent to the Governor-General in Rajputana, one Walterkrit Rajputra Hitkarini Sabha was formed in 1889 at Ajmer to undertake social reforms in Rajasthan.

The Shuddhi movement, however, created tension between the caste Hindus and the Muslims in Rajasthan. In order to counteract it, the Muslims formed the Ajmer Muhammadan Association, called the Hami-i-Association in 1889 at Ajmer. The Christians also intensified their missionary activities. Undoubtedly, the Arya Samaj was the pioneer organization in respect of social reforms in Rajasthan, but, it "failed in shaking the foundations of the caste system, for it persists within staunch Arya Samajis themselves".[22]

The sects like Kabir Panth, Gorakhnath Panth, Nanak Panth, Dattatreya Panth, were in vogue in Rajasthan. However, their impact in the field of social reforms was negligible.

The Dalit liberation movement could not grow much stronger and vital in Rajasthan. The Dalit leaders like Swami Balinath Buntinath (Nagaur), Naval Ram (Nagaur), Umaid Ram (Jodhpur), Gopalanand Maharaj (Jodhpur), Berupal Pannalal (Bikaner), Harichand Jathia (Ajmer), Narsing Deo Gujarathi (Jodhpur), Shriram Sarvate (Jodhpur), Onkarlal Chouhan (Kota), Rahul Suman Chhavara (Ajmer), Durga Singh Sisodia (Ajmer), Parasram Jathia (Kota) and others tried to awaken their brethren.

No legal measures for the abolition of untouchability were taken before the passage of PCR Act, 1955.

---

21. V.K. Vashishtha, Arya Samaj Movement in Rajasthan during nineteenth century, in *Disssent, Protest and Reform in Indian Civilization* ed. by *S.C.* Malik p. 231.

22. *Ibid.* p. 233.

TAMIL NADU

The British people came to Madras in 1611, but the large area from the Northern Circars to Cape Comorin had been brought under British rule by 1801. Under the provisions of SRA, 1956, the Malabar district and the Kasargode district, a Taluka of South Kanara, were transferred to Kerala. Some parts of South Kanara district and Coimbatore district were transferred to Karnataka. Four Talukas of Trivandrum district and a Taluka of Quilon district were transferred to Tamil Nadu on 1 April 1960. In August 1968 the State of Madras was renamed as Tamil Nadu.

Shri Kasi Viswanatha Mudaliar (1806-1871) was one of the earliest adherents of Brahmo Samaj in Madras. He tried to propagate the message of Brahmo Samaj and the social reforms in Madras.

Colonel Olcott and Madam Blavatsky founded the Theosophical Society at Adyar near Madras in 1880. The Society opened a school for the Pariah untouchables in 1894 near Adyar. The second school was opened in 1898, and the third one in 1899. In 1901, there were 384 boys and 150 girls in the schools of the Society wherein 16 teachers were to teach.[23]

The American missionaries came to Madras as early as 1833. In 1877 John E. Clough tried to convert the untouchables to Christianity.

The Depressed Classes Mission opened its branch in Madras in 1909. It maintained two schools, one at Vyasarpady with 55 students under two teachers and the other at Perambur with 25 students.

In 1877 Shri Kanchi Subba Rao founded Madhava Siddhantonnatini Sabha (Association for the strengthening of the Madhava system) at Madras. In 1892 the Madras Hindu Social Reforms Association was formed to promote social reforms among the Hindus.

---

23. V.R. Shinde. *Bharatiya Asprushyancha Prashna* p. 235.

The South Indian Liberal Federation, popularly called, the Justice Party was formed in 1916 in Madras. In 1925 the Self Respect movement was started. Shri Ramaswamy Naicker, P. Sundaram Pillai and C.N. Annadurai were its leaders. These organizations had the credit of awakening the backward castes including the Depressed Classes in Madras.

Dalit movement in Madras had a very long history of valiant struggle and achievement. The leaders from among the Dalits were R.B. Madurai Pillai (Madras), Kotteshwar V. Subramaniam (Madras), M. Palaniswamy (Madras), R.B.V. Dharmalingam Pillai (Madras), I.N. Iyakannu Pulavar (North Arcot), R.B.R. Srinivasan (Chengalpet), A.S. Sahajanandam Swamy (North Arcot), R.Veerian (Madras), R.B.M.C. Rajah (Madras), R.B. L.K. Gurupadswamy (Madras), R.B.N. Sivaraj (Madras), Keshav Pillai (Madras), R.B.V.I. Munuswamy Pillai (Madras), J. Shivashanmugham Pillai (Madras), Vasudev G. Pillai (North Arcot), A.K. Kuppuswamy (Chengalpet), M.K. Mariappa (Dharmapuri) S.C. Balkrishnan (Madurai), Pallikonda Krishnaswamy (North Arcot), Aryashankar (Madras), Smt Maragatham Chandrashekhar, Smt Jyoti Venkatachalam (Madras), R.S. Arumugham (Tirunelveli) and many others endeavoured to uplift their brethren in Tamil Nadu.

The Removal of Civil Disabilities Act, 1948, the Madras State Disabilities Act, 1947, and the Madras Temple Entry Authorization Act, 1947, were in implementation before the passage of the PCR Act, 1955.

Pandit C. Iyodhi Dass (1845-1914) was the pioneering leader of the Dalit liberation in Tamil Nadu. He tried his best to revive Buddhism in South India. Places like Madras, Kolar Gold Field, Hubli and Hyderabad were the important centres of Buddhism.

Formerly, the Dalits were politically affiliated to Justice Party from its very inception. However, after having come to know the apathy of the Justice Party towards their problem, they shunned it and associated with Ambedkarite movement.

This State provided to the nation the first Dalit leader as member of the Central Legislative Assembly namely Diwan

Bahadur M.C. Rajah, who was for sometime under the influence of caste Hindu leaders like Dr Moonje, but later on he joined the Ambedkarite movement. Rao Bahadur R. Srinivasan was the trusted friend and companion of Dr Babasaheb Ambedkar who along with the later participated in the RTC (1930-32). Rao Bahadur N. Shivaraj headed the SCF and RPI almost from 1942 to the end of his life in 1964. The State of Tamil Nadu provided a good number of able leaders to the movement.

UTTAR PRADESH (UTTAR PRADESH AND UTTARAKHAND)

Previously it was called North-West Province. It was a part of Bengal before 1833. In 1856 Oudh was annexed to the British Empire. In 1877 Agra and Oudh were brought under one Lieutenant Governor. In 1902 its name was changed to United Provinces of Agra and Oudh. In 1921 it became a full fledged Province. In 1935 its name was shortened to United Provinces. After independence, the States of Rampur, Banaras, and Tehri Garhwal were merged with the United Provinces. In 1950 the name of United Provinces was changed to Uttar Pradesh.

The American Presbyterian Mission started its activities at Allahabad as early as 1836. The Wahabi movement started by Saiyid Ahmad of Rai Bareilly (1786-1831) was in vogue from 1820 to 1871. Later Sir Sayed Ahmad Khan (1817-1898) started the Mohammadan Anglo-Indian Oriental College in 1875, which became the precursor of Aligarh Muslim University. Pandit Madan Mohan Malviya (1861-1946), the leader of the Hindu Maha Sabha founded Banaras Hindu University.

The Radha Soami Satsang movement founded by Radha Soami of Agra (1818-1878) followed by Rai Saligram Saheb Bahadur (1828-1898), Brahma Sankar Misra (1861-1907) was in vogue in Uttar Pradesh. The Dev Samaj founded (1887) by Siva Narayan Agnihotri of Kanpur was also in existence.

Bhadant Bodhanandji Mahasthvir (1874, Lucknow) took *Pravarja* in Buddhism in 1914 and started preaching and propagating Buddhism especially to the backward classes communities. He founded the UP Hindu Backward Classes League in 1928. He wrote *Mool Bharatvasi Aur Arya*. He was of the view that the caste system should be abolished before independence itself. Rai Saheb Ram Charan, Shivadayal Sinh Chourasia, Gouri Shankar Pal, Chandrika Prasad Jigyasu cooperated with him.

The Brahmo Samaj and Arya Samaj were already in existence and they were trying to awaken the caste-ridden Hindu society. The Kabir Panth and Ravidas Panth were popular especially among the Depressed Classes.

Dalit movement in Uttar Pradesh was quite strong and influential. From among the Dalit leaders Babu Nandlalji Choudhari (Allahabad), Swami Prabhutanand Vyas (Agra), Khemchandji Bohare (Agra), Pandit Sundarlal Sagar (Agra), Rai Saheb Ramcharanji (Kanpur), Dr Manik Chand Jatav Veer (Agra), Karan Singh Kaen (Agra), Mahant Baba Lachmandas (Unnao), Kanoji Lal Jatav (Fatehgarh), Babu Gopichandra Pipal (Agra), Dr Dharam Prakash (Bareilly), Mahadeo Prasad (Gorakhpur), Ram Narayan Yadvendu (Agra), Masuria Din (Allahabad), Kalyan Ramji Das (Muzaffarpur), Rajvaidhya Mata Prasad Sagar (Lucknow), Prem Chand Arya (Lucknow), Swaminath Prasad (Deoṛia), Tilak Chand Kureel (Kanpur), Master Mansing (Agra), Mata Prasad Mitra (Jaunpur), Gaya Prasad Prashant (Lucknow), Choudhari Lachhiram (Jalon), and many others tried to liberate their brethren in Uttar Pradesh.

Before the passage of PCR Act, 1955, The United Provinces Removal of Social Disabilities Act, 1947 was in operation in Uttar Pradesh.

WEST BENGAL

From 1833 to 1947 Bengal was ruled by the British people. The North-Western Provinces were separated from it in 1833, Assam in 1874, Bihar and Orissa in 1912. Under the Indian Independence Act, 1947, its Muslim majority region (Chittagong and Dhaka Divisions) became part of Pakistan and now Bangladesh.

In 1792 the Baptist Mission under the stewardship of William Carey from England started its missionary activities in Bengal. He started the first Bengali newspaper named *Samchar Darpan* in about 1818. Raja Ram Mohan Roy (1772-1833) founded Brahmo Samaj in 1828. Raja Ram Mohan Roy started his crusade against suttee and other superstitions. It was because of his initiative the Lord William Bentick finally promulgated The Regulation XVII against it in 1829. In 1866 Keshav Chandra Sen (1838-1884) founded Brahmo Samaj of India as separate from the Adi Brahmo Samaj and tried to awaken the people almost throughout India.

Shri Shashipad Bandopadhyaya, a Brahmo, established a girls school, at Baranagar. Till 1873 he started four girls schools. In 1887 he founded a Home for Hindu Widows and a night high school for working women at Baranagar. In 1874 he founded one Toilers Association, through which he tried to organize the mill workers at Baranagar. He tried to awaken the untouchables and tried to imbibe in them the habits of cleanliness and temperance. He used to organize community dinners to break the barriers of castes.

Shri Shivanath Shastri united the factions of Brahmo Samaj into one Sadharan Brahmo Samaj. He worked for the Depressed Classes Mission also. He performed commendable work in spreading education and awakening the Depressed Classes in Bengal.

Swami Ramkrishna Paramhansa (1834-1886) believed that all the religions are true and equal. God is impersonal and every body should practise good moral conduct. His disciple Swami Vivekananda (1863-1902) was a great philosopher and a missionary. He founded Ramkrishna Mission in 1896 at Belur near Calcutta and tried to awaken the ignorant masses. He pleaded for liberalization of the rigid rules of the religion. Later on, the branches of the Mission were opened at Banaras, Allahabad, Mayavati, on the Himalayas and at Bangalore.

Dalit liberation movement in Bengal was very strong and influential. Its leaders were Harichand Thakur (Faridpur – now in Bangladesh), Guruchand Thakur (Faridpur), Jananayak Mukund Behari Mullick (Khulna - now in Bangladesh), Rai Bahadur K.B. Mullick and Pulin Behari Mullick (Khulna - now in Bangladesh), Sarat Chandra Majumdar (Jessor–now in Bangladesh), Sarat Chandra Bal (Faridpur), Man Mohan Das (Burdwan), Mahapran Jogendra Nath Mandal (Barisal), P.R. Thakur (24 Pargana), Krishna Dhan Biswas (Jessore), Shyama Prasad Barman (Calcutta), Purna Chandra Mullick (Faridpur), Birat Chandra Mondal (Calcutta), Rai Bahadur Kamini Kumar Das (Calcutta), Dr Keshablal Majumdar (Calcutta), Jatin Bagchi (Calcutta), Dr Sarat Chandra Boral (Barisal - Calcutta), Sitanath Mondal (Khulna), Rasik Lai Biswas (Calcutta), Hemchandra Naskar, Rai Bahadur Anukul Chandra Das (24 Parganas), Sakti Kumar Sarkar (Calcutta), Manohar Dhali (Calcutta), Aditya Kumar Maitru (Calcutta), Apurba Lal Majumdar (Howrah) and many others.

Thakur Hari Chand, who started the Matua sect was the pioneering leader of the untouchables. Mukund Behari Mullick and Jogendra Nath Mandal were very important leaders of the Dalit movement in Bengal which was based on the thoughts of Dr Babasaheb Ambedkar. However, most of the leaders of the movement were from that region which ceded to East Pakistan and are now in Bangladesh.

The West Bengal Hindu Social Disabilities Removal Act, 1948 was in operation in West Bengal till the passage of PCR Act, 1955.

DELHI

Since 1911 Delhi has been the capital of India. It has witnessed many upheavals and movements. Dalit liberation movement in Delhi was strong and influential. Its leaders were Devidas Jatav, Swami Prakashanand, Sardar Devi Singh, Rai Saheb Puran Chand, Pandit Patram Sinh Jatav, Chotti Ram, Swami Darshanand and many others.

Thus, the Dalit liberation movement spread to almost all the parts of the country from 1857 to 1956. During this period also almost all the endogenous as well as exogenous factors which gave rise to Dalit movement were in operation in their more developed and sophisticated forms and they contributed much for the development and success of the movement.

The cultural encounter of Islam and Christianity with the Hindu caste culture produced a chain reaction in India. Brahmo Samaj, Arya Samaj, Ramkrishna Mission and many others came into existence to check the growing proselytization which was posing threat to Brahmanic superiority. These movements and counter-movements were responsible for the growth of a general consciousness in India. The expanding imperialism, new scientific and technical education, new philosophy and constitutionalism, increasing industrialization, communication and Press had also contributed to the growth of a new awareness.

'Dalit consciousness' was also not separate from the general consciousness. The martial service, social protest movements, able leadership and the general political atmosphere in the country was obviously conducive for the all-round development.

It could not be a mass movement in some parts of the country. However, its object was one, that is, liberation of the Dalits from untouchability and casteism so that they could regain their identity as human beings.

Of all the factors, the quality of leadership assumes important place. The Dalit leadership was, of course, objectively determined to liberate their brethren from clutches of the untouchability. Especially, Dr Babasaheb Ambedkar could provide a well determined, exceptionally able and highly 'charismatic' leadership to the Dalit liberation movement. His leadership was accepted by the whole nation in his capacity as Chairman of the Drafting Committee of the Constitution. He could take the Dalit movement to its logical conclusion.

8

Dynamics of Dalit Movement

The object of Dalit movement was obviously to emancipate the Dalits from the thraldom of untouchability and caste system. However, the strategies, ideologies, approaches, ways and means were varied from leader to leader, place to place and time to time. The 'Dalit consciousness' came to the fore in different forms and shades. However, the process of Dalit movement which was in continuation during the study period could be characterized as follows:

SANSKRITIZATION

The term 'Sanskritization' was used by M.N. Srinivas while analysing the process of change in the traditional social structure in India. He states that sanskritization in "the process by which a 'low' Hindu caste, or tribal or other group, changes its customs, ritual, ideology and way of life in the direction of a high and frequently, 'twice born' caste. Generally such changes are followed by a claim to a higher position in the caste hierarchy than that traditionally conceded to the claimant caste by the local community".[1] In this process the low caste people by imitation follow the Brahmanical customs and manners, with an intention to claim a higher status in the traditional social order.

---

1. M.N. Srinivas. *Social Change In Modern India,* Orient Longman Ltd., Bombay, p.6. 1972.

The phenomenon of sanskritization had been apparently explained long ago by Dr Babasaheb Ambedkar in his *Castes in India* (1916) by the term 'imitation', in the context of formation of the castes. He had very categorically stated that almost all the classes in the pre-caste society followed the priestly Brahmin class in their attempt to upgrade their social status by way of 'imitation' of certain Brahmanic manners and customs and by 'differentiation' from other groups. This process led to the formation of the castes. It was but natural because the 'propensity to imitate is a deep-seated one in the human mind'. He stated that the laws of imitation flows from the higher to the lower. The extent or intensity of imitation varies inversely in proportion to social distance from the superior caste, and the source of imitation must enjoy prestige in the group. The Brahmin priestly class was treated as 'semi-Gods', as such the other groups followed them. Thus, each group deliberately prevented its members from fusing into another through the custom of endogamy and formed its own caste. They imitated certain manners, customs and rituals of Brahmins to raise their status.

In the traditional Hindu society, the religion (Dharma) and the religious elites (the Brahmins) were treated in high esteem. Naturally, they were treated as 'models' or 'reference groups' to be followed by the lower castes. The lower castes began thinking that by emulating or imitating certain manners and rituals of the Brahmins and the higher castes, their position would be elevated in the view of others.

Some of the Dalit leaders also thought that by following the Brahmanic manners, including vegetarianism, temperance, putting sandalwood paste on forehead, wearing sacred thread around the neck, and by adopting Brahmanic dialects, dress, manners, ceremonies, rituals and clean professions, they would be able to elevate themselves to the higher position in the caste hierarchy.

The Dalit leaders like Maharshi Balinath and Umaid Ramji Maharaj (Rajasthan), Swamy Thykkad and Shubhanand

Gurudevan (Kerala), Pandit Sundarlal Sagar and Prabhutanand Vyas (UP), Muldas Vaishya (Gujarat), Moon Vithoba Raoji Pande (Maharashtra) and others tried to adopt the established cultural norms and practices of the higher castes.

Some of the leaders followed purely the Brahmanical pattern of life, whereas others were attracted towards Brahmo Samaj, Arya Samaj, Mahanubhav sect, Warkari Panth and other liberal Hindu sects. All these sects believed in one God, spiritual equality and high moral and cultural life.

The lower castes were strictly prohibited to follow the high caste way of life. However, at some places the higher castes preferred to give some concessions to the lower castes, at the cultural level so as to keep them in the Hindu fold. It is also true that some of the higher castes were very much against the sanskritization of Dalits. They had shown their wrath against them.

Although, the untouchables imitated the Brahmins and other locally dominant high caste groups, their social status remained unaltered. At the most they were treated equally at the public functions and ceremonies, but the high caste mentality remained intact. There was no change in the material condition of the Dalits. The process of sanskritization, however, Hinduised the Dalits to a great extent.

However, it should be noted that the imitation of the high caste manners by the Dalits, which was strictly prohibited, was but an assertion of their right to equality in the initial stages of the liberation movement. Some of the families could develop the habit of maintaining cleanliness and cultural standard. Though it was not a protest, it was a craving for a better life standard at least according to the established norms.

DICHOTOMIZATION

In the words of Owen Lynch, dichotomization is 'concerned with dyadic relationships of a status and a counter-status but analytically specifies what happens to the dyad when a third party enters into the relationship".[2] The third party, however, tries to change the dyadic relationship through redefinition of "the roles of statuses". "The case of the Scheduled Castes in India", as observed by Owen Lynch, "offers a good example of dichotomization." "The status of untouchable *vis-a-vis* non-untouchable has become the concern of the Indian Government (here the third party). The government has redefined the status of untouchable into that of Scheduled Castes and implicitly all other castes become non-Scheduled castes... In creating this differentiation of statuses the government has also brought those who occupy these new statuses into a special relationship to itself through integrating institutions at a higher level than caste."[3]

The classification of the Dalits as against non-Dalits is not a new phenomenon. From time immemorial the Dalits were treated as separate and outside of the fourfold varna system. They were 'outcastes' or 'Panchama', They were deliberately asked to maintain spatial distance from the main village caste community. They were culturally different from the caste Hindus. Their food habits, recreation, language, rituals and ceremonies, deities, manner of worship, etc, were different from those of the caste Hindus. They consequently developed a sense of separateness or isolation from each other. There was absolutely no endosmosis between the caste Hindus and the Dalits. The situation became worse due to increasing incidents of atrocities, suppression and exploitation. They were subjected to harsh and uneven legal system. The race theory dividing the caste Hindus and' the Dalits on Aryan and non-Aryan line further accentuated the evil.

This situation, naturally gave rise to a new movement called Adi-Hindu movement. This movement explained the Dalit identity in terms of Adi-Hindus. The pioneering leaders of Adi-Hindu movement were Gopalbaba Walangkar (Maharashtra),

---

2. M. Owen Lynch, *The Politics of Untouchability*, p. 17.

3. *Ibid*. p. 18

Swami Achhutanandji (UP), Bhagya Reddy Varma and B. Shyamsundar (AP) and Mangu Ram (Punjab). They thought that the Dalits were the original inhabitants of India and they were not Hindus. The Aryans or Brahmins who invaded this country forcibly imposed untouchability on the original inhabitants of this land, so that they would not rise in rebellion in future.

Further, they thought that if Hinduism was discarded, untouchability would automatically come to an end. The Dalits being the original inhabitants, the land and other sources of production belonged to them. They felt that denial of Hinduism was necessary for the abolition of sub-casteism among them, as it was resulted out of divisive Hinduism.

Accordingly, they called themselves as Adi-Andhras in Andhra, Adi-Karnataka in Karnataka, Adi-Dravidas in Tamil Nadu, Adi-Hindus in Uttar Pradesh and Adi-Dharmis in Punjab. The Adi-Hindu movement became popular in those states. The concerned authorities also accepted the new nomenclature in all those states except in Uttar Pradesh.

Later on, Dr Babasaheb Ambedkar gave a new dimension to the 'theory of original inhabitants'. He put forward his 'Broken Men' theory for explaining the origin of untouchability in the light of anthropological and anthropometrical exploration. He stated that the untouchables and the caste Hindus were not racially different from each other. The untouchables were broken men from the rest of the society and in the course of time, they became Buddhists. However, they continued to eat beef and declined to accept the supremacy of the Brahmins. Therefore, the Brahmins, out of sheer hatred for the Buddhists, imposed untouchability on them.

Nevertheless, he argued for separate settlement and separate electorate for them as a necessary measure for a certain period in order to achieve their healthy socio-economic development. He thought that it was but a pre-condition to bring them to the mainstream. His scientific view had a good bearing upon social cohesion.

In the whole dichotomic situation, the government positively intervened to settle the communal problem through the historic Round Table Conference held during 1930-32, but in vain. However, the matter was amicably settled between the Dalits and caste Hindus under the Poona Pact, 1932. Accordingly, the government prepared the list of Scheduled Castes for the purpose of seeking certain benefits under the Act of 1935. Thereafter, several measures were taken to ameliorate the socio-economic condition of the Dalits. The process of dichotomization could not last for long, but it proved to be effective in awakening the Dalits to their problems. It could, however, instil in them a sense of self-identity and self pride.

DE-HINDUIZATION

Untouchability was ruthlessly and widely practised by the caste Hindus. Naturally the Dalits thought that unless they desert that exploitative order, there was no liberation for them.

The term de-Hinduization implies complete distant and protest against Hinduism, and acceptance of any other non-Hindu religion like Islam, Christianity, Sikh or Buddhism, with a purpose of getting rid of untouchability and to develop their moral and financial conditions.

In the process of de-Hinduization, the Dalits in many parts of the country embraced Islam and Christianity. Under the census of 1901 there were 47,048,581 Muslims in northern India (Punjab, Kashmir, UP, Bihar, Bengal and Orissa) out of which 8,628,566 were shown as *Arjal* (inferior) Muslims. Shri V.R. Shinde thinks that the Muslims enumerated as inferior in the north were probably original Antyaj or the untouchables.[4] A good number of Dalits were converted to Christianity, especially in Kerala. Under the census of 1931, among the Pariah untouchables, 70,684 were Hindus, whereas 71,680 were

4. V.R. Shinde, *Bharatiya Asprushyantecha Prashna* (Marathi), p. 200.

Christians.[5] Among the Pulayas 207,337 were Hindus, whereas 157,813 were Christians.[6] The Dalit leaders like Pampady John Joseph (Kerala), Rev. John Rathnam (Tamil Nadu) and Gurram Jashua (AP) were prominent among the converts.

However, the Christian Dalit leader Poykayil Yohanan (Kerala) severed his relations with the church and formed his own sect known as PRDS (Pratyaksha Raksha Deiva Sabha) and Shri Gabriel Appaduraiyar (Tamil Nadu) embraced Buddhism.

Some of the Dalits, especially in Punjab, were converted to Sikhism. They are known as Mazhabis, Namdharis, Sikaligares and Kabir Panthis. Some of the Dalits, especially in Maharashtra, embraced Mahanubhav sect, a somewhat liberal sect.

As a protest against Hinduism some of the Dalit leaders founded their own sects or religions. Guru Ghasi Das (MP) founded Satnami Sect, Guruchand Thakur (Bengal) founded Matua sect, Ayyan Kali (Kerala) founded SJPY (Sadhu Jana Paripalan Yogam), Poykayil Yohanan founded PRDS (Pratyaksha Raksha Deiva Sabha) and Mangu Ram (Punjab) founded Ad Dharm.

Some of the Dalits were converted to Buddhism. Pandit Iyodhi Dass (Tamil Nadu), Gabriel Appaduriyar (Tamil Nadu), Iyakanu Pulawar (Karnataka) and M.Y. Murugesan (Karnataka) took the initiative in reviving Buddhism. Bhagya Reddy Varma (AP) was also attracted towards Buddhism. Dr Ambedkar converted to Buddhism along with his millions of followers at Nagpur in 1956. It was, undoubtedly a protest against the Vedas, Smritis, Puranas, plurality of Gods, idolatory, Karma theory, concept of hell and heaven and the caste-based social order. Moreover, it was an attempt to establish a new rational and moral society, based on liberty, equality and fraternity. Buddhism could bring about the philosophical, attitudinal and behavioural change in the life of the Dalits. It could give them a new identity, self-pride and self-confidence.

---

5. L.A Iyer Krishna. *The Travancore Tribes and Castes,* Vol. II, p. 83.
6. *Ibid.* p. 118.

SOCIAL DIALECTICISM

Due to untouchability the whole Hindu society was divided into touchables and the untouchables. The touchables were to enjoy all the civil rights, whereas the untouchables were not to enjoy any right. The untouchables were to fulfil the duties imposed by the touchables. Their interests were diametrically opposed to each other.

However, with the advent of British in India, the whole legal system was changed. The principle of rule of law came into implementation in India. Due to centralized, efficient and democratic administration the whole anarchy of the villages was almost lost. New avenues of livelihood came into existence. The system of new education was giving rise to a new awareness. This situation was naturally ripe for the growth of the 'Dalit consciousness'. With this new consciousness, the Dalits began to break the bondage of untouchability. Every fallen community has to struggle for its rights. There cannot be any sympathy among the dominant class for the servant class. Only the process of struggle may bring a desired change in the attitude of the former. This was true in the case of Dalits also.

The struggle for regaining the civil rights was in continuation till its logical conclusion. However, the struggle was peaceful and constitutional. Dr Babasaheb Ambedkar gave a clarion call to his brethren that they must 'educate, agitate and organize' for their emancipation. They, followed their leader. The Vaikom Satyagraha, Mahad Satyagraha, Kalaram Temple Satyagraha, etc, could be stated as milestones in the movement. Ultimately they could achieve all the civil rights under the Constitution.

The dialectic was not limited to civil rights only. It was in vogue in the field of economic uplift. In Kerala the bulk of the Dalits were constrained to earn their bare subsistence as agricultural bonded labourers. They were attached to the land, subject to sale, mortgage, lease, exchange and gift along with the land. Therefore, Dalit leaders like Ayyan Kali had to give a fight against serfdom.

With a view to accelerating the Dalit liberation movement, Dalits could have joined the Communist movement roughly in the second half of the study period, as it claimed to be a vanguard of the exploited people. However, this did not happen. It was obviously because communism could not create the necessary confidence in the minds of Dalits. The Communist movement was invariably in the hands of the high caste people and they could not realize the crucial role of caste in the Indian social structure. Neither had they any plan to exterminate untouchability nor had they any grasp of that problem. On the contrary they thought that if the base of material conditions is changed, the superstructure of caste, untouchability and all the vices which crept in the body politic will be automatically changed. But they could change neither the base nor the superstructure.

In order to fight against the socio-economic problems, Dr Babasaheb Ambedkar formed the Independent Labour Party in 1936. He tried to abolish the exploitative *Khoti* system prevailing in the Konkan part of Maharashtra, and *Veti* or *Maharaki* system - a wage free hereditary service to the caste Hindus in the local administration. He was of the view that all the key industries, including agriculture should be nationalized in the interest of the nation as a whole.

The Dalit leaders had to give a very tough fight against social tyranny. The caste Hindus were orthodox and aggressive, whereas the Dalit masses were illiterate, poor and ignorant. The British rulers were, more or less, sympathetic to the Dalits, but their main interest was in maintaining their empire in this country. The native princes were more or less indifferent towards the problems of Dalits, except the Maharajas of Kolhapur, Baroda and Pithapur. The caste Hindu leaders, except a few, were busy in the struggle for Swaraj. In that adverse situation, the Dalit leaders had to struggle for their rights. The way of struggle, of course, proved to be efficacious to the Dalits.

POLITICIZATION

Politicization means, "The orientation of people to political perspectives and political actions ,"[7] It is necessary in respect of a community which is 'apolitical' and ignorant. However, Dr Babasaheb Ambedkar said that, "the problem of the Depressed classes will never be solved unless they get political power in their own hands. If this is true, and I do not think that the contrary can be maintained, then the problem of the Depressed classes is, I submit eminently, a political problem and must be treated as such."[8] Thus, the problem of Dalits was viewed by him from the political aspect. However, the Dalits were not politically conscious. They, of course, needed the orientation and inspiration to enter the power structure of the state in order to solve their problems.

The first attempt to politicize the Depressed Classes was made by Shivram Janba Kamble, Subedar Ramji, Subedar Major Ghatge and others when the British Government abandoned recruitment of the Mahars in the military. The military service was the first and foremost avenue of participation in power structure of the state. Later on, Dr Babasaheb Ambedkar also tried to convince the government to recruit the Mahars in the military. Ultimately, he became successful in 1941 when the first Mahar Regiment was formed.

In order to organize the castemen, a number of caste associations were formed, for example Adi-Dravida Mahajan Sabha (1890), All Bengal Namasudra Association (1912), Jatav Veer Maha Sabha (1917), Adi-Andhra Mahajan Sabha (1917), etc. All these associations had tried to politicize their members.

With the growing process of democratization, a new avenue of participation in the power structure of the state was opened. Dr Babasaheb Ambedkar rightly thought that the Dalits must win political power in order to bring the desired changes. Therefore, he demanded adequate representation for the Dalits

---

7. R.T. Jangam, *Political Sociology*, p. 167.

8. Bhagwandas (ed.), *Thus Spoke Ambedkar*, Vol.I. p. 24.

in the legislatures and in the administration. He thought that due to the stigma of untouchability the Dalit candidates would not win in the elections. Hence, they ought to be elected through reserved constituencies and by the method of separate electorate. Mahatma Gandhi, however, opposed the scheme of separate electorate on the ground that this would separate the Dalits from the Hindus. Eventually, both the parties came to a compromise and signed the Poona Pact in 1932, which envisaged reserved seats and certain other special rights for the Dalits. The Constitution of India, which envisaged justice-social, economic and political-provided certain special safeguards to the Dalits.

During this period organizations like the Independent Labour Party, Depressed Classes League, Scheduled Castes Federation, etc, tried to aggregate and articulate the interests of the Dalits, tried to mobilize mass support for their interests, tried to inspire the Dalits to organize and agitate for the acquisition of their due share in political power. The Dalit masses also positively responded to the call of their leaders.

To avail of an employment opportunity in the government service has been an important avenue of entering the power structure. Dr Babasaheb Ambedkar rightly said that the Dalits must enter the government service and capture the strategic positions, so that they would be able to serve their brethren in a right manner. He tried to get reservation facilities for the Dalits and ultimately became successful in 1943. The Constitution of India, *inter alia,* provides for reservations in the services for the Dalits.

The process of politicization had a greater impact on the then apolitical and ignorant Dalits. They could successfully evolve their identity as a separate group, they evinced their keen interest and performed their historic role in the national politics. The British Government, Indian National Congress and Muslim League had to take cognizance of the separate identity of Dalits. Everybody tried to win over their confidence. Mahatma Gandhi, with his well-knit organization of Harijan Sevak Sangh tried to win the confidence of Dalits, and he could become successful in his endeavour, to some extent. However, he could not counter the overall impact of Ambedkarite movement on the masses. Dalits could not trust him because of his love for Varnashram Dharma and the ideology of Ramrajya in which they had no faith. However, the contribution of Mahatma Gandhi to the Dalit liberation cannot be ignored. He tried to convince non-Dalit masses to give up untouchability and tried to bring the Dalit elites into politics. Thus, both Dr Babasaheb Ambedkar and Mahatma Gandhi tried to raise the political level of Dalits in their own way.

DALIT UNIFICATION

A social movement requires a strong unity amongst the members of the community for which it is meant. However, to achieve unity among the Dalits, who were internally divided into several castes and sub-castes, externally scattered almost throughout the vast country and who were prone to be a prey of divisive Hindu forces, was a challenging task. Therefore, the Dalit leadership had to strive consistently for bringing about unity among the Dalits to fight against their common woes and enemies. In the process of unification, they devised certain means and methods, including arranging common programme of devotional songs, inviting and associating with the men of other castes at marriages and funerals, arranging inter-caste and inter-sub-caste dining and bringing them together in the conferences, where there could be proper orientation of the people of all the castes and sub-castes.

There were certain common factors among them, which were skilfully utilized to unite them. The social status of all the untouchables was more or less equally degraded in the view of the caste Hindus. All the untouchables were treated by the caste Hindus as the most despised and polluting castes. Almost all the untouchables were engaged in hereditary unclean professions like sweeping, tanning, shoe making etc. Majority of them were agricultural labourers and very few of them were small farmers. All of them were poor and economically exploited people.

Spatially, all of them were living outside the village in separate ghettos.

The untouchables became socially segregated, economically exploited, religiously boycotted, culturally degraded and politically persecuted. They could not break the traditional shackles and could not come out of that trap. They naturally thought that all the miseries were caused by the oppressive Hindu religion and the caste Hindus. Thus, they could rightly identify their common enemy as orthodox Hinduism.

Dalit leaders could find out from their past history the saints like Shambhuka, Chokhamela, Ravidas, Kabirdas, etc, and they were treated as their common cultural heroes. Their teachings and movements lured them. The stories of those saints were taught to the people with great admiration and devotion.

Since they were kept aloof from the large Hindu society, they tried to inquire into their origin as a community. They found that they were not Hindus, but Adi-Hindus. They asked their brethren to abandon their Hindu identity and adopt their own 'Adi-Hindu' identity. However, Dr Babasaheb Ambedkar advanced 'the Broken Men theory' (1946) through which he stated that the so-called untouchables were Broken Men from the main bulk of the society and they were Buddhists, they were against the supremacy of the Brahmins. Therefore, the Brahmins out of hatred for the Buddhists, imposed untouchability and thereby degraded them to the level of untouchables, unapproachables and unseeables. In the immemorial past they were Broken Men and Buddhist. Thus the Adi-Hindu theory culminated into a logical conclusion that they were Buddhists.

Due to increasing democratic process in India, the Dalits also got an opportunity to participate in the political power. As a result of their politics, the then government duly identified the so-called untouchables and prepared a comprehensive list of 435 castes with the nomenclature of "The Scheduled Castes". Subsequently the Scheduled Castes were known as a 'community' whose interests were seemingly 'common'. Their collective name gave them strength and confidence.

The message of the new 'consciousness' was meticulously spread by the elite strata of the community including primary teachers, railway workers, mill workers, retired army personnel, peons, masons, private physicians, butlers, pedlars and the saints. They were the first harbingers of the community. They used to preach and propagate, organize the meetings and conferences, mobilize mass-support and tried to represent the grievances of their brethren. Eventually, the able efficacious and comprehensive leadership of Dr Babasaheb Ambedkar proved to be instrumental in uniting the Dalit masses to a great extent.

Thus, from 1857 to 1956 the Dalit liberation movement witnessed several forces and processes in its development. It is very difficult to explain the whole complicated process of its development. Every process was virtually followed by a counter-process. With the process of sanskritization, there arose a process of de-sanskritization. With the process of dichotomization, there arose a process of integration. With the process of de-Hinduization, there arose a process of Hinduization. Many of the converted Dalits positively responded to the process of *shuddhi.* With the process of social and political dialecticism, some of the people thought that their problem could be solved not by confrontation but by 'change of the heart'. The process of Westernization and Islamization were also in existence in certain parts of the country depending on the influence of these religions and the local situation. There was, however, unanimity on the spread of education among the Dalits. Dalit leadership viewed that education was the *sine-qua-non* of the liberation of their brethren.

Some of the Dalits migrated to cities to find employment and to get rid of thraldom. Thus, it is difficult to analyse and describe the whole process of Dalit movement.

It is true that if a movement is objectively well defined and determined, and if it is supported by sufficient activism to achieve its set objective, the movement becomes organically living one. It requires a continuous flow of 'qualitatively' and quantitatively good and sufficient leadership to take it to its logical conclusion.

No movement can be expected to be a monolith of one organism and idealism. It may be ideologically and strategically divided, but not objectively. In the fair competition of internal ideological forces, everyone would get a fair chance to prove his individual worth. The ideology and strategy proved to be suitable to the cause and superior to the others. It proved that the internal dialectic will give to the movement sufficient spirit and strength, courage and confidence.

The movement is always opposed by external forces. It is, however, necessary to identify and oppose the enemy tooth and nail. If the cause is right and leadership is good, the movement will certainly grow even in adverse situation and will win over the mightiest force. Every step of success will give a vigour to the movement to fight till the last.

Dalit movement was, of course, based on a well-defined objective which was to abolish untouchability and establish a new social order based on liberty, equality and fraternity. During the period of 100 years (1857-1956) several leaders and their ideologies and strategies became popular. The leadership of some of them was confined to certain regions and fields. After 1920 onwards the mission of Dr Babasaheb Ambedkar became more popular and efficacious; and it spread almost throughout India.

During 1857 to 1956 several exogenous factors including the Hindu reformist movements, Hindu-Muslim rivalry, Western education and missionaries, new industrial growth, new legal system, means of communications, etc, greatly contributed to the growth of Dalit movement.

To give a decisive fight against the age-old ugly practice of untouchability which was spread throughout the country and was deeply rooted in the minds of the people, was not a simple task. Firstly, the Dalit leaders had to lift their brothers and sisters from their ignorance; to teach them to agitate against injustice and to organize them into a force. The response was at first, weak, clumsy and slow, but later it became positive and healthy. Secondly, they had to face the reactionary caste Hindus. Every step towards the liberation of Dalits was followed by sharp reactions from the caste Hindus in the form of boycotts, atrocities, arson and all other crimes. In all such critical and crucial situations the Dalit leaders had to stand by their poor brethren, to raise their morale and to wage a peaceful and legal battle against the forces of reactionaries. Thirdly, the Dalit leadership had to convince the government to accept their genuine demands of human rights. In all these situations the Dalit leaders had to exemplify their exceptional qualities of wisdom, courage and missionary zeal. Ultimately, the leadership became successful in the task of emancipation of Dalits in spite of several odds and obstacles.

9

Observations

The practice of untouchability had virtually dehumanized a significant section of Indian society. It came into existence out of mere hatred and jealousy of the Brahmins in respect of the Broken Men who became Buddhists and who were unwilling to accept the supremacy of the Brahmins. It was so widespread that in almost every part of India, it was recklessly observed by the caste Hindus. It slowly intruded in other religions also; it was so much exploitative, oppressive and inhuman that the untouchables had lost their very *persona* and all the fundamental rights.

No exploitation can last for a longer period. It cannot command acceptance of the exploited voluntarily. They may not be able to overtly express their protest against it due to the adverse situation in which they are constrained to lead their life. However, as and when that adverse situation becomes unable to sustain the shock of the emergence of new diametrically opposite forces, the protests of the exploited would be heard. They would gain the strength to break the foundations of the old decadent situation. It exactly happened so with the advent of the British in India. The new philosophy of social reconstruction and the material advancement which they progressively brought to India paved the way for a new social order. The new awakening which the British brought had a deep penetrating impact on the Hindu social structure. Several thinkers and social minded people began to search for the causes of the downfall of the Hindu society. Ultimately, they came to the conclusion that unless the traditional Hindu social order is changed and new thoughts absorbed, the Hindu social system could not be able to survive honourably. Therefore, they came forward individually and collectively to bring a new awakening in the society.

In the process of development and spread of the new awakening in India, the Dalit consciousness also started gaining momentum. It came to the fore in the form of dissent and protest against the oppressive untouchability, and which culminated in the meeting in 1857. Thereafter, the new consciousness was steadily consolidated in India, both among the Dalits as well as non-Dalits.

With the growth of democratic institutions and 'politics of number' the Dalits began to assume some importance in the national politics. The Dalit leaders, in order to take due advantage of the situation and bring about their liberation, began to mobilize forces in their favour. They started organizing their brethren to struggle to eliminate untouchability and caste system. They had launched several satyagrahas and agitations to assert their human rights. They tried to convince the men in power and politics to accept their genuine demands of human rights. Eventually, they became successful in accomplishing their objective of liberation of their brethren. The age-long practice of untouchability came to an end at the instance of the Constitution in 1950. The Constitution had not only abolished "untouchability" in all its forms and practices, but it declared the practice of untouchability an offence punishable by law. Subsequently, the protection of Civil Rights Act was passed in 1955 which provided punishment to the offences of untouchability. The other provisions of the Constitution including the provisions of protective discriminations under Articles 15 (4), 16 (4), 46, 330 and 332, aim to ameliorate the socio-economic condition of the Dalits and to give them due share in power which hitherto had been denied to them. The final and far-reaching blow was given in 1956 to the Hindu traditionalism, when the unprecedented conversion of the untouchables to Buddhism took place under the leadership of Dr Babasaheb Ambedkar at Nagpur. It was not a mere protest against

Hinduism. It was but a revival of a rational and moral philosophy. Buddhism was accepted to liberate the mind from all the superstitions and ignorance.

Dalit liberation movement was against the whole oppressive Hindu system and values, and it was active, more or less throughout India. The role of Dalit and non-Dalit leaders in the Dalit liberation movement was of great value. The contribution of impersonal factors like the new education, industrialization, land-system, democratic process, means of communication, etc, to the Dalit movement, cannot be ignored. Thus, the personal and impersonal factors were responsible for the rise and growth of the "new Dalit consciousness", which brought a new vigour to the "untouchables."

The ideological and operational trends which were in vogue in the Dalit movement in the pre-Mutiny period seem to have been reflected in the post-Mutiny period also. For instance, sanskritization, conversion and politicization were again resorted to by the Dalit leaders for the liberation of the Dalits. It was rightly thought by Dr Babasaheb Ambedkar that the problem of the Dalits was basically political and the solution was in politics. Accordingly, he channelized the strength and formulated the strategies to accomplish the end. His dictum 'educate, agitate and organize' added vigour to the movement. Ultimately the acceptance of constitutionalism, and rationalism in the form of Buddhism, proved to be efficacious in the emancipation of Dalits. Some of the leaders were divided among themselves either because of their personal rivalry, or ideological differences, or the inherent divisive Hindu philosophy of caste and sub-caste, and because of spatial and communication gaps. However, all of them were united in one objective of abolition of untouchability and they were ceaselessly working to achieve the same to the best of their abilities.

The success of the Dalit liberation movement could rightly be attributed to the dynamic, well-determined and value-oriented leadership of Dr Babasaheb Ambedkar. He viewed the problem of Dalits from politico-religious point of view and tried to brilliantly mobilize the forces for the Dalit liberation. He was very clear in his conviction that unless the Dalits search for their lost identity, strive to regain political power and resort to rationalism, there would be no future for them. He was, undoubtedly opposed by some of the community leaders, but their opposition resulted in his sharpening his strategy and thereby adding vigour to the movement. It was he who could channelize the strength of the Dalits into a nationwide movement to strive for their liberation. The Constitution which he gave to the nation has abolished "untouchability" and provided certain special privileges for the socio-economic development of the Dalits. He could liberate them not only from the thraldom of untouchability and caste system, but from the bondage of mental slavery by reviving Buddhism.

The contributions of other leaders before him and during his time also cannot be ignored. The pioneering role played by leaders like Wastad Lahuji Salve, Umaidramji Maharaj, Harichand Thakur, Swami Thykad, Guru Balak Das, Gopalbaba Walangkar and Rev. John Ratnam is of great importance. All of them had protested against the oppressive practice of untouchability.

Dalit movement became successful in the sense that the Dalits could legally and constitutionally come to the level of non-Dalits. They have to march ahead with the help of the Constitution in one hand and Buddhism in the other to achieve their moral and material well-being. They have to derive benefit of the politico-legal set-up to a great extent.

Dalit movement was, obviously, based on the sublime principles of liberty, equality and fraternity. Dalit leaders tried to propagate social equality among the Dalit as well as non-Dalit masses, and tried to assert their right to social equality. It was because of Dalit movement, that the Dalits were conspicuously known in the country and even outside the country. They were recognized as a separate and significant community and their assistance was invariably sought in the national governance since 1919. Dr Babasaheb Ambedkar and R. Srinivasan were invited at the Round Table Conference held in London during 1930-32. The Poona Pact was signed in 1932. Some of the Dalit leaders participated in the national independence movement. Dr Babasaheb Ambedkar was nominated as Labour Member in the Governor General's Executive Council in 1942. He was even, elevated as Chairman of the Drafting Committee of the Constituent Assembly. The Dalit leaders firmly stood for national interests, while protecting the interests of their brethren. Their role in the national politics cannot be ignored. They viewed the problem of Dalits as a part of the national problem.

Dalit leaders, undoubtedly, tried their best to protect the interests of their brethren. Though they did not work under one banner as such, their aim was common that is the liberation of their brethren. Dr Babasaheb Ambedkar viewed the problem of Dalits as political rather than social, and accordingly started his mission. His ideas and strategy of the Dalit liberation could bring success to the movement.

The uplift of *Dalits* on a par with the privileged classes of the society is necessary for social unity. Dalit movement had endeavoured to uplift the Dalits so as to bring them into the mainstream. The struggle for the liberation of Dalits ought to be treated as equal to the struggle for the independence of the nation. National independence cannot be complete unless all the segments of the society are free. It is, therefore, necessary to record it with due respect and with the same sense of gratitude to those leaders and their struggle for the liberation of Dalits as that of the struggle for national independence. Even, it was more difficult to wage a war against the social tyranny than against political hegemony. They fulfilled that difficult task.

The present study is a macro level study of the movement. It could be studied at micro level. In other words it could be studied at regional and state level, individual and organizational level. It could be studied from various point of view like social, economic, educational, religious, political and cultural. The studies pertaining to the role of non-Dalits, ideological currents and cross-currents and research pertaining to certain periods could be undertaken. There is very wide scope for undertaking these tasks.

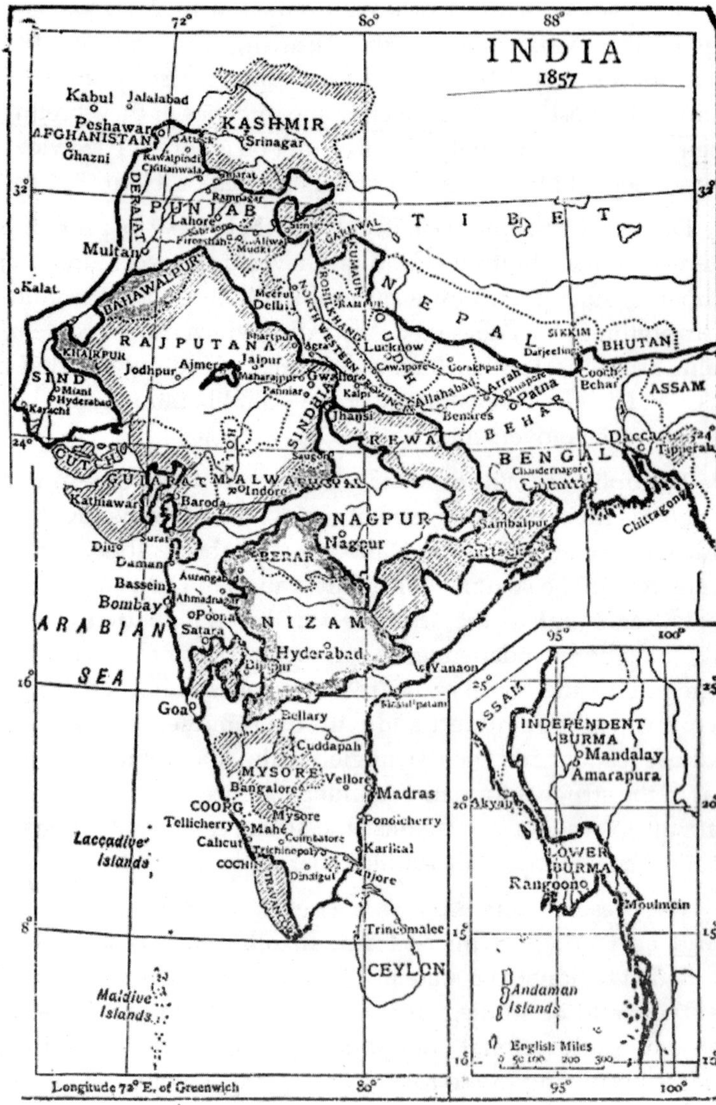
INDIA
1857
KASHMIR
Srinagar
Kabul
Jalalabad
Peshawar
AFGHANISTAN
Ghazni
PUNJAB
Lahore
Multan
Kalat
BAHAWALPUR
TIBET
NEPAL
SIKKIM
Darjeeling
BHUTAN
ASSAM
RAJPUTANA
KHAIRPUR
Jodhpur
Ajmer
Jaipur
SIND
Karachi
Delhi
Meerut
Lucknow
OUDH
Allahabad
Benares
Patna
BEHAR
BENGAL
Chandernagore
Calcutta
Dacca
Chittagong
Cooch Behar
Jhansi
Gwalior
REWA
CUTCH
GUJARAT
MALWA
Indore
Kathiawar
Baroda
Surat
Diu
Daman
Bassein
Bombay
NAGPUR
Nagpur
Sambalpur
BERAR
Poona
Satara
NIZAM
Hyderabad
ARABIAN
SEA
Goa
Bellary
Cuddapah
MYSORE
Vellore
Bangalore
Madras
COORG
Mysore
Tellicherry
Mahé
Calicut
Pondicherry
Karikal
Laccadive Islands
Maldive Islands
Trincomalee
CEYLON
INDEPENDENT BURMA
Mandalay
Amarapura
Akyab
LOWER BURMA
Rangoon
Moulmein
Andaman Islands
English Miles
Longitude 72° E. of Greenwich

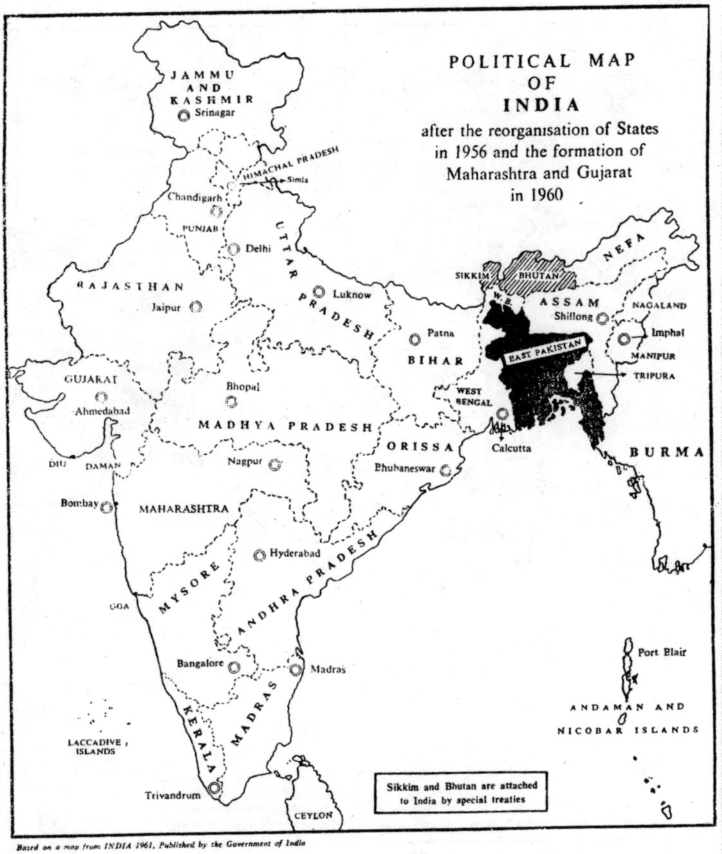

Based on a map from INDIA 1961, Published by the Government of India

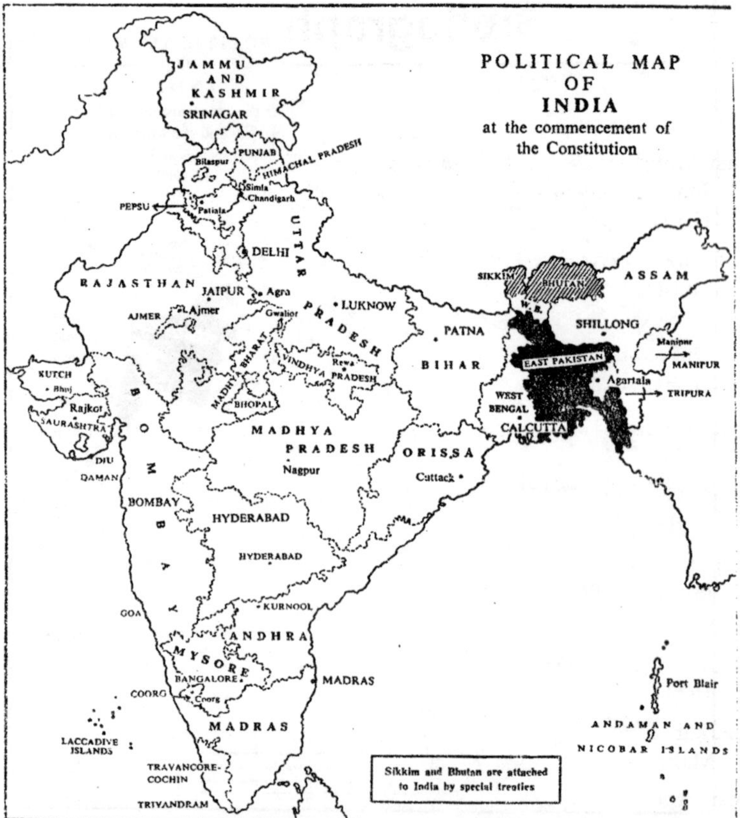

Based on a map from INDIA 1954 published by the Government of India

Bibliography

Abbasi Mohd. Yusuf, *The Genesis of Muslim Fundamentalism in British India,* Indian Institute of Applied Political Research, New Delhi, (2nd ed.) 1987.

Abraham, C.E. *The Rise and Growth of Christianity in India,* The Cultural Heritage of India, Calcutta, 1956.

Abraham M. Fancis *Modern Sociological Theory–An Introduction,* Oxford University Press, Delhi, 1982.

Agrawal, C.B. *The Harijans in Rebellion,* Taraporwala, Bombay, 1934.

Ahmad Manazir *Lord William Bentinck,* Chugh Publications, Allahabad, 1978.

Ahmad Qeyamuddin, *The Wahabi Movement in India,* Firma Mukhopadhyaya, Calcutta, 1966.

Aiyappan, A. *Social Revolution in a Kerala village,* Asia Publishing House, Bombay, 1965.

Ambedkar B.R. *Castes in India: Their Mechanism, Genesis and Development.*

Ambedkar B.R. *Annihilation of Caste,* Vol. I (ed.) Govt,.of Maharashtra, 1979.

Ambedkar, B.R. *Pakistan or the Partition of India,* Vol. 8, (ed.) Govt. of Maharashtra, Bombay 1990.

Ambedkar, B.R. *What Congress and Gandhi Have Done to the Untouchables?* (Vol.. 9), Govt. of Maharashtra, Bombay, 1991.

Ambedkar B.R. *The Untouchables,* Vol. 7, Govt. of Maharashtra, Bombay, 1990.

Ardythe Basham, *Untouchable Soldiers,* Bhagwan Das (ed), Ambedkar Sahitya Prakashan, Bangalore, 1980.

Athavale Sadashiv *UmajiRaJe, Mukkam Dongar,* Continental Prakashan, Pune, 1991.

Atre, T.N. *Gawagada,* Varada, Pune, 1989 (ed.).

Ayrookuzhiel A.M. Abraham, *Swami Anand Thirth* CISRS, Bangalore 1987.

Bagchi Jatin *Jati Dharma O Samaj Bibartan* Smt Ramala Bagehi, Calcutta, 1987.

Bailey, F.G. *Politics and Social Change,* Oxford University Press, London, 1963.

Baird Robert D. *Religion in Modern India,* Manohar Publications, New Delhi 1981.

Banaji D.A. *Slavery in British India,* Tarapoorwala Sons & *Co.* (2nd ed.), 1933.

Bansod Shyamrao (Eli) *"Pradeep"* by Kisan Fagu Bansod, Jagruti Prakashan Siraspeth, Nagpur, 1959.

Basu, D.D. *Constitutional Law of India,* Prentice-Hall of India, New Delhi 1977.

Beteille, *A. Caste, Class and Power: Changing Patterns oj Stratification in a Tanjore Village,* Oxford University Press, Bombay, 1966.

Bhagwandas (ed.). *Thus Spoke Ambedkar,* Vol. I, Bheem Patrika Publications, Jullundur, 1963.

Bhagwandas (ed.) *Thus Spoke Ambedkar,* Vol. I & II, Bheem Patrika Publications, Jullundur, 1969.

Bharadwaj, A.N. *Problems of Scheduled Castes and Scheduled Tribes in India,* Light & Life Publishers, New Delhi, 1979.

Bhargave Bhavana *Padmashri Dadasaheb Gaikwad,* Ramabai Ambedkar Vidyarthini Hostel, Nasik, 1968.

Bhavanishankar *Veerangana Zalkaribai,* Anand Sahitya Sadan, Cantt., Aligarh, 1964.

Bivalkar, R.M. and Kamble Zumbarlal *Mahadchya Mukti Sangram* (Marathi), Rajhans Prakashan, Sadashiv Peth, Pune, 1977.

Boag, G.T. *The Madras Presidency 1881-1931,* Govt. Press, Madras, 1933.

Borale, P.T. *Segregation and Desegregation in India-A Socio-legal Study.* P.C. Manaktala & Sons Pvt. Ltd., Bombay, 1968.

Brigg Geo W. *The Chamars,* Oxford University Press, London, 1920.

Buhler. G. *The Laws of Manu,* Motilal Banarasidas, Delhi, 1964.

Chakrabartty Syamal *Iswar Chandra Vidyasagar,* NCERT, New Delhi, 1971.

Chakravarti, S. and S.N. Ray *Brahmo Samaj, The Depressed Classes and Untouchables,* Calcutta, 1933.

Chandrasekar S. *Dimensions of Socio-Political Change in Mysore, 1918-40,* Ashish Pub.House, New Delhi, 1985.

Chentarassery, T.H.P. *Ayyankali* (Malayalam), Prabhath Book House, Trivandrum, 1979.

Chentharassery, T.H.P. *Poykayil Sree Kumara Gurudevan,* Navodhanam Publications, Trivandrum, 1983.

Chentharassery, T.H.P. *Pampady John Joseph,* Backward People's Development Corporation, Tiruvalla, 1989.

Choudhari Mulkiram *Hridayodgar,* Shanti Prakashan, Saharanpur, 1983.

Das Amalkumar Choudhari Raha *Handbook on Scheduled Castes and Scheduled Tribes of West Bengal,* Tribal Welfare Department, Govt. of West Bengal, 1966.

Das Bhakta *A Glimpse of the Scheduled Castes in Assam,* Omson Publications, New Delhi, 1968.

Das Gupta B.N. *The Life & Times of Rajah Rammohan Roy,* Ambica Publications, New Delhi, 1980.

Das, K.K.S. *Ayyankaly Kerala Charithrathil,* (Malayalam) P.B. Centre, Chathanthara, Kerala, 1986.

Desai, A.R. *Social Background of Indian Nationalism,* Popular Book Depot, Bombay, 1959.

Dhatavkar Bhaskar *Rajarshi Shahu Chhatrapatinche Niwadak Adesh* (I & II), Archaeology Dept., Maharashtra Govt., Bombay, 1988.

Dinkar D.C. *Swatantra Sangram mein Achhutonka Yogadan* (Hindi)) Tula Chandani, Lucknow, 1986.

Dronberger IISC *The Political Thought of Max Weber,* Meredith Corporation, New York, 1971.

Durge V.G. *Sphurti Devata Ramabai Ambedkar,* Prabha Prakashan, Nagpur, 1989.

Dutt Palme R. *India Today,* Peoples Publishing House, Bombay, 1947.

Farauhar J.N. *Modern Religious Movements in India,* Munshiram Manoharlal Oriental Publishers & Booksellers, Delhi, 1967.

Forester Duncan B. *Caste and Christianity,* Centre for South Asian Studies, School of Orient and African Studies, University of London, 1980.

Fuchs S. *Children of Hari: A Study of the Nimar Balahis in Madhya Pradesh,* India, New Order Book Co., Ahmedabad, 1949.

Fuchs, Stephen *Rebellious Prophets,* Asia Publishing House, Bombay, 1965.

Fuchs Stephen *At the Bottom of Indian Society,* Munshiram Manoharlal Pub. Pvt. Ltd., 1981.

Gaikwad Narendra *Marathwadyatil Dalit Chalwal Ani Hyderabadcha Swatantry Sangram*, Sugava Prakashan, Pune, 1990.

Gandhi M.K. *Removal of Untouchability,* Navajivan Publishing House, Ahmedabad, 1954.

Gautam M.B. *Bhagyadayam,* Adi-Hindu Social Service League Trust, Hyderabad, 1991.

Gedam, Ashtikar Kulkarni *Shri N.R. Shende Vyakti Ani Sadhana,* Sudha Prakashan, Nagpur, 1975.

Gedam T.V. *Shri Balasaheb Tirpude: Vyakti Ani Karya,* Yugandhar Shikshan Sanstha, Sadar, Nagpur, 1967.

Gorge, K.M. *Kumaran Asan,* Sahitya Akadami, Rabindra Bhavan, New Delhi, 1972.

Ghodeswar Ramaji *Barrister Rajabhau Khobragade Yanchi Bhashane,* Buddha Vihar Bandhkam Samiti, Chandrapur, 1987.

Ghosh S.K. *Protection of Minorities and Scheduled Castes,* Ashish Publishing House, New Delhi, 1980.

Ghurye G.S. *Caste, Class and Occupation,* Popular Book Depot, Bombay, 1961.

Gour H.S. *The Penal Law of India* Vol. I-IV, Law Book Co. Allahabad.

Goutam Pradnyawant *MeeAni Mangaon Parishad,* The Rahul Publications, Kolhapur, 1991.

Govt. of Maharashtra *Dr. Babasaheb Ambedkar Writing sand Speeches,* 1979.

Gupta S.K. *Scheduled Castes in Modern Indian Politics: Their Emergence as a Political Power,* Munshiram Manoharlal Publishers, New Delhi, 1985.

Hajarika B.B. *Political Life in Assam: During the Nineteenth Century,* Gian Publishing House, Delhi, 1987.

Harit Dropati *Hamein Jin Par Garva Hai,* Harit Sahitya Prakashan, New Delhi, 1990.

Hate B.S. *Jithe Pani Petala,* Sambodhi Prakashan, Bombay, 1977.

Hutton J.H. *Caste in India,* Oxford University Press, London, (4 ed.) 1969.

Ilbert C. Sir *Government of India,* Neeraj Publishing House, Delhi (Third ed.) 1984.

Ingle Ramchandra Thakaji *Maharancha Sanskrutik Itihas,* Abhijit Prakashan, Prabhanivas, Lakshmi Nagar, Nagpur, 1987.

Iyer Krishna L.A. *The Travancore Tribes and Castes,* Govt. Press, Trivandrum, 1939.

Jangam R.T. *Political Sociology,* Oxford & IBH Publishing Co. New Delhi, 1980.

Janjal Prakash *Ambedkari Kranti Senani N.Shivaraj,* Smt. Nandini Gavali, Sagarmal, Kolhapur, 1992.

Jatav D.R. *Dr. Ambedkar's Role in National Movement,* Boudha Sahitya Sammelan, New Delhi, 1979.

Jatava D.R. *The Indian Social System,* Marathwada University, Aurangabad, 1982.

Jawadekar S.D. Acharya *Adhunik Bharat,* Sulabh Rashtriya Granthmala, Pune, 1953.

Jha Shashishekhar *Political Elite in Bihar,* Vora & Co. Pub. Pvt. Ltd., Bombay, 1972.

Jigyasu Chandrika Prasad *Shri 108 Swami Achhutanandji Harihar,* Bahujan Kalyan Prakashan, Lucknow, 1960.

Jigyasu Chandrika Prasad *Swami Bodhanand,* Bahujan Kalyan Prakashan, Lucknow.

Jogan Shankar *Devadasi Cult,* Ashish Publishing House, New Delhi, 1990.

Joshi Barbara (ed.) *Untouchable Voices of the Dalit Liberation Movement,* Selected Book Service Syndicate, New Delhi, 1986.

Joshi Mahesh *Satyashodhak Samajacha Itihas,* Sahitye Ani Samaj Sanskriti Mandal, Govt. of Maharashtra, Bombay, 1987.

Joshi P.C. (ed). *Rebellion 1857,* K.P. Bagachi Co. 1957-1986, Calcutta, 1986.

Joshi P.L. (ed) *Political Ideas and Leadership in Vidarbha,* Deptt. of Pol Sci, Nagpur University, Nagpur, 1980.

Juergensmeyer Mark *Religion as Social Vision,* University of California Press, Berkeley, 1982.

Juergensmeyer Mark *Religious Rebels in the Punjab. The Social Vision of Untouchables*, Ajantha Publications, Delhi, 1988.

Kadam K.N. *Dr Babasaheb Ambedkar and the Significance of his Movement,* Popular Prakashan, Bombay, 1991.

Kamble J.R. *Rise and Awakening of Depressed Classes in India,* National Publishing House, New Delhi, 1979.

Kamble M.C. *Dristidata Dr Ambedkar,* Bombay, 1985.

Kamble N.D. *Deprived Castes and their Struggle for Equality,* Ashish Publishing House, New Delhi, 1983.

Kamble N.D. *The Scheduled Castes,* Ashish Publishing House, New Delhi.

Kananoikil Jose *Scheduled Castes and the Struggle Against Inequality,* Indian Social Institute, New Delhi, 1983.

Kanti Mohan *Premchandra Aur Achhut Samasya,* Jansulabh Sahitye Prakashan, Delhi, 1982.

Kardak Bhimrao Dhondiba *Ambedkari Jalase,* Abhinav Prakashan, Bombay, 1978.

Keer Dhananjay *Dr Ambedkar: Life and Mission,* Popular Prakashan, Bombay, 3rd ed, 1971.

Keer Dhananjay, *Mahatma Jyotirao Phule,* Popular Prakashan, Bombay, 1964.

Kelkar S.V. *The History of Caste in India,* Cosmo Publications New Delhi, 1979.

Khairmode C.B. *Dr Bhimrao Ramji Ambedkar,* Vol. I. Pratap Prakashan, Bombay, 1978.

Khairmode C.B. *Asprushyancha Lashkari Pesha,* Maharashtra Rajya Sahitye Ani Sanskrit Mandal, Bombay, 1987.

Khan M.A. *History of the Faraidi Movement in Bengal.* Karachi, 1965.

Kharat Shankarrao (ed.) *Dr Babasaheb Ambedkaranchi Patre,* Idrayani Sahitye, Shanwar Peth, Pune, 1990.

Khare R.S. *Untouchables or himself; Ideology, Identity and Pragmatism Among the Lucknow Chamars,* Cambridge University Press, Cambridge, 1984.

Kosare H.L. *Vidarbhatil Dalit Chalwalicha Itihas,* Dnyan Deep Prakashan, Nagpur, 1984.

Kothari Rajani (ed.) *Caste in Indian Politics,* Orient Longman Ltd., New Delhi, 1970.

Kshirsagar R.K. *Bharatiya Republican Paksh,* Nath Publishers, Aurangabad, 1979.

Kshirsagar R.K. *Untouchability in India: Implementation of Law and Abolition,* Deep & Deep Publishers, New Delhi, 1986.

Kusuman K.K. *Slavery in Travancore,* Kerala Historical Society, Trivandrum, 1973.

Lavanam Hemalata *Ma Nana Garu,* Atheist Centre, Vijayawada, 1986.

Leel K.C. *Ambedkari Andolan Mein Punjabiyon ka Role,* Bhim Patrika Publications, Jullundur, 1976.

Lokhande Bhalchandra *Maharanche Mahan Divya,* Bhim Bodhi Mission Society, Nagpur, 1986.

Lokhande H.G. *Dr Ambedkari Krantiveer,* Samata Mitra Mandal, Kalyan (East), 1983.

Longer V. *Forefront for Ever the History of the Mahar Regiment.* The Mahar Regimental Centre, Saugar (MP) 1981.

Lynch Owen *The Politics of Untouchability,* S.Chand and Co., New Delhi, 1972.

Mac Munn, Sir George *The Martial Races of India,* Sampson Low, Marston & Co.Ltd., London.

Madan G.R. *India's Social Transformation,* Allied Publishers Pvt.Ltd., New Delhi (2nd ed.). 1979.

Mahar Michael J. (Editor) *The Untouchables in Contemporary India,* The University of Arizona Press, Tucson Arizona, US, 1972.

Maharshi Dayanand *Satyarth Prakash,* Vaidik Sahitye Sadan, Delhi.

Mahasthavir Sadanand *Anagarik Dharmapal,* Saddhammaditye Prakashan, Dhammarajik Mahavihar, Wardha, 1986.

Mahatma Gandhi *My Philosophy of Life,* A.T. Hingorani (ed), Pearl Publications Pvt. Ltd., Bombay, 1961.

Mahesh Shiromani *Hamare Harijan Neta,* Konark Prakashan, Delhi, 1981.

Malik S. C. (ed.) *Indian Movements, Some Aspects of Dissent, Protest and Reform,* Indian Institute of Advanced Studies, Shimla, 1978.

Malik Yogendra K. (ed) *South Asian Intellectuals and Social Change,* Heritage Publishers, New Delhi, 1982.

Malkani N.R. *Clean People and Unclean Country,* Delhi, 1965.

Mandal *Mahapran J.N. Mandal,* Vol. I & II (Bengali), Calcutta.

Mangudkar M.P. *Dr Ambedkar and Parliamentary Democracy, Poona, 1976.*

Mankar D.F. *Karmaveer Babu Haridas Awale Yancha Jeevan Sangharsh,* Karmaveer Awale Prakashan Samiti, Nagpur.

Mathew Joseph Ideology, *Protest and Social Mobility Case Study of Mahars and Pulayas.* Inter India Publications, New Delhi, 1986.

Menon V.P. *The Story of the Integration of Indian States,* MacMillan, New York, 1956.

Metcalf R. Thomas *The Aftermath of Revolt: India 1857-1870,* Princeton, 1965.

Michael Mofatt *An Untouchable Community in South India: Structure and Consensus,* Princeton University Press, Princeton, New Jersey.

Moon Vasant *Madhya Prant Varadatil Dr.Ambedkar-Poorva Dalit Chalwal,* Sugava Prakashan, Pune, 1987.

Moore Wilber E. *Social Change,* Prentice Hall of India Ltd., New Delhi, 1965.

More S.S. *Maharashtratil Buddha Dhammacha Itihas, Trirutna* Granthmala, Yervada, Pune, 1985.

Mudroch J. *Review of Caste in India,* Rawat Publications, 11, Jaipur, 1977.

M. Mujeeb *Mirza Ghalib,* NCERT, New Delhi, 1970.

Mujumdar, R.C. *British Paramountcy and Indian Renaissance,* Bharatiya Vidyabhavan.

Mukherjee Prabhati *Beyond the Four Varnas,* Indian Institute of Advanced Studies, Shimla, 1988.

Mukherji Neelmani *The Ryotwari System in Madras,* Calcutta, 1962.

Murkot Kunhappa *Sree Narayana Guru,* National Book Trust of India, New Delhi, 1982.

Murthy B.S. *Depressed and Oppressed,* S. Chand & Co. Pvt. Ltd., New Delhi, 1971.

Nag Jamuna *Social Reform Movements in Nineteenth Century India,* RBSA Publishers, Jaipur, 1988.

Narwade S.S. *Dr. Babasaheb Ambedkar Ani Hyderabad Sanathan,* Sugava Prakashan, Sadashiv Peth, Pune, 1988.

Natrajan K. *A Century of Social Reforms in India,* Asia Publishing House, Bombay, 1959.

Nath Trilok *Politics of the Depressed Classes,* Deputy Publications, Delhi, 1987.

Natrajan J. *History of Indian Journalism* Publication Division Govt. of India, New Delhi, 1955.

Navalkar H.N. S.G. *Kamble Yancha Charitra,* Pune.

Nirmale H.S. *Dalitanchi Niyat Kalike,* Sugava Prakashan, Sadashiv Peth, Pune, 1967.

Oddie G.A. *Social Protest in India,* Manohar Publications, New Delhi, 1979.

O'Malley L.S.S. *Indian Caste Customs,* Vikas Publishing House, Delhi, 1974 edn.

O'Malley L.S.S. *Bengal District Gazetters: Jessor,* Bengal Secretariat Book Deptt. Calcutta, 1912.

O'Malley L.S.S. (Ed.) *Modern India and the West,* Oxford University Press, London, 1968.

Omvedt Gail *Cultural Revolt in a Colonial Society,* Scientific Socialist Edu. Trust, Bombay, 1976.

Omvedt Gail (ed) *Land, Caste and Politics in Indian States,* Authors Guild Publications, Delhi, 1982.

Pagare Haribhau *Dadasaheb Gaikwad: Jeevan Ani Karya,* Anil Prakashan, Nasik, 1987.

Pande A.B. *Society and Government in Medieval India,* Central Book Deptt. Allahabad, 1965.

Panikkar K.M. *The Foundations of New India,* George Allen & Unwin Ltd.. London, 1963.

Pantawane Gangadhar *Vidrochache Pani Petale Ahe,* Vijay Prakashan, Nagpur, 1978.

Pantavane Gangadhar *Vadalache Vanshaj* (Marathi), Prachar Prakashan, Kolhapur, 1982.

Pantavane Gangadhar *Patrakar Dr. Babasaheb Ambedkar,* Abhijit Prakashan, Nagpur, 1987.

Parvate T.V. *Mahadev Govind Ranade : A Biography,* Asia Publishing House, Bombay, 1963.

Pathak Shekhar *Uttarakhand Mein Kooli Begar Pratha,* Radhakrishna Prakashan Pvt. Ltd., New Delhi.

Patwardhan Sunanda *Change Among Indian Harijans,* Orient Longmans Ltd., Delhi, 1973.

Pawar Urmila / Moon Meenakshi *Ambihi Itihas Chandavila,* Bombay, 1989.

Phadake Bhalchandra *Shri Bapusaheb Rajbhoj Yani Bharatatil Anusuchit Jatijamati Va Boudh Yanchyasathi Kaya Kele?* Pune.

Phadake Y.D. *Visavya Shatkatil Maharashtra,* Vol. I II, Shrividya Prakashan, Shaniwar Peth, Pune, 1989.

Phadake Y.D. *Ambedkari Chalwal,* Shrividya Prakashan, Pune, 1990.

Phillips Godfrey E. *The Untouchables' Quest: The Depressed Classes of India and Christianity,* Edinburgh House Press, London, 1936.

Pradhan Ganesh Prabhakar (ed.) *Agarkar Lekh Sangrah,* Sahitye Akadami, New Delhi, 1960.

Pradhan G.R. *Untouchable Workers of Bombay City,* Karnataka Publishing House, Bombay, 1938.

Prakash D.R. *How to Erase Untouchability? R.P.* Bookwala, New Delhi, 1972.

Prasad Rajeshwar *Social Reforms: An Analysis of Indian Society,* Y.K. Publishers, Agra, 1990.

Pylee M.V. *Constitutional History of India,* Asia Publishing House, Bombay, 1972.

Radhakrishnan S. *The Hindu View of Life,* George Allen and Unwin, London, 1928.

Raju G.G. *The Life of Dr B.R. Ambedkar,* Dr Ambedkar Memorial Society, Hyderabad, 1979.

Ramakrishna V. *Social Reform in Andhra (1848-1919),* Vikas Publishing House, New Delhi, 1983.

Ramanujam G. *Indian Labour Movement,* Sterling Pub., New Delhi. 1986.

Ramasami *Untouchability: History of Vaikom Agitation,* Periyar Self-Respect Propaganda Institution, Madras, 1980.

Ram Jagjivan *Caste Challenge in India,* Vision Books, New Delhi. 1980.

Ranpise A.S. *Dalitanchi Vrutpatre,* Maharashtra Boudh Sahitye Parishad, Bombay, 1956.

Rao C. Hayavadana *Mysore Gazetteer,* Govt. Press, Bangalore, 1930.

Rao Shiva B. *The Framing of India's Constitution,* Vol. I, The Indian Institute of Pub. Admn., New Delhi, 1968.

Ravindran T.K. *Vaikom Satyagraha and Gandhi,* Shri Narayana Institute of Social & Cultural Development, Trichur, 1975.

Rice Stanly *Hindu Customs and Their Origin,* George Allen Unwin, London, 1937.

Rodage Shrirang *Subhedar Ramji Ambedkar,* Ramaji Prakashan, Wakvali, Dapoli, 1989.

Rudolp Lloyd, Rudolph Susanne Hoeber, *The Modernity of Tradition* Orient Longmans Ltd., New Delhi, 1967.

Sabine G.H. *History of Political Theory,* Oxford Publishing Co., Calcutta, 1961.

Sachchidananda *The Harijan Elite,* Thomson Press (India) Limited, Faridabad, 1976.

Sagar Sundarlal *Jatav Jeevan,* Jatav Pracharak Mahamandal, Agra, 1924.

Sagar S.L. *Achhut Aur Achhut Sthan,* Sagar Prakashan Mainpuri, UP, 1977.

Samagra Savarkar Vangmaya Prakashan Samiti, Maharashtra Hindu Sabha, Pune, 1965.

Sampla B.R. *Yug Purush Ambedkar,* Bheera Patrika Publications, Jullundur, 1978.

Sanjana J.E. *Caste and Outcaste,* Thakkar and Co. Ltd., Bombay, 1946.

Sankrutyan Rahul *Atit Se Vartaman,* Vidya Mandir Press, Varanasi, 1956.

Santoshi Harkishan *Daliton Mein Dalit,* Nav Sahitye Academy, New Delhi, 1990.

Saradamoni K. *Divided Poor: A Study of a Kerala Village,* Ajanta Publications, Delhi, 1981.

Saraswati S. *Minorities in Madras State,* Impex India, Delhi, 1974.

Sarkar Sumit *Modern India (1885-1947),* MacMillan India Ltd., Madras, Bombay, Delhi, 1985.

Sautar J.A. / Bernard Miall *Among the Brahmins and Pariahs,* London, 1924.

Sen S.P. *The Indian Press,* Institute of Historical Studies, Calcutta, 1967.

Senart Emile *Caste in India.* Trans. Sir E. Denison Ross, Datta Book Centre, Delhi-7, 1977 Ed.

Shah Ghanshyam *Politics of Scheduled Castes and Tribes (Adivasi & Harijan Leaders of Gujarat),* Vora & Co. Publishers Pvt. Ltd., Bombay.

Shah Ghanshyam *Social Movements in India,* Sage Publications, New Delhi, 1990.

Shahir Yogesh *Guruvarya Krantikarak Lahuji Vastad,* Bharatiya Vichar Sadhana, Shanivar Peth, Pune, 1990.

Shakir Moin *Politics of Minorities,* Ajanta Book International, Delhi, 1980.

Sharma G.S. *Legislation and Cases* on *Untouchability and S.C. in India,* Allied Publishers, Bombay, 1975.

Sharma Satish Kumar (ed.) *Reform, Protest and Social Transformation,* Ashish Publishing House, New Delhi, 1987.

Sharma Satish Kumar *Social Movements and Social Change,* BR Publishing Corp., Delhi, 1985.

Shastri Shankaranand *Poona-Pact-Banam Gandhi,* Bahujan Kalyan Prakashan, Lucknow, 1977.

Shastri Sohanlal *Babasaheb Dr. B.R. Ambedkar ke Sampark Mein Pachhis Varsh,* Siddharth Sahitya Sadan, New Delhi.

Shende N.R. *Thavare: Charitra Ani Charitre,* Yugantar Shikshan Sanstha, Sadar, Nagpur, 1968.

Shende N.R. *G.A. Gavari: Vyakti Ani Karya,* P.P. Bhatkar, Chhya Cine Agencies, Amravati, 1963.

Shetty V.T. Rajshekar *Dalit Movement in Karnataka,* The Christian Literature Society, Madras, 1978.

Shinde B.S. *Amritnak* (Marathi), Mayur Prakashan, Pune, 1980.

Shinde V.R. *Bharatiya Asprushyancha Prashna* (Marathi), Mangudkar (ed.), Maharashtra Govt. Bombay, 1976.

Shiva Rao, B. *The Framing of India's Constitution,* Vol. I, The Indian Institute of Public Administration, New Delhi, 1968.

Shivatarkar Shankar Sitaram *Shri Sitaram Shivatarkar Mastar: Samarpit Pravas,* Pradeep Prakashan, Mahim, Bombay, 1991.

Shyamlal (Dr.) *The Bhangis in Transition,* Inter India Publications, New Delhi, 1984.

Shyamlal (Dr.) *Caste and Political Mobilization: The Bhangis,* Panchsheel Prakashan, Jaipur, 1981.

Singh T.R. *The Madiga,* Department of Anthropology, University of Lucknow, Lucknow, 1969.

Singh Yogendra *Social Stratification and Change in India,* Manohar Book Service, New Delhi, 1977.

Singh Yogendra *Modernisation of Indian Tradition,* Rawat Publications, Jaipur, 1986.

Sinh Kanwarpal (ed.) *Premchand Aur Janvadi Sahitya ki Parampara,* Bhashya Prakashan, New Delhi, 1981.

Smith George *The Conversion of India,* John Murray, London, 1893.

Somvanshi B.C. *Mahar-Mang Sambandh,* Anand Prakashan, Jaisingpura, Aurangabad, 1989.

Srinivas M.N. *Caste in Modern India and Other Essays,* Asia Publishing House, Bombay, 1962.

Srivastav D.K. *Religious Freedom in India,* Deep & Deep Pub., New Delhi, 1982.

Srivastav, Tripathi, Dwivedi *Bharat Mein Samajik Andolan Aur Parivartan,* Kashi Vishwavidyalaya Prakashan, Varanasi, 1987.

Subramanyam Y. Subhashini *Social Change in Village India. An Andhra Case Study,* Prithvi Raj Publishers, New Delhi, 1955.

Survade Vijay Gangaram (ed.) *Dr B.R. Ambedkar Through Correspondence,* Vol. I, Kalyan (East), Dist. Thane, 1986.

Tapase G.D. *From Mudhouse to Rajbhavan,* UBS Publisher's Distributors Ltd., New Delhi, 1983.

Thakur-Khadas *Narak Safaichi Gost,* Majestic Prakashan, Bombay, 1989.

Ulakanathan A.S. *Leaders of Equality* (Tamil), Sangappalagai Publications, Kottoor, Madras, 1990.

Vaishya Brahmadatta *Guruji,* Harijan Ashram Trust, Ahmedabad, 1985.

Varale B.H. *Dr Babasaheb Ambedkarancha Sangati,* Shrividya Prakashan, Pune, 1988.

Vatkar Namdeo *Katha Majhya Janmachi,* Majestic Book Stall, Girgaon, Bombay, 1983.

Veeramani K. *The History of the Struggle for Social and Communal Justice in Tamil Nadu,* The Dravidar Kazhagam Publications, Madras, 1981.

Venkataswamy P.R. *Our Struggle for Emancipation,* Vol. I & II, Hyderabad, 1955.

Vidrohi M.R. *Dalit Dastavaij,* Dalit Sahitya Prakashan Sanstha, New Delhi, 1989.

Wagh C.M. *Eka Karmavirachi Kahani,* 'Guha' Nagsen Vana, Aurangabad, 1972.

Walker David *The Prince of India,* Bennet Coleman & Co. Bombay, 1923.

Wallace Paul / Chopra *Political Dynamics and Crisis in Punjab,* Guru Nanak Dev University, Amritsar, 1988.

Walter H.A. *The Ahmadia Movement,* Oxford University Press, London, 1918.

Webster John C.B. *The Christian Community and Change in Nineteenth Century North India,* MacMillan Comp. Ltd., Delhi, 1976.

Wheeler J. Talboys *The History of the Imperial Assemblage at Delhi,* R.K. Publishing House, Delhi, 1982.

William-Monier, Sir *Hinduism,* Society for Promoting Christian Knowledge, London, 1894.

Yoshino I.R. and Murakoshi Sueo *The Invisible Visible Minority – Japan's Burakumin,* Buraku Kaiho Kenkyusho Osaka, Japan, 1977.

Zinkin Taya *Caste Today,* Institute of Race Relations, Oxford University Press, London, 1962.

Diary, Dictionary, Directory

'Directory' Times of India

Kulkarni Atul, Vilas Chaphekar, Vipul, *Asprushyata Nivarana Dainandini,* Pune University Housing Society, Pune, 1983.

Mugale Chandrakant and others *Ambedkar Directory,* Dalit/Boudh Sahitye Prakashak Vikrate Parishad, Nagpur, 1992-93.

Patil R.R., Sheela R. Patil *Kranti Parva* (calendar) Shivaji Housing Society, Ahmednagar, 1991-94.

Rao Parameshwar B. *Ambedkarite Diary,* Mozam Janhi Market, Hyderabad, 1985.

Sen S.P. *Dictionary of National Biography,* Vol. I, II & III Institute of Historical Studies, Calcutta-17, 1972, 1973 & 1974.

Encyclopaedia

Edwin R.A. Seligman Alvin Johnson, *Encyclopaedia of the Social Sciences,* The MacMillan Co., New York.

Hastings, James T. Clark, *Encyclopaedia of Religion and Ethics,* New York.

Election Reports

Chandidas & others (eds) *India Votes,* Popular Prakashan, Bombay, 1968.

Singh V.B., Shankar Bose *Elections in India (1952-80),* Sage Publications, New Delhi, 1984.

Annual Register/Year Book

India (Year book) Publications Division, Ministry of Information & Broadcasting, Government of India.

Indian Annual Registers 1922-1935.

Journals

Babb L. A. "The Political Involvement of a Religious Movement: The Satnamis", *South Western Journal of Anthropology,* 1970.

Bahu Jan Uttham (Bombay) June 1989, July 1989.

Bairava Jyoti, New Delhi, Jan. 1989.

Cohen S.P. "The Untouchable Soldier. Caste, Politics and the Indian Army", *Journal of Asian Studies,* vol xxviii. No. 3, 1969.

Dharma Jyoti Pune, Oct. 1971.

Dalit Karavan Bharatiya Dalit Sahitya Akademi, UP, 1991.

Jhalkari Sandesh (monthly) Agra, June 1989.

Karant. K.S. "Four Great Saints of India and Spiritual Equality", *Janata,* Sept. 7, 1980.

Lai Shyam, Sanskritization and Social Change among Bhangis of Jodhpur city, A case study, *Indian Journal of Social Work,* Vol. 34, No.l, 1973.

Pantawane Gangadhar (ed) *Asmitadarsh* Diwali Special Numbers, 1980, 1981.

Parvattama C. "*Case for Indian Untouchables*", United Asia, Sept-Oct, 1968.

Right View (monthly), Mahabodhi Ashoka Press, Ajmer, April 1963.

Srivastava S.I. "The concept of Sanskritization", *Eco & Pol. Weekly,* April 1970.

The Maha Bodhi Calcutta, Aug. 1971.

The Oppressed Indian New Delhi, Feb. 1981, July 1982, April. 1983.

Uprell H.C. "Status Determinants in Caste Hierarchy", *Indian Journal of Social Work,* Vol. 28, No. 2, 1967.

Reports

AIR (1936) Allahabad, p. 534. Jasnani & others V. Emperor

AIR (1938) Bombay, p. 147. Nahari Damodar. V. Bhimrao Ramji Ambedkar.

AIR (1938), Madras, p. 714 Shanmuga Sundaram, V.K. Ponnuswami Iyer.

AIR (1958) SC 255, Venkataramana Devaru. V. State of Mysore.

AIR (1966) SC 1119, Shastri Yagnapurushdasji. V. Muldas Bhundardas Vaishya.

Census of India 1941 by M.W.M. Yeatts (1943) Manager of Publications, Delhi.

Hutton J.H. Census of India: 1931, Gian Publishing House, Delhi, 1986.

Kitts Eustace J. *A Compendium of the Castes and Tribes Found in India (1885).* The Academic Press, Gurgaon, Haryana, 1982.

Report of the Commissioner of SC, ST, New Delhi 1953, 1955.

Souvenir

Akhil Bharatiya Dalit Natya Sammelan, Ambajogai, 1986.

All India Political Science Conference, Mysore, December 1980 "The Politics of Violence" Communal Atrocities in Madras Presidency - 1920-1945 by G. Thangavelu.

Punjab History Conference, 1982 Communal Award and the Movement for the Upliftment of the Untouchables in the Punjab by D.R. Grover, Punjab Historical Studies Department, Punjab University, Patiala, 1982.

Ambedkari Chalvaliche Ardh Shatak: Akola Zilla 1925-75.

Andhra Pradesh Scheduled Castes Welfare Association, Hyderabad, 1978.

Andhra Pradesh State Harijan Conference, 1976.

Ayyankali Smaraka Trust, Trivandrum, 1982.

Dalit Sahitya Sammelan, Nagpur, 1976.

Delhi Scheduled Castes Welfare Association, New Delhi, 1986.

Paschim Khandesh Dalit Shikshan Prasarak Mandal, Dhulia, 1986.

People's Education Society, Bombay, 1974.

S.C., S.T. Students Asso., Kashi Vidyapeeth, Varanasi, 1986- 87, *Babuji Smriti Visheshank.*

S.C., S.T. Karamchari Sangh, Bihar, 1989.

Index